HOW SHOULD CHRISTIANS LIVE THEIR FAITH IN THE PUBLIC ARENA?

Twenty years ago, the first edition of Chuck Colson's *Kingdoms in Conflict* became a bestseller, a must-read for people interested in politics and the relationship between church and state. Now, with a passion for truth and moved by the urgency of the times we live in, *God and Government* has been published, re-voicing Colson's powerful and enduring message for our post-9/11 world.

In an era in which Christianity is being attacked from every side—when books are published charging Christians with being theocrats who attempt to impose their views on an unwilling culture—what is the message of the Christian church? What does the Bible say, and what do we learn from history about the proper relationship between faith and culture? Appealing to Scripture, reason, and history, this book tackles society's most pressing and divisive issues. New stories and examples reflect the realities of today, from the clash with radical Islam to the deep division between "reds" and "blues." In an era of angry finger-pointing, Colson furnishes a unique insider's perspective that can't be pigeonholed as either "religious right" or "religious left."

Whatever your political or religious stance, this book will give you a different understanding of Christianity. If you're a Christian, it will help you to both examine and defend your faith. If you've been critical of the new religious right, you'll be shocked at what you learn. Probing both secular and religious values, *God and Government* critiques each fairly, sides with neither, and offers a hopeful, fair-minded perspective that is sorely needed in today's hypercharged atmosphere.

CHARLES COLSON, well-known syndicated columnist, author, and international speaker, is founder of Prison Fellowship and host of the daily radio commentary *BreakPoint*. An honors graduate of Brown University and George Washington Law School, he served from 1969 to 1973 as special counsel to President Richard M. Nixon. Colson's articles appear in national secular and Christian magazines. He has written twenty-five books, the most recent of which is *The Good Life*. Charles Colson donates the royalties from his books to Prison Fellowship.

Books by Charles Colson

Born Again

Life Sentence

Loving God

Kingdoms in Conflict

Against the Night

Why America Doesn't Work
(with Jack Eckerd)

Gideon's Torch

The Body

Being the Body

How Now Shall We Live?

Justice that Restores

The Good Life

CHARLES COLSON

WITH ELLEN SANTILLI VAUGHN

G&D

GOVERNMENT

AN INSIDER'S VIEW
ON THE BOUNDARIES BETWEEN
FAITH & POLITICS

Formerly titled *Kingdoms in Conflict*

ZONDERVAN®

ZONDERVAN.com/
AUTHORTRACKER
follow your favorite authors

We want to hear from you. Please send your comments about this book to us in care of zreview@zondervan.com. Thank you.

God and Government
Copyright © 2007 by Charles W. Colson

Requests for information should be addressed to:
Zondervan, *Grand Rapids, Michigan 49530*

Library of Congress Cataloging-in-Publication Data

Colson, Charles W.
    God and government : an insider's view on the boundaries between faith and politics /
Charles W. Colson.
      p. cm.
    Rev. ed. of: Kingdoms in conflict / Charles Colson with Ellen Santilli Vaughn. c1987.
    Includes bibliographical references and index.
    ISBN-13: 978-0-310-27764-4
    ISBN-10: 0-310-27764-7
   1. Christianity and politics. 2. Church and state. I. Colson, Charles W. Kingdoms in conflict.
II. Title.
    BR115.P7C614   2007
    261.7 — dc22   2007006574

All Scripture quotations, unless otherwise indicated, are taken from the *Holy Bible, New International Version*®. NIV®. Copyright © 1973, 1978, 1984 by International Bible Society. Used by permission of Zondervan. All rights reserved.

Internet addresses (websites, blogs, etc.) and telephone numbers printed in this book are offered as a resource to you. These are not intended in any way to be or imply an endorsement on the part of Zondervan, nor do we vouch for the content of these sites and numbers for the life of this book.

Interior design by Beth Shagene

Printed in the United States of America

07 08 09 10 11 12 13 • 26 25 24 23 22 21 20 19 18 17 16 15 14 13 12 11 10 9 8 7 6 5 4 3

❧

To those
who serve in
"the little platoons"
around the world, faithfully
evidencing the love and justice
of the Kingdom of God
in the midst of the
kingdoms of
this world

❧

CONTENTS

PROLOGUE

MARCH 24, 2014

General Brent Slocum's T-shirt stuck to his sweaty back and powerful, heaving shoulders. He grinned at his twenty-nine-year-old adjutant, whose urgent breathing filled the small handball court.

"Gonna make it through the last point, Rob?" the general asked. It was a pleasure, at fifty-four, to whip a younger man.

Suddenly there was a pounding on the door. "General," another aide shouted from outside. "Command Center on the line, sir."

Slocum hesitated. He wanted to finish the game. The pounding resumed.

"All right, Sloan," the general bawled. "I hear you. Those boys better have something worth my time." Someone was forever using the channels. He wondered whether anybody could get through in a real emergency — like war.

The youthful voice on the other end of the mobile communications line was shaking, probably scared half to death to be speaking to the chairman of the Joint Chiefs of Staff. "It's the White House signal agency calling, sir. Shall I patch it in?"

"Of course," Slocum grunted. Almost instantly he heard a second voice, crisp and precise.

"General Slocum, POTUS has asked you to come immediately, sir. The diplomatic entrance. Enter through the south gate. Can I give an affirmative, sir?"

"Of course," he grunted again, then tossed the receiver in his aide's direction as he headed for the locker room. The White House? Six in the morning? Why on earth do they use an acronym for every last living thing in this city, Slocum grumbled to himself, including the President of the United States?

Eight minutes later he strode toward his waiting car in full-dress uniform. From Fort Myer to the White House was a ten-minute drive without traffic. His driver, the Army's best, had practiced many times. Fortunately, the city was just coming to life. Most of the streets were gray and deserted.

The general sat back and tried to gather his swirling thoughts as his limousine raced toward its destination. He had seen the president only a few times since becoming chairman in January. Never had he entered the White House outside regular hours. Something hot was up. He ran through the possibilities.

It might be Venezuela. Former President Chavez had ordered his supporters into the streets on Friday. Slocum still didn't have an op. plan ready to protect the new, U.S.-friendly government; he'd be in trouble if the chief wanted that.

The Middle East? That very morning, before leaving for the handball court, Slocum had glanced over a report of Turkey moving troops onto the border of Kurdistan.

Or perhaps, though less likely, it was France. Nobody had anticipated the vehemence of the Zidane government when they discovered two Poseidon subs in their waters.

Go to the Residence, he had been ordered. Whatever it was, it was important.

The blue-jacketed White House policeman saluted and waved the general's car through the heavy black-steel gates and up the long curved driveway that cut across the South Lawn of the White House. Slocum counted five limousines, all larger than his, at the door. The secretary of defense … the secretary of state. … Getting out of the car, he stood for a moment and gazed up at the light scum of late snow clinging to the gutters of the Residence. *This could be war*, he thought in wonder.

"Right this way, sir," announced a young marine. He steered the general through the oval-shaped Diplomatic Receiving Room and up the flight of marble steps to the Great Center Hall. From there Slocum followed another flight of stairs carpeted in thick red pile. They led, he knew, to the family quarters, a sacred territory he had never before entered.

At the head of the stairs stood a secret-service agent, a plug in one ear. He glanced at the general and then seemed to look through him. The agent's suit sagged as though he'd worn it for a week. It annoyed Slocum. After a life in the military, sloppy civilian dress was difficult to accept.

His Marine escort clicked his heels softly and announced, "The Lincoln Sitting Room, sir." The secret-service agent leaned to one side and swung the door open, never taking his eyes off the stairway.

Larry Parrish, the sandy-haired, ivy-league White House chief of staff, was the only one to nod at Slocum as he entered. The others were preoccupied in knots of uneasy conversation. Parrish waved the general into the last empty seat, a hard-backed antique chair next to the president. He then caught President Hopkins's eye.

"Everyone's here," he said.

The small room, which had once served Abraham Lincoln as an office, was crowded with antiques. This morning it seemed even more crowded by the egos of the handful of powerful men and one woman the president had summoned. Parrish had taken their measure long ago, and he somehow managed to make these egos work together for whatever goals the president chose. He knew people, he knew the system, and he had a finely tuned political sense of how to work the news cycle. "I'm a technician," he would say with a smile when pressed about his role in the government.

His eyes went around the circle. To the president's immediate left—an uncomfortable chair in an uncomfortable position, he thought—sat Brent Slocum. Parrish had known Slocum through a decade of Washington receptions. A bundle of powerful muscles on a long frame, Slocum prided himself on physical toughness. The general was the best sort of military man: politically unimaginative, but quick to seize the main issues. Neither a paper pusher nor a cowboy, he had just the kind of solid, capable confidence to command any situation. In that respect he was like the president, which explained why they got on so well and why the president had wanted him to head the Joint Chiefs.

Seated next to Slocum was Alexander Hartwell, the secretary of defense, revered as the nastiest infighter in Washington's brutal bureaucracy. Parrish had often thought he was glad Hartwell was *their* hatchet man. He would make a formidable enemy.

A veteran of twenty years in the House, Hartwell had worked the deals reconciling evangelicals to the anti-terror realists. As a reward for bringing such opposites together, Hartwell had demanded and received Defense. He sometimes acted, however, as if he had been given the White House. Parrish worked hard to stay one jump ahead of Hartwell—and to remind him who was president.

Next to Hartwell was Secretary of State Henry Lovelace. Parrish suspected Henry was out of his depth, and so did a lot of other people. They referred to him privately as Secretary Love. Lovelace owed his job to his friendship with the president, dating back to college days. The president was comfortable with him, and his weaknesses were compensated for by the strength of Mary-Ellen Davies, the national security advisor. It was doubtful anyway whether Davies could have worked with a strong counterpart at State.

MaryEllen Davies had the silver-haired, matronly appearance of a top-drawer school superintendent. It was a facade that some men expected they could bully, but those who tried usually learned to regret it. She remembered slights, she never lost track of her objectives, and she could face down much larger men with a stare that reminded them of their mothers, assuming that their mothers were unstinting disciplinarians. The president had come to rely on her during his fourteen months in the White House. Almost dangerously so, Parrish thought.

Finally, slumped on a rosewood chair purchased by Mary Todd Lincoln, was the professorial attorney general, Hyman Levin. How the man could talk! He kept the right-wingers happy, crusading with the vigor of the recently converted. Fortunately, he was a pragmatist who knew how to talk on one line and compromise on another.

Any one of the five, with the possible exception of Lovelace, would have dominated another setting. But bluster as they would, in the end they did the president's bidding. Parrish loved watching Hopkins manage them, the greatest exhibit of political skill and personal magnetism he had ever observed. Partly it was physical. Hopkins looked like a president should: tall, with a magnificent silver mane, a jutting jaw that suggested strength, and soft sparkling eyes that drew people to him. And he sounded like God Almighty, his thunderclap voice rising out of some lower register known only to pipe organs and synthesizers. As a Marine, Colonel Hopkins had been a great warrior, absolutely revered by his men. He carried all that sense of authority into the Oval Office.

Lately, though, Parrish had come to believe another, newer factor was just as important to Hopkins' authority. Parrish didn't believe morality mattered a fig in politics, and yet he had almost begun to believe that Hopkins dominated these egos through sheer goodness. Ever since the election, and increasingly so over the past months, Hopkins radiated something indefinably admirable. You felt it; and you felt that if you should oppose him you would do it at a cost to yourself, becoming shriveled and small.

It had not always been so. Parrish had worked closely with Hopkins through his term as governor of Oklahoma and on through the presidential campaign. The Hopkins he had signed on with was impressive and commanding, but also cold and almost demeaning toward those who worked with him. They feared him; they didn't like him. Something had happened since the election, and the "something," Parrish knew, was religion. Hopkins had experienced some kind of religious conversion. The word alone made Parrish feel itchy, but he had watched with his own eyes as Hopkins became deeper, more three-dimensional, one might almost say more *human*. So far Parrish had to admit that it was a change for the good. Hopkins seemed to have expanded into something above politics, something beyond human power struggles.

Parrish's thoughts were interrupted now as the president looked up from some papers, smiled briefly, and looked at each of the men. "Gentlemen, let's get started. Sorry to call you in so early this morning. I appreciate your promptness." There was just a trace of Oklahoma in his voice.

"I've asked you here to the Residence because if we were seen at this hour in the West Wing, the press would be onto things in nothing flat. We can't have that.

"We seem to have a little trouble brewing in Israel. You all know that the Knesset has been paralyzed for some time, with neither Kadima nor Labor able to get a stable majority to form a government."

Hopkins held up the black-leather notebook engraved with gold letters, *For the President's eyes only*, and continued.

"But this morning's intelligence summary suggests that the logjam is breaking. Both parties have been bargaining with small fringe parties, as you know. Our sources say that the Kadima party is very close to striking a deal with the Yisrael Beiteinu party. In fact, since it's well past noon in Israel now, they may have already reached an agreement. I talked this over with MaryEllen earlier this morning and decided we'd better get to work on it right away."

The news surprised Parrish. Was this truly an emergency? The difference between the two Israeli parties appeared minuscule, especially in their attitudes toward their Middle Eastern neighbors. So far as the U.S. was concerned, it made little difference which actually gained power.

At the president's invitation MaryEllen Davies leaned forward and, consulting a red notebook that looked like the president's but without the lettering, told them more than anyone could possibly want to know at 6:30 in the morning about the tiny fanatical party known as Yisrael Beiteinu, a recent merger with the religious party known as Mopet.

The leader was Yosef Tzuria, an Albanian refugee who favored stripping Israeli citizenship from all Arabs and driving all Palestinians out of the occupied territories. Tzuria also believed that God had given Israel title to all land west of the Euphrates River—territory inconveniently known as Iraq, Lebanon, and Syria. But—Parrish almost missed the emphasis because of Davies's impassive reporting—Tzuria's biggest, latest scheme was religious. He wanted to blow up the Dome of the Rock, the sacred Muslim shrine in Jerusalem, and build a temple in its place.

Davies concluded her briefing with a quote from Tzuria: "'We must establish a permanent place of prayer on the mount. It is a desecration of God to enter the mount under the authority of an Islamic guard.'

"I might add," Davies said dryly, "that they're quite serious. They're being bankrolled by some big industrialists in Israel, along with a fundamentalist group in Texas, which, we gather, has handed them at least twenty-five million dollars. They've got men in training." An inappropriately perky smile suddenly curved her lips. "Not only commandos, but priests. They're in training to perform Jewish sacrificial rites."

Priests? Sacrificial rites? Parrish searched the faces of the other men. Did they understand the significance here? He didn't. Nor could he decipher the strange, excited light in the president's eyes.

"I hate to sound uninformed," Parrish said finally, "but so what?"

"So what?" the president echoed slowly. "*So what?* This could mean war!"

"The Kadima party isn't going to let some marginal crowd of fanatics carry them into war," Parrish said. "Anyway, it sounds to me like their big thing is religion, not politics."

"Yes, that's right, Larry," the president said, nodding his silvery head. "That's just the problem. They take the Old Testament prophecies very seriously. And on the question of whether Kadima would allow them to carry the nation into the war, that's why I called you together. This morning's briefing says, and MaryEllen tells me the sources are impeccable, that Tzuria and the Kadima leader, Ehud Arens, are in negotiations right now. And Arens has tentatively agreed to look the other way when Tzuria's commandos blow up the Dome of the Rock. What they've yet to agree on is whether Arens will promise to declare Israeli sovereignty over the whole Temple Mount. It looks as though it could actually happen. The Jewish Temple could be rebuilt."

"And that would mean violence like you can't imagine," added Attorney General Levin. "The Dome of the Rock is one of the most sacred sites in Islam."

Parrish shifted uncomfortably. Given his nominal Episcopalian background, he felt out of his depth when it came to the finer nuances of the religious world.

"I'm sorry, Mr. President," he said apologetically. "Maybe everyone else understands this, but I'm not with it. Could you bear with me here until someone explains about the Temple? I must have missed that briefing." He saw to his relief that at least Hartwell and Slocum were in the same boat he was, for Slocum nodded at his request and Hartwell was wearing a tight, bemused smile.

"Maybe I can get Hyman to brief us on that, Larry. He was quite a Levitical scholar up at Yale, you know. Explain it, will you Hy?" The president and his attorney general grinned at each other.

This suggestion did not set Parrish at ease. He had heard about Levin's recent conversion to Christianity, but what in heaven's name was a Levitical scholar? And the glances exchanged by Levin and the president, as if they shared some secret fraternity ritual, made him extremely nervous.

Levin had a high choirboy voice and held his chin up slightly when he talked. He loved the chance to lecture.

"I suppose you know, Larry, that the ancient Israelites worshiped in a Temple built by Solomon in Jerusalem. By the time of King Hezekiah, in 715 B.C., worship was allowed nowhere else. That Temple was destroyed, however, by Babylonian armies in 586 B.C. Then came the Babylonian captivity, after which the returning Jews built a second Temple. That was later replaced by an elaborate monument for King Herod." Levin grinned. "You have heard of King Herod?"

Parrish nodded.

"Good," continued Levin in a tone that suggested mockery. "But the main fact you need to know is that in A.D. 70 the Jews revolted against Rome, and the Romans retaliated by destroying their Temple. It was never rebuilt. The Muslims erected a mosque over the ruins centuries later. During the

Crusades the Christians gained control and turned it into a church, but in recent centuries it has reverted to the Arabs. Today it is the Dome of the Rock, one of the holiest Muslim shrines. They would view its desecration as an unspeakable outrage.

"Now that, Larry, poses quite a problem. Because the devout Jew cannot just forget the Temple. They consider the site sacred. The Temple originally built there contained the Holy of Holies where no one could set foot — except the high priest, once a year — without desecrating God's holy name. So the Muslim control of that spot is ... a desecration of all that is sacred to them."

"So somebody gets desecrated no matter what," Parrish interjected.

"Very good, Larry. Furthermore, the Jews cannot fulfill the Old Testament sacrificial laws unless a Temple is rebuilt on that site. Promises of Messiah's return to a new Temple are found in Scripture; there and only there does He wish to make His residence. So for the truly devout Jew a rebuilt Temple is more important than the renewal of the state of Israel."

"But ... they have synagogues," Parrish said.

"A synagogue is not the Temple. A synagogue is a house of prayer. You cannot do the blood sacrifices there."

Parrish's eyebrows went up. "Blood sacrifices?"

"Yes, a sheep, a goat, a bull. Killed on the altar and burned on the perpetual fire."

"What in the world — "

"There is one more thing I should add," Levin interrupted him. "To the devout Christian who pays attention to prophecy, the rebuilding of the ancient Temple will set the stage for the last great act of history. It will signal Armageddon. That explains why Christian groups are funding Yisrael Beiteinu in this effort. The Temple will pave the way for Christ's triumphant return."

Levin leaned back, pleased with his presentation. The president looked inquiringly at Parrish.

"Does it make sense now, Larry? Obviously, while these reports are frightening, there's some excitement that comes with them too. You can't help but wonder if these could be events we've all waited for."

Brent Slocum listened intently to the discussion, struggling to accommodate his six-foot-three frame to the undersized antique chair and his mind to the subject matter. He had visited Israel several times, but to observe Israeli defenses on the Golan Heights, not mosques in Jerusalem. He was a man of war, comfortable talking about supply operations and air support. Not Armageddon.

He glanced at Hartwell, knowing that behind his narrowed eyes and high forehead the secretary of defense was computing fast. Slocum didn't particularly like Hartwell, but he did expect him to talk in terms that made some sense.

Hartwell didn't disappoint him. "So the gist of it is, Mr. President, Armageddon or no Armageddon, we need to head off this deal. It's explosive. Why would Arens even entertain it? He must know all this better than we do."

Davies leaned forward and answered before Hopkins could respond.

"Arens is an old fool," she said flatly. "He'd do anything to regain power. And this issue, strange as it sounds to us, is really quite popular within certain powerful segments of the Israeli population."

"Not with Arens!" Slocum blurted. "I know the man. He doesn't have a religious bone in his body."

"Right," Davies said. "But he is a politician who knows how to play religious issues."

"If he's a politician," Hartwell scoffed, "then he ought to know that Israel's existence depends on the good opinion of the United States. If this cockamamie scheme is as serious as you seem to think, then why don't we get him on the phone and tell him to forget it? No ifs, ands, or buts."

"Now hold on," Secretary Lovelace interjected. "That's no way to treat our ally."

"What if he says no?" Parrish asked, looking up from his note taking. "Could you back it up?"

Slocum grabbed onto a possibility that made some sense to him. "I can have the Delta Force in the area ready to go in twelve hours, sir."

"Hold on, now," said Parrish. "If I understand it correctly, the question isn't military in nature. We could drop an atom bomb on Jerusalem, if it came to that. The question is, could we back it up politically? Do you really think we can dictate policy to Israel, our only reliable ally in the Middle East? You think the Israel lobby would give us room to maneuver? Or the evangelicals, for that matter? And Arens knows just how much leeway we have."

"Come off it, Larry," said Hartwell. "We can make Arens come around if we're willing to get rough."

Parrish suddenly became aware that President Hopkins had not spoken in some time. It was unusual for him not to take part in the discussion; he enjoyed a spirited debate. But at the moment he seemed far away, his eyes fixed on some distant point. As Parrish looked his way the discussion stopped, and all eyes shifted expectantly to the president.

"Gentlemen," he said finally, "we must keep in mind the very real possibility that this situation is beyond us all." The words hung suspended in the air for a long, awkward moment. Only Levin nodded.

Hartwell shook his head with annoyance and reflexively reached into his jacket pocket for a cigarette. Then he remembered that no one smoked in the White House anymore.

"Mr. President," he said angrily, "whatever cosmic forces may be involved here, Tzuria must be stopped. There's nothing more dangerous than allowing religious fanaticism to replace reasoned political judgment."

"Are you talking about me or Tzuria?" the president asked coldly. He disliked it intensely when anyone hinted that his newfound faith skewed his judgment.

"No, Mr. President, of course not. I'm talking about Tzuria. He's the menace."

"Good," said Hopkins, putting on his half-circle reading glasses and picking up a well-worn brown-leather Bible. "At the risk of appearing fanatical, I'd like to read you all a passage from Ezekiel. It was written five centuries before the birth of Christ, and I believe it applies to Israel today." He flipped a few pages until he located his text. "Listen to this: 'They will live in the land I gave to my servant Jacob, the land where your fathers lived. They and their children and their children's children will live there forever, and David my servant will be their prince forever. I will make a covenant of peace with them; it will be an everlasting covenant. I will establish them and increase their numbers, and I will put my sanctuary among them forever. My dwelling place will be with them; I will be their God, and they will be my people. Then the nations will know that I the Lord make Israel holy, *when my sanctuary is among them forever.*'"

President Hopkins put down the Bible, removed his glasses, and ran a hand through his hair. "That sanctuary," he said solemnly, "is what we're talking about today." He stared into the eyes of each of them one by one. Slocum felt self-conscious. Parrish, who usually had his head down taking notes, stared back at Hopkins.

"I feel a little strange reading that to you all," Hopkins said. "A couple of years ago I thought the Bible belonged in a discussion of foreign policy about as much as a Baptist preacher in a casino. But how in the world can you read that—something written what, twenty-five hundred years ago?—and not see the relevance to what is going on?"

Slowly the president shook his head. "Now let's get down to business. We've talked enough. You know the situation. I want strategy options out of all of you by noon. Keep the subject as mysterious as possible to your aides. I don't want any leaks. Repeat—*no* leaks."

Turning to Parrish, he asked, "Larry, one key question. Is there any hint of this in the press? Do they know about the Arens-Tzuria deal at all?"

"Not to my knowledge," said Parrish. "I'll check, but I don't think there's been anything in the wind."

"Good," the president said tersely. "In fact, just to be sure we keep it that way, steer them a little. Put out a story, Larry. Something from, you know, 'informed sources.' Say there will be a labor-left-wing coalition. Or whatever you think is best. We need to buy some time here."

The president sat down, took off his watch, and wound it. "Anything else?" he asked. There was no response. "Then at the risk of again appearing to be a religious zealot, may I suggest that before you leave to prepare your recommendations, we invoke God's blessings upon us and upon this nation. Henry, will you lead us in prayer?"

Slocum watched in horror as the secretary of state stood up, turned around, and knelt before his chair. The president and Parrish followed suit. So did Levin. Davies, looking annoyed, got slowly onto her knees.

Brave enough to have won a Silver Star in the Gulf War, Slocum was not sure he had the courage for this. He looked over at Hartwell who sat obstinately in his chair, his eyes on the floor, his chin on his fist.

But Slocum was a soldier, and a soldier follows his commander-in-chief. Awkward though it felt, he turned his long body around and knelt.

Secretary Lovelace began to pray in a deep, passionate voice. "We humble ourselves before You, the one true God, who governs the affairs of this beloved nation. We serve You only because You have granted us this privilege and authority, and so we ask You, dear Father, to lead us. We seek Your will. Whatever all this means, give us the eyes to see and the ears to hear. Have it Your way, not ours, and forgive us the sin that would make us blind to Your truth.... "

8:45 A.M., THE WHITE HOUSE

Each day at 8:00 A.M. the senior aides to the president gathered around a giant mahogany table in the Roosevelt Room, the windowless conference chamber just across from the Oval Office. This morning Parrish's eyes had been drawn to the famous painting on the north wall, Teddy Roosevelt charging up San Juan Hill. The chief of staff had sighed inwardly, wondering exactly what they were charging into in Israel.

Now, almost an hour later, Parrish sat hardly listening as self-important aides held forth on a variety of matters—the latest nomination to the Supreme Court; the plan to abolish the Department of Education; and the drive in the Senate for Social Security reform. At the moment James Shepherd, head of the Budget Office, was off on his usual tirade about agencies refusing to cooperate with the 10-percent across-the-board budget cut.

A master at disguising his true feelings behind an impassive mask, Parrish stared soberly at Shepherd as his mind churned. One mishandled crisis, especially in Israel, could destroy a popular president's ratings overnight. And as volatile as the Middle East was, one incident there could escalate into a major situation. Concerned as he was about that, however, Parrish was more troubled by another matter. He was beginning to worry about the president.

Parrish had followed Hopkins onto the 2012 campaign trail knowing that his political positives were terrific. As a decorated war hero he brought strength to the fight against terrorism, along with a reputation for unimpeachable honesty. But Parrish had known Hopkins' political negatives as well. He came off on television as an icicle—cold and colorless. Parrish had tried to coach him on warmth but he wasn't truly interested. A man who had commanded a thousand Marines in battle thought he knew more about leadership than a draft-dodging graduate of Princeton.

Despite a core of loyal followers, and a ton of money from the oil industry, Hopkins had done poorly in the first two primary rounds. He came out of them still breathing, but barely. Then something extraordinary happened, the kind of mind-boggling change in public opinion that Parrish, like all political veterans, dreamed of but didn't truly believe possible. It had come because of dreadful news: Hopkins' twelve-year-old daughter, Julie, was suddenly diagnosed with inoperable spinal cancer.

Hopkins, true to form, wouldn't mention the tragedy on the campaign trail, and when word leaked out he absolutely refused to answer questions about a subject he considered completely personal. He was going to tough it out, utterly stoic. Yet somehow, despite his attempt to wall off his private life, people all over America began to see him with a new set of eyes. Instead of seeming cold and unfeeling, he appeared heroic and tragic. Everything he did and said was touched by feeling for his plight and his daughter's. The evangelical bloc, which had been repelled by his worldly and secularized outlook, began to pray for him, especially when they heard through the rumormill (aided surreptitiously by Parrish) that Hopkins had accepted Oklahoma City megachurch pastor Bart Methune's offer to pray for his daughter. There were even rumors of a miraculous healing.

It left the opposition sputtering. How could they fight against a twelve-year-old girl with cancer? Elevated by the public feeling, Hopkins swept through the remaining primaries, won the Republican nomination, and proceeded to a landslide electoral victory. During the last three weeks of the campaign he had been buoyed by unexpected brio, campaigning with a vigor Parrish had never seen in him. Parrish knew the reason, though few others did: Hopkins' daughter's tumor had shrunk, to the astonishment of her doctors. How could any parent help feeling overwhelming elation at the possibility that his daughter was healed, whether he believed in miracles or not?

Then, in the interim between the election and the inauguration, tragedy: Julie took an overnight turn for the worse and suddenly died. When Parrish got the phone call it struck him like a blow. He could hardly imagine what this would do to the president, a man who had never learned how to grieve, who had always commanded his way through every obstacle.

Even less could Parrish have imagined that Hopkins would turn to Pastor Bart Methune for comfort. Or that through Hopkins' devastating loss he would end up not cursing God but embracing him in a full-scale Billy-Graham-style religious conversion. Parrish remembered vividly his shock when Hopkins called him into his private quarters, read his Bible aloud to him, and began to weep while telling Parrish that Jesus had entered his heart and forgiven his sins and promised him eternal life. Hopkins had put his hand on Parrish's shoulder and said he now had hope he would see Julie again. He had tried to explain to Parrish that he could be forgiven too, despite Parrish's hurried reference to his Episcopal background. It had surely been the most uncomfortable moment of Parrish's whole political life, and the most alarming. And little had he known there would be plenty more of the same to come.

Yet until today Parrish would have sworn the results were nearly all good. Yes, Hopkins read the Bible more than his briefing papers. True, he constantly wanted to squeeze in time with religious senators and pastors. Those were minor problems. Making up for them by far, Hopkins made a better leader. He was warmer. People wanted to follow his lead, even some very hardened and egotistical career politicians. It was true that Hopkins quoted from the Bible more than was comfortable in Washington, but the people in the hinterlands hardly seemed to mind — in fact, they loved it. Weird as it seemed to Parrish, he had been forced to accept that Hopkins' conversion had made him a better president.

Now, for the first time, Parrish had begun to wonder whether this new religious fervor had a truly dark side. He didn't understand the currents moving in Hopkins's mind on the Israeli situation. He had left the president just an hour before, staring into the big brown Bible open before him. Parrish told himself that it was perfectly reasonable for a president to draw strength from the Bible at such a time. What bothered him was that Hopkins didn't seem to be reading his Bible for inspiration. He seemed to be looking for directions.

10:00 A.M., THE PENTAGON

Once back at the sane world of the Pentagon, General Brent Slocum almost wondered whether he had imagined the strange scene at the White House. The praying and Bible reading seemed impossibly distant from this familiar territory among the uniformed brass and the bureaucrats. Slocum watched the secretary of defense pace back and forth behind his desk. Shirtsleeves rolled up, tie loosened, collar open, Hartwell punctuated his lecture to a gathering of high-ranking officials with readings from intelligence reports clutched in his left hand. His right hand held a cigarette, which he rubbed out whenever it burned down to a stub, only to light another. Ashes floated like dirty snow onto the navy-blue carpet, the desk, and Hartwell's beautifully tailored pants.

He talked as quickly as he walked, a practice he had developed during his twenty years as a congressman.

Of all the cabinet members, the former representative from Wisconsin was the least in tune with the new, born-again Hopkins. Hartwell was as profane as the president was pious. A party loyalist since the eighties, he had stuck staunchly with the big-business conservatives and hard-line foreign policy realists who reclaimed the party from the evangelicals in the '08 election. But when values voters sat on their hands and Democrats won in a landslide, he had seen the necessity of a reconciliation. More than any other single person he had done the deals behind the scenes that brought evangelicals back in. Always a realist, he had swallowed hard and publicly lauded the leaders of the religious right. He had negotiated the promises of appointments and programs on behalf of Hopkins' campaign, including a new cabinet-level office for Faith-Based Initiatives. And he had made the evangelicals believe that, while Hopkins might not be a terribly religious man, he was in tune with their values.

It was almost funny that the evangelicals, having swallowed an irreligious Hopkins, had gotten a brother.

Hartwell's pre-election negotiations did not endear him to a man like Slocum, who distrusted politicians. But the secretary of defense had other qualities. He was a formidable debater, quick with the facts or, if necessary, his mesmeric personality. He knew how the government worked—had it down cold—and could store more information about the budget in his head than any of Slocum's technological wizards could access with their laptops.

Now Hartwell was jabbing his cigarette in the air like a weapon, lecturing them on the immediate action required. "Arens must be ordered to drop Tzuria like a piece of pork. If not, we withdraw all support, military or otherwise. The subject is nonnegotiable." Stopping his pacing for a moment, he glared at his audience. "Anybody disagree?"

Slocum shook his head and the others followed suit.

General Curt Oliver of Central Intelligence, who sat beside Slocum, had delivered actual transcripts of the Arens-Tzuria meetings. They showed Arens as depressingly querulous and erratic, while Tzuria had the constancy of a hungry predator. Tzuria offered to deliver the votes Kadima needed to form a government, but there was a price. Arens must look the other way when commandos took out the Dome of the Rock; then he must claim Israeli sovereignty over the site. Tzuria would do the rest. They would move so fast the Palestinians wouldn't have time to react. Marble slabs had been precut. The Temple could be up within thirty days.

By now Slocum understood what had earlier sounded like an old Paramount biblical epic. On reaching his Pentagon office, he had called in a young captain whom he knew to be highly religious. "What do you know about the Temple Mount?" Slocum had asked. Captain Bryce had confirmed just what Slocum had heard at the White House, and more. The Temple must be rebuilt within the next generation, according to prophecy, Bryce said. As far as he knew, all born-again Christians believed it because the Bible taught it.

Slocum cleared his throat. "Mr. Secretary, I confirm your objectives. But I think we need to optionalize contingencies. What if Arens refuses to listen to us? What then? This thing could slip out of gear in a hurry."

"Refuse to listen?" Hartwell snapped. "Absolutely not. We own him. Three of his Knesset members work for us. Oliver here signs their paychecks." Hartwell gestured toward the deputy director of the CIA.

"Yes, sir," Slocum said, "I'm sure that's right. However, it seems optimal to prepare for all contingencies. People do strange things when religion gets involved. Also Arens might think he can call our bluff. He knows that this administration will never abandon Israel."

Hartwell flushed. He took a long drag on his cigarette. "General," he said scornfully, "I think I know where this administration stands. The abandonment of Israel is not at stake. The abandonment of Ehud Arens is more to the point."

"Yes, sir," said Slocum, "but the Israelis have been known to confuse the two. And they have a track record of maximizing independence. I'd propose we optionalize the possibility—however infinitesimal—that they ignore our counsel."

Hartwell fumed, stared at Slocum, blew smoke. He detested Slocum's Pentagonese but knew the general was right. The president's loyalty to Israel was a matter of faith, and the Israelis would play that for all they could.

"What do you propose then, General?" Hartwell asked, lighting another cigarette and leaning on the back of his overstuffed, shiny-blue leather desk chair.

"The Marines, sir. We have an LPH with the Sixth Fleet that could be off the coast in a little under twenty-four hours. It's up to T/O requirements—and ready ... one battalion ... good troops. We'd be able to put twenty choppers with six hundred men into Jerusalem thirty minutes after lift-off. The Israelis wouldn't know how to react, especially if we told them we were on an antiterrorist maneuver. It's now 5:00 P.M. in Tel Aviv. My men could have the Dome of the Rock sealed by this time tomorrow."

Hartwell smiled but didn't interrupt.

"Of course, sir," Slocum continued, "I don't have an op. plan approved by the chiefs. We haven't even contemplated ... that is, no one ever figured on defending a mosque in Jerusalem."

"Wasn't part of the war games, eh General?" Hartwell burst into laughter, which started a coughing spasm. It took a full minute before he could stop his smoker's hack.

Drying his eyes with a rumpled handkerchief, Hartwell said, "Sorry, General. Just the thought of American Marines—probably Christians— defending an Islamic mosque against our closest allies, the Jews—" With that he started laughing and coughing again. "Hopkins'll have kittens."

Slocum's military operation was both bold and simple, and thus likely to succeed. They kicked it around, discussing logistics. Nobody had a better idea. But their conversation lacked energy, drifting to a halt whenever they moved from the military to the political situation. None of them could imagine the president authorizing the Marines to invade Jerusalem.

As he thought of this ridiculous limitation on his power, Alexander Hartwell gradually warmed into a fury. He slammed his fist on the desk, jumped to his feet, and began to pace again.

"Something has to move him," he muttered. "Something has to make it too hot for him. Not State. The little pipsqueaks there will be wringing their hands all through afternoon tea. Nobody has the guts for this kind of crisis. Congress'll go berserk."

The others stopped talking, watching Hartwell pace from one end of the room to the other.

Suddenly he whirled around and stabbed a finger at the general. "Slocum, what did you make of Parrish? Where is he in all this?"

"Sir?"

"Could we use Parrish? He seems to know the inside of the president's skull. Do you think he'd work with us?"

Slocum found the very idea of outflanking the president offensive. "Parrish is the president's man. He might agree with us, but I don't believe he'd scheme against his own boss."

Hartwell scowled but passed over the implicit warning. "You're right, I suppose. But we need some way ..." He paused, his gaze fixed on the vivid colors of his desk pad, etched with the giant seal of the secretary of defense.

A smile twitched the corners of his lips. He muttered, "Of course, of course. Why hasn't anyone thought of this until now? Yes, we'll have to." He looked up at his assistant. "Frank, that's it."

After twenty years Flaherty knew enough to say, "Yes, sir."

"Get the story to the press. Leak it fast, and make sure they go after it full speed ahead. But be careful." He grinned widely. "If Hopkins ever found out it would be my—that is, all of our necks, right on the chopping block."

Slocum sat up stiffly, as though coming to attention. "Sir, the president gave us strict instructions not to allow this story out."

"Yes, he did, didn't he, General? That's why I want it kept in this room. If it gets out who's responsible, you'll go down with me. Clear enough?" He was leaning across his desk, staring directly at Slocum. Then he sat down slowly. "General, I appreciate that this may go against your grain. But this is a case when following protocol may not be in the best interest of the commanding officer. When the enemy's aiming a gun at your commander's head, you just shove him into a foxhole. You don't wait to say, 'sir!' Am I right?"

"Yes, sir," Slocum said grudgingly.

"That's all we're gonna do," said Hartwell with a smile. "Give our commander a little shove into the foxhole. You see?"

Slocum said nothing.

Hartwell was on his feet again, pacing behind his desk, his attention back to the leak. "I can't believe this story hasn't broken yet anyway. Well, no ... it's a religious thing, so the press probably wouldn't even understand. And the Israelis know how to keep things quiet. I wish we did as well."

He pointed a nicotine-stained finger at his assistant. "Okay, Frank, move on it. Call Stuart or Marvin. No, they're too well plugged in. Call Nolan. He'll buy it in a minute. And let it all out: 'Arens is dealing with the Devil ... would constitute the worst offense against Palestinian rights in forty-five years of occupation ... fanatical religious elements are gaining control of Israeli foreign policy.' Just make sure we're well under cover—'informed sources,' you know. Once we point the press in the right direction, they'll scare themselves half to death without our help. But it needs to move fast."

"Yes, sir." Flaherty never looked up from his notes.

"But the Palestinians will be tipped off too," General Oliver added. "And that may force Arens's hand. Tzuria may strike before the Marines are in position."

"No, no. Think it through, gentlemen. The Israelis can't move except by surprise. This'll create confusion for them, and it'll force Hopkins to intervene. Otherwise he'd appear weak." Hartwell licked his lips. He was obviously pleased with himself.

"General." He wheeled around and jabbed his finger at Slocum. "Order the Marines to head due east, full steam ahead. Put the Sixth Fleet on standby alert, and have your battle plan ready to issue as soon as possible. That means in the next hour."

Hartwell took one long satisfied look at the military men arrayed before him and chuckled. "From the Halls of Montezuma to the Dome of the Rock, eh? All right. Get to it."

LATE AFTERNOON, THE WHITE HOUSE PRESS ROOM

At 2:30 in the afternoon Hartwell's leak exploded in the middle of an otherwise routine Washington day. First, Robert Nolan came on Cable News with the bizarre story. Then the wire services ran their versions, crediting "informed sources" saying that U.S. policymakers were working day and night to head off a militant Yisrael Beiteinu party takeover of Israeli foreign policy; intelligence experts considered war in the Middle East a real possibility.

A separate story, pulled up on short notice out of the files, told the history and objectives of the Yisrael Beiteinu party, including last year's merger with the religious Mopet party and financial links to American groups who shared their belief that these were the "last days." The Beiteinu rallying cry was "they must go," referring to the Palestinians. The party had also called for the trial and execution of any Israeli officials who talked to Hamas.

Reporters began to congregate in the White House Press Room, first reading the story on computer monitors in the little cubicles lining the back of the room, then jabbering into their cell phones.

By 3:00 P.M. the Associated Press cited unconfirmed reports that the U.S. Sixth Fleet had been ordered to the eastern Mediterranean. The Pentagon press office issued a flat denial. But only a half hour later there were reports from naval headquarters in Naples, Italy, that all leaves had been cancelled.

That triggered a flood of dispatches from Middle East correspondents eager to catch up. These included wild and vitriolic quotations from various leaders of Yisrael Beiteinu; of the Waqf, the Jordanian-backed Muslim group that controlled the Temple Mount; and others.

At 4:15, ABC broke into daytime programming with a brief report. The other networks were on the air by 4:25.

The Christian Broadcasting Company interrupted its regular programming for what they called their "Last Things Report." This included continuous live satellite coverage of the Dome of the Rock, using the site as the backdrop for their news set. The host, an Australian named Sydney Halford, interviewed several Bible scholars, evangelists, and a retired Navy admiral. The White House and Pentagon telephone numbers flashed across the screen at five-minute intervals, and Halford urged everyone who wanted to hasten the return of Christ to call and express unqualified support for Israel.

By 5:00 P.M. the White House switchboard was overloaded, and the signal agency was called in to help.

As the network evening-news deadline drew near, Press Secretary Dolores Lawrence pleaded with Larry Parrish for some kind of release. The White House Press Room was like a den of underfed animals, she said. Parrish told her tersely to stick with "no comment." Finally, after she had interrupted him three times, Parrish checked with the president and then sent MaryEllen Davies down with a written statement reaffirming the government's faith in Israel's democratic processes and stating that no unusual military maneuvers were being called for or contemplated.

5:00 P.M., THE OVAL OFFICE

It was clear to Larry Parrish that Hopkins was angry and flustered. An ordinary observer would not have recognized this; Hopkins had his reading glasses on and was perusing reports as though he were reading birthday cards. But his chief of staff had learned the signs. When the president was angry, he would take off his watch, chafe the inside of his wrist, and then put the watch back on—sometimes four or five times in a row. Today his watch was on and off incessantly.

"Larry," the president said in a voice that should have been accompanied by lightning bolts, "I want to know who did it. You find out. I don't care what means you have to take. Well, you know what I mean. I don't want Nixon's plumbers or Reagan's polygraphs. Nothing dirty, understand. But spare no effort. This kind of thing can destroy us. It has us up against the wall right now."

"Yes, sir," Parrish said.

The president took off his glasses, tossed them onto the desk, and rubbed his hands through his hair. "I don't know, Larry. What do we do next? Wait and see what Arens says to Ambassador Walker? This is the first time I've really felt what I've read so often of other presidents: to have the responsibility for the world and yet so little power to do anything. I don't think I've ever prayed like I have today."

"You have the option papers from Hartwell and Davies, sir," Parrish said crisply. "They both want to see you, quite urgently. They're rather insistent. Also, Dolores is begging you to make a statement."

The president was silent for a moment, then said softly, "Larry, I read those option papers. And frankly, I just couldn't believe it. I ran on a platform of military strength, it's true, but not against our allies. And certainly not against *Israel*. I can't see any point in talking to Hartwell or Davies right now. It'd just disturb me."

The president flipped through a few of the reports on his desk, indicating that the subject was closed for the moment. "Did you see this report on phone traffic between Jerusalem and the U.S.? It says a lot of money — millions — is being offered to Tzuria. From Arizona, Colorado, California, Florida, Alaska. Some from people I know: the Temple Foundation, the International Christian Embassy, the Thromos, the Merchessens. But what I found interesting is that a lot of big money is coming from the oil men, especially in Alaska."

"Davies has a theory on that, Mr. President," Parrish said. "She says some of the big oil companies would like nothing better than a Middle East war to send oil prices soaring again. The oil crowd could be stirring this thing up."

Hopkins peered over his reading glasses. "Yes, yes, I suppose. We'll watch that. You call Hy Levin and tell him to alert the FBI. Christians and Zionists have pure motives, but those oil boys, well, that's another story."

Then Hopkins gestured with his left hand, as if he were brushing away an annoying insect, and reached across the desk for his Bible. Parrish had never seen Hopkins so preoccupied.

"You know, Larry, I never thought of it before, but isn't there a prophecy of that in Luke? Yes. Here. Listen to this. 'It was the same in the days of Lot.

People were eating and drinking, buying and selling, planting and building. But the day Lot left Sodom, fire and sulfur rained down from heaven and destroyed them all. It will be just like this on the day the Son of Man is revealed.' That's Luke 17:28. You see, people will keep right on doing business up to the very moment of Christ's return." The president smiled, the first break in his gloom. "Can you imagine the looks on the faces of those oil boys?"

The president paused, looking up as though he were trying to see through the ceiling. "You know, Larry, I can't help thinking — this really could be *the time*. The generation that saw the Jews return to their homeland is all but gone. It almost has to happen soon. All that is left is for the Temple to be built. That's the last big sign before ..."

Parrish stood to his feet as though facing a firing squad. "Mr. President, I feel it's my duty to beg you not to pursue such thoughts. The people of the United States didn't elect you to be their ..." Parrish groped for the right term ... "to be their crystal-ball gazer. They elected you to protect and defend the Constitution of the United States."

Hopkins looked at Parrish with more sadness than anger. "Larry, as you well know, at one time I would have agreed with you. I thought God-talk had no place in government. But now I believe my thoughts have penetrated a little deeper. I took an oath to defend the Constitution, but I believe God is the ultimate defender of this nation and the Constitution. He's the one who enables this nation to stand, and if we stand against him, how long do you think he'll let us go on? If we stand against God, we're not defending the Constitution at all."

"Sir, I understand that. But you're the president, and as such, you have clear duties. You took an oath of office — "

Hopkins cut him off. "Larry, you called me a crystal-ball gazer. But that's the furthest thing from what I'm doing. Don't you believe that Ezekiel was a prophet inspired by God? We can't just close our ears to those words and pretend they're irrelevant to this situation."

"No, sir. But when you're in this room, you represent all the people — Christian, Jew, Muslim, atheist. You can't let one view of Bible prophecy influence you. Your job is to protect the nation — and everyone's religious views. I mean, we're talking about war and peace, Mr. President, not church."

"Larry, Larry. You should know better. Separation of church and state doesn't mean keeping God out of everything that truly matters. Yes, we're talking about war and peace. Do you think God doesn't care about war and peace? Furthermore, the God I serve isn't just God of the Christians. He's the God of the universe. What he says goes for everyone. It's not *my* views we're discussing Larry. I've come to understand that my views don't matter that much. These are *God's* views, clearly spelled out in the Bible. If I am going to live up to my oath of office I need to bring the wisdom of God into the conduct of our affairs. And if the wisdom of the Bible doesn't have anything to say about Israel, I guess I don't know much about the Bible."

Parrish was about to respond, but the president's phone beeped gently and a light flashed. Hopkins punched the speaker button hard.

"Sir," said his secretary's gentle voice, "Secretary Davies insists she must see you right away."

MaryEllen Davies strode into the office two minutes later, her cheeks flushed and her eyes abnormally bright. She seemed to be breathing heavily.

"What happened to you, MaryEllen?" the president said jovially.

"Those vultures." Davies gestured in the direction of the Press Room. "They're after red meat."

"Tell me about it," the president said dryly. "And if you have any information about who leaked this business, I want to know."

"Yes, Mr. President," said Davies. "That's not my concern at the moment, however." She pulled a Queen Anne side chair up to the president's massive mahogany desk and began talking even before she sat down. "Ambassador Walker visited Arens an hour ago at his residence, conveyed your concern, and got no satisfactory response. Nothing. The old coot just sat there and said, 'You tell your president that Israel has never had a better friend than Shelby Hopkins.' That's the same thing they've been telling every president since Truman. Now, Mr. President, we need a tough note from you that I can fax to Tel Aviv. It can be handed to Arens at 8:00 A.M. their time. I have a draft here, sir."

Hopkins put on his reading glasses and took the sheet from Davies. His lips hardened as he quickly scanned it.

"Paragraph three will have to go. I will not threaten any kind of military action against Israel." Hopkins swept his pen angrily across the center of the page.

"You must, sir. It's all they'll listen to," Davies insisted.

"That goes against my deepest convictions." Hopkins glared over his glasses. "And this could be leaked and destroy my credibility. Furthermore, it's unnecessary. Ehud Arens is a friend and a reasonable man."

Davies started to protest, but Hopkins held up his left index finger and kept scratching on the paper, mumbling to himself as he wrote. "There. That's more like it." He leaned back and read through his revisions, then spun the piece of paper across the polished desktop.

"Will that do, MaryEllen?"

Parrish knew Davies was steaming. Hopkins wrote well, often drafting his own speeches, but Davies wasn't looking for subtlety. She wanted a sledgehammer.

Davies also knew, however, how far Hopkins could be pushed. She shrugged slightly and smiled demurely. "It may work, Mr. President. I'll have it typed up and returned at once for your signature." She inserted the paper into a green folder and left immediately.

"Larry," the president said, "I want you to handle Hartwell and Slocum for me. Tell them I've read their papers and I'm weighing the whole thing. Hold their hands a little and let them know they're important. Tell them … tell them I fully understand their feelings about Tzuria.

"Call me if anything important happens tonight. But only important matters, please. I'll trust your judgment. I'm going to be in the Lincoln sitting room after dinner. I want time to think and pray some more … and I may call Dean Roberts."

"Who's that, sir?"

"Dean Roberts?" For a moment the stress of crisis disappeared from Hopkins' eyes. "He's a great old man Pastor Methune introduced me to. Roberts was president of the Mid-South Seminary, but he's retired now, living in Alexandria. A complete gentleman of the old school, and according to Methune one of the world's foremost Bible scholars. I have a feeling he might help me."

Not knowing what to say, Parrish began to gather his papers.

"Larry," the President said, "I'm sorry if I lost my temper with you. This has been a trying day, but that's no excuse."

"No problem, Mr. President. I probably had it coming."

"Oh, and one more thing, Larry. When you talk to Hartwell, see if you can find out where this leak came from."

7:00 P.M., THE WHITE HOUSE SITUATION ROOM

Parrish had a strong suspicion who had leaked the story, but he needed to confirm it and find out whether any other secrets were about to hit the fan. He descended the narrow staircase in the West Wing, moved past the basement security desk, then followed the long corridor toward the White House staff dining room. Beyond that he came to an unmarked door and entered the Situation Room, the Security Council nerve center.

Designed for use in World War II, the Situation Room bore little resemblance to its Hollywood counterparts. There were no flashing lights or electronic displays. It was merely a large room with open-office furnishings, strangely silent except for the gentle, steady hum of computers. Men and women moved about in tightly controlled frenzy, transporting the paper that continuously spit from printers.

Parrish entered the nondescript conference room in the center. On one wall was a blackboard, on another a global map, and on a third, a giant video screen used for conferences with the national military command center in the Pentagon. Parrish had chosen to talk to Hartwell and Slocum from here because it was absolutely secure. Listening devices from several different embassies in Washington could pick up most digital transmissions, but this room was surrounded by an impenetrable electronic shield.

At precisely 7:00 Hartwell and Slocum appeared, full size, on the video screen. The simulation was so real that participants soon forgot they were five miles apart. A puff of smoke trailing from Hartwell's mouth drifted lazily across the screen. When he realized the video was on, he stared directly at Parrish.

"I don't want to talk with you," he snapped. "I want to talk to the president. We need action. Tell him I must talk to him. We have critical new intelligence."

Parrish deliberately spoke in a soft tone, almost too soft to hear. "The president understands the situation fully. He asked me to update *you*. He wants you to be fully informed at all times of *our* initiatives." He paused to let that sink in and then continued. "A very strong note signed by the president will be delivered to Arens first thing in the morning. We believe that once he realizes our displeasure, he'll reject Tzuria's offer."

"What're you guys smoking over there?" Hartwell exploded. "That's bull and you know it, Parrish. Words aren't going to stop Arens. We need action."

Parrish calculated quickly and decided to risk a slight evasion. "We'll know what we need soon. It's 2:00 A.M. in Jerusalem. In a few hours we'll have Arens's response. We can then proceed to other options as necessary." Hartwell began to interrupt, but Parrish raised his voice just enough to continue. "The president has read your option paper and has it fully in mind."

"What's that mean?" Hartwell asked sarcastically. "He's thinking about it? Don't run that White House we-know-it-all stuff at me, Parrish. Come tomorrow, we'll be in a dogfight. I guarantee it. You tell the president the task force'll be sixty miles off the coast, the Second Battalion Eighth Marines ready to go by tomorrow morning, fourteen hundred hours Jerusalem time."

"And we have an airtight op. plan," Slocum added. "We can secure the Temple Mount in thirty minutes from lift-off."

Parrish deliberately looked down at his fingernails until he had his anger under control. "Who authorized that?" he asked softly.

"No authorization was necessary," Hartwell said. "Those are routine precautions—"

"Routine, my foot," Parrish snapped. "Hartwell, I know what you're up to. The president doesn't ... yet. I haven't told him. But you should know you can't keep secrets from me."

"What are you talking about, Larry?"

"You know what I'm talking about. The leak. What a clumsy move." Watching closely, Parrish thought he saw Slocum flinch.

"Are you accusing me of leaking sensitive military secrets? Because if so—"

"Not me, Al." Parrish raised his hands in a gesture of peace. He knew Hartwell would like nothing better than a shouting match. "No accusations here. Just mind me from now on. And listen to what I'm saying. You don't get your way with this president by pushing him into a corner. He'll push you right back. This leak has made a bad situation worse. It's distracting him. And it's fired up his fundamentalist brothers too. They've been calling him all day. So don't try anything with those ships and guns. I'm giving you the word right now: the policy of the United States government is that we will not interfere in the domestic affairs of our ally, the sovereign state of Israel. Period. Until you hear differently from here."

Hartwell blew a cloud of smoke over his right shoulder. "I know all that stuff the State Department puts out. By tomorrow the president will be more than grateful that we're ready for action when we have to be. So remember that, Larry, when tomorrow morning comes.

"Now look," Hartwell continued, narrowing his brown eyes slightly. "We've got something new. If the president won't talk to me, you better get this to him. You know we have a man in Arens's inner circle. And we now have absolute intelligence that the decision is made. There will be a deal; Arens will go along fully with Tzuria. And Arens doesn't for a moment believe that Hopkins will lift a finger. In fact, he believes that Hopkins is sympathetic with them." He paused, waiting for a reaction.

"Go on," Parrish said.

"So they'll move on the mosque. We don't know when, but it could be very soon. You can bet Hamas will respond with everything they have. Their honor's at stake. But we're most worried about Iran. They're the only players who can match Israel militarily."

"Bomb for bomb," Parrish said gloomily.

"Yes. So far they've kept the nuclear option under wraps. But you have to wonder why they went to all the trouble to develop a bomb, if they wouldn't use it to defend the Dome of the Rock. There would be internal pressures to launch. Some of Iran's leading elements, possibly including their president, have a theology that leads them to seek maximum chaos."

"Is that so?" Parrish said. This was worse than he had thought. "Any suggestion that they're mobilizing their launchers?"

"Nothing so far," Hartwell said. "We've got all the eyes trained on them, but so far no movement that we've detected. But then, nobody has blown up the mosque yet, either."

"You're saying," Parrish repeated after taking a deep breath, "that the Arens-Tzuria deal is confirmed. You expect the mosque to be invaded shortly. Is that correct?"

"That's it."

"I'll inform him immediately," Parrish said. "I'll phone him from here. Call MaryEllen Davies if anything changes." He punched a button and the screen went blank.

Parrish wanted to get outdoors and clear his head with some fresh air; he wanted to see his wife and kids. He had eaten only a sandwich for lunch — hours ago — yet he felt uncomfortably bloated. He reached for a telephone, but the operator couldn't put his call through. The president was with Dean Roberts and could not be interrupted, she explained.

7:25 P.M., THE LINCOLN SITTING ROOM

"Dean, that is so, so helpful." President Hopkins was seated in a yellow brocade wing chair, an open Bible splayed in his lap. Dean Roberts had his own straight-back chair pulled alongside, so they could examine the text together. He was a balding man with round glasses and a small white goatee. His resemblance to an owl was often noted, a wise old owl.

Hopkins fumbled in a nearby table drawer and drew out a yellow legal pad. "If you don't mind, Dean, it would help me to summarize some of the key points. Number one is that we must stand with the Jews. Genesis 12:3 and all that about the blessings God will offer through them." He paused and scribbled on the pad. "And it doesn't matter whether the Israeli government has faith in God or whether they are unbelieving nationalists. The point is that Israel today is the biblical nation to which Jesus returns."

At that point the door swung open. The Secret Service would admit only his wife or Parrish without advance permission, so Hopkins scarcely looked up.

"And point two, God has been kind to America because America has been kind to the Jews. 'Those who bless you I will bless,' as the Bible says." The president motioned for Parrish to sit down. "And point three, you say it is clear in Ezekiel and Daniel that the attack on Israel will come from the north."

Dean Roberts had glanced curiously at Parrish when he entered, but his mind was clearly engrossed in the discussion. He cleared his throat. "Yes, Mr. President, that's very clear, but I must honestly tell you there's some controversy about how to apply it. We used to think it referred to Russia. That seemed a perfect fit during the Cold War. Some people still think it's about Russia, but others wonder about other candidates."

"Lebanon is the closest country to the north," Hopkins mused.

Dean Roberts cleared his throat again. "Yes, Mr. President, but it's a tiny, weak nation. As I don't have to tell you. How could it hurt Israel?"

Parrish had remained standing, staring a hole in the deep pile carpet. His stomach was beginning to churn again. What he was hearing, added to what Hartwell had just told him, made the burden in his stomach heavier.

Hopkins paused, momentarily pondering Roberts' point about Lebanon. Then he switched his attention back to the yellow pad, which he tapped twice with the tip of his pen. "So you believe that the 1967 war was a signal—of sorts, that is—that God has given Israel full sovereignty over the Promised Land." Again he signaled Parrish to sit. "So point number four is that the Jews must redeem the land. Is that the word, Dean? Redeem?" At an enthusiastic nod from Roberts he continued. "Which brings us to the Temple. Rebuilding the Temple would be the final step, along with preaching the gospel to the whole world. Which, heaven knows, is already happening with all our satellites for television and radio."

Parrish wandered over to a window and looked out while the conversation continued. He couldn't listen to this stuff. It disturbed him too much. But he couldn't entirely filter it out, especially when the two men began to use words like "Armageddon," as they did now. He had been brought up Episcopalian, with no place at all for matters like the rapture and the tribulation, words Hopkins and Roberts also used enthusiastically. Parrish had very little idea what those words actually meant.

Parrish saw that the president was standing and shaking hands with Roberts. "I guess that will about wrap up the whole story, won't it?" Hopkins was asking. "As far as these events are concerned?"

Roberts had both the president's hands clasped in his, and he was beaming as at a star pupil. "Yes, the end of the story, Mr. President. That's why they call it the End Times."

"Well, Dean, I can't tell you how much you've helped me. A lot of this is new to me, and confidentially we're facing some difficult matters in the Middle East just now. I can't tell you more than that, but pray for us. Do pray. I find it so helpful to know what the Bible says about it all. Step by step, as though by a secret plan."

Roberts lifted an admonitory finger. "Not a secret, Mr. President. All of it written down for our encouragement."

Roberts saw himself out while Hopkins threw his muscular body into the wing chair again. He glanced at Parrish but waited to speak until Roberts was gone.

"A brilliant man," Hopkins said. "He's eighty-three and hasn't lost a step."

"Yes, sir," Parrish said.

The enthusiasm on Hopkins's face drained away slowly as he confronted his aide's grim expression. "Larry, don't 'yessir' me. Say what's on your mind."

"I don't know what's on my mind, Mr. President. Frankly, sir, you're scaring me to death."

"You mean that, don't you, Larry?" The president stood, half turned away, then whirled back to face him. "Tell me why."

"I don't know how to explain it, if you can't see it for yourself, sir," Parrish replied. "You're responsible for hundreds of millions of lives, including mine, including my wife and kids. And you seem to be guiding us by some obscure, kooky theory about the end of the world."

"What if the obscure, kooky theory happens to be true?"

"I'm happy to leave that decision up to God. The end of the world is His business. Our business here in the White House is to *prevent* the end of the world."

"Well, according to my theology, Larry, the end of the world—"

Parrish interrupted, something he never would have done had he not been deeply distressed. "Your theology is irrelevant right now! You weren't elected to be the nation's theologian."

Hopkins was visibly shocked by his aide's words. He turned and walked over to the window and looked out across the South Lawn at the Washington monument, floodlit against the darkened sky. "Larry, you're right, I wasn't elected to be the nation's theologian. Even if I were, I'm not qualified. But I was elected to be the nation's leader. And I don't happen to think it's just an accident that it says on our money, 'In God we trust,' or that it says in our pledge, 'one nation, under God, indivisible.' I'm the leader of a country that lives under God. America needs a president who will listen to God. I'm sure that's what people want, at least people outside of the Beltway."

"Mr. President, you know better than that. The people want a president who has one wife, 2.5 well-mannered kids, and uses an occasional quote from the Bible. They would never have elected you if they thought you would be setting foreign policy according to pronouncements from a book in the Bible most of them have never heard of, let alone read. That scares me to death, and it would scare them too. They want their president to be tough and strong and to use common sense."

"The only common sense I know is to trust God's Word," Hopkins said stubbornly. He seemed genuinely irritated by Parrish's words. Parrish felt as though he was crossing a line. But he had to. He had to try to talk sense.

"Does God's Word tell you to sit back and let the Israelis blunder into war? Hartwell has information that Tzuria and Arens have reached an agreement. If we don't stop them, they'll destroy the mosque, probably within the next twenty-four hours. We have to move militarily or there'll be war."

"No," Hopkins said vehemently. "I will not lift a hand against God's chosen people."

"Then you shouldn't have taken that oath last year, Mr. President. You didn't promise you'd defend us against anybody but God's chosen people. You said you'd defend the Constitution — period. And by the way," Parrish said, looking at his watch, "the fleet will be off the coast of Israel in about twelve hours."

"Who ordered that?" Hopkins demanded, taking off his watch to chafe the inside of his wrist.

"Hartwell said it was a routine precaution."

"Routine, my foot."

"That's what I said. But at least it keeps your options open."

Hopkins accepted that with a grunt and dropped into the yellow chair again, stretching out his legs and running his fingers through his hair. "By the way, did you learn anything about the leak?"

Parrish hesitated. "Nothing solid, sir. But I suspect Hartwell was behind it."

The president accepted that too with a grunt, his mind obviously elsewhere. Parrish wondered whether he should leave.

"The truth is, Larry, I'm not sure what to think," Hopkins said gloomily. "You're talking political sense. And my Christian friends are talking another kind of sense. It's almost as though two worlds are colliding here, and I'm in the middle. I wouldn't say this to anyone but you, but maybe I just don't belong in this place."

For the first time ever, Parrish saw a hint of weakness in Hopkins's eyes, an almost pleading look.

"Larry ..." The president's voice was tentative, hesitant ... "Larry, how did we ever get into this mess?"

He sat forward, took a deep breath as if drawing on hidden reserves, and forced a smile. "Well, I guess we've done what we can for tonight. Arens will get my letter shortly. And the fleet, you say, is moving. Why don't you go home and spend some time with your family, Larry? It's been a long, frustrating day. Let's pray tomorrow is better."

As Parrish moved toward the door, Hopkins called to him. Parrish saw that the president had picked up his yellow legal pad. "Larry, one more thing. Is there any indication that Lebanon could be involved in what's going on?"

Parrish recognized immediately that the president had reverted to Dean Roberts' step-by-step rendition of the end times. "No," he said, feeling the queasiness in his stomach once more. "Not that I know of. Hartwell considers Iran to be the big worry. The Palestinians will go berserk if something is done to the Dome of the Rock, but they're militarily impotent. Iran is another matter. We're monitoring their rocket launchers very carefully. So far, nothing."

"Just a thought, Larry. Tell Hartwell I want a very careful workup on Lebanon. See if there is anything suspicious there. It's just possible the attack on Israel will come from there."

3.00 A.M., GEORGETOWN

The phone woke Parrish — the special secure phone. It rang five times while he tried to straighten the confusing shapes in his head; he was always slow to awaken. Finally his wife sat up in bed and turned on the light.

"Why don't you answer it?" she asked.

He picked up the receiver and heard MaryEllen Davies's dry tones. "Larry, there has been a very interesting development. The president was on to something in Lebanon. The CIA says the Hezbollah have got an operation cooking in the Bekaa Valley. Our on-the-ground people say Hezbollah have cordoned off an area the size of a small county. Nobody, not even their own people, can come and go from there. We're still studying the satellite data but it looks as though they are putting some rocket launchers on the ready, launchers that they must have got from Iran, because they're big. Big enough to go nuclear."

Parrish felt his own heart thumping madly. "So what's going on, MaryEllen?"

"It's all theoretical, but the CIA thinks that Iran may have word about Tzuria's deal. They could attack Israel through the Hezbollah and have plausible deniability."

"Why would they do that?"

"Larry, not even the Iranians want to go up in a mushroom cloud."

"No, I mean why would they risk everything because of a Jerusalem mosque? They have had these weapons for a decade, and they've never put them in play before."

He could almost hear her shrug over the telephone. "You know, the Iranians have a curious theology. Most of them are what is known as 'Twelvers.' They are waiting for the twelfth imam to reappear and bring the world to an end. He's a kind of messiah figure. Some of them believe that since he will only appear at a time of maximum chaos, it's a good thing to stir up maximum chaos. According to certain sources President Ahmadinejad himself believes that. It's possible those kinds of views have become ascendant."

What immediately passed through Parrish's mind, though he did not say it, was that they had found President Hopkins' mirror image. Two men, staring into the vast differences of culture, religion, and national interest, were trying to steer their nations according to a kooky, apocalyptic version of the end of history. Parrish realized that he was trembling slightly as he thought of it. They were steering straight into each other. They were steering the world into a black hole.

Parrish hung up and called the president. Hopkins answered on the first ring. His voice sounded fresh and awake.

"Mr. President," Parrish began, "You seem to have been right about Lebanon." He tersely described what Davies had said about the Hezbollah and Iran, fully expecting Hopkins to crow that Bible prophecy had been proven right.

The response, however, was unexpectedly muted. "Sounds like we better put our diplomats to work. I know we don't have too much to go on with Hezbollah, but what about Lebanon's PM? Can he serve as a go-between with them? He might be reminded that he doesn't want to preside over a nuclear wasteland.

"And Iran, let's work all our contacts there. Not just the official channels, the undercover links. This is important enough to risk blowing some covers. And better bring Syria in too. If Iran has sent nuclear weapons into Lebanon, the Syrians are certainly in on it."

"You're tracking with Davies, sir. She suggested all those moves. She also suggested that we put our forces on alert. If war breaks out, we want to be ready to respond immediately."

"You don't suppose, Larry, that by putting our forces on alert we might spook the Iranians? That they might think we are backing up Tzuria, for example? Could we get ourselves in the thick of a fight we don't want?"

"It's possible, sir. We could get our diplomats to reassure them on that point."

"Which assumes, doesn't it, that they believe what we say. Which, if they trust us as much as we trust them, isn't very likely. But we can't be caught with our pants down. Let's go on alert. And have Davies get on those calls immediately. Anything else, Larry?"

"No, sir."

"No word on a response from Arens, is there?"

"Nothing so far."

"Well, let's all meet at 6:00 A.M. Make it the Oval Office—it doesn't matter now. Hartwell, Slocum, Lovelace, Davies, you, and me.... Larry, are you still scared? I've been praying for you and your family."

"Thank you, sir. No, I guess I'm not scared," he lied.

"Well, good. The Lord has been speaking to me, telling me there is no need to be afraid. When this is all over, we're going to praise Him for the magnificent wonders He has wrought. Be of good courage. That's the Lord's message to us both."

7:15 A.M., THE OVAL OFFICE

Alexander Hartwell stood before the president's desk and pounded on it with his fist. The cigarette in his hand trailed ashes across the carpet—the first cigarette in the Oval Office in fourteen months, Parrish thought as he watched in horrified astonishment.

"Mr. President!" Hartwell was almost shouting. "The Marines are ready. They'll be in the air within sixty seconds if you say the word. I'm telling you, our information is absolutely certain. Tzuria has the okay from Arens. He'll move on the mosque if we don't get there first. And Hezbollah are just waiting for an excuse to fire away. It could be nuclear. You've got to move!" Hartwell punctuated his last words with two desk-shuddering blows.

The president stood to majestic height. "Hartwell, that's enough," he said in a splendid, controlled bass. "Go sit down. You've had your say."

To Parrish's surprise, Hartwell obeyed. As he sat down, he glanced at his cigarette as though surprised to find it in his hand. Parrish picked up a cup and saucer, and shoved it toward him. Hartwell ground out the cigarette.

For a long minute there was complete silence. They had been in the Oval Office since sunrise; they had talked themselves out. Everyone except Lovelace favored immediate military action, reasoning that there was no point in having a CIA if they couldn't trust information it said was firm.

Lovelace wanted to wait for a definite response from Arens. But the president's note had been given to the Israeli leader almost eight hours before, and there was still no reply. Arens was holed up in his office and had put off the American ambassador repeatedly.

"Nobody wants to say anything else? That's amazing, isn't it? Who would have thought it? Silence from this group." Hopkins smiled wanly. "I'll tell you what I've decided then. I can't in conscience move our troops, with all the risks that entails, until I've heard from Arens. If he won't talk to our ambassador, I guess he'll have to talk to me. MaryEllen, get Arens on the phone for me."

Hartwell exploded again, jumping to his feet. "That'll take time, and we don't have time. Let's at least get our men in the air. We can always recall them."

"No, no, I'm not ready to raise a hand against Israel," the president said decisively.

Davies got up and walked briskly out of the room.

Then the president began to talk, the music of Oklahoma in his voice, something that happened when he reached for his full eloquence. Using his big hands like a television evangelist, he tried pulling his listeners into his point of view, changing the shape of things by massaging the air. He took them back to the campaign and his pledge to fight terrorism anywhere in the world. They had promised America strength, and they would give America strength.

It is the plight of politicians, Parrish thought, to believe that words still make a difference when events are racing past them. Speeches like this one had gotten Hopkins to the White House. No wonder, when he didn't know what to do, he talked.

The president spoke of the meaning of Israel, how it embodied the hopes the Jews kept through the millennia. He quoted the Bible from memory. He recited America's enduring commitments, suggesting that America's great blessings were linked to its protection of the Jews. On and on and on he went.

Suddenly the door burst open. "Mr. President," Davies announced, "the Dome of the Rock has been destroyed. One minute ago Israeli commandos blew it up!"

Hopkins, interrupted midsentence, stood with mouth open. Hartwell began to swear.

After a brief, stunned silence, Slocum asked, "Any casualties?"

"Definitely. Hundreds of worshipers were in and around the mosque. There were Palestinian militants all around it too. How many, we don't know yet. Israeli troops are trying to seal the area."

Parrish stood and walked to a wall cabinet. He opened the doors, switched on the large television screen inside, and flipped across several channels. The morning talk shows were blathering on, still unaware of the event. But the picture on the Christian Broadcasting Company channel looked like something straight out of hell. Two broadcasting voices were talking on top of each other. The picture seemed out of focus or full of dust.

"That's the mosque," President Hopkins said in a low voice.

Out of the dust appeared two tiny blurred objects. The camera zoomed in on them. They were trucks. When they stopped, small dark particles seemed to scatter from them.

"They're deploying their men," said Slocum. "Throwing up a perimeter, I would guess."

"Extraordinary," murmured Lovelace. "I assume this is live?"

"MaryEllen," said the president softly, "you weren't able to get Arens on the telephone?"

"No, sir."

They watched the picture for another minute. No more movement was discernible. Both broadcasting voices had stopped; the background sound was now a choir singing "The Battle Hymn of the Republic."

"What do you suggest we do, MaryEllen?" the president asked.

Parrish thought he saw just a flicker of the earlier how-did-we-get-into-this-mess look cross Hopkins's grim face.

"I think we'd better try to get President Ahmadinejad on the telephone," Davies said.

The president nodded and turned to his desk.*

---

*Although this story is fictional, certain quotations attributed to Israeli and U.S. political and religious leaders have been taken from actual public statements; material regarding the takeover of the Temple Mount is also taken from public records.

PART ONE

NEED
FOR THE
KINGDOM

1

KINGDOMS
IN CONFLICT

Men never do evil so completely and cheerfully as when they do it from religious conviction.

BLAISE PASCAL

Without Christian culture and Christian hope, the modern world would come to resemble a half-derelict fun-fair, gone nasty and poverty-racked, one enormous Atlantic City.

RUSSELL KIRK

"How did we get into this mess?" Our fictional president's anguished query echoes a cry heard across our country. For while this story of a decent, moral leader who lets the world slip to the brink of Armageddon would have seemed outrageous fiction just a few years ago, for millions today, a similar scenario looms as a terrifying possibility. Equally disturbing to many is the realization that if this nightmare came true, millions of others would welcome it as a long-awaited consummation of human history.

These tensions run deep. On one side are those who believe that religion provides the details for political agenda. On the other are those who see any religious involvement in the public arena as dangerous. Not since the Crusades have religious passions and prejudices posed such a worldwide threat—if not through a religious zealot or confused idealist whose finger is on the nuclear trigger, then certainly by destroying the tolerance and trust essential for maintaining peace and concord among peoples.

Radical, Islamo-fascist terrorists have spread fear throughout Europe, Asia, the Middle East and the United States. In recent decades, Iraq, Northern Ireland, Sudan, India, and Indonesia are grim examples of nations deeply torn by sectarian strife. Where once people of faith endured horrific persecution under oppressive Marxist regimes—and still do today in North Korea, China, and Cuba—today millions are persecuted under equally oppressive Islamic regimes in Iran, Saudi Arabia, and Pakistan. Even where radical Muslims do not rule, Islamic terrorists do not hesitate to engage in murderous attacks, as we have tragically seen in England, Spain, Indonesia, Italy, and the United States—most horrifically in the September 11 attacks which killed nearly 3,000 innocents. In the West, church-state confrontations are multiplying. As one prominent psychologist observed, this strife "has little to do with whether the state espouses a leftist or rightist political philosophy";[1] the fires rage amid a variety of political systems.

Diverse as they may seem, these tensions all arise from one basic cause: confusion and conflict over the respective spheres of the religious and the political. What Augustine called the City of God and the city of man are locked in a worldwide, frequently bitter struggle for influence and power.

Nowhere has this conflict been more hotly debated than in America. Throughout most of its history, the U.S. has enjoyed uncommon harmony between church and state. The role of each was regarded as essential, with religion providing the moral foundation upon which democratic institutions could function. As recently as 1954 the Supreme Court explicitly rejected the contention that government should be neutral toward religion. Justice William O. Douglas stated that "we are a religious people whose institutions presuppose a Supreme Being."[2] But only nine years later, barbed wire was flung up on the "wall of separation" between the two as the court reversed itself in its landmark school-prayer decision. Though the expulsion of formal prayer from the schoolroom did not impede people's ability to talk to God wherever they wished, the decision reflected the shifting public consensus about the role of religiously based values in public life. It set off major tremors along long-dormant fault lines in America's political landscape.

At the same time the works of such writers as Camus and Sartre were enjoying enormous popularity on American college campuses. These existentialists argued that since there is no God, life has no intrinsic meaning. Meaning and purpose must be boldly created through an individual's actions, whatever they may be.

This relativistic view of truth perpetuated a subculture whose password was "do your own thing"—which for many meant a comfortable spiral of easy sex and hard drugs. Personal autonomy was elevated at the expense of community responsibility. Even as many pursued these new freedoms in search of fresh utopias, some acknowledged the void left by the vacuum of values. Pop icon Andy Warhol spoke for the mood of a generation: "When I got my first TV set," he said, "I stopped caring so much about having close relationships ... you can only be hurt if you care a lot."[3]

Liberal theologians eagerly adapted to the powerful trends of the day. The late Bishop Robinson's book *Honest to God*, published the same year as the school-prayer decision, gave birth to the God Is Dead Movement, popularized on the cover of *Time* magazine.

By the seventies, religion was fast becoming an irrelevant, even an unwanted intruder in politics and public affairs. The Supreme Court often practiced what one dissenting justice in the school-prayer case had warned against: a "brooding and pervasive devotion to the secular and a passive or even active hostility to the religious."[4]

Roe v. Wade, the 1973 decision legalizing abortion, was the final blow for traditionalists. Not only was it seen as a rejection of America's commitment to the sanctity of life, but as a repudiation of moral values as a factor in court decisions. For the first time the justices excluded moral and philosophical arguments from their determination.

Roe v. Wade triggered a counter-reaction, sending tremors from another direction. Determined to preserve moral values in the public sphere, conservative church members who had long disdained politics began organizing furiously; the pro-life movement spread quickly across the country. By 1976 evangelicals were flexing their muscles behind a "born-again" presidential candidate. In 1979 a group of conservative Christian leaders met privately in Washington; the result was the Moral Majority and the Christian New Right. Within only six years this movement became one of the most formidable forces in American politics, registering millions of voters, raising vast war chests for select candidates, and crusading for its "moral agenda" with the fervor of old-time, circuit-riding preachers.

In 1984 the fault line broke wide open with a presidential campaign that resembled a holy crusade more than an election.

First, the Democratic candidate for vice-president, Geraldine Ferraro, questioned whether President Reagan was "a good Christian" because of his policies toward the poor.[5] Days later, the Catholic archbishop of New York challenged Mrs. Ferraro's Catholic faith because of her support for pro-abortion legislation. At the Republican convention President Reagan told 17,000 foot-stomping partisans that "without God democracy will not and cannot long endure."[6] His Democratic challenger, former Vice President Mondale, said that faith is intensely personal, should never be mixed up with politics, and that Reagan was "trying to transform policy debates into theological disputes."[7] Governor Cuomo of New York gave a widely heralded address at Notre Dame, in which he stated that as a Catholic he could personally oppose abortion, yet support it as governor as a "prudential political judgment," since he was following the will of the majority.[8]

In thousands of precincts across the country, fundamentalist ministers organized voter-registration campaigns, equating conservative political positions with the Christian faith. New Right spokesmen trumpeted the call for God, country, and their hand-picked candidates, and compared abortion clinics to the Nazi holocaust.

Civil libertarians reacted with near hysteria. Some labeled the late Jerry Falwell an American version of the Ayatollah Khomeni. People for the American Way, a group organized by liberal activists to counter the Moral Majority, launched a slick media campaign attaching the Nazi slur to the religious right.

Never had religion become such a central issue in a presidential campaign; never had the church itself been so dangerously polarized.

The fissures that broke open in 1984 remain wide and deep today. On one side are certain segments of the Christian church, religious conservatives who are determined to regain lost ground and restore traditional values. "America needs a president who will speak for God," proclaimed one leader. Whether out of frustration or sincere theological conviction, Christian conservatives have become politicized, attempting to take dominion over culture through legislation and court decisions handed down by strict-constructionist judges.

Those on the other side are no less militant. Believing (or at any rate, claiming to believe) that Christian political activists will cram religious values down the nation's unwilling throat, they heatedly assert that faith is a private matter and has no bearing on public life. The New York Times, for example, accused Ronald Reagan of being "primitive" when he publicly referred to his faith: "You don't have to be a secular humanist to take offense at that display of what, in America, should be private piety."[9]

The mainstream media took the same open-minded approach when President George W. Bush told a reporter that his favorite political philosopher was Jesus Christ. New York Times columnist Maureen Dowd sneered: "Translation: You're either in the Christ club or out of it, on the J.C. team or off. This is the same exclusionary attitude, so offensive to those with different beliefs, that he showed in 1993 when he said that you must believe in Jesus Christ to enter heaven." Yet, most of the media looked the other way when the president of Iran publicly prayed at the United Nations during a visit in 2006.

Meanwhile, the 2000 and 2004 elections were extremely close, revealing a country closely (and dangerously) divided, politically and culturally, stereotyped along "Red State" (Republican, rural, church-going, NASCAR-watching, country-music loving) and "Blue State" (Democratic, urban, latte-drinking, brie-nibbling, rock-and-roll loving) ideologies. A British videogame designer had some fun at America's expense with his Internet meme "Jesusland" map, in which "blue" voters ended up in "The United States of Canada" (California, New England, and Canada), while "red" voters lived in "Jesusland:" the Midwestern and Southern states plus Alaska. Secession, anyone?

The real tragedy is that both sides are so deeply entrenched and polarized that neither can listen to the other. Invective and name calling have replaced dialogue. Nothing less than obliteration of the enemy will suffice; America must be either Christianized or secularized. Many citizens feel that they must choose sides, either enlisting with People for the American Way and the ACLU, or joining up with one of the many evangelical activist groups, from the Family Research Council to Concerned Women for America to the American Center for Law and Justice.

However we got to this point, the fact is that both extremes—those who want to eliminate religion from political life as well as those who want religion to dominate politics—have overreacted and overreached. Richard John Neuhaus does not overstate the case when he argues that this confrontation can be "severely damaging, if not fatal, to the American democratic experiment." Furthermore, both exclusivist arguments are wrong.

There is another way, however. It's a path of reason and civility that recognizes the proper and necessary roles of both the political and the religious. Each respective role is, as I hope this book will demonstrate, indispensable to the health of society.

Wise men and women have long recognized the need for the transcendent authority of religion to give society its legitimacy and essential cohesion. One of the most vigorous arguments was made by Cicero, who maintained that religion is "indispensable to private morals and public order ... and no man of sense will attack it."[10] Augustine argued that the essence of public harmony could be found only in justice, the source of which is divine. "In the absence of justice," he asked, "what is sovereignty but organized brigandage?"[11]

In the West the primary civilizing force was Christianity. According to historian Christopher Dawson, Christianity provided a transcendent spiritual end that gave Western culture its dynamic purpose. It furnished the soul for Western civilization and provided its moral legitimization; or, as was stated somewhat wistfully in *The London Times* some years ago, "The firm principles which could mediate between the individual and society to provide both with a sense of proportion and responsibility in order to inform behavior."[12]

The American experiment in limited government was founded on this essential premise; its success depended on a transcendent reference point and a religious consensus. John Adams wrote, "Our constitution was made only for a moral and religious people. It is wholly inadequate for the government of any other."[13] Tocqueville credited much of America's remarkable success to its religious nature; it was later called a nation with "the soul of a church."[14]

Today, many thinkers, even those who reject orthodox faith, agree that a religious-value consensus is essential for justice and concord. Polish newspaper editor Adam Michnik, a dissident during Poland's Communist era, who describes himself as a "pagan," applauds the church for resisting tyranny. Religion, he says, is "the key source of encouragement for those who seek to broaden civil liberties."[15] To disregard the historic Western consensus about the role of religion in culture is to ignore the foundation of our civilization.

But men and women need more than a religious value system. They need civic structures to prevent chaos and provide order. Religion is not intended or equipped to do this; when it has tried, it has brought grief on itself and the political institutions it has attempted to control. An independent state is crucial to the commonweal.

Both the City of God and the city of man are vital to society—and they must remain in delicate balance. "All human history and culture," one historian observed, "may be viewed as the interplay of the competing values of these ... two cities";[16] and wherever they are out of balance, the public good suffers.

This is why today's conflict is so dangerous. It would be a Pyrrhic victory indeed should either side win unconditionally. Victory for either would mean defeat for both.

I have brooded over this dilemma since the mid-seventies. My concerns deepened each year as the conflict intensified between the body politic and the body spiritual. A variety of questions plagued me: To what extent can Christians affect public policy? Is there a responsible Christian political role? In a pluralistic society, is it right to seek to influence or impose Christian values? How are the rights of the nonreligious protected? Are there mutual interests for both the religious and the secular? Is it possible to find common ground? What does the experience of history say to us today? What would God have us understand about this torn and alienated world—or, considering the mess we've made, has He given up on us?

Friends urged me to write on the subject since I've been on both sides—first, as a non-Christian White House official, and now as a concerned Christian citizen and the head of a Christian ministry. But the task always appeared too daunting. I couldn't sort out all the questions raised in the blistering American debate. Both sides seemed hopelessly intractable.

Oddly enough, it was on a visit to India in the fall of 1985 that I came to the unmistakable conviction that I must write this book.

At a friend's home in New Delhi, I listened to shocking stories of conflict between Indian Christians and their society. One young man who was converted to Christ after reading Christian tracts had been forced to leave his rural village by his outraged family. Another man who had been preaching on the street was cornered and beaten by an angry crowd. Many others, after converting to Christianity, had been tried by civil authorities.

The same day I was in New Delhi, opposition leader Charan Singh called upon Prime Minister Gandhi to "stamp out" all Christian missionaries lest their converts in certain states seek political independence.[17] Why, I wondered, is there such hostility to one faith in this Hindu culture that believes all roads lead to heaven? They should be the most tolerant of all. What is it about the Judeo-Christian message that makes it so offensive? Ironically, the Indians may understand the heart of the gospel—that Christ is King, with all that portends—better than many in the "Christian" West.

Later that day as my flight lifted off for Bombay, I looked down on New Delhi, which was shrouded in a dense smog from the open cooking fires of its crowded streets. Then, as we broke through to the blue sky above, it was as though the clouds surrounding these issues also broke open for me. I began to see the struggle in America—and around the world—more clearly than ever before.

So it was high in the skies between New Delhi and Bombay that I first wrote, "The kingdoms are in conflict, both vying for ultimate allegiance. Not just in America, but around the world. By his nature man is irresistibly religious—and he is political. Unless the two can coexist, mankind will continue in turmoil. Tragically, we have lost sight of both the nature of man and the nature of God and His rule over the world."

To put it simply, humanists—using that term in its best sense—fail to understand humanity and Christians fail to understand the message of Christ.

I first published *Kingdoms in Conflict* in 1987. I was motivated to bring out a twentieth anniversary edition by the fact that *Kingdoms* has continued to sell briskly all these years since its first publication. In my travels, I've found copies of *Kingdoms*, translated into Russian, being shared by members of the Russian Parliament. When I was in Canada recently, virtually every member of Parliament was reading *Kingdoms*.

I have substantially updated the book to address the tremendous changes that have occurred in the last twenty years. While the anecdotes may be different, however, the principles enunciated in the original edition are the same.

The truths *Kingdoms* contains are even more relevant today than they were in 1987. That was the heyday of the Moral Majority and the emergence of what was referred to as the New Christian Right. Twenty years later, the term "Christian Right" has morphed into "Right-Wing Extremist"—the most pejorative term in American politics. In the view of many, the goals of conservative Christians are considered synonymous with the Republican Party (leading to the bumper sticker quip "God is Not a Republican" [in large letters] "Or a Democrat" [in small letters]—a condemnation of the Christian Right by liberal evangelical Jim Wallis). This identification is tragic, because it diminishes the role of the Kingdom of God—and it's why the messages of this book are needed today more than ever.

Men and women have always been spiritual beings. But modern culture, in its zeal to eliminate divisive influences and create a self-sufficient, "enlightened" society, has ignored this fundamental truth. Along with denying God, today's social visionaries have denied man's intrinsic need for God. At the same time, Christianity has become a pale shadow of the radical Kingdom its Founder announced.

The shock waves that threaten the very foundations of our culture today, then, emanate from society's failure to understand man's need for God and the Christians' failure to accurately present Christ's message of the Kingdom of God. So before we can hope to deal with the modern religious-political conflict, we must take what at first may seem to be a digression. But bear with me. For until we understand the true nature of man and the true nature of Christ's message, we cannot hope to understand the story of President Hopkins and why we are in the mess we are in today—or, more importantly, the way out.

The place to begin, then, is with human nature itself. We'll start with a man who embraced the spirit of the twentieth century and lived it to its logical conclusion.

2

AFTER THE FEAST

*Our Nada who art in nada, nada be thy name thy kingdom nada
thy will be nada in nada as it is in nada. Give us this nada our daily
nada and nada us our nada as we nada our nadas and nada us not
into nada but deliver us from nada; pues nada. Hail nothing full of
nothing, nothing is with thee.*

"A CLEAN, WELL-LIGHTED PLACE"

The last party went on that entire summer. Papa had come to Spain to relive memories from earlier, happier days. He delighted in the rough red Spanish wines, the fresh flowers of the countryside, the uproar of the *fiera*. He ran with the bulls in Pamplona and crisscrossed the country following his favorite bullfighters, hanging over the edge of the ring in his *barrera* seat, tanned and squinting in the sun and dust, cheering the skill of the matadors. He loved the moment of death: the immense bull, thrusting and dancing with the slim figure of the matador; the glittering sword raised high in the air above the deadly horns; and finally the blade plunging deep between the animal's shoulders. Sometimes, when the bull could not be killed with the sword, the matador used a short knife, or *puntillo*. "I love to see the puntillo used," Papa would say happily. "It is exactly like turning off an electric light bulb."[1]

After the bullfights came the midnight feasts with the matadors and a variety of guests. American college coeds who had hesitantly approached Papa for his autograph suddenly found themselves swept into the party, mingling with Hollywood stars and Papa's old friends from the Spanish Civil War. They clustered around him, toasting his health, laughing at his stories.

That summer of 1960 was Papa's last happy time before the depression set in. It was as if he had gathered all his forces—the friends, the wine, the feasts, the women, the bullfights—for one final tribute to the things

56

that had filled his life so well over the years. The highlight was his sixtieth birthday party, a grand event designed to make up for all the birthdays that had slipped by while he was pursuing lions on safari, marlin off Key West, or lime daiquiris at his favorite Havana bar. Even if the passing of years was no great pleasure for Papa, the fact that he had survived to sixty was cause for celebration.

Guests arrived from the corners of Spain, from Paris, Washington, and Venice. The party began at noon on July 21 at a friend's seaside estate in Malaga. Mary, Papa's wife, had imported champagne from Paris, Chinese food from London, a shooting booth from a traveling carnival, fireworks and flamenco dancers from Valencia. An enthusiastic Spanish orchestra played on the balcony.

Papa declared it the best party ever. He danced through the house, a champagne glass in one hand, shotgun in the other. As the evening spilled on, he entertained guests by shooting cigarettes from the pursed—and presumably drunken—lips of two guests, the Maharajah of Cooch Behar and Antonio Ordonez, Spain's premier bullfighter. When the fireworks erupted, cheers resounded through the estate, and Papa led his guests in the *riau-riau*, the festive dance of the bullfights.

Evening spiraled into dawn, and at noon the next day the last guest staggered home. Before going to bed Papa plunged into the ocean, swimming in long, steady strokes parallel to the shore. A friend swam beside him. As they emerged from the water, Papa said with a sigh, "What I enjoyed most is that these old friends still care enough to come so far. The thing about old friends now is that there are so few of them."

Papa had made hundreds of friends over the years, collected everywhere he had lived and worked. He had lost many as well, abruptly cutting ties with those who disappointed him by being weak or dishonest. With his grizzled white beard, barrel chest, and baggy clothes, he was a man's man who in his fame had become almost a caricature of himself: the world traveler equally at home in Spain, France, Italy, Cuba, Idaho; the mighty big-game hunter of African lion, elephant, kudu. He had collected many women as trophies as well and had married four of them.

Papa started collecting adventures early. Born in Illinois in 1899 into a staunchly religious home, he had escaped during World War I to drive ambulances for the Italian Army. He was nineteen and relished the sweat, the blood, the spectacle of it all. Later a critic would write that he had been born twice—once in Oak Park, then born again to the reality of death on the Italian battlefields of Fossalata.

A few days after he volunteered for frontline duty, an Austrian mortar landed almost on top of him. The man it did hit disintegrated. Papa was severely wounded. He felt life begin to slip from his body "like you'd pull a silk handkerchief out of a pocket by one corner."

But he survived, even carrying a wounded comrade to safety, and spent half a year convalescing in Italian hospitals and back home in the States. (As the years went by, his wounds would continue. Plate glass sliced his head in Paris; a car crash crushed him in London; two plane crashes in Africa left him wounded and burned; boating accidents off the coast of Cuba resulted in concussions.)

After recovering from his war wounds, Papa became a journalist, writing crime stories in Chicago and feature stories in Toronto. He married and decided that Paris was the best place to refine his craft. For first and foremost Papa was a writer. Journalism had given him clean declarative sentences and the beginnings of a style; Paris was to provide a feast of experience that would last the rest of his life.

Papa wrote in cafes of the city. Using a stubby pencil and a small notebook, sipping a *cafe au lait*, he transformed his experiences into stories. When a story was done, he leaned back and splurged on a carafe of crisp white wine and a dozen oysters fresh from the sea, feeling empty and happy as if he had just made love.

Paris in the twenties had become a haven for writers and artists, and Papa was friends with many of them: Pablo Picasso, James Joyce, Gertrude Stein, Ezra Pound, F. Scott Fitzgerald. From these fellow expatriates, Papa learned how to write dialogue and refine his style. Of their philosophy he learned little, for the prevailing mood already matched his own. Papa had long since given up on the orthodox faith taught in his childhood—what he called "that ton of [manure] we are all fed when we are young." God was irrelevant, if He existed at all. The measure of a man's life was what he did—his experiences, actions, his courage in the face of death. Life was a wine glass to be filled to the brim and relished.

Papa's books of short stories and his first novel brought him recognition and success, granting him the freedom to pursue what suited him best: writing hard, loving hard, eating and drinking well, war, the hunt, and the bullfight.

When the writing flourished, he exuded a vitality, a sense of keen enjoyment that others could not help but admire.

But beneath that fulfillment was a vacuum that sometimes sucked him under. All his life Papa suffered bouts of depression — he called it "Black Ass." As long as there was another fiesta, another party, another good day's work ahead of him, the depression eventually lifted.

But in the end, when he had nothing with which to fill his life, it didn't.

By 1961 Papa had high blood pressure and diabetes. He was overweight and tired of dieting. His liver was corroded from alcohol. He was no longer able to function like a man's man. He had mental problems.

After all, Papa told a friend, "What does a man care about? Staying healthy. Working good. Eating and drinking with his friends. Enjoying himself in bed. I haven't any of them — none of them." Maybe the time had come, he thought.

Papa felt he had already died. After watching the failure, years earlier, of a once-great matador, he had said, "The worst death for anyone is to lose the center of his being, the thing he really is. Retirement is the filthiest word in the language. Whether by choice or by fate, to retire from what you do — and what you do makes you what you are — is to back up into the grave."

For even as he had danced with death over the years — he called it "that old whore" — he believed that when it came time to take her upstairs, that was his choice and his right. What else could a man control in his life if not the time and means of his death? His own father had killed himself years earlier.

If God existed, He might be fair reason to reject the whore; but if not, nothing made much difference after all. Papa had given up on God long before. Taking his life would prove he was master of his own fate.

What interested him most was how to do it. Dying, he said, was easy; it meant "no more worries." But a real man would die "intelligently, the way you would sell a position you were defending ... as expensively as possible, trying to make it the most expensive position ever sold."

Papa woke up early that Sunday morning, put on his red robe, and padded down the carpeted stairway of his Idaho home, which faced the magnificent Sawtooth Mountains. His wife knew he wanted to make his assignation, so she had locked his hunting guns in the basement. But she had left the keys on the window ledge above the kitchen sink. Perhaps she felt she had no real right to keep Papa from his choice.

He got the keys, went down the basement stairs, and unlocked the dark storage room. He chose a custom-made twelve-gauge Boss shotgun, inlaid with silver, which he had used for years to shoot pigeons. It was his favorite gun — not just a firearm, but a near-sacred object. He selected ammunition, locked the door, and climbed back up to the bright living room.

In the front foyer, a five-by-seven entryway walled with oak, he pushed a shell into each barrel and carefully lowered the gun butt to the floor. He stooped slightly, took a deep breath, and placed the cold metal inside his mouth. Then he tripped both triggers.

Thus did Ernest Hemingway give in to death's seduction. His work and his pleasures were gone; his once-full life had emptied. With no God, it was up to him to assert control over the one thing he still could — his own death.

His immediate legacy was the ruin of blood, bones, teeth, and hair that his wife found blasted onto the foyer walls that sunny morning, July 2, 1961. The legacy of his writing and his philosophy lives on.

In one sense Ernest Hemingway is the quintessential twentieth-century man. Born the year before the century began, he experienced its rapid advance of technology and depersonalization, its growing faith in science and government, and its declining belief in orthodox religion.

The week after the shotgun blast heard throughout the literary world, *Time* magazine reflected,

> Though he was leery of metaphysical systems, Hemingway was really on a metaphysical quest ... a tenacious observer of the crisis in belief and values which is the central crisis of Western civilization.... Hemingway's "ingenuous nihilism" was early set, but ... [if] life was a short day's journey from nothingness to nothingness, there still had to be some meaning to the "performance en route." In Hemingway's view, the universal moral standard was nonexistent ... [so] he invented the Code Hero, the code being "what we have instead of God."[2]

Hemingway was never far from his characters. He extended the drama of his books and stories into the stream of his own life — or vice versa: "The characters Hemingway creates drink everything, see everything, feel everything, do everything. Life to them is a chain of varied links, each different, each exciting and uniquely interesting, and the last link is the largest and most interesting of all, the link of death."[3]

And why not? If Hemingway and his existentialist friends who frequented the cafes of Paris were correct, their code is reasonable and even heroic. If this life is merely a glass to fill, when the glass is emptied, why not smash it against the living-room wall?

As Hemingway's friend Jean-Paul Sartre put it, "On a shattered and deserted stage, without script, director, prompter, or audience, the actor is free to improvise his own part."[4]

This view sounds both reasonable and romantic in literature or discussions in cafes and coffee bars. But the prospect in real life is stark. Among those who "tie a lamp to the masthead and steer by that" when "the stars are quenched in heaven,"[5] few take their existential belief to the ultimate conclusion. For this comfortless doctrine shreds the very fibers and design of the human psyche.

We need more. And most of us—deep down—cannot deny it. There is a core of truth buried in every heart, a truth that we can't escape.

Papa Hemingway thought he had when he consciously resisted it. The man in the next chapter knew he couldn't.

3

CROSSING
THE RUBICON

The heart has its own reasons which Reason does not know; a thousand things declare it. I say the heart loves the universal Being naturally, and itself naturally, according to its obedience to either; and it hardens against one or the other, as it pleases.... The heart has reasons which Reason can never know.

BLAISE PASCAL

On a cool March morning in 1984, a rumpled middle-aged man checked the lock on the solid-iron security door of his apartment, then headed toward his office at Cable News Network's Beirut Bureau. Cool Mediterranean breezes rippled the dust of the street as he rounded the corner from his cul-de-sac and turned onto Rue Bliss.[1]

The dark expressive eyes held concern. Late last night there had been shooting between rival Muslim and Christian militia along the Green Line, the barrier dividing East from West Beirut. There had also been reports of scattered shooting in the mountains. *I hope the camera crew's okay*, he thought. He had sent them to the front in the south with a local guide.

He was also thinking about yesterday's surprising announcement. The leaders of Lebanon's major political factions had agreed to meet the following Monday in Switzerland for a reconciliation conference. *Doubt if it'll make any difference*, he thought. *Reconciliation seems out of the question here.* Even the American-sponsored peace treaty between Lebanon and Israel was in danger of being cancelled. Syria was making headway in forcing Lebanon to end the agreement designed to keep the PLO out of an already chaotic Lebanon.

The light tap on his shoulder startled him. He turned and a short bearded man in his early twenties pushed a green handgun into his stomach, propelling him toward a small gray car pulling up to the curb. The back door gaped open. He didn't struggle when his assailant shoved him into the back seat and jumped in behind him.

"Close eyes. Close eyes," the man shouted, waving the revolver as the car sped away. "You see, I kill."

Life in Beirut before that morning had been exhilarating for Jerry Levin and his wife Sis. They had seen his assignment as Middle East bureau chief as a new adventure and had not been disappointed. Though the fifty-one-year-old newsman regularly put in fourteen- and fifteen-hour days reporting on the political situation, he relished the challenge of trying to unravel the enigma of Lebanon.

For her part, Sis had willingly interrupted her classes at the University of Chicago's divinity school and enrolled in the Near East School of Theology in Beirut. Typical of her enthusiasm, she had plunged into Arabic lessons, found the local Episcopal church, and made friends with the neighbors in their apartment building. Sis had already received several elegant invitations for teas and soirees, all neatly lettered with the disarming clause, "situation permitting."

Once the seaside Paris of the Mediterranean, Beirut was now a maze of gun emplacements, armed checkpoints, and patrolling militiamen. The civil war that began in 1975, the Israeli invasion of 1982, and the increasingly provocative rule by the Christian minority that had spurred the Shiite Muslim and Druze takeover of West Beirut just a few weeks earlier had all created chaos. No individual or military presence had been strong, willing, or able enough to impose order. Bombings, political assassinations, and kidnappings were the norm.

Jerry Levin was just one more victim.

Jerry and his colleagues at CNN had talked about the possibility of kidnapping. You couldn't live in Beirut with its almost daily "situations" without at least having it cross your mind. Now, the gun digging into his back was a sharp reminder that he had underestimated the reality. Jerry Levin was scared.

His captors had blindfolded him, but once they reached their destination, he could vaguely make out the shapes of shadowy figures who shoved guns up under the blindfold. They accused him of being a CIA agent, an Israeli spy, or a defender of the American foreign policy designed to eliminate them and their political goals. After several hours of inquisition they gagged him, wrapped him in heavy packing tape, and threw him in the back of a truck.

Jerry used all his senses to try to track their route. They had left Beirut and were climbing mountain roads that eventually stretched into level highways. They must have driven about two and a half hours. Jerry had studied maps of the area; he guessed they were in the Bekaa Valley, northeast of Beirut, somewhere near its main city, Baalbeck, and that his kidnappers were militant Shiite Muslims who favored the establishment of *Sharia* law in Lebanon. He was correct on both counts.

When they stopped, he was led into a building and shoved into a room. There they shackled his right arm and leg to a radiator. Then they left. Jerry waited, listened. He was alone.

He lifted his blindfold and blinked, not so much from the light — the blindfold wasn't that impenetrable — as the reality of the situation. The room was tiny and bare except for the narrow foam-rubber mattress he was sitting on. The one small window had been painted over. His arm and leg were secured to the wall by a bicycle-length chain that stretched only enough for him to sit or lie on his left side. He turned and with his free hand carefully scratched a tiny mark on the dingy wall. Day one.

The days passed in a blur of monotony and fear. Once a day his guards led him to the bathroom next door. That was the outer limit of his world for months. Otherwise, he was alone in his small room.

At first Jerry willed himself to think only pleasant thoughts. He blotted out his situation by reliving his first meeting with Sis. He saw her smile at him across the ballroom of an elegant opera party in Alabama. He pictured family and friends. He created long lists of major-league baseball teams and players. It took three days to mentally list every opera he had ever seen — all ninety-eight of them. He envisioned resplendent scenes from his favorites, playing out such roles as Floristan, the political prisoner in Beethoven's *Fidelio*. Chained to the wall in the depths of a dungeon, he sang, "God! This is miserably dark. How horrible the silence, here in my lonely cell." At the end of the aria Floristan's wife, Leonore, came to save him. "I see her. An angel. She leads me to freedom and heavenly life." Jerry imagined Sis rescuing him from his Lebanese prison.

All his escape routes led back to his prison. The labyrinth of his memories could take him only so far. The bicycle chain held him fast to dismal reality.

He lost weight. His back and left shoulder ached from the cramped position. Then the scary thing happened: he began talking to himself. That worried him. *I'm going crazy*, he thought. *But if I don't talk to myself, I'll go crazy anyway.*

What if he talked to someone besides himself? People had been talking to something they called God for several thousand years and hadn't gone crazy. Rabbis did it. Priests did it. Lots of different kinds of people did it. Maybe he could too.

No.

He had no right to talk to God unless he believed in God. He couldn't talk to someone who didn't exist. "If one-millionth of one percent of me doubted, then — I reasoned — I really would not be talking to God; but I would be doing what I was afraid would happen after all — be talking to myself. So I would go crazy anyway."

Jerry had long been an atheist, or perhaps an agnostic. It was a toss-up. His Jewishness was more a cultural than religious force in his life, but he had long since dismissed Christianity as irrelevant. Sis was a Christian, and though he respected the strength of her faith, it held no appeal for him. To him Christianity called up childhood memories of neighbors' rural country churches in Michigan, musty smells, faded lace doilies — a quaint, American-Gothic experience that had little to do with his fast-paced, urbane life. And besides, what about the Christian persecution of Jews, the Inquisition, the atrocities committed in the name of Christ?

Hunched on his foam-rubber mattress, Jerry remembered as best he could the scene from Dostoyevsky's *Brothers Karamazov* in which the story is told of a village in Spain during the Inquisition. As he recalled it, Christ Himself returns to the town and begins preaching the gospel. The Grand Inquisitor has Christ thrown into prison, then sentences Him to be burned at the stake. "We can't survive on these teachings," says the Inquisitor. "What you're saying is seditious as far as the church is concerned." Then he pauses and suddenly orders that Jesus be released. "Say all you want," he concludes. "It won't make any difference anyway."

I keep coming back to choices, Jerry thought. Believe God or don't believe. Reject Jesus for His followers' perversions of the faith He taught, or accept Him as the Son of God because of His incredible "extrahuman" life and teachings. Days went by. Jerry's mental struggle continued.

"It was a cosmic Catch-22, definitely not something to be fooled with. Ten days after my meditating began, on April 10, 1984, I approached and then crossed a kind of spiritual Rubicon, a diminishing point in time, a shrinking thousandth, then millionth of a second, on one side of which I did not believe and then on the other side I did."

When he crossed that line, things began to make sense. For example, he had always thought of Jesus' teaching about forgiveness as incredibly tacky, wimpy, and weak-kneed. Now, in his solitary cell, Jerry saw that "the bully with the gun is the wimp. The man who says go ahead and shoot is not." His first prayer was for Sis and his family. Then these words came out: "God, please forgive men like these—like I'm doing now—because they are in part responsible for bringing me to You and Your Son." He learned to forgive his captors even as he saw more clearly their bitter rage and desperation.

The hostile, bitter men who were holding him had actually done God's work. God had used their bondage to get his attention. *After all*, he thought, *why else would a middle-aged grandfather be sitting in his underwear here in a bare little room in Lebanon, chained to a wall?*

Within a few months Jerry was moved to a different house. There he was allowed to use the bathroom unaccompanied. When he was ready to leave, he had to tie his blindfold back on and knock on the door. Then his captors would lead him back to his room next door.

As the spring and summer passed, he heard the knocks of other hostages being shuffled in and out of the bathroom. The terrorists must have rounded up more Americans for bargaining chips.

In July he understood for the first time why he was a hostage. Looking into the lens of a video camera, he was forced to read a statement written by his captors, appealing to Ted Turner, founder of Cable News Network, to urge the U.S. government to intercede with the government of Kuwait to free the prisoners there. "My life and freedom," said Jerry's message, depended on the "life and freedom of the prisoners in Kuwait."

The prisoners were seventeen Shiite Muslims convicted of bombing the United States and French embassies in Kuwait in December 1983. Six people had been killed, eighty others wounded. Three of the men had been sentenced to death, the others to long prison terms. Some of Jerry's kidnappers were relatives of these prisoners.

Jerry was certain the U.S. government would never make such a deal. Again he was faced with a choice. Should he try to escape? The youths guarding him had been careless with his chains on several occasions. Would it happen again? He needed to be ready.

The opportunity he had been praying for finally came on February 13, 1985. About midnight he worked his way out of the chain. He tied three thin blankets together and climbed through the window onto the balcony. He then secured the blankets on the railing and lowered himself to the ground. He couldn't let himself even think about the fact that he was free. He zigzagged down the mountain as fast as he could, tripping over loose stones, his heart pounding.

As he neared the bottom, a dog began to bark. The refrain was picked up by dozens of others. Then he heard voices in the dark. He threw himself under a parked truck. Guns fired into the air; lights pointed in his direction. They had caught him.

When he crawled out, however, he saw not his kidnappers, but Syrian soldiers. He began babbling in a mixture of English and French. The soldiers agreed to help, and within thirty-six hours Jerry Levin stepped off an airliner in Frankfurt, West Germany. He walked straight into Sis's waiting arms.

It was then he learned that for eleven and a half months Sis had been practicing what he was just learning. Praying passionately for him, she had traveled to the Middle East with a radical message of forgiveness and reconciliation. Behind the scenes she was helped by Christian, Muslim, and Jewish friends. One Muslim leader in Beirut told her that never in a thousand years had so many people of different faiths worked together on behalf of one man.

"The irony," says Jerry Levin today, "is that they thought they were working for someone who was a godless man. They could not have known that the skeptic had become a reconciler himself.

"I am convinced now that none of us is ever really godless. I know now that He is always there for us whether or not we are there for Him."

4

FAITH AND
THE EVIDENCE

*Now it is our preference that decides against Christianity,
not arguments.*

FRIEDRICH NIETZSCHE

Experiences like Jerry Levin's are frequently described as foxhole conversions. Maybe so. My own conversion in the midst of Watergate certainly was greeted with skepticism. The cartoonists were busy for months with caricatures of Nixon's tough guy turned to God. But thirty-four years later I can write that I, like Malcolm Muggeridge, am more certain of the existence of God than I am of my own.

I understand, however, how people can listen sympathetically to stories like Levin's or mine and still doubt. Just because we need God does not prove He exists. This was, of course, Sigmund Freud's central point: that religion perseveres because people need it. "A theological dogma might be refuted [to a person] a thousand times," he wrote, "provided, however, he had need of it, he again and again accepts it as true."[1]

The influential German philosopher Ludwig Feuerbach believed that God was made in the image of man, a creation of the human mind projecting man into the universe. He picked up the Freudian belief that God was an illusion, Someone we created ourselves. And Karl Marx saw religion as nothing more than an opiate used by the powerful to tranquilize the exploited masses.

If these arguments are correct, then today's battle over the role of religion relates to the need for a psychological prop. If we create God for our individual needs and to civilize culture, then the secularist is right: religion *is* merely a personal illusion and has no place in political affairs.

68

But if there is strong objective evidence for the existence of God, if He is not a psychological prop but a fact, then we are dealing with the central truth of human existence. And if that is the case—if He exists—then God's role in human affairs, or religion's role in public life, is indeed the most crucial issue of this or any age.

So while it may seem an intrusion, please join me briefly as I relate a few of the evidences of God's existence and character that I have found convincing. For without such evidence, there is no point in your reading this book—or my writing it.

It was the very question of God's existence that created the most serious stumbling block to my own conversion. That August night in 1973 when my friend Tom Phillips first told me about Christ, I told him that I wanted no part of foxhole religion. And though later I tearfully called out to God, my mind still rebelled. I needed to know: Was this simply an escape from the trouble I was in? Was I having some sort of emotional breakdown? Or could Christianity be real? I needed evidence.

I started with the copy of *Mere Christianity* that Tom had given me. In C. S. Lewis's book I confronted powerful intellectual arguments for the truth of Christianity for the first time in my life.

Whether or not God's existence can be proved, the evidence can be rationally probed and weighed. Lewis does so compellingly, and he cites moral law as a key piece of evidence. Clearly it is not man who has perpetuated the precepts and values that have survived through centuries and across cultures. Indeed, he has done his best to destroy them. The nature of the law restrains man, and thus its very survival presupposes a stronger force behind it—God.

Or consider the most readily observable physical evidence, the nature of the universe. One cannot look at the stars, planets, and galaxies, millions of light years away, all fixed in perfect harmony, without asking who orders them.

For centuries it was accepted that God was behind the universe because otherwise "the origin and purpose of life [would be] inexplicable."[2] This traditional supposition was unchallenged until the eighteenth century's Age of Reason, when enlightenment thinkers announced with relief that the origins of the universe were now scientifically explainable.

But in the past few decades, science has completely reversed itself on the question of the origin of the universe. After maintaining for centuries that the physical universe is eternal and therefore needs no creator, science today has uncovered dramatic new evidence that the universe did have an ultimate origin, that it began at a finite time in the past — just as the Bible teaches.

In the early twentieth century, several lines of evidence began a curious convergence: the implication from general relativity theory that the universe is expanding; the finding that the stars exhibit a "red shift," implying that they are moving outward; and finally, the realization that the two laws of thermodynamics actually make it imperative to believe in a beginning to the universe.

The second law of thermodynamics, the law of decay, implies that the universe is in a process of gradual disintegration — implacably moving toward final darkness and decay. In other words, the universe is running down, like a wound-up clock. And if it is running down, then there must have been a time when it was wound up. In the eloquent words of Lincoln Barnett in *The Universe and Dr. Einstein*, "the inescapable inference is that everything had a *beginning*; somehow and sometime the cosmic processes were started, the stellar fires ignited, and the whole vast pageant of the universe brought into being."[3]

What's more, the first law of thermodynamics (the conservation of matter) implies that matter cannot just pop into existence or create itself. And therefore, if the universe had a beginning, then something *external* to the universe must have caused it to come into existence — something, or Someone, transcendent to the natural world. As a result, the idea of creation is no longer merely a matter of religious faith; it is a conclusion based on the most straightforward reading of the scientific evidence. British physicist Paul Davies, though not a professing Christian, says the big bang is "the one place in the universe where there is room, even for the most hard-nosed materialist, to admit God."[4]

These various lines of evidence coalesced in the 1960s and led most scientists to conclude that the universe began in a much hotter, denser state and is still expanding from those initial moments. The new theory hit the scientific world like a thunderclap. It meant that the idea of an ultimate beginning was no longer merely religious dogma. Science itself now indicated that the universe burst into existence at a particular time in the remote past.

Big bang theory delivers a near fatal blow to naturalistic philosophy, for the naturalistic credo regards reality as an unbroken sequence of cause and effect that can be traced back endlessly. But the big bang represents a sudden discontinuity in the chain of cause and effect. It means science can trace events back in time only to a certain point; at the moment of the big bang explosion, science reaches an abrupt break, an absolute barrier.

In fact, when the theory was first proposed, a large number of scientists resisted it for that very reason. The great physicist Arthur Eddington summed up the feelings of many of his colleagues when he stated that the idea of a beginning is philosophically "repugnant." Albert Einstein fiddled with his equations in the vain hope of avoiding the conclusion that the universe had a beginning. Astronomer Robert Jastrow, an agnostic who nevertheless delights in tweaking the noses of his naturalistically minded colleagues, maintains that science has reached its limit, that it will never be able to discover whether the agent of creation was "the personal God of the Old Testament or one of the familiar forces of physics."[5]

Many secularists are still squirming to avoid the clear implications of the theory. Some argue that the big bang actually advances naturalistic philosophy — that it has extended naturalistic explanations back to the moment of the origin of the universe itself. That means that if God exists, he has been pushed back to a shadowy first cause who merely started things off, with no role to play after that. But this is sheer bluster. Far from supporting naturalism, big bang theory shows the *limits* of all naturalistic accounts of reality by revealing that nature itself — time, space, and matter — came into existence a finite period of time ago.*

Nobel Prize-winning astronomer George F. Smoot (who shared the 2006 prize in physics with astronomer John C. Mather for their work uncovering evidence on the origin of the universe and how it grew into galaxies) sums it up this way: "It really is like finding the driving mechanism for the universe, and isn't that what God is?"[6]

Dr. Arno Penzias — also a Nobel Prize winner — would agree. Some forty years ago, while adjusting an antenna for a radio astronomy experiment, he and Dr. Robert Wilson encountered an annoying noise that wouldn't go away — no matter what direction they rotated their directional antenna. Eventually the realized they had discovered "cosmic background radiation," that many physicists now call "the radio echo of creation."

As Dr. Penzias explains, "The creation of the universe is supported by all the observable data astronomy has produced so far. As a result, the people

---

*I deal with this subject in greater depth in *How Now Shall We Live?* (with Nancy Pearcey), Tyndale, 1999.

who reject the data can arguably be described as having a 'religious' belief." That is, people who refuse to consider the evidence because it conflicts with their preconceived ideas are following a "dogma" in the most stubborn sense of the word.

In an article in *Perspectives in Science and Christian Faith*, Penzias told Dr. Jerry Bergman of the American Scientific Affiliation, "I invite you to examine the snapshot provided by half a century's worth of astrophysical data and see what the pieces of the universe actually look like ... In order to achieve consistency with our observations we must ... assume not only creation of matter and energy out of nothing, but creation of space and time as well."[7]

"The best data we have," Penzias added, rubbing it in, "are exactly what I would have predicted had I had nothing to go on but the five books of Moses, the Psalms, the Bible as a whole."[8]

One word that shows up in discussion of whether or not the universe had a beginning is "singularity." This interpretation visualizes all the matter of the universe concentrated in a "singular" location of infinitesimally small size and expanding to form all the galaxies, stars, and planets. But this interpretation fails the test of mathematical physics. Penzias points out that when the distance between objects decreases, the gravitational attraction between them increases. So if all the matter of the universe had once been compressed into an infinitesimally small "singularity," the gravitational pull would have been so massive that the matter never would have spread out and formed today's universe. "It would collapse into a black hole and stay that way," Penzias explains.[9]

So what does Penzias think that the Big Bang was? The most logical explanation is "a moment of discrete creation from nothing!"

Although the big bang theory has captured the imagination of many, it leaves serious questions unanswered—not only who or what made the big bang, but what came before it. And how in the big bang process—a presumably random explosion—did planet earth achieve such a remarkable, finely developed state?* William Paley, the eighteenth-century English clergyman,

---

*The big bang thesis is not by itself antithetical to the Christian biblical view. Professor Owen Gingerich, noted Harvard astronomer, frequently lectures on the "strange convergence" between the biblical and modern scientific explanation of the universe's origin. He relates the scientific evidence for the so-called big bang event to the biblical affirmation that the universe flashed instantly into existence in a great showering of light. Gingerich believes, however, that science deals strictly with the question of "how," while the biblical account addresses the equally critical question of "who."

told what has become a well-known parable on this point. A man walking through a field discovers first a stone, then an ornate gold watch. The stone, the man may reasonably conclude, has simply always been there, a sliver of mineral chipped from the earth by chance. But the watch, which has beauty, design, symmetry, and purpose, did not just happen. It had to have been made by an intelligent, purposeful Creator.

Some have asserted that the universe was self-generated. This violates, however, a primary law of logic: the law of non-contradiction that says the universe cannot be itself *and* the thing it creates at the same time.

Others simply state that the universe itself is self-existent and infinite; it has always been. Yet modern science has discovered no element in the universe that is self-existent.* Granted, the whole can be greater than the sum of the parts, but can it be of a different character altogether? Clearly not.

Nonetheless this is the view widely expressed today. One of its most popular defenders was the late Carl Sagan, who proposed that "the Cosmos is all that is or ever was or ever will be."[10] That is simply another way of saying that the universe itself is transcendent. Though Sagan's films and books are widely used in schools as science, his assertion is, in fact, only an assertion. It is also no more than an acknowledgment that we do not know how the universe began.

At one point or another even the most obstinate atheist or agnostic must deal with this question of first cause.

During the Watergate scandal, though a new Christian, I approached one of my colleagues to offer spiritual help. "No thanks," he replied. "I'm a rationalist." He tapped his head and said, "It's all in human will. I've thought it all through." He was a confirmed atheist and proud of it.

Since that time I've watched this man not only survive but recover remarkably. He served his prison term without apparent ill-effect, wrote memoirs, built a successful business, and kept his family intact. If anything, he appeared stronger for the ordeal.

Then, a few years ago, I learned that he was reading Christian literature. I wrote to him, and he replied that he was indeed seeking. "I'm now an agnostic," he wrote. "I can no longer be an atheist, for I cannot get by the question of the first cause — that is, how life began. The scientific rationales are simply irrational."

---

*A tentative theory exists today with respect to quantum physics that may raise questions about this conclusion.

Even if modern scientific theories provided satisfactory explanations for the origin of the universe, however, the question of the origin of man would still be unanswered.

The prevailing view of Sagan and others is that a serendipitous stew of chemicals gave rise to the first life, then natural selection sifted mutations over billions of years and an extraordinarily complex creature evolved that we know as man.

If this is true, man is nothing more than an accident that started as slime or, as one theologian has put it, we are but grown up germs. Our intuitive moral sense rejects such a trashing of human dignity.

Interestingly enough, even modern scientific research is beginning to question some of its own theories. Given the laws of probability and even allowing for the oldest possible dating of the universe, they ask, has there been enough time for life to begin from mere chemistry and for a creature like man to evolve?*

Weighing the evidence, it is not unfair to suggest that it takes as much faith, if not more, to believe in impersonal mechanisms as it does to believe in a Creator. One can understand why no less a scientist than Albert Einstein, though not of an orthodox faith, felt "rapturous amazement at the harmony of natural law, which reveals an intelligence of such superiority that compared with it all the systematic thinking and acting of human beings is an utterly insignificant reflection." Einstein's belief in the harmony of the universe caused him to conclude, "God does not play dice with the cosmos."[11]

---

*A *Washington Post* article by Eugene F. Mallove, an astronautical engineer, science writer, and Voice of America broadcaster, noted that "some cosmologists are proposing that the universe has been perfectly 'designed' for life in a way that could not have happened 'by chance.' ... There is an infinity of ways that the universe could have been set up that would have been more 'simple,' with fewer improbable coincidences.... Of course in almost any of these 'simpler' universes, the odds for the development of anything as complicated as life—no matter how you imagined it—would be nil." Eugene F. Mallove, "The Universe as Happy Conspiracy: There are Too Many Coincidences for Life to Have Happened by Chance," *Washington Post* (October 27, 1985), B 1–2.

Actually such odds may indeed be nil. The French mathematician, Lecompte de Nouy, examined the laws of probability for a single molecule of high dissymmetry to be formed by the action of chance. De Nouy found that, on an average, the time needed to form one such molecule of our terrestrial globe would be about 10 to the 243 power billions of years.

"But," continued de Nouy ironically, "let us admit that no matter how small the chance it could happen, one molecule could be created by such astronomical odds of chance. However, one molecule is of no use. Hundreds of millions of identical ones are necessary. Thus we either admit the miracle or doubt the absolute truth of science." Quoted in "Is Science Moving Toward Belief in God?" Paul A. Fisher, *The Wanderer* (November 7, 1985).

Scientific arguments also fail to take man's basic nature into account: we are imbued with a deep longing for a god. Even an obstinate unbeliever like philosopher Bertrand Russell wrote,

> One is a ghost, floating through the world without any real contact. Even when one feels nearest to other people, something in one seems obstinately to belong to God, and to refuse to enter into any earthly communion — at least that is how I should express it if I thought there was a god. It is odd, isn't it? I care passionately for this world and many things and people in it, and yet ... what is it all? There *must be* something more important, one feels, though I don't *believe* there is. [12]

When people try to suppress their essential nature, they must either admit the haunting desire for a god, as did Russell, or deal with the inner turmoil through their own means, often with disastrous consequences. Hemingway chose the latter course, as, for that matter, did Marx, Nietzsche, and Freud. Near the ends of their lives they were all bitter and lonely men. Nietzsche's insanity, many believe, was due as much to the despair of nihilism as to venereal disease. Freud could not be comforted after his daughter's death, as if he was grieving at the finality of life without God. In his last days Marx was consumed with hatred. All these men were simply reaping the logical consequences of their own philosophies.

But even should we concede that man just happened, and that he creates his own need for God, how do we explain his need for purpose? Consistent evidence points not only to man's deep spiritual longings, but to a purposeful nature in his desire for community, family, and work.

The great Russian novelist Fyodor Dostoyevsky said that not to believe in God was to be condemned to a senseless universe. In *The House of the Dead* he wrote that if one wanted to utterly crush a man, one need only give him work of a completely irrational character, as the writer himself had discovered during his ten years in prison. "If he had to move a heap of earth from one place to another and back again — I believe the convict would hang himself ... preferring rather to die than endure ... such humiliation, shame and torture." [13]

Some of Hitler's henchmen at a Nazi concentration camp in Hungary must have read Dostoyevsky. There, hundreds of Jewish prisoners survived in disease-infested barracks on little food and gruesome, backbreaking work.

Each day the prisoners were marched to the compound's giant factory, where tons of human waste and garbage were distilled into alcohol to be used as a fuel additive. Even worse than the nauseating odor of stewing sludge was the realization that they were fueling the Nazi war machine.

Then one day Allied aircraft blasted the area and destroyed the hated factory. The next morning several hundred inmates were herded to one end of its charred remains. Expecting orders to begin rebuilding, they were startled when the Nazi officer commanded them to shovel sand into carts and drag it to the other end of the plant.

The next day the process was repeated in reverse; they were ordered to move the huge pile of sand back to the other end of the compound. A *mistake has been made*, they thought. *Stupid swine.* Day after day they hauled the same pile of sand from one end of the camp to the other.

And then Dostoyevsky's prediction came true. One old man began crying uncontrollably; the guards hauled him away. Another screamed until he was beaten into silence. Then a young man who had survived three years in the camp darted away from the group. The guards shouted for him to stop as he ran toward the electrified fence. The other prisoners cried out, but it was too late; there was a blinding flash and a terrible sizzling noise as smoke puffed from his smoldering flesh.

In the days that followed, dozens of the prisoners went mad and ran from their work, only to be shot by the guards or electrocuted by the fence. The commandant smugly remarked that there soon would be "no more need to use the crematoria."

The gruesome lesson is plain: Men will cling to life with dogged resolve while working meaningfully, even if that work supports their hated captors. But purposeless labor soon snaps the mind.

You might argue that our need to work was acquired over centuries of evolution. But we must do more than work just to survive; we must do work that has a purpose. Evolution cannot explain this. More plausible is the belief of Jews and Christians that man is a reflection of the nature of a purposeful Creator.

But for those who insist that God is created by man, perhaps the most telling argument is to consider the nature and character of the God revealed in the Bible. If we were making up our own god, would we create one with such absolute demands for justice, righteousness, service, and self-sacrifice as we find in the biblical texts? (As someone has said, Moses didn't come down from the mountain with the Ten Suggestions!)

Would Israel's powerful elite have concocted such declarations as, "He defended the cause of the poor and needy ... Is that not what it means to know me?"[14] Would the pious New Testament religious establishment have created a God who condemned them for their own hypocrisy? Would even a zealous disciple have invented a Messiah who called His followers to sell all, give their possessions to the poor, and follow Him to their deaths? The skeptic who believes the Bible's human authors manufactured their God out of psychological need has not read the Scriptures carefully.

But can we rely on the biblical accounts? When I first became a Christian, I certainly raised such questions. In fact, I began to study the Bible with a lawyer's skepticism. I suspected it was a compilation of ancient fables that had endured through the centuries because of its wisdom.

I made some startling discoveries, however. The original documents from which the Scriptures derive were rigorously examined for authenticity by early canonical councils. They demanded eyewitness accounts or apostolic authorship. Today, a growing body of historical evidence affirms the accuracy of the Scriptures. For example, the prophecy recorded in Psalm 22 explicitly details a crucifixion, with its piercing of the hands and feet, disjointing of the bones, dehydration. Crucifixion, however, was a means of execution unknown to Palestine until the Romans introduced it—several hundred years after the Psalms were written. So modern critics concluded the Psalms were written later, such "prophecies" perhaps even recorded after the fact. Then came the discovery of the Dead Sea Scrolls, which made possible the scientific dating of portions of the Psalms to hundreds of years before Christ.*

Modern technology and archeological discoveries are also adding substantial support to the historical authenticity of Scripture.† As historian Paul Johnson has written, "A Christian with faith has nothing to fear from the facts."[15]

---

*Similarly, modern critics insisted there was no Hittite empire, since the only references to the Hittites were found in the Bible. But earlier last century the great Hittite civilization of ancient Asia Minor was discovered. Today no scholar would deny the authenticity of the Hittite civilization.

†Researchers in Israel, for example, after subjecting the first five books of the Bible to exhaustive computer analysis, came to a different conclusion than expected.

The Torah, or Books of Moses, had long been assumed by skeptics to be the work of multiple authors. But Scripture scholar Moshe Katz and computer expert Menachem Wiener of the Israel Institute of Technology analyzed the book's material through sophisticated

But sometimes personal experience offers the most convincing evidence. As I have written elsewhere, it was, ironically, the Watergate cover-up that left me convinced that the biblical accounts of the resurrection of Jesus Christ are historically reliable.

In my Watergate experience I saw the inability of men—powerful, highly motivated professionals—to hold together a conspiracy based on a lie. It was less than three weeks from the time that Mr. Nixon knew all the facts to the time that John Dean went to the prosecutors. Once that happened Mr. Nixon's presidency was doomed. The actual cover-up lasted less than a month. Yet Christ's powerless followers maintained to their grim deaths by execution that they had in fact seen Jesus Christ raised from the dead. There was no conspiracy, no Passover plot. Men and women do not give up their comfort—and certainly not their lives—for what they know to be a lie.

Finally, many of the world's greatest philosophers and scientists have gone beyond deductive assent to the confidence that God exists because they have experienced Him. Were Augustine, Aquinas, Luther, Newton, and the great social reformers of the nineteenth century victims of infantile wish fulfillment? Did some psychological whim motivate St. Francis or George Fox to expend their lives in protest against economic elitism? Was Louis Pasteur, who labored against great physical handicaps to achieve scientific breakthroughs to benefit man, simply mistaken in his motivation to do so for the glory of God?

What is it that motivates people, both Christian and nonbeliever, to do works of mercy? The goodness of the human heart? Hardly. Man's basic nature, as we shall see in the next chapter, suggests just the reverse. Rather, love for others, like the need for purpose, is implanted in the hearts and minds of men and women—even those who don't acknowledge it—by a loving and purposeful Creator.

Faith requires no surrender of the intellect. It is not blind, unthinking, and irrational. Nor is it simply a psychological crutch. For me, the objective evi-

---

computer analysis. They discovered an intricate pattern of significant words concealed in the canon, spelled by letters separated at fixed intervals. Mr. Katz says that the statistical possibilities of such patterns happening by chance would be one to three million. The material suggests a single, inspired author—in fact it could not have been put together by human capabilities at all. Adds Mr. Wiener, "So we need a non-rational explanation. And ours is that the [Torah] was written by God through the hand of Moses." From an Associated Press news story in the *Washington Times* (July 18, 1986), D-5.

dence for God's existence is more convincing than any case I argued as an attorney.

But most rebellion against God is not intellectual. I have met few genuine atheists who would argue passionately that there can be no God. Instead, the preponderance of objections are moral and personal. Before his eventual conversion, when the late philosopher Mortimer Adler was pressed on his reluctance to become a Christian, he replied,

> That's a great gulf between the mind and the heart. I was on the edge of becoming a Christian several times, but didn't do it. I said that if one is born a Christian, one can be light-hearted about living up to Christianity, but if one converts by a clear conscious act of will, one had better be prepared to live a truly Christian life. So you ask yourself, are you prepared to give up all your vices and the weaknesses of the flesh?[16]

Adler believed in transcendent truth and realized there had to be a source of that truth. But for years he couldn't cross the "great gulf." He resisted the moral challenges Christianity would demand of him.

Adler's move from belief in "the god of the philosophers" to the God of the Cross was a long time coming. But he recognized that if the God he knew must exist really did exist, he would have to make the leap from logic to faith. In 1984 — bedridden with illness — Adler made that leap. Seeking solace in prayer, he received what he called the "gift of grace" and professed belief "not just in the God my reason so stoutly affirms," as he said, "but the God ... on whose grace and love I now joyfully rely."[17]

Adler showed us that faith does indeed have its reasons — and in that he was a wonderful model for worldview thinking. Maybe that's why, when he died on June 28, 2001, the media ignored his conversion. The idea that the Christian faith is logically coherent and reasonable was too great a leap for secular-minded journalists to make.

It is on the moral level that the most intense battle is being fought for the hearts of modern men and women. If Hemingway and the twentieth-century skeptics are right — if God is dead or irrelevant — then the prospect for true harmony and justice is grim.

Sometimes children understand this profound truth better than adults. Several years ago my son Chris and I were discussing the evidences for God. As I argued that if there were no God, it would be impossible to account for moral law, my grandson Charlie, then four, interrupted.

"But Grandpa," he said, "there is a God." I nodded, assuring him I agreed.

"See, if there wasn't a God, Grandpa," he continued, "people couldn't love each other."

Charlie is right. Only the overarching presence and provision of God assures that both Christian and non-Christian enjoy human dignity and a means to escape our naturally sinful condition. Without His presence, we could not long survive together on this planet.

5

NEITHER
APE NOR ANGEL

*They that deny God destroy man's nobility; for certainly, man is
akin to the beasts by his body; and if he be not of kin to God by
his spirit, he is a base and ignoble creature.*

FRANCIS BACON

In Aleksandr Solzhenitsyn's masterful novel *The Cancer Ward*, a young,
cancerous political prisoner named Oleg finds momentary escape from the
hospital's horrors in an attractive nurse, Zoya.[1] One day Oleg volunteers
to help Zoya with her reports. Reading from patient records, Oleg notices
hardly any deaths in the hospital.

"I see they don't allow them to die here," he says. "They manage to discharge them in time."

"What else can they do?" responds Zoya. "Judge for yourself. If it is obvious a patient is beyond help and there is nothing left for him but to live out
the few last weeks or months, why should he take up a bed?... People who
could be cured are kept waiting...."

Days later, one of Oleg's gravely ill friends is told he is being released from
the hospital. The man struggles to dress, weakly bids adieu to his comrades,
and sets out for the streets. The best he can hope for is an empty bench
where he can lie down and wait to die.

This approach to dying people may be cruel, but it is not illogical.

The now-defunct Soviet system was committed to the eradication of
any vital practice of religion; God was officially dead. But the death of God
ultimately spells the death of what it means to be truly human. For if worth
is not God-given, it must be established by man. And atheistic philosophies, such as the old Soviet system, treat man as an object whose value is
determined solely by his usefulness to society. Why not, then, subject him

to whatever will achieve the government's objectives: oppression, torture, genocide? In utilitarian terms, sending terminal patients out to die is not inhumane, but eminently sensible. Why waste a bed on someone who will not survive?

Contrast *The Cancer Ward* with the wards of the late Mother Teresa. For decades this faithful nun provided shelter and help for the homeless, the sick, the poor; for AIDS patients dying in pain, afraid and alone. Sometimes she was criticized: "Why care for those who are doomed anyway?" She explained, "They are created by God; they deserve to die with dignity." Christianity can never be utilitarian; it holds every human being as precious because human beings are created in the image of God.

To understand the unique nature of this Judeo-Christian view, we need only compare the ancient Hebrew law codes in the Old Testament with, say, the Assyrian laws of Hammurabi, another Middle Eastern legal code from the same period. Historian Paul Johnson has noted that the Assyrian code made the rights of property ultimate, while "the Hebrew [laws] emphasized the essential rights and obligations of man, and their laws were framed with deliberate respect for moral values."[2]

Jesus continued—and expanded—the Old Testament law. He constantly affirmed the dignity and worth of the lowest members of first-century society—women, children, Gentiles, tax-collectors, lepers.

Today's clamor for human rights is ironic. Much of the activism emanates from those who claim no belief in God. But consider the beliefs of those who have had a major influence on some human-rights activists.

Karl Marx, for example, thought man a victim of economic forces. Sigmund Freud believed all was lost in the dark web of the psyche. B. F. Skinner insisted that freedom was an illusion and dignity a lost cause. More extreme philosophers, such as Princeton's Peter Singer, get downright angry at the snobbery of speciesists—those of us who see man as the highest species—and assert that man enjoys no special standing in the universe. As Singer writes:

> We can no longer base our ethics on the idea that human beings are a special form of creation, singled out from all other animals, and alone possessing an immortal soul. Once the religious mumbo-jumbo has been stripped away, we may continue to see normal members of our species as possessing greater capacities ... than members of any other species; but

we will not regard as sacrosanct the life of each and every member of our species.... Species membership alone ... is not morally relevant.[3]

In this light, human dignity and human rights are tenuous assertions. If man is merely a fortuitous collection of molecules in a meaningless cosmos, why should he have any inherent rights?

Spinoza once observed that man builds his kingdoms in accord with his concept of God.[4] The rise of atheism in the twentieth century thus provided unlimited license for tyrants. If there is no morally binding standard above the state, it becomes god and human beings mere beasts of bureaucratic burden. A government cannot be truly just without affirming the intrinsic value of human life.

The Judeo-Christian ethic does more than affirm human dignity, however; it also insists that we are inclined to do evil. Man is more than a beast, but he is not an angel. This dual nature is not properly understood apart from what theologians call *original sin*.

No modern parable portrays man's sinful nature more powerfully than Nobel prize-winning author William Golding's novel *The Lord of the Flies*, in which a planeload of English schoolboys is wrecked on a tropical island.[5] Good British subjects that they are, they attempt to organize themselves into an orderly society while awaiting rescue.

But darker urges soon grip the boys. The veneer of civilization melts away, and many of them revert to savagery, first as a game, then in deadly earnest.

One of them wounds a boar. Suddenly, "the desire to squeeze and hurt was overmastering." Soon the boys are chanting with ritualistic fervor, "Kill the pig! Cut his throat! Bash him in!"

A sow is caught and killed in a primitive sacrifice, the head cut off and placed on a post, allegedly to assuage the "beast" some of the boys have encountered. Great black and iridescent green flies buzz insistently around the severed head. The boys' "chieftain" giggles as he rubs his bloodied hands on the next boy's face.

The young savages soon turn on a fat, asthmatic, bespectacled lad nicknamed Piggy, who retains more civility than they care to have on their island. "Which is better," Piggy asks plaintively as they advance on him, "to have rules and agree, or to hunt and kill?"

Moments later, Piggy is knocked off a cliff. His skull cracks open, his arms and legs twitching. Eventually the pounding waves suck his body into the sea.

Piggy's friend Ralph collapses in a spasm of grief. "With filthy body, matted hair, and unwiped nose, Ralph wept for the end of innocence, the darkness of man's heart, and the fall through the air of the true, wise friend called Piggy."

Later, when the group is rescued, a shocked naval officer asks how such savagery could have happened. "I should have thought that a pack of British boys — you're all British, aren't you? — would have been able to put up a better show than that — I mean ..."

Civilization, empire, education, all the trappings of human progress had clothed these young innocents. Now, their faces smeared with blood, their consciences apparently inoperative, they bear the guilt of the death of two playmates.

When William Golding was awarded the Nobel Prize for Literature in 1983, the Swedish Academy declared that his novels "illuminate the human condition in the world today." They reflect as well what Golding described as "an attempt to trace the defects of society back to the defects of human nature. The shape of a society must depend on the ethical nature of the individual and not on any political system, however apparently logical or respectable."[6]

Golding's views may sound grimly anachronistic in a culture constantly heralding man's ability to achieve utopia through modern science, education, and technology. This notion of boundless possibility was given impetus by, among others, Jean-Jacques Rousseau, the Enlightenment writer who insisted that human misery was rooted in the structures of society. Change the structures and you change the man, he said.

Rousseau looked to primitive human experience as a rosy time of innocence free of socially induced vices. From the beginning of man's history, however, we see not guilelessness, but betrayal and evil. After the account of the Garden of Eden the Bible tells the story of the first four people on the planet — and before long, one of them killed his brother. This first murder was committed long before urban blight and social deprivations. It set the standard for human society ever since. Whenever we learn about primitive societies, we learn about revenge, murder, human sacrifice, tyranny. There were — and are — no noble savages.

So it is with modern societies as well. Human nature has not changed since Cain. This is vividly illustrated in the memoirs of Cuban poet Armando Valladares, *Against All Hope*, in which he recounts his twenty-two-year imprisonment by Fidel Castro for speaking out "against Communism because it went against my religious beliefs and some of my more idealistic notions of the world."[7] For such treason, Valladares was thrown into the man-made hell of a Cuban prison. He was given showers of human urine and excrement by sadistic guards. During an escape attempt he broke three bones in his leg and was captured and brought back to his cell. "Guards ... stripped us again," he writes.

> They were armed with thick twisted electric cables and truncheons. Suddenly, everything was a whirl—my head spun around in terrible vertigo.... The beatings felt as if they were branding me with a red-hot branding iron, but then I suddenly experienced the most intense, unbearable, and brutal pain of my life. One of the guards had jumped with all his weight on my broken, throbbing leg.[8]

One cannot explain the torture, the sadism, and the evil only in terms of godless political systems. The problem is human nature. The only progress between Cain and the Communist jailers of Armando Valladares has been the technological sophistication of cruelty.

Given the wealth of such examples today, why is it so difficult for modern man to acknowledge the inherent evil in the human heart? Why is *sin* an outmoded term, used only by Bible-thumping preachers, born-again zealots, or the titillating covers of paperback thrillers?

English historian Paul Johnson contends that the great obstacle to modern belief in human sin began with the loss of belief in individual responsibility. Coupled with the ascendancy of Freud's theories and Marx's ideology, collectivism encouraged the belief that "society could be collectively guilty in creating conditions which made crime and vice inevitable. But personal guilt-feelings were an illusion to be dispelled. None of us was individually guilty; we were all guilty."[9]

This misreading of the nature of man, which resulted in the denial of personal responsibility, was institutionalized into various social reforms in the sixties; these contributed markedly to the social pathologies of American inner cities. Charles Murray, W. H. Brady Scholar at the American Enterprise Institute, has noted: "What many of these reforms shared (in varying ways and degrees) was an assumption that people are not in control of their own behavior and should not properly be held responsible for the consequences of their actions. The economic system is to blame; the social environment is to blame; perhaps accidents and conceivably genetics are to blame."[10]

Any effort to encourage individual initiative and responsibility among America's urban poor was derided as "blaming the victim." Blaming the system rather than the "victim" further eradicated individual responsibility and dignity. As Polish philosopher Leszek Kolakowski once wrote: "I remember seeing on American television a young man who was convicted of brutally raping a child, a little girl; his comment was, 'Everybody makes mistakes.' And so, we now know who raped the child; 'everybody,' that is, nobody."[11]

This elimination of individual responsibility is matched by the corresponding utopian belief in man's collective perfectibility. While Christian teaching emphasizes that each person has worth and responsibility before God, utopianism argues that salvation can only be achieved collectively. Mao Tse-tung could assert, therefore, that "our God is none other than the masses of the Chinese people."[12] And in the name of that god, millions of Chinese people were murdered and starved to death.

Utopianism always spells disaster because "the utopian holds that, if the goal is goodness and perfection, then the use of force is justified," as Thomas Molnar writes.[13] In contrast, the Christian who knows that perfection cannot be realized in this life will resist the tyrannical dictator who promises a brave new world.

With God dead or ill, twenty-first-century men and women are stripped of their source of dignity and reduced to sophisticated beasts. At the same time, society denies individual sin, blaming all social ills on environment, and illogically assumes human perfectibility.

Such propositions run counter to the evidence of history. Man is neither ape nor angel. And as Jerry Levin and countless others have experienced, deep down inside we know we are created by God. We desperately long to know the Power beyond us and discover a transcendent purpose for living. We long as well to shed the guilt of sin, to be free people, forgiven in the sight of the God we know is there.

Many search for Him through bizarre spiritual journeys, attested to by the popularity of Eastern religions, the neo-paganism arising out of extreme environmentalism, Scientology, Wicca, Kabala, and shamanism. Such counterfeits only intensify frustration — and often ultimately lessen belief in any God at all. Sometimes the end of the journey is gruesome and shocking — like the piles of bodies at Jonestown in 1978, the Heaven's Gate suicides in

1997, and the mass murder of innocents on September 11 — murder committed by Islamic extremists who believe the god they serve wants them to kill themselves in order to murder others.

Diverted from the one source that can provide meaning and a sense of worth and responsibility, modern men and women are left to thrash about for themselves. Their frustration inevitably deepens into despair. For some like Hemingway, who accept the logic of this age, the despair turns to tragedy; for millions of others it fosters a brooding sense of alienation and helplessness.

And so we come full circle, back to where we began. For it is this pervasive sense of impotence that has paved the way for the emergence of political saviors and the all-powerful state that promise salvation through changed structures. Before we discuss our situation today, though, we need to make one more stop. Having looked at the nature of man, we must now look at the nature of the two kingdoms in which he lives.

We can do this by stepping back to a time that bears a striking parallel to our day: Palestine in the first century, where a volatile population eagerly awaited the long-expected political Messiah who would deliver them.

PART TWO

ARRIVAL
OF THE
KINGDOM

6

KING WITHOUT
A COUNTRY

My kingdom is not of this world.
JESUS CHRIST

Two thousand years ago Palestine was (as it is today) a land in turmoil, its two and a half million inhabitants bitterly divided by religious, cultural, and language barriers. An unlikely mix of Jews, Greeks, and Syrians populated the coastal towns and fertile valleys of the ancient land, and tensions among them often erupted in bloody clashes. Rome did little to discourage this volatile bitterness. As long as the people's passions were spent on each other, they weren't being vented on their conquerors.

Among these disparate groups, the Jews alone had hope for the future, for they clung to the promise that a Messiah, sent from God, would one day come to set them free. According to their Scriptures, this savior would bring swift judgment to Israel's oppressors and triumphantly reestablish *the* mighty throne of the great King David. "The God of heaven will set up a kingdom that will never be destroyed," the prophecies said.

Some Jews were not content to wait and hope, however. Small groups of incendiaries, known as Zealots, mapped political strategies for supremacy, including terrorist plots and assassinations. Rome responded with deadly force.

In the midst of this oppression and chaos, a rumor began to spread. It harked back thirty years to a time when stories had circulated about angelic visitations attending the birth of a peasant child named Jesus in the village of Bethlehem. The child had grown up in Nazareth, a dusty stopping place on the caravan route to Damascus, where He had learned the carpentry trade from His father. Now stories about this Jesus were igniting the countryside. Apparently He had abandoned His carpentry tools and was going about preaching a spiritual message and gradually amassing followers. There had even been reports that He had supernatural powers.

Early one Saturday morning Jesus returned to Nazareth to speak in the synagogue. His friends and relatives and neighbors gathered in great excitement. They had watched Him grow to manhood; they knew His parents, Mary and Joseph. So they were astonished at His air of authority as He strode to the center of the crowded stone room and was handed the book of the prophet Isaiah from the Torah shrine. He found the passage He wanted, then read the ancient prophecy: "The Spirit of the Lord is on me, because he has anointed me to preach good news to the poor. He has sent me to proclaim freedom for the prisoners and recovery of sight for the blind, to release the oppressed, to proclaim the year of the Lord's favor."[1]

Jesus handed the Scriptures back to the attendant and stared quietly at the rows of townspeople. "Today," He said slowly, "this scripture is fulfilled in your hearing."

At first there were gasps, then excited murmurings. Was Jesus claiming that their hopes were to be realized? Had the long-dreamed-of day of the Lord—the coming of Messiah—arrived?

Then one of the elders called out sarcastically, "Isn't this Joseph's son?" Others laughed. After all, this young man was merely a hometown boy, a carpenter and the son of a carpenter. What could He know of Messiah?

Jesus knew what they were thinking. "No prophet," He said steadily, "is accepted in his hometown." Then He reminded them of two stories they knew well from their heritage: During a great drought, the prophet Elijah had brought water not to the dying widows of Israel, but to a heathen widow; and his successor Elisha had ignored Jewish lepers and cleansed a Syrian instead.

His words were like a dash of cold water in the faces of the crowd. They expected liberation for the Jews and judgment for all others. Now this arrogant young man was extending the long-awaited promise of their liberation with one hand and insinuating their own judgment with the other.

The crowd surged forward and dragged Jesus out of the building, shoving Him to the brow of the hill on which the synagogue perched. But when they reached the edge, they discovered that in the confusion, Jesus had slipped away.

This humble message at the remote Nazareth synagogue was the inaugural address for Jesus' entire ministry. Through it He formally announced His messiahship and the rule of God in this world. As a result, human history was forever altered.

The Kingdom of God had come.

I've used this message of human liberation from the Gospel of Luke countless times as the centerpiece of my message to prisoners. "He has sent me to proclaim freedom for the prisoners ... to release the oppressed...." It speaks of men and women set free by the good news of the gospel. Not until I began to research this book did I understand its wider significance.

Of all the Scriptures Jesus might have read, He chose the one that unmistakably announced the coming of the Kingdom of God. Furthermore, the listening Jews understood that in this particular passage of Isaiah, the one speaking *is* the messenger—the Messiah who ushers in the Kingdom era. To those in that synagogue, Jesus' words could only mean that He was claiming to be the Messiah. And if that was true, the Kingdom of Heaven had become a present reality.

One reason I, like many others, missed this deeper meaning of Christ's radical declaration is that I had always read the term *kingdom* metaphorically. Like the Jews in that Nazareth synagogue, most of us think of kingdoms as geographic entities, physical realms with boundaries and defenses and treasuries. But the Kingdom of God is a rule, not a realm. It is the declaration of God's absolute sovereignty, of His total order of life in this world and the next.*

Throughout His ministry Jesus repeatedly returned to the Kingdom theme. In the Sermon on the Mount, He told His followers to "seek first his kingdom and his righteousness."[2] He consistently defined His work as ushering in the Kingdom of God. Almost all His parables focused on the Kingdom in one aspect or another, while His miracles authenticated His message. In converting water to wine, calming storms, multiplying loaves and fishes, healing the sick, and raising the dead, Jesus was not working magic to gather crowds; nor was He showing His power to gain credibility. He was demonstrating the reality of His rule. By exercising dominion over every phase of earthly existence, He revealed that in fact the Kingdom of God had come.

---

*That this Kingdom is a rule not a realm makes it no less an actual kingdom, nor its laws less binding than those of nations and states, any more than unseen physical laws are less binding than the laws of legislatures.

Many Jews of first-century Palestine missed Christ's message because they, like many today, were conditioned to look for salvation in political solutions. More than anything else they wanted to be set free of Roman rule. They longed for a military messiah who would stamp out their hated oppressors. It is not surprising, then, that support for the Zealots was widespread.

The Zealot political vision was too narrow, however; for Jesus to embrace it would have been to limit the Kingdom of God to Israel. Though, ironically, Jesus was later tried and convicted as a Zealot, He dashed the hopes of those whose narrow political expectations blinded them to His real message.

The same could be said of the Jewish hierarchy. They might have welcomed Jesus because of their messianic expectations. Instead, they jealously guarded their own arrogant, self-righteous interpretation of the Jewish law, as well as the limited autonomy the Romans had given them.

Palestine's factions were embroiled in a struggle over the political and religious future of a limited ethnic group confined and defined by geographic borders. In pointing to a far larger Kingdom, Jesus was a leader without a constituency. Even His closest followers had times of doubt.

Another reason that many Jews missed the full significance of the message of the Kingdom of God was that Jesus spoke about a Kingdom that had come and a Kingdom that was still to come — one Kingdom in two stages. This still confuses people today. Perhaps a contemporary analogy will make it clearer.

Probably the most significant event in Europe during World War II was D-Day, June 6, 1944, when the Allied armies stormed the beaches of Normandy. That attack guaranteed the eventual destruction of the Axis powers in Europe. Though the war continued with seeming uncertainties along the way, the outcome was in fact determined. But it wasn't until May 8, 1945 — VE Day — that the results of the forces set in motion eleven months earlier were realized.

We can compare this two-stage process to the strategy of the Kingdom of God.

A holy God would not force his dominion over a sinful world. So He first sent His Son, Jesus Christ, to die on the cross to pay the debt for man's sin and thereby provide for men and women to be made holy and fit for God's rule. To extend our war analogy, Christ's death and resurrection — the D-Day of human history — assure His ultimate victory. But we are still on the beaches. The enemy has not yet been vanquished, and the fighting is still

King Without a Country 95

ugly. Christ's invasion has assured the ultimate outcome, however—victory for God and His people at some future date.

The second stage, which will take place when Christ returns, will complete God's rule over all the universe; His Kingdom will be visible without imperfection. At that time there will be a final judgment of all people, peace on earth, and the restoration of harmony unknown since Eden.

Many soldiers died to bring about the victory in Europe. But in the Kingdom of God, it was the death of the King that assured the victory. And this leads to the third reason that the Kingdom is often misunderstood: the nature of the King Himself.

What king would ever sacrifice himself for his people? Kings sacrifice their subjects, not themselves. What king would wash his servants' feet, as Jesus did, or freely befriend his lowest subjects? Potentates maintain the mystique of leadership by keeping a distance from those they rule. A certain grandeur seems to robe those who occupy high office.

I vividly recall a glimpse of this from my White House days. One brisk December night as I accompanied the president from the Oval Office in the West Wing of the White House to the Residence, Mr. Nixon was musing about what people wanted in their leaders. He slowed a moment, looking into the distance across the South Lawn, and said, "The people really want a leader a little bigger than themselves, don't they, Chuck?" I agreed. "I mean someone like de Gaulle," he continued. "There's a certain aloofness, a power that's exuded by great men that people feel and want to follow."

Jesus Christ exhibited none of this self-conscious aloofness. He served others first; He spoke to those to whom no one spoke; He dined with the lowest members of society; He touched the untouchables. He had no throne, no crown, no bevy of servants or armored guards. A borrowed manger and a borrowed tomb framed His earthly life.

Kings and presidents and prime ministers surround themselves with minions who rush ahead, swing the doors wide, and stand at attention as they wait for the great to pass. Jesus said that He Himself stands at the door and knocks, patiently waiting to enter our lives.

This was not the kind of messiah the Jews expected. The symbol of the tribe of Judah was a lion, majestic and powerful. The Jews waited for the descendant of this tribe—a man like David, the lion warrior of Judah, to come with chariots and armies. Instead, Christ came as "the Lamb of God."

But lambs were for sacrifice. Where was the mighty warrior who would tear Rome to shreds?

Because of the nature of the King and the price He paid for His Kingdom, much is required of its citizens, and Jesus made these demands of the Kingdom clear.

Through the centuries, however, many of His followers have watered down His teaching, stripped away His demands for the building of a righteous society, and preached an insipid religion concerned only with personal benefits. This distorted view portrays Christianity not as the powerful source of spiritual rebirth and the mediating force for justice, mercy, and love in the world, but as the ultimate self-fulfillment plan. The gospel is not a release for the captives, but confidence for the shy. It is the spiritual equivalent of racy sports cars, designer clothes, and Gordon's Gin — a commodity to help one get more out of life.

As we've seen in a previous chapter, many humanists have failed to understand human nature. But many Christians have failed also — failed to understand the utterly radical nature of the central message of Christianity. Other great leaders have expounded creeds, philosophies, and mystical visions. Many are wise and moral, but they are only belief systems: rules to live by, value codes. Men and women require more than rules; they require what Jesus' message of the Kingdom uniquely provides: answers to their most basic needs.

What are these needs?

To know God. "The heart of man is restless until it finds its rest in Thee."[3] With these simple words Augustine expressed man's most primal yearning — the need to know God. In announcing His messiahship Jesus was saying that God's love and just rule had come to earth — in Him. Men and women would thereafter be able to find rest not in a law they could never hope to fulfill, but in the actual person of Jesus Christ.

To find salvation. But how does one come to a personal relationship with this Christ? That is the archetypal question asked by the apostle Paul's jailer: "What must I do to be saved?"[4]

Because we interpret it from our perspective and not God's, salvation has always been misunderstood. The Jew wanted salvation from his oppressor, the Roman centurion. Instead, Christ came to save him from a much greater oppressor — the sin within him.

Sin is essentially rebellion against the rule of God. This is why Jesus coupled the message of the Kingdom with the call to repent and believe. Faith and repentance, the opposite of rebellion, are the necessary human responses to the divine initiative of spiritual rebirth, resulting in salvation.

When Christ first used the term *born again*, it was not the evangelical cliché or secular slur it is today. He used it in a late-night conversation with Nicodemus, a member of the Jewish religious community, telling him it was the key to entering into the Kingdom of God. Imagine the shock of the religious elite when they heard Jesus' words: Salvation was not to be found in proud piety or scrupulous adherence to religious rules, but in a turning from evil and in humble faith in One greater than oneself. Just as a person is born physically in a particular nation, so he or she is born spiritually by submitting to God's rule in His holy nation.

To find meaning. This relationship with God meets man's deepest psychological need. As we have already seen, human beings cannot live in a vacuum. We are not a chance collision of atoms in an indifferent universe or islands amid cold currents of modern culture. We each have a personal purpose in history, which is to be found under the purposeful rule of God, as a beloved citizen of His Kingdom.

To find authority. Christianity is more than simply a relationship between man and God, however. The Kingdom of God embraces every aspect of life: ethical, spiritual, and temporal, and it determines the "pattern, purpose and dynamic by which God orders life of the heavenly polis in this world."[5]

In announcing this all-encompassing Kingdom, Jesus was not using a clever metaphor; He was expressing the literal theme of Jewish history — that God was King and the people were His subjects. This tradition dated back to the days of Abraham and the patriarchs, when God made His original covenant with the Jews to be His "holy nation."*

David, the first great king of the Jews, consolidated a visible kingdom for the people of God, but it was to be only a reflection of the ultimate rule of God, their true King. From David, the scepter passed to his son Solomon

---

*As R. C. Sproul notes, Americans, steeped in the tradition of democracy, find a monarchy, even with Christ on the throne, an alien concept. We think in terms of human rulers whose limitless lust for power is a constant peril to mankind. But God is not a mirror reflection of human rulers. He is God — and as such, is entitled to rule over all things. His character, as revealed in the Bible and in the person of Christ, reveals absolute justice, mercy, and love. R. C. Sproul, *If There Is a God, Why Are There Atheists?* (Minneapolis: Dimension Books, 1978), 137.

and on through a succession of rulers, some good, some bad, but all serving as a link between God and His subjects. Later, when the Jews were conquered and sent into exile, prophets promised the coming of Messiah and the eventual establishment of the Kingdom of God. Christ was the fulfillment of that prophecy; He was the final king in David's royal line. But Jesus was not just a king for Israel; He was King for all people.

His message, then, assumes the ultimate authority man requires: God rules every aspect of what He has made. Life, death, relationships, and earthly kingdoms are all in His hands.

This totality of God's authority is a major reason many non-Christians resent Christianity, seeing it as an excuse for religious zealots to try to cram absolute orders from their God down others' throats. But when Christ commanded His followers to "seek first the kingdom of God," He was exhorting them to seek to be ruled by God and gratefully acknowledge His power and authority over them. That means that the Christian's goal is not to strive to rule, but *to be ruled*.

While God's rule *is* authoritarian, it is also *voluntary*. The Good News is that the price has been paid, and His Kingdom is open to all who desire admission.

7

POLITICS
OF THE KINGDOM

If the joyful news of the rule of God is proclaimed, if men humble themselves and do justice to its claims, if evil is overcome and men are made free for God, then the Rule of God has already become actual among them, then the Reign of God is "in their midst."

HEDDA HARTL

"Mr. Colson," a college student asked following a lecture I'd given, "How can you try to live by the Sermon on the Mount and at the same time support the use of military might?"

It's a fair question. Jesus teaches that we should love our enemies and return good for evil. But is this realistic in a world in which evil so often triumphs? Can one forgive seventy times seven and still restrain wrongdoers? Turn the other cheek to terrorists who fly jets into buildings, murdering our friends and loved ones?

These dilemmas lead many to conclude that either Jesus was not speaking literally or if He was, one must live a monastic life to be a Christian. We reach such conclusions, however, because we misunderstand Jesus' teaching about the Kingdom.

When Jesus announced the Kingdom, He did indeed set forth radical standards by which its citizens are to live. He knew such a lifestyle would be both costly and complex, but it would witness the values of God's Kingdom even in the midst of the evil of this world. Christ was not suggesting, however, that the obedient Christian would be able to usher in the Kingdom of God on earth. Only Christ Himself will do that when He returns.

But for this period between the two stages—the announcement of the Kingdom and its final consummation—God has provided structures to restrain the evil of this world. The state is even ordained to wield the sword when necessary; and the Christian is commanded to obey the state and to respect its authority as God's instrument.

The Christian, therefore, follows two commandments: to live by Christ's teaching in the Sermon on the Mount, modeling the values of God's Kingdom — *the one yet to come in its fullness* — and at the same time to support government's role in preserving order as a witness to God's authority over the *present* kingdoms of this world. So while the Christian is not to return evil for evil (he must instead exercise forgiveness, breaking the cycle of evil), he may participate in the God-ordained structure that restrains the evil and chaos of the fallen world by the use of force.

In addition to the state, which preserves order, God has provided two other institutions for the ordering of society: the family for the propagation of life and the church for the proclamation of the Kingdom of God. Each of these three institutions has been established to fulfill a distinct role.

The family is the most basic unit of government. As the first community to which a person is attached and the first authority under which a person learns to live, the family establishes society's most basic values. Paul Johnson observed that the family "is an alternative to the state as a focus of loyalty and thus a humanizing force in society. Unlike the state, it upholds nonmaterial values — makes them paramount indeed."[1]

In most Eastern cultures the family remains the fundamental unit of society. In the West, however, relativism has encouraged the belief that family is a matter of convenience rather than convention. The result is that the traditional family has all but disintegrated. Today, 68 percent of all black children are born to unmarried mothers, as are 45 percent of Hispanic children and 25 percent of white children.[2] Unwed childbearing is at an all-time high: 1.5 million babies were born to unmarried parents in 2004.[3] Children living in mother- or father-only homes has gone from 11 percent in 1970 to 23 percent in 2004.[4]

Even worse, many young people today have no idea how to go about forming the families they desire. As poverty expert Robert Rector recently put it, most young, urban, single mothers "want to be married, to have a house in the suburbs, two kids, a dog, and a minivan. The problem is that they have absolutely no practical plan to get there.... Liberal nostrum complaints about lack of access to birth control are completely irrelevant. The mothers have all the birth control they could want, they know all about it, but they are having children because children are absolutely essential to their vision of what they want to be and to their life fulfillment. The problem is that they have the sequence mixed up." They meet a man, have a child, and then the mother seeks commitment—although "not necessarily to the father of the child, because he may not be the right guy—and then she ultimately seeks marriage perhaps ten or fifteen years down the road … These young women do not see that the sequence that I just described as in any way abnormal; it's absolutely normal to them."[5]

More than 40 percent of cohabiting households today include children—households that are more likely than married-couple homes to break up over a short period of time, and more likely to involve infidelity, domestic violence, and child abuse.[6] We are also seeing a rise in "multiple partner fertility"—individuals having children with more than one partner.[7]

Some school textbooks encourage this familial chaos, going so far as to describe the family as any voluntary grouping of people living together, including homosexual couples and any children they have adopted. This attitude is reflected in our laws, our court decisions, our public mores—and in our crime rates.

The widely acclaimed seventeen-year study of Stanton Samenow and the late Samuel Yochelson concluded that crime is not the result of environment or poverty, but of wrong moral choices.[8] Harvard professors James Wilson and the late Richard Herrnstein concluded in 1985 that such moral choices are determined by moral conscience, which is shaped early in life and most profoundly by the family. Without the lessons the family alone can teach, commitment to God and duty to fellow man become alien concepts.[9] Little wonder that many of today's youth have been lost to the streets.

Though it is not my purpose here to examine the issue of the modern family, the situation today merits a word of warning. The widespread loss of the God-ordained role of the family leads, as the late theologian Carl Henry has written, to the "deterioration of society and [the] eventual collapse of the nation."[10] The humanizing force of the family can never be replaced by political or bureaucratic means.

The *state* was instituted by God to restrain sin and promote a just social order. Western political thought often mistakenly assumes that the role of government is determined solely by the will of the people. The biblical reality is different. On the eve of His execution, Jesus told Pilate that he held his office of political authority only because it had been granted him by God. The apostle Paul spoke of civil authority as "God's servant, an agent of wrath to bring punishment on the wrongdoer."[11] Peter used similar language, saying that governments were set by God to "punish those who do wrong and to commend those who do right."[12]

Government is, in one sense, God's response to the nature of the people themselves. Man "can adapt himself somehow to anything his imagination can cope with ... but he cannot deal with chaos."[13] While it cannot redeem the world or be used as a tool to establish the Kingdom of God, civil government does set the boundaries for human behavior. The state is not a remedy for sin, but a means to restrain it. Its limited task is to promote "the good of the community in temporal concerns, the protection of life and property and the preservation of peace and order."[14]

When God established ancient Israel as a nation, His first order of business was the propagation of law, not just for religious purposes, but for the ordering of civil life. Even before the giving of the Ten Commandments there was great need for civil adjudication.

The biblical text records that "Moses took his seat to serve as judge for the people and they stood around him from morning till evening."[15] (Court dockets seem to have been clogged from the very beginning.) Moses explained that "the people come to me to seek God's will. Whenever they have a dispute, it is brought to me, and I decide between the parties and inform them of God's decrees and laws."[16]

Thus the Israelite involved in a dispute looked not to the whim of a judge or to an arbitrary settlement but rather to a ruling based on divine laws. The judicial role was not a mechanism to advance the state's perception of social equilibrium, but to discern God's revealed law.

This is the origin of what we call the rule of law; it stands in stark contrast to modern moral relativism. Without transcendent norms, laws are either established by society's elites or are merely bargains struck by competing forces in society. In the Judeo-Christian view, law is rooted in moral absolutes that do not vacillate with public taste or the whim of fashion.

Thus rooted, government can perform not only the negative function of restraining evil, but the positive function of promoting a just social order so that people can live in harmony. The apostle Paul had this in mind when he urged his young colleague Timothy to pray "for kings and all those in authority, that we may live peaceful and quiet lives in all godliness and holiness."[17]

In the words of the late sociologist Robert Nisbet, man is engaged in a continual "quest for community."[18] It is important to remember, however, that the state is not itself that community. Can anyone cozy up to the mammoth machine of big government?

But the state can protect people's voluntary efforts to shape community by granting equal protection of the law, by upholding principles of justice so the weak and powerless are not exploited, and by guaranteeing liberty and providing security. In this way the government sustains a stable environment in which people can live, producing art, literature, music, and children. Or as C. S. Lewis suggested, they can partake of one of the primary benefits of democracy: the simple freedom to enjoy a cup of tea by the fire with one's family.

Christianity teaches, then, that the state serves a divinely appointed and divinely defined task, although it is not in itself divine. Its authority is legitimate, though limited.

The *church* is the community that administers and encourages the worship of God and meets the spiritual needs of God's people, by teaching, offering the sacraments, and encouraging us to bear one another's burdens. "The primary purpose of the church in relation to the world is evangelization."[19]—that is, to proclaim in word and deed the same gospel that Christ announced.

The church is not the actual Kingdom of God, but is to reflect the love, justice, and righteousness of God's Kingdom within society.*

Though the church as a human institution often fails in this high calling, its most potent social weapon is its commitment to live out the Lord's command to love one's neighbor, the law of love. "In essence," writes historian Floyd Filson, "the program of the church disregarded the social divisions of society; it made the church a home for all classes; its democratic basis was a common worship and fellowship and mutual love."[20]

The church's transcendent vision holds the world accountable to something beyond itself. In doing so, its members serve as ambassadors, citizens of the heavenly Kingdom at work in this world. The late French theologian Jacques Ellul well summarized the duty of those in the church:

---

*The church is, as one authority notes, "the community in which through its behavior and mission the reign of God becomes visible, serving as the precursor and avant-garde of the society that will be fulfillment of all hope." Stephen Charles Mott, *Biblical Ethics and Social Change* (New York: Oxford University Press, 1982), 106.

The Christian who is involved in the material history of this world is involved in it as representing another order, another master (than the "prince of this world"), another claim (than that of the natural heart of man).... Thus he must plunge into social and political problems in order to have an influence on the world, not in the hope of making it a paradise, but simply in order to make it tolerable — not in order to diminish the opposition between this world and the Kingdom of God, but simply in order to modify the opposition between the disorder of this world and the order of preservation that God wills for it — not in order to "bring in" the Kingdom of God, but in order that the gospel may be proclaimed, that all men may really hear the good news of salvation through the death and resurrection of Christ.[21]

Thus, the church, while not the Kingdom of God, is to live out the values of the Kingdom of God in this world, resisting the ever-present temptation to usher in the Kingdom of God by political means. Yet this is the temptation to which the church has most commonly succumbed, and certainly this is its greatest temptation today. We will discuss this in depth in later chapters.

Pope John Paul II may well have had this temptation in mind when he addressed Latin American Catholics at Puebla, Mexico, in 1979:

The gospels make it clear that in Jesus' eyes anything that would distort his mission as servant of the Lord was a temptation. He did not accept the view of those who confuse the things of God with attitudes that are purely political. He rejects unequivocally any recourse to violence. He offers his message of conversion to all, not excluding even the tax collectors. The purpose of his mission embraces far more than political order. It embraces the salvation of the entire person through transforming and peace-giving love.[22]

Unlike the politics of the world, the politics of the Kingdom is the politics of "faith, hope and love: faith that confesses the Risen Savior, hope that looks for His appearing, love that is inflamed by His sacrifice on the cross."[23] The church "anticipates the form of the world to come and thus it transcends the social and political forms of this world."[24]

While Jesus did not come to establish a political kingdom, the announcement of the Kingdom had profound consequences for the political order.

When Jesus said to Pilate, "My kingdom is not of this earth," Pilate may have breathed a sigh of relief. He should have reconsidered. Which is more threatening to a ruler—an external foe with mighty but visible armies or an eternal king who rules the very souls of men and women? The latter can command the will and affections, demand absolute obedience, impart unlimited power to His subjects, and radically change their values and lives; His followers fear no earthly power and His Kingdom has no end. In the face of such a potentate, any mere political leader must shudder.

This is why the Kingdom of God has had such an astonishing effect upon the most powerful of human empires in every age. It is not a blueprint for some new social order; nor does it merely set the forces of radical cultural change in motion. Rather, God's Kingdom promises radical changes in human personalities.

This is the crucial point. While human politics is based on the premise that society must be changed in order to change people, in the politics of the Kingdom it is people who must be changed in order to change society.

Through men and women who recognize its authority and live by its ethical standards, the Kingdom of God invades the stream of history. It breaks the vicious and otherwise irreversible cycles of violence, injustice, and self-interest. In this way the Kingdom of God equips its citizens, as Augustine said, to be the best citizens in the kingdoms of man.

Such was certainly the case in early nineteenth-century England, when one man dared—against great personal and political odds—to represent the standards of the Kingdom of God for the good of his nation.

8

FOR THE GOOD
OF THE NATION

Things have come to a pretty pass when religion is allowed to invade public life.

LORD MELBOURNE
(opposing abolition of the slave trade)

Scudding clouds obscured the moon as the heavy schooner pitched forward in the dark waters. A lone sailor walked the deck on late watch; at the helm, three others held the wheel against the high seas. Below, the rest of the crew tossed in their hammocks, while in the main cabin the captain dipped his quill in a well of sepia ink and began the day's log. He squinted in the poor light from the tallow candle. " ... 1787 ... a fair wind today ... five hundred miles off the coast of Africa ... bound due east now for Jamaica with cargo ..."

Packed into the dark hold beneath his feet was the ship's cargo—five hundred African men and women layered like fish packed in brine. Barely able to breathe in the air heavy with the stench of human waste and vomit, they lay chest to back, legs drawn into fetal position, feet resting on the heads of those in the next row.

Some had been taken prisoner during tribal wars; some had been jailed as petty criminals; and others had been unsuspecting dinner guests of Englishmen visiting their country. But all had been forcibly enslaved and held in a stockade on the African coast until sold to the highest bidder. That bidder was the captain in the cabin above.

Once purchased they had been branded and rowed to the schooner waiting offshore, their screams and cries ignored by the seamen who hoisted them aboard and chained them in the stinking hold. For the women, however, there was a further torture. The crew, diseased and ill-treated themselves, claimed the one sordid privilege of their trade—the pick of the slave women. Once under way, the ship had become half bedlam, half brothel.

Now, several weeks into the voyage, sixty slaves had already died. Fever had taken some. Others, driven insane by the horror of their lot, had been killed by the crew. Each morning when the lower decks were opened, several dead or near-dead bodies were thrown to the sharks trailing the ship.

The captain cursed as the bodies hit the choppy water. Each body overboard meant lost profits.

For those who survived the hellish three-month journey, an equally gruesome future awaited. They would be auctioned naked in the marketplace to planters who would work them to death on their Caribbean plantations. Never again would these African men and women see their homeland.

Thousands of miles to the north, in a country that profited richly from this human misery, another man sat at his desk. He too gazed into the flickering flame of his lamp, for the early morning darkness still filled his second floor library at Number 4 Old Palace Yard, London. Only his piercing blue eyes reflected the turmoil of his thoughts as he eyed the jumble of pamphlets on his cluttered desk.

He ran his hand through his wavy hair and opened his Bible to begin the day, as was his custom, with Scripture reading and prayer. But his thoughts kept returning to the pamphlets, grisly accounts of human flesh sold like mutton for the profit of his countrymen. No matter how he tried, William Wilberforce could not wipe these scenes from his mind.[1]

William Wilberforce was the only son of prosperous merchant parents. Though an average student at Cambridge, his quick wit had made him a favorite among his fellows, including William Pitt, with whom he shared an interest in politics. Often the two young men had spent their evenings in the gallery of the House of Commons watching the heated debates over the War of Independence in the colonies.

After graduation Wilberforce had run as a conservative for a seat in Parliament from his home county of Hull. Though only twenty-one at the time, the prominence of his family, his speaking ability, and a generous feast he sponsored for voters on Election Day carried the contest.

The London of 1780, when Wilberforce arrived to take his office, was described as "one vast casino" where the rich counted their profits through a fog of claret. Fortunes were lost and won over gaming tables, and duels of honor were the order of the day. The city's elegant private clubs welcomed young Wilberforce, and he happily concentrated on pursuing both political advancement and social pleasure.

High society revolved around romantic intrigue and adulterous affairs. An upper-class couple might not be seen together in public for weeks during the social season, for no popular hostess would invite a husband and wife to the same event.

The poor, of course, had no such opportunity to escape from one another. Crammed together in shabby dwellings, they were cogs grinding out a living in the Empire's emerging industrial machines. Pale children worked eighteen hours a day in cotton mills or coal mines to bring home a few shillings a month to parents who often wasted it on cheap gin.

Highwaymen were folk heroes. Newgate and other infamous prisons overflowed with debtors, murderers, rapists, and petty thieves—often children. The twelve-year-old who had stolen a loaf of bread might be hanged the same day as a celebrated highwayman, providing public entertainment.

In short, London was a city where unchecked passions and desires ran their course. Few raised their voices in opposition.

So it is not surprising that few argued against one of the nation's most bountiful sources of wealth—the slave trade. In fact, the trade was both a successful business and a national policy. Political alliances revolved around commitments to it. It became known euphemistically as "the institution," the "pillar and support of British plantation industry in the West Indies." In a celebrated case in England's high court only four years earlier, slaves had been deemed "goods and chattels."

Corruption in government was so widespread that few members of Parliament thought twice about accepting bribes for their votes. Planters and other gentlemen involved in the slave trade paid three to five thousand pounds to "buy" boroughs, which sent their representatives to the House of Commons. Their political influence in Parliament grew until a large bloc was controlled by the vested influence of the slave trade. The same attitude reigned in the House of Lords.

The horrors of the trade were remote and unseen, the cotton and sugar profits they yielded very tangible. So most consciences were not troubled about the black men and women suffering far away on the high seas or on remote plantations.

Early in 1784 Wilberforce's friend William Pitt was elected prime minister at the age of twenty-four. This inspired Wilberforce to make a big political gamble. He surrendered his safe seat in Hull and stood for election in Yorkshire, the largest and most influential constituency in the country.

It was a grueling campaign; the outcome was uncertain until the closing day when Wilberforce addressed a large rally. James Boswell, Samuel Johnson's celebrated biographer, stood in the cold rain and watched the young candidate, barely five feet tall, climb onto a table so the wet, bored crowd could see him. The power of his oratory, however, soon gripped them.

"I saw what seemed a mere shrimp mount upon the table," Boswell wrote, "but as I listened the shrimp grew and grew and became a whale."

Wilberforce was elected. As an intimate of the prime minister and as a man respected by both political parties, he seemed destined for power and prominence.

After the election, Wilberforce's mother invited him to take a tour of the Continent with his sister and several cousins. Subsequently, he happened to meet his old schoolmaster from Hull, Isaac Milner, and on impulse asked him to join the traveling party. That invitation was to change Wilberforce's life.

Isaac Milner was a large, jovial man with a mind as robust as his body. Called "an evangelical Dr. Johnson," Milner's forceful personality had contributed to the spread of Christian influence at Cambridge. Not unnaturally, then, he raised the matter of faith and religion to his former pupil as their carriage ran over the rutted roads between Nice and the Swiss Alps.

When Wilberforce treated the subject flippantly, Milner growled at his young companion's derisive wit and declared, "I am no match for you, but if you really want to discuss these subjects seriously, I will gladly enter on them with you." Provoked, Wilberforce eventually agreed to read the Bible.

The summer session of Parliament forced Wilberforce to make a break in his travels, and his visit to the social scene of London revealed subtle changes in his tastes. Parties he had once attended routinely now seemed "indecent." Letters to family and friends indicated his growing distaste for corruption he had scarcely noticed before.

When he and Milner continued their Continental tour in the fall of 1785, Wilberforce was no longer the same frivolous young man. In fact, the rest of the traveling party complained about his preoccupation when he and Milner studied a Greek New Testament in the coach.

Wilberforce returned to London in early November, but his travels had not rested him. Instead, he felt weary and confused. In need of counsel, he sought advice from John Newton.

Son of a sailor, Newton had been impressed into the Royal Navy when he was eleven. He deserted, was caught in West Africa, flogged, and placed into service on a slave ship. Eventually he became involved in the slave trade and in 1750 was given command of his own ship. On one especially stormy passage to the West Indies, however, Newton was converted to faith in Jesus Christ. He renounced slaving and expressed his wonder at the gift of salvation in his famous hymn, "Amazing Grace."

By the time Wilberforce knew of him, Newton was a clergyman in the Church of England, renowned for his outspokenness on spiritual matters. He counseled Wilberforce to follow Christ but not to abandon public office: "The Lord has raised you up to the good of His church and for the good of the nation." Wilberforce heeded his advice.

The responses of his old friends were predictable. Some thought his mind had snapped; others assumed he would now retreat from political life since religion could have little to do with politics. Many, however, were simply bewildered. How could a well-bred, educated young man with so much promise get caught up in a religious exuberance that appealed only to the common masses?

The reaction Wilberforce cared about most, however, was that of his friend Pitt. He wrote to the prime minister, telling him that though he would remain his faithful friend, he could "no more be so much of a party man as before." Pitt's understanding reply revealed the depth of their friendship, but after their first face-to-face discussion, Wilberforce wrote in his diary: "Pitt tried to reason me out of my convictions but soon found himself unable to combat their correctness, if Christianity was true. The fact is, he is so absorbed in politics, that he has never given himself time for due reflection on religion."

Thus Wilberforce arrived at that foggy Sunday morning in 1787 when he sat at his desk and stared out the window at the gray drizzle, thinking about his conversion and his calling. Had God saved him only to rescue his own soul from hell? He could not accept that. He could not be content with the comfort of life at Palace Yard and the stimulating debates of Parliament. If Christianity was true and meaningful, it must go deeper than that. It must not only save but serve. It must bring God's compassion to the oppressed as well as oppose the oppressors. And at the moment, all he could envision were loaded slave ships leaving the sun-baked coasts of Africa.

He turned back to the journal filled with his tiny, cramped writing and dipped his pen in the inkwell. "Almighty God has set before me two great objectives," he wrote, his heart suddenly pumping with passion. "The abolition of the slave trade and the reformation of manners."

With those words, an epic offensive was launched against a society pock-marked by decadence and the barbaric trafficking of human flesh that underwrote those excesses.

"As soon as ever I had arrived thus far in my investigation of the slave trade, so enormous, so dreadful, so irremediable did its wickedness appear that my own mind was completely made up for the abolition. A trade founded in iniquity and carried on as this was must be abolished."

Wilberforce knew the issue had to be faced head-on in Parliament. Throughout the damp fall of 1787 he worked late into the nights on his investigation, joined by others who saw in him a champion for their cause. There was Grenville Sharp, a hook-nosed attorney with a keen mind who was already well-known for his successful court case that had made slavery illegal in England itself—ironic in a time when the country's economic strength depended on slavery abroad. Another was Zachary Macaulay, a quiet, patient researcher who sifted through stacks of evidence to build damning indictments against the trade. A dedicated worker who took pen in hand at four o'clock every morning, he became a walking encyclopedia for the rest of the abolitionists. Whenever Wilberforce needed information, he would look for his quiet, heavy-browed friend and say, "Let us look it up in Macaulay."

Thomas Clarkson was another compatriot. The red-headed clergyman and brilliant essayist with a passion for justice and righteousness was Wilberforce's scout. He conducted exhausting—and dangerous—trips to the African coast. Once, needing some evidence from a particular sailor he knew by sight though not by name, Clarkson questioned dozens of men from slave vessels in port after port until finally, after searching 317 ships, he found his man.

In February 1788, while working with these friends and others, Wilberforce suddenly fell gravely ill. Doctors predicted he would not live more than two weeks. Cheered by this news, the opposition party in Yorkshire made plans to regain his seat in Parliament. Wilberforce, however, recovered. And though not yet well enough to return to Parliament, in March he asked Pitt to introduce the abolition issue in the House for him. On the basis of their friendship, the prime minister agreed.

Lacking Wilberforce's passion but faithfully citing his facts, Pitt moved that a resolution be passed binding the House to discuss the slave trade in the next session. The motion provoked a lukewarm debate and was passed. Those with interest in the trade were not worried about a mere motion to *discuss* abolition.

Then another of Wilberforce's friends, Sir William Dolben, introduced a one-year experimental bill to regulate the number of slaves that could be transported per ship. After several members of Parliament visited a slave ship lying in a London port, the debates grew heated with cries for reform.

Now sensing a threat, the West Indian bloc rose up in opposition. Tales of cruelty in the slave trade were mere fiction, they said; it was the happiest day of an African's life when he was shipped away from the barbarities of his homeland. Besides, warned Lord Penrhyn ominously, the proposed measure would abolish the trade upon which "two thirds of the commerce of this country depends."

Angered by Penrhyn's hyperbole, Pitt himself grew passionate. Threatening to resign unless the bill was carried, he pushed Dolben's regulation through both houses in June of 1788.

The success of Dolben's bill awakened the slave traders to the possibility of real danger. By the time a recovered Wilberforce returned to the legislative scene, they were furious and ready to fight, shocked that politicians had the audacity to press for morally based reforms in the political arena.

"Humanity is a private feeling, not a public principle to act upon," sniffed the Earl of Abingdon.

Lord Melbourne angrily agreed. "Things have come to a pretty pass when religion is allowed to invade public life."

James Boswell, who had initially been astounded by Wilberforce's oratorical prowess, penned a bit of snide verse aptly reflecting the abuse heaped by Wilberforce's enemies:

Go, W_____ with narrow skull,
Go home and preach away at Hull.
No longer in the Senate cackle
In strains that suit the tabernacle;
I hate your little witling sneer,
Your pert and self-sufficient leer.
Mischief to trade sits on your lip,
Insects will gnaw the noblest ship
Go, W, begone, for shame,
Thou dwarf with big resounding name.

But Wilberforce and the band of abolitionists knew that a private faith that did not act in the face of oppression was no faith at all.

Wilberforce's first parliamentary speech for abolition shows the passion of his convictions as well as his characteristic humility:

> When I consider the magnitude of the subject which I am to bring before the House—a subject, in which the interest, not of this country, nor of Europe alone, but of the whole world, and of posterity, are involved ... it is impossible for me not to feel both terrified and concerned at my own inadequacy to such a task. But I march forward with a firmer step in the full assurance that my cause will bear me out ... the total abolition of the slave trade....
>
> I mean not to accuse anyone, but to take the shame upon myself, in common, indeed, with the whole Parliament of Great Britain, for having suffered this horrid trade to be carried on under their authority. We are all guilty—we ought all to plead guilty, and not to exculpate ourselves by throwing the blame on others.

But the passionate advocacy of Wilberforce, Pitt, and others was not sufficient to deter the interests of commerce in the 1789 session. The House's vote spurred Wilberforce to gather further evidence that could not be ignored. He and his co-workers spent up to ten hours a day reading and abridging factual material, and in early 1791 he again filled the House of Commons with his thundering eloquence. "Never, never will we desist till we ... extinguish every trace of this bloody traffic, of which our posterity, looking back to the history of these enlightened times, will scarce believe that it has been suffered to exist so long a disgrace and dishonor to this country."

The opposition was equally determined. One member asserted, "Abolition would instantly annihilate a trade, which annually employs upwards of 5,500 sailors, upwards of 160 ships, and whose exports amount to £800,000 sterling; and would undoubtedly bring the West Indies trade to decay, whose exports and imports amount to upwards of £6,000,000 sterling, and which give employment in upwards of 160,000 tons of additional shipping, and sailors in proportion." He paused dramatically, pointed to the gallery where a number of his slave-trading constituents watched, and exclaimed, "These are my masters!"

Another member, citing the positive aspects of the trade, drew a chilling comparison: the slave trade "was not an amiable trade," he admitted, "but neither was the trade of a butcher ... and yet a mutton chop was, nevertheless, a very good thing."

Incensed, Wilberforce and other abolitionists fought a bitter two-day battle; members shouted and harangued as spectators and press relished the fray. But by the time votes were cast, "commerce clinked its purse," as one observer commented, and Wilberforce was again defeated.

In 1792, when it became apparent that the fight would be long, Henry Thornton suggested to Wilberforce that they gather and work at his home in Clapham, a village four miles south of Westminster; there they would be convenient to Parliament, yet set apart. Thornton's home, Battersea Rise, a Queen Anne house on the grassy Clapham Common, was a lively household. As abolitionist friends came to live or visit, Thornton added extra wings until eventually Battersea Rise had thirty-four bedrooms as well as a large, airy library designed by Prime Minister Pitt. Here, in the heart of the house, many an intense prayer meeting and discussion lasted late into the night as the "cabinet councils" prepared for their parliamentary battles.

Wilberforce took up part-time residence in Thornton's home until his marriage in 1797, at which time he moved to Broomfield, a smaller house on the same property.

As the Clapham community analyzed their battle in 1792, they were painfully aware that many of their colleagues in Parliament were puppets, unable or unwilling to stand against the powerful economic forces of their day. So Wilberforce and his friends decided to go to the people, believing, "It is on the general impression and feeling of the nation we must rely ... so let the flame be fanned."

The abolitionists distributed thousands of pamphlets detailing the evils of slavery, spoke at public meetings, and circulated petitions. The celebrated poet William Cowper wrote "The Negro's Complaint," a poem that was set to music and sung in many fashionable drawing rooms. Josiah Wedgwood, a master of fine china, designed a cameo that became the equivalent of a modern-day campaign button. It depicted a slave kneeling in bondage, whispering the plea that was to become famous: "Am I not a man and a brother?" Ladies sympathetic to the cause bought the cameos and wore them as bracelets and brooches, or turned them into hair ornaments.

A boycott of slave-grown sugar was organized, a tactic even Wilberforce thought could not work. To his astonishment, it gained a following of some 300,000 people across England. Later in 1792 Wilberforce was able to bring to the House of Commons 519 petitions for the total abolition of the slave trade, signed by thousands of British subjects. This surging tide of public popularity along with Wilberforce's usual impassioned eloquence combined to profoundly disturb the House:

> In the year 1788 in a ship in this trade, 650 persons were on board, out of whom 155 died. In another, 405 were on board, out of whom were lost 200. In another there were on board 402, out of whom 73 died. When captain Wilson was asked the causes of this mortality, he replied that the slaves had a fixed melancholy and dejection; that they wished to die; that they refused all sustenance, till they were beaten in order to compel them to eat; and that when they had been so beaten, they looked in the faces of the whites and said, piteously, "Soon we will be no more."

Even the vested economic interests of the West Indian bloc could not gloss over these appalling facts or ignore the public support the abolitionists were gaining. But again the slavers exercised their political muscle and the House moved that Wilberforce's motion be qualified by the word *gradually*. And so it was carried. Again the traders relaxed, knowing a bill could be indefinitely postponed by that seemingly innocuous word.

Though Wilberforce was wounded by yet another defeat, he had a glimmer of hope. For the first time the House had actually voted for an abolition motion; with the force of the people behind the cause, it would only be a matter of time.

That hope was soon smashed by events across the English Channel. The fall of the Bastille in 1789 had heralded the people's revolution in France.

By 1792 all idealism vanished. The September massacres loosed a tide of bloodshed as the mob and the guillotine ruled France.

Fears of a similar revolt abounded in England until any type of public agitation for reform was suspiciously labeled "Jacobinic," after the radicals who had fanned the flames of France's Reign of Terror. This association and the ill-timed slave revolts in the West Indies stemmed the tide of public activism for abolition.

Sensing the shift in the public mood, the House of Commons rejected Wilberforce's motion. The attitude in the House of Lords was summed up by the member who declared flatly, "All abolitionists are Jacobins." Wilberforce saw his hopes wither and his cause lampooned in popular cartoons and ridiculed by critics.

Weary with grief and frustration, he often sat long into the night at his old oak desk, wondering whether he should abandon his hopeless campaign. One night as he sat flipping through his Bible, a letter fluttered from between the pages.

Wilberforce stared at the shaky handwriting. The writer was dead. In fact, this letter was one of the last he had ever written. Wilberforce had read it dozens of times, but never had he needed its message as much as he did now.

My dear Sir,

Unless the Divine power has raised you up to be as Athanasius contra mundum,* I see not how you can go through your glorious enterprise in opposing that execrable villainy, which is the scandal of religion, of England, and of human nature. Unless God has raised you up for this very thing, you will be worn out by the opposition of men and devils, but if God be for you who can be against you? Are all of them together stronger than God? Oh, be not weary of well-doing. Go on in the name of God, and in the power of His might, till even American slavery, the vilest that ever saw the sun, shall vanish away before it. That He that has guided you from your youth up may continue to strengthen in this and all things, is the prayer of,

Your affectionate servant,
John Wesley

---

*This Latin phrase, which means "against the world," characterizes anyone who makes an unpopular moral stand against prevailing social opinions. Athanasius (c. A.D. 296—373) was an early church father who opposed many of the heresies of his time.

"Be not weary of well-doing." Wilberforce took a deep breath, carefully refolded the letter, and blew out the candle. He needed to get to bed; he had a long fight ahead of him.

Wilberforce's resolution returned and for the next several years he doggedly reintroduced, each year, the motion for abolition; and each year Parliament threw it out.

An abrupt reversal came early in 1796 after the fall of Robespierre in France and the resultant swing of public sentiment toward peace. Popular favor again began to swing toward Wilberforce, surprisingly reinforced by a majority vote in the House of Commons for his annual motion for abolition. Victory suddenly seemed within reach.

But the third reading of the bill took place on the night a long-awaited comic opera opened in London. A dozen supporters of abolition, supposing the bill would be voted in this time, skipped Parliament for the opera—and a grieving Wilberforce saw his bill defeated by just four votes.

And so it went—1797, 1798, 1799, 1800, 1801—the years passed with Wilberforce's motions thwarted and sabotaged by political pressures, compromise, personal illness, and the continuing war in France. By 1803, with the threat of imminent invasion by Napoleon's armies, the question of abolition was put aside for the more immediate concern of national security.

During those long years of struggle, however, Wilberforce and his friends never lost sight of their equally pressing objective: "the reformation of manners," or the effort to clean up society's blights. Several years before, backed by Pitt and others, Wilberforce had sent a proposal to King George III that Wilberforce hoped would capture public attention. He asked the king to reissue a "Proclamation for the Encouragement of Piety and Virtue and for the Preventing of Vice, Profaneness and Immorality." On June 1, 1787, the king issued the proclamation, citing his concern at the deluge of "every kind of vice which, to the scandal of our holy religion, and to the evil example of our loving subjects, have broken upon this nation."

Copies of the proclamation were distributed to magistrates in every county. Wilberforce mounted his horse and followed after them, calling on those in government and positions of leadership to set up societies to develop such a moral movement in Britain.

One prominent leader, Lord Fitzwilliam, laughed in Wilberforce's face. Of course there was much debauchery and little religion, he said, but after all, this was inevitable in a rich nation. "The only way to reform morals," he concluded, "is to ruin purses."

In many areas, however, the proclamation was received seriously. Magistrates held meetings to determine how to follow its guidelines, and long-ignored laws were dusted off and enforced.

The years of battle had welded Wilberforce and his Clapham group into a tight-working unit; with five of them serving as members of Parliament, they exerted an increasingly strong moral pressure on the political arena of the day. They organized the Society for the Education of Africans, the Society for Bettering the Condition of the Poor, the Society for the Relief of Debtors, which over a five-year period obtained the release of 14,000 people from debtor's prisons. Various members were involved in prison reforms, establishing hospitals for the blind, helping war widows and distressed sailors. Zachary Macaulay, at one time a wealthy man, gave away all he had and died penniless. Derisively labeled "the saints," they bore the name gladly, considering such distinction a welcome reminder of their commitment not to political popularity but to biblical justice and righteousness.

As the abolitionists prepared for their fight in Parliament in 1804, the climate had changed. The scare tactics of Jacobin association would no longer stick, and public sentiment for abolition was growing.

The House of Commons voted for Wilberforce's motion by a majority of 124 to 49, but victory was short-lived. The slave traders were better represented in the House of Lords, which adjourned the bill until the next session.

In 1805 the House of Commons reversed itself, rejecting the bill by seven votes. A well-meaning clerk took Wilberforce aside. "Mr. Wilberforce," he said kindly, "you ought not to expect to carry a measure of this kind. You and I have seen enough of life to know that people are not induced to act upon what affects their interests by any abstract arguments."

Wilberforce stared steely-eyed back at him. "Mr. Hatsell," he replied, "I do expect to carry it, and what is more, I feel assured I shall carry it speedily."

But Wilberforce went home in dismay, his heart torn by the notion of "abstract arguments" when thousands of men and women were suffering in the bonds of slavery. "I never felt so much on any parliamentary occasion," he wrote in his diary. "I could not sleep …. The poor Africans rushed into my mind, and the guilt of our wicked land."

Once more he went to Pitt to press for the cause, but his old friend seemed sluggish. Wilberforce pushed harder, reminding him of old promises. The prime minister finally agreed to sign a formal document for the cause, then delayed it for months. It was finally issued in September 1805. Four months later Pitt was dead.

Wilberforce felt his death keenly, sad that he had never seen the conversion of his dear friend. "I have a thousand times wished and hoped that he and I might confer freely on the most important of all subjects," he said. "But now the scene is closed — forever."

William Grenville became prime minister. He and Foreign Secretary Fox were both strong abolitionists. After discussing the matter with Wilberforce, Grenville reversed the pattern of the previous twenty years and introduced the bill into the House of Lords first. A bitter and emotional month-long fight ensued before the bill passed at four o'clock on the morning of February 4, 1807.

On February 22 the second reading was held in the House of Commons. Outside a soft snow fell. Inside candles threw flickering shadows on the cream-colored walls of the long room, filled to capacity but unusually quiet.

Lord Howick opened the debate with a nervous, disjointed speech that reflected the tension in the chambers. Then, one by one, members jumped to their feet to decry the evils of the slave trade and to praise the men who had worked so hard to end it. They hailed Wilberforce and praised the abolitionists.

As the debate came to its climax, Sir Samuel Romilly gave a passionate tribute to Wilberforce and his decades of labor, concluding, "When he should retire into the bosom of his happy and delighted family, when he should lay himself down on his bed, reflecting on the innumerable voices that would be raised in every quarter of the world to bless him; how much more pure and perfect felicity must he enjoy in the consciousness of having preserved so many millions of his fellow-creatures."

Stirred by Romilly's words, the entire House rose, cheering and applauding. Realizing that his long battle had come to an end, Wilberforce sat bent in his chair, his head in his hands, tears streaming down his face.

The motion carried, 283 to 16.

Late that night Wilberforce and his friends burst out of the stuffy chambers and onto the snow-covered streets. They frolicked like schoolboys, clapping one another on the back, their joy spilling over. Later, at Wilberforce's home, the old friends crowded into the library, recalling the weary years of battle and rejoicing for their African brothers and sisters.

Wilberforce, surely the most joyous of all, looked into the lined face of his old friend Henry Thornton. Years of illness, defeat, and ridicule had taken their toll. Yet all of it was worth this moment.

"Well, Henry," Wilberforce said with joy in his eyes, "what do we abolish next?"

After the outlawing of the slave trade in 1807, Wilberforce fought another eighteen years for the total emancipation of existing slaves. Despite increasingly poor health, he continued as a leader of the cause in Parliament until his retirement in 1825. He also continued his work for reforms in the prisons, among the poor, and in the workplace. And on July 29, 1833, three days after the Bill for the Abolition of Slavery passed its second reading in the House of Commons, sounding the final death blow for slavery in the British Empire, Wilberforce died. "Thank God," he whispered before he slipped into a final coma, "that I should have lived to witness a day in which England was willing to give twenty millions sterling for the abolition of slavery!"

The story of Wilberforce's long battle has been beautifully told in the film *Amazing Grace*, released on February 23, 2007 — the two hundredth anniversary of perhaps the noblest votes in history. I happened to see a preview of the film on November 6, 2006 — Election Eve. It was, as it turned out, the eve of a conservative rout: Democrats retook both the House and the Senate. Many moral conservative despaired, convinced the election doomed their efforts to restrict abortion, cloning, and embryo-destructive research, pass an amendment protecting marriage, and confirm strict constructionist judges.

Amazing Grace is a potent reminder that ultimate success does not ride on a single election. Wilberforce's half-century campaign reminds us that we must faithfully persevere in battles against modern moral horrors including, tragically, the continued enslavement of African Christians and animists by Muslims. We are not given the option of abrogating this command — of "fasting" from politics, as conservative activist Paul Weyrich advised in 1999 and as David Kuo, former aide to President George W. Bush, suggested in 2006.

Amazing Grace is a reminder, as well, that at the same time we are fighting moral battles in the public square, we must also open our neighbors' eyes to the truth: A sturdy moral standard must undergird a just society. Once they understand this, our neighbors can say, in the word of former slave trader John Newton, "I once was blind, but now I see!"

9

THE CROSS
AND THE CROWN

I die the king's good servant, but God's first.

SIR THOMAS MORE

*If I am faced with the choice between religion and my country...
I will choose my fatherland.*

FATHER MIGUEL D'ESCOTO,
Nicaraguan Foreign Minister

Wilberforce's dogged campaign to rid the British empire of the slave trade shows what can happen when a citizen of the Kingdom of God challenges corrupt structures within the kingdoms of man. One excellent Wilberforce biography is aptly titled *God's Politician*, and truly he was, holding his country to God's standard of moral accountability.

The kind of conflict that Wilberforce and other activist Christians experience—between their Christian conscience and their politician mandates—is unavoidable. Both church and state assert standards and values in society; both seek authority; both compete for allegiance. As members of both the religious and the political spheres, the Christian is bound to face conflict.

The conflict is particularly apparent in the Judeo-Christian tradition because of the assertion that the God of both the Old and New Testament Scriptures is King. That has been an offense to the proud and powerful since the beginning—and one of the reasons Jews and Christians alike have been systematically persecuted.

The tension between the Kingdom of God and the kingdoms of man runs like an unbroken thread through the history of the past two thousand years. It began not long after Christ's birth. Herod, the Roman-appointed king over the Jews and as vicious a tyrant as ever lived, was gripped with fear when the Magi arrived from the East seeking the "King of the Jews." Though not a believer, Herod knew the ancient Jewish prophecies that a child would be born to reign over them, ushering in a Kingdom of peace and might.

Herod called the Magi to his ornate throne room. In what has become common practice in the centuries since, he tried to manipulate the religious leaders for political advantage. He told them to go find this King in Bethlehem so he too could worship Him.

The rest of the story is familiar. The Magi found Jesus but were warned in a dream to avoid Herod and return to the East. Jesus' parents, similarly warned, escaped with their son to Egypt—just ahead of Herod's marauding soldiers who massacred all the male children of Jesus' age in and near Bethlehem.

Herod didn't fear Jesus because he thought He would become a religious or political leader. Herod had suppressed such opponents before. Herod feared Christ because He represented a Kingdom greater than his own.

Jesus was later executed for this same reason. Though He told Pilate His Kingdom was not of this world, the sign over His cross read "INRE"—King of the Jews. The executioner's sarcasm was double-edged.

His followers' faithfulness to Christ's announcement of His Kingdom led to their persecution as well. An enraged mob in Thessalonica threatened Paul and Silas, shouting, "These men who have caused trouble all over the world … are all defying Caesar's decrees, saying that there is another king, one called Jesus."[1] During the early centuries Christians were martyred not for religious reasons—Rome, after all, was a land of many gods—but because they refused to worship the emperor. Because they would not say, "We have no king but Caesar," the Roman government saw them as political subversives.

Christians who refused to offer incense before the statue of the emperor were flogged, stoned, imprisoned, condemned to the mines. Later, when Christianity was officially outlawed, they were tortured mercilessly and fed to the lions, to the delight of bloodthirsty crowds.*

*In the second half of the second century, Christians were systematically persecuted. This account of a massacre in the Rhone Valley is not atypical: "Many Christians were tortured in the stocks or in cells. Sanctus, a deacon from Vienna, had red-hot plates applied to his testicles—his poor body was one whole wound and bruise having lost the outward form of a man. Christians who were Roman citizens were beheaded. Others were forced through a gauntlet of whips into the amphitheater and then … given to the beasts. Severed heads and limbs of Christians were displayed, guarded for six days, then burned, the ashes being

With the conversion of Constantine, however, Christianity was legalized in A.D. 313. This marked the end of persecution and ushered in a second phase in church-state relations.* In A.D. 381 Christianity became the official religion of Rome, and in an ironic turnabout, church leaders began exploiting their new-found power. As historian F. F. Bruce has written: "Christian leaders ... exploit[ed] the influential favor they enjoyed even when it meant subordinating the cause of justice to the apparent interest of their religion ... they were inclined to allow the secular power too much control in church affairs.... Where church leaders were able to exercise political as well as spiritual authority, they did not enjoy any marked immunity from the universally corrupting tendency of power."[2]

Even Augustine, the great church father who provided the classic definition of the roles of the City of God and the city of man, was beguiled by the lure of temporal power; after a wrenching internal struggle he endorsed the suppression of heretics by the state.

Through succeeding centuries the church relied increasingly on the state to punish heresy. By the time of the Byzantine empire in the East, the state had become a theocracy with the church serving as its department of spiritual affairs. In the West both church and state jockeyed for control in an uneasy alliance. In the thirteenth century, for example, Frederick II, king of Sicily, was first excommunicated for not going on a crusade, then excommunicated for going on one without the Pope's permission. The state conquered territory, but the Pope distributed the land to the more faithful crusaders.

The consequences of this alliance were mixed. Certainly Christianity provided a civilizing influence on Western culture through art, music, litera-

---

thrown into the Rhone.... One lady, Blandina, was the worst treated of all, tortured from dawn until evening till her torturers were exhausted and marveled that the breath was still in her body. She was then scourged, roasted in the frying pan and finally put in the basket to be tossed to death by wild bulls." Paul Johnson, *History of Christianity* (New York: Atheneum, 1979) 72–73.

Many Christians went to their death praising their King, and such martyrdom became the church's most potent witness. Pagan Romans were convinced that Christ had taken away his followers' pain. As has often been said, the church was built on the martyrs' blood.

*Historians have questioned Constantine's motives. Some believe it was an effort to save a dying empire, though one contemporary historian has come to a different conclusion. Christianity was practiced only by a small minority. Its universality, the message of Christ Himself, the reliability of written revelation as opposed to myths, began to attract pagan masses. Robin Lane Fox, *Pagans and Christians* (New York: Knopf, 1986).

ture, morality, and ultimately in government. One eminent historian concluded that "society developed only so fast as religion enlarged its sphere."[3] On the darker side, however, the excesses of the politicized church created horrors Augustine could not have imagined.

The church turned to military conquest through a series of "holy wars" that became more racial than religious. Jews, Muslims, and dark-skinned Christians were massacred alike. The goal was not to convert the populace, but to conquer it.

In the twelfth and thirteenth centuries a system was organized for adjudicating heresy. Like many well-intentioned reforms, however, the Inquisition simply produced a new set of horrors. Unrepentant heretics were cast out by a church tribunal that regularly used torture, and were executed by the state.

The spiritual corruption of the church led to the Reformation of the sixteenth century, which innovated several streams of church-state relations. One, believing the state to be essentially coercive and violent, rejected participation in any form of government. A second stream of Reformation thought dictated that the religion of a resident king or prince would be the church of the state. Thus, many kings became their own pope. A third stream encouraged church independence. Scottish church leaders like Samuel Rutherford revived the biblical view that God's law reigns over man and his kingdoms. This profoundly influenced the experiment in constitutional government then beginning in the New World.

A new phase of hostility between church and state began in the eighteenth century when waves of skepticism washed over the continent of Europe. Voltaire, one of the most influential philosophers of the day, was vehemently dedicated to the extirpation of what he called "this infamous superstition."

Religions had been assaulted before but always in the name of other religions. With the French Revolution, de Tocqueville noted, "Passionate and persistent efforts were made to wean men away from the faith of their fathers.... Irreligion became an all-prevailing passion, fierce, intolerant and predatory."[4] For a time this all-prevailing passion was successful. Wrote de Tocqueville: "The total rejection of any religious belief, so contrary to man's natural instincts and so destructive of his peace of mind, came to be regarded by the masses as desirable."[5] The French Revolution was a conscious effort to replace the Kingdom of God with the kingdoms of man.

But the state must have some moral justification for its authority. Thus France's irreligion was soon replaced by a new faith—man's worship of man.

Against this backdrop Wilberforce and other heirs of John Wesley's Christian renewal in England brought the Christian conscience to bear on a society that was nominally Christian but engaged in vile practices. Their stand strengthened the church in England at the very moment it was under its most vicious assault.

Meanwhile, in the New World a radical experiment opened another chapter in church-state relations. There a group of gentlemen farmers, who were neither naïve about human nature nor pretentious about human society, were drawing up the American Constitution. By refusing to assign redemptive powers to the state or to allow coercive power to the church, the American experiment separated these two institutions for the first time since Constantine.

What might be considered the modern phase in church-state history emerged in the twentieth century. It is an amalgam of elements from the previous eras. The rise of totalitarian regimes has brought back the kind of persecution the church experienced in early Rome; the rise of Islamic fundamentalism has meant persecution, not only of Christian populations in Africa, the Middle East and Indonesia, but also of more moderate Muslims. Like Herod, modern dictators tolerate no other kings. In the West, secularism has aggressively spread irreligion, turning Europe into a post-Christian culture and America into a battleground with orthodox religion under constant attack by those who want to force it out of the public square.

Can we conclude from this cursory overview that the church and the state must inevitably be in conflict? To some extent the answer is yes. Dual allegiances always create tension. And in a sinful world the struggle for power, which inevitably corrupts, is unavoidable. When the church isn't being persecuted, it is being corrupted. Man's own nature has created centuries of conflict.

But every generation has an obligation to seek anew a healthy relationship between church and state. Both reflect man's nature; both have a role to play. Christ's teaching clearly delineates these roles.

Jesus was remarkably indifferent to those who held political power. He had no desire to replace Caesar or Pilate with His apostles Peter or John. He gave civil authority its due, rebuking both the Zealots and Peter for using the sword.

This infuriated the religious right of His day. Eager to discredit Jesus, the Pharisees and Herodians tried trapping Him over the question of allegiance to political authority.

"Tell us," they asked, "is it right to pay taxes to Caesar or not?"

The question put Jesus in the middle: if He said no, He would be a threat to the Roman government; if He said yes, He would lose the respect of the masses who hated the Romans.

Jesus asked them for a coin. It was a Roman denarius, the only coin that could be used to pay the hated yearly poll tax. On one side was the image of the Emperor Tiberius, around which were written the words *Tiberius Caesar Augustus, son of the divine Augustus.*

"Whose portrait is this?" He asked, rubbing His finger over the raised features of the Roman ruler. "And whose inscription?"

"Caesar's," they replied impatiently.

"Give to Caesar what is Caesar's and to God what is God's," replied Jesus, handing the coin back to them. They stared at Him in stunned silence.

Not only had He eluded the trap, but He had put Caesar in his place. Christ might simply have said, "Give to Caesar what is Caesar's." That's all that was at issue. It was Caesar's image on the coin, and Caesar had authority over the state.

What made Him add the second phrase, "Give ... to God what is God's"?

The answer, I believe, is found on the reverse face of the coin, which showed Tiberius's mother represented as the goddess of peace, along with the words *highest priest.* The blasphemous words commanded the worship of Caesar; they thus exceeded the state's authority.

Jesus' lesson was not lost on the early church. Government is to be respected, and its rule honored. "It is necessary to submit to the authorities," wrote the apostle Paul. "If you owe taxes, pay taxes."[6] But worship is reserved solely for God.

The distinction Christ made is clear; as discussed in chapter 7, both church and state have clear and distinct roles ordained by God. The issue is how to apply these teachings to each institution in today's volatile world.

"Christ did not give the keys of the Kingdom to Caesar nor the sword to Peter," writes a contemporary scholar.[7] In God's provision the state is not to seize authority over ecclesiastical or spiritual matters, nor is the church to seek authority over political matters. Yet the constant temptation of each is to encroach upon the other.

Governments, with rare exceptions, seek to expand their power beyond the mandate to restrain evil, preserve order, and promote justice. Most often they do this by venturing into religious or moral areas. The reason is twofold: the state needs religious legitimization for its policies and an independent church is the one structure that rivals the state's claim for ultimate allegiance.

A recent example, though admittedly extreme, was the former Soviet Union and its Act of 1918 on separation of church and state. This sounded benign enough, but what the Soviets decreed, reinforced in a 1929 law and in subsequent constitutions, was that churches could conduct worship services when licensed by the government but could not give to the poor, carry on education, or teach religion outside of church. State publishing houses in turn could not publish religious literature; schools could not teach religion but must actively teach atheism; and the government embarked on a campaign to discourage orthodox religious participation and aggressively promote atheism.[8]

So while the edifice of the church was retained, it was a hollow structure; the work of the people of God, which is the true church, was forbidden. Yet in officially promoting atheism, the state was offering its own substitute religion to legitimate its own structure.*

Encroachment upon faith in the West is usually not as dramatic as it has been in modern totalitarian states. It begins in minor ways, such as a county zoning commission barring Bible studies in homes, suppers in church basements, or religious activities on public property. And then, as we have seen in recent years, the state becomes more aggressive. For example, in Massachusetts, adoption agencies must be licensed by the state and adhere to the state's anti-discrimination laws, including laws prohibiting discrimination against homosexual couples. This law put Catholic Charities in a bind. The Vatican has called gay adoptions "gravely immoral" and said that they do "violence" to children. By "violence" it mans taking advantage of the children's "dependency" to place them "in an environment that is not conducive to their full human development."[9]

---

*Oscar Cullman has written, "According to the Jewish, as to the early Christian, outlook the totalitarian state is precisely the classic form of the Devil's manifestation on earth." Oscar Cullman, *The State in the New Testament* (New York: Scriber's, 1956), 74.

At the same time, Catholic Charities wants to help children in need of a home. The most obvious way out of the dilemma is an exemption from the law, what's commonly called a "conscience clause," which is done all the time. So, the bishops of Boston, Worcester, Springfield, and Fall River hired a law firm to "explore legal and political strategies for opting out of gay adoptions."

In February of 2006, Governor Mitt Romney informed them that "he was not authorized to give such an exemption," and State Representative Eugene L. O'Flaherty told them that the legislature was unlikely to enact one. That left the bishops, who at least nominally control Catholic Charities, with two choices: allow gay adoptions or get out of the adoption business altogether. Actually, there was a third option: find ways around the law. This is what the Worcester branch did. It refers prospective gay adopters to other agencies. But even this prompted hostile state officials to investigate the agency for possibly "flouting" the laws against discrimination.

This is hardly surprising. What motivates regulations like this is not the interests of the children — it's the interests of adults. Legally and culturally, religion is increasingly being treated as a purely private affair whose teachings must yield to any so-called public purpose. You're free to believe what you want — so long as it doesn't affect how you behave.

What's more, rules like the Massachusetts one embody a cynical calculation: The enforcers are betting that, in the end, the desire to help these kids will trump the desire to adhere to Catholic teaching. In other words, it's a kind of hostage-taking: "You do what we say or you're going to risk the well-being of these kids."

Those in the adoption business are not the only ones being affected by regulations deliberately hostile toward religious belief (much of it instigated by radical homosexual groups). Some legal scholars believe that if gay "marriage" becomes the law of the land, Christian ministers and priests will be ordered to marry same-sex couples — or see the state yank their licenses to perform marriages. School children and their parents are fighting for the right for children to leave school to perform religious duties — such as attending Ash Wednesday or Yom Kippur services — without being punished with a black mark on their attendance record. Catholic hospitals are pressured to offer abortion services; churches and mosques are fighting "eminent domain" attempts to seize their property. At some medical schools, students are told it's not enough to learn how to remove a deceased fetus from a patient. They're also ordered to take part in the abortion of *live* fetuses—even though they are learning nothing new, because the procedure is identical.

In 2004, the California Supreme Court upheld a state law requiring that Catholic Charities, a religious employer, include contraceptive coverage in health plans that cover other prescriptions—in effect, demanding that Catholic Charities violate Church teachings. The sole dissenter, Justice Janice Rogers Brown, wrote: "Here we are dealing with an intentional, purposeful intrusion into a religious organization's expression of its religious tenets and sense of mission."[10] Joseph Starrs, director of American Life League's Crusade for the Defense of Our Catholic Church, agreed. Justice Brown, he said, "clearly identified the real agenda behind this decision when she wrote, 'The government is not accidentally or incidentally interfering with religious practice; it is doing so willfully by making a judgment about what is or is not a religion.'"[11]

It goes on and on. All over the country, Catholic and evangelical pharmacists are fighting for the right to obey their conscience (or Church teachings) when it comes to prescribing oral contraceptives or the so-called morning-after pill, the drug that causes the spontaneous abortion of an embryonic human being. For instance, Heather Williams spent five years working as a pharmacist at a Target store in St. Louis, Missouri. Target willingly accommodated Williams's desire not to take part in dispensing the morning-after pill. But then Planned Parenthood threatened to boycott the Target chain over Williams's employment—so Target fired her.[12]

There are more than 300 other pharmacies in St. Louis—a fact Planned Parenthood was well aware of. So this was hardly a matter of great public concern. Some observers, like the *Washington Post*, argue that the moral objections of pharmacists must be sacrificed if they interfere in medical decisions made between doctors and patients. This argument is both ethically confused and false. For every pharmacist who refuses to dispense the morning-after pill, there are hundreds who will. So what is really going on here?

It's an effort to silence any reminder, any public witness, that abortion is a moral evil, an offense against God. The proof is in the fact that attacks on pharmacists came at the very time that the California Medical Association attempted to bar doctors from getting involved in death-row executions—even if the doctors have no objections to taking part. In other words, you can't execute convicted murderers, but you *must* kill innocent babies. Health-care providers, it appears, are allowed to have a conscience, as long as those consciences object only to politically correct moral evils.

Even when it appears that the state is accommodating religious viewpoints, its action may well be a Trojan horse. Though my opinion is perhaps a minority one, I believe the much-debated issue of prayer in schools is a case in point.

Children or teachers who want to pray in schools should have (and, according to the Supreme Court, do have) the same constitutional rights of free expression and the same access to public facilities as any other group; six-year-olds who whisper prayers over their peanut-butter sandwiches should not be punished by teachers hostile to religion. But organized prayer, even if voluntary, is another matter. The issue is who does the organizing. If it is the school board, Caesar is being given a spiritual function; admittedly a small crack in the door, but a crack nonetheless. I, for one, don't want my grandchildren reciting prayers determined by government officials. And in actual practice they would be so watered down as to be of no effect except perhaps to water down my grandchildren's growing faith.

Whenever the state has presumed on God's role, whether in ancient Rome or modern America, the first liberty, freedom of conscience, suffers.

On the other side of the coin, the church, whose principal function is to proclaim the Good News and witness the values of the Kingdom of God, must resist the tempting illusion that it can usher in that Kingdom through political means.* Jesus provided the best example for the church in His wilderness confrontation with Satan when the Devil tempted Jesus to worship him and thus take dominion over the kingdoms of this world.

No small temptation. With that kind of power, Christ could enforce the Sermon on the Mount; love and justice could reign. He might have reasoned that if He didn't accept, someone else would. This rationalization is popular today, right up through the highest councils of government: compromise to stay in power because there you can do more for the common good.

---

*James Schall reminds us that "if there is any constant temptation of the history of Christianity, from reaction to Christ's rejection of Jewish zealotism on to current debates about the relation of Marxism to the Kingdom of God, it is the pressure to make religion a formula for refashioning political and economic structures." James Schall, "The Altar as the Throne," in *Churches on the Wrong Road* (Chicago: Regnery/Gateway, 1986), 227.

And think of the popularity Jesus could have gained. After all, the people wanted a Messiah who would vanquish their oppressors. But Jesus understood His mission, and it could not be accomplished by taking over the kingdoms of the world in a political coup.

Yet the church has persistently succumbed to the very temptation that Christ explicitly denied: In the Middle Ages this produced bloody crusades and inquisitions; in modern times it has fostered a type of utopianism expressed in a stanza from one of William Blake's most famous poems:*

> I will not cease from mental fight,
> Nor shall my sword sleep in my hand,
> Till we have built Jerusalem,
> In England's green and pleasant land.[13]

The last century's social-gospel movement echoed Blake's sentiments, dissolving Christian orthodoxy into a campaign to eliminate every social injustice, often through governmental means. Objectives became political and economic to the detriment of the spiritual. The reformers' well-intentioned efforts were shattered as social programs failed to produce the promised utopia, leaving observers to conclude, "Things are no better. Where is your God now?"

A kind of utopianism is often articulated today in contemporary Christian circles; it crosses political lines, from left-leaning Catholics and mainline leaders to evangelicals on both the left and the right. Such preoccupation with the political diverts the church from its primary mission.

The political right is also subject to this temptation; many want to impose religious and cultural values by force of law, irrespective of the wishes of the electorate. This is as wrong, and as dangerous, as the secular left attempting to impose *its* values on society by force of law — usually via the

---

*The problem is, as historian Christopher Dawson observed, "There are quite a number of different Jerusalems.... There is the Muscovite Jerusalem which has no temple, there is Herr Hitler's Jerusalem which has no Jews, and there is the Jerusalem of the social reformers which is all suburbs. But none of these are Blake's Jerusalem, still less [the Kingdom of God]." Christopher Dawson, "Religion and Politics," *Catholicism in Crisis* (June 1985), 8.

All these New Jerusalems are earthly cities established by the will and power of man. And if we believe that the Kingdom of Heaven can be established by political or economic measures, then we can hardly object to the claims of such a state to embrace the whole of life and to demand the total submission of the individual will and conscience.

courts—particularly activists for abortion and radical gay rights. Some, such as those in the theonomist movement, even want to reinstate Old Testament civil codes, ignoring Christ's teaching in the parable of the wheat and the tares in which He warns that we live with both good (the wheat) and evil (the tares), and cannot root out the tares. Only God is able to do that and He will—when the Kingdom comes in its final glory.

It is on this point that the church most frequently has stumbled in its understanding of the Kingdom of God. The late Oscar Cullman writes: "In the course of history the church has always assumed a false attitude toward the state when it has forgotten that the present time is already fulfillment, but not yet consummation."[14] Even if Christians advocating dominion gained power, they would be doomed to failure.* As Martin Luther once wrote, "It is out of the question that there should be a Christian government even over one land ... since the wicked always outnumber the good. Hence a man who would venture to govern ... with the gospel would be like a shepherd who should place in one fold wolves, lions, eagles and sheep together and let them freely mingle."[15]

It was perhaps because he realized this truth—that the present world cannot be ruled by spiritual structures and that the church has long abused power—that John Paul I at his inauguration in 1978 refused to be crowned with the papal tiara, the vestigial symbol of the claim to temporal power. John Paul II followed his example. These dramatic gestures renounced a centuries-old tradition that has contributed to the darkest moments for the church.

But while the church must avoid utopianism and diversion from its transcendent mission, it is not to ignore the political scene. To the contrary, as will be explored in later chapters, its members, who are also citizens of the world, have a duty, as the late Carl Henry put it, "to work through civil authority for the advancement of justice and human good." They may provide

---

*Cullman amplifies his point: "The church's task with regard to the state which is posed for all time is thus clear. First, it must loyally give the state everything necessary to its existence. It has to oppose anarchy and all zealotism within its own ranks. Second, it has to fulfill the office of watchmen over the state. That means it must remain in principle critical towards every state and be ready to warn it against transgression of its legitimate limits. Third, it must deny to the state which exceeds its limits, whatever such a state demands that lies within the province of religio-ideological excess; and in its preaching, the church must courageously describe this excess as opposition to God." Cullman, *The State in the New Testament*, 90–91.

"critical illumination, personal example and vocational leadership."[16] Wilberforce is a prime example. There are proper ways as well for the institutional church to provide society with its moral vision and hold government to moral account.*

Through the individual Christian's involvement in politics, as we will discuss later, the standards of civic righteousness can be influenced by the standards of righteousness of the Kingdom of God. Such an influence is what theologians call common grace (as distinguished from God's special grace that offers citizenship in the Kingdom of God to all who desire admission). Common grace is God's provision for the welfare of all His created beings, both those who believe in Him and those who don't.

As I wrote in *How Now Shall We Live?*, common grace is the means by which God's power sustains creation, holding back the sin and evil that result from the Fall and that would otherwise overwhelm his creation like a great flood.[17] As agents of God's common grace, we are called to help sustain and renew his creation, to uphold the created institutions of family and society, to pursue science and scholarship, to create works of art and beauty, and to heal and help those suffering from the results of the Fall. It is a Christian's duty to participate in public affairs because it is a part of his responsibility to bring all areas of life into conformance with the created order.

When advancing the biblical perspective in public debate, we ought to interpret biblical truth in ways that appeal to the common good. So although we believe that Scripture is God's inerrant revelation, we do not have to derive all arguments directly from Scripture. For example, when I argue in state legislatures that criminals should be required to pay restitution to their victims, I do not say, "Do this because the Bible says so." Rather, I present it as sound public policy. It makes sense to give back what you have taken, to restore what you have destroyed.

---

*Some Christian traditions similarly believe that they can best model Kingdom values not by involvement in politics but by the establishment of alternative communities in which they live out the teachings of the Kingdom. In its proper form, this is not a withdrawal from the world or abandonment of Christian responsibility; nor is it a privatization of Christian values as with those who profess to believe but live as if they do not. It is instead a different strategy to the same end of providing a witness in the kingdoms of man of the values of the Kingdom of God. While I do not agree with the generally negative view of government held by such groups, I respect the faithfulness by which they live their convictions.

The critical dynamic in the church-state tension is separation of institutional authority. Religion and politics can't be separated—they inevitably overlap—but the institutions of church and state must preserve their separate and distinct roles. In this regard, the American experiment merits closer examination.

America is not the New Jerusalem or a "city upon a hill," though some of its founders harbored that vision. Nor are Americans God's chosen people. The Kingdom of God is universal, bound by neither race nor nation. But Abraham Lincoln used an interesting phrase; Americans, he said, were the "almost chosen people."[18] If there is any justification for that term—not theologically but historically—it is because in the hammering out of a new republic, the combination of wisdom, reason, and providence produced a church-state relationship that uniquely respected the differing roles of each.

The basis of this radical idea came from the partial convergence of at least two conflicting ideologies: confidence in the eighteenth-century Enlightenment belief that both public and private virtue were possible without religion; and a reaction against the excesses of the state church in Europe. The first view was held by the Deists among America's founders, while the second particularly motivated the avowed Christians among them.

These men and women believed that Christ had given the church its own structures and charter, and the state, ordained in God's providence for the maintenance of public order, was not to tamper with it. The church was ordained principally for the conversion of men and women—conversion grounded in individual conscience and wrought by the supernatural work of a sovereign God upon the soul. So the state could neither successfully establish nor destroy the church, since it could not rule conscience nor transform people's hearts and souls.*

Thus two typically mortal enemies, the Enlightenment and the Christian faith, found a patch of common ground on American soil. Both agreed (for different reasons) that the new government should neither establish nor

---

*The comment of Baptist minister Isaac Backus is representative: "Nothing can be a true religion but a voluntary obedience unto his revealed will, of which each rational soul has an equal right to judge for himself, every person has an unalienable right to act in all religious affairs according to the full persuasion of his own mind." "A Declaration of the Rights of the Inhabitants of the State of Massachusetts-Bay in New England," in Edwin S. Gaustad, ed., *A Documentary History of Religion in America, Vol. 1* (Grand Rapids, Mich.: Eerdmans, 1982), 268.

interfere with the church.* It was this reasoning that led to the adoption of the First Amendment, expressly to protect the individual's right to freedom of conscience and expression, and to prevent the establishment of a state church.

But contrary to the belief of many today, this separation of church and state did not mean that America was to be a nation free of religious influence. From the very beginning the American Revolution itself was fueled by the conviction that man is a creature of God, and his political life conditioned by that truth. As James Madison insisted, "This duty [homage to the Creator] is precedent, both in order of time and degree of obligation, to the claims of civil society. Before any man can be considered as a member of civil society, he must be considered as a subject of the governor of the universe."[19] A nation under God was no idle phrase.

Nor did the separation of church and state mean religion and politics could be separated or religious values removed from the public arena. For one's political life is an expression of values, and religion, by definition, most profoundly influences values.†

The Founding Fathers were well aware that the form of limited government they were adopting could only succeed if there was an underlying consensus of values shared by the populace. I am always reminded of this when I visit the House of Representatives. A beautiful fresco on the upper walls of the chamber itself contains the portraits of history's great lawmakers. Standing at the speaker's desk and looking straight ahead over the main entrance, one's eyes meet the piercing eyes of the first figure in the series: Moses, the one who recorded the Law from the original Lawgiver.

John Adams eloquently acknowledged the understanding of our constitutional framers when in 1798 he wrote: "We have no government armed

---

*One phrase in James Madison's "Memorial and Remonstrance," presented to the Commonwealth of Virginia in 1785, succinctly sums up the thinking of our Founding Fathers: "... that Religion or the duty which we owe to our Creator and the manner of discharging it, can be directed only by reason and conviction, not by force or violence. The Religion then of every man must be left to the conviction and conscience of every man; and it is the right of every man to exercise it as these may dictate." "James Madison's Memorial and Remonstrance, 1785," in Gaustad, ed., A Documentary History of Religion in America: Vol. I, 262.

† The concept of a "wall of separation," a phrase incidentally first used by Jefferson fifteen years after the Constitution was adopted, applied to institutions of church and state, not religious and political values.

in power capable of contending with human passions unbridled by morality and religion.... Our constitution was made only for a moral and religious people. It is wholly inadequate for the government of any other."[20]

Many of these original American visionaries believed that Christian citizens would actively bring their religious values to the public forum. George Washington faintly echoed Augustine when he asserted, "Of all the dispositions and habits which lead to a political prosperity, religion and morality are indispensable supports. In vain would that man claim that tribute of patriotism, who should labor to subvert these great pillars of human happiness."[21]

Thus, when laws were passed reflecting the consensus of Christian values in the land, no one panicked supposing that the Christian religion was being "established" or that a sectarian morality was being imposed on an unwilling people. The point of the First Amendment was that such convictions could only become the law of the land if a majority of citizens could be persuaded (without coercion) of the merits of a particular proposition, whether they shared its religious foundation or not.

Today's widespread attempt to relegate religion to the privacy of homes or churches would have been unimaginable to the founders of the republic — even those who personally repudiated orthodox Christian faith. Though America has drifted far from the vision of its founders, this system continues to offer one of the world's most hopeful models in an otherwise contentious history of conflict.

The record of the centuries should not cause despair, however. Tension between church and state is inherent and inevitable. Indeed, it is perhaps the outworking of one of God's great mysteries, part of the dynamic by which He governs His universe. For from the constant tension — the chafing back and forth — a certain equilibrium is achieved.

To maintain this balance the church and the state must fulfill their respective roles. One cannot survive without the other; yet neither can do the work of the other. Both operate under God's rule, each in a different relationship to that rule.

Certainly one thing is clear. When they fail in their appointed tasks — that is, when the church fails to be the visible manifestation of the Kingdom of God and the state fails to maintain justice and concord — civic order collapses. The consequences can be catastrophic, as the tumultuous events described in the next two chapters demonstrate.

PART THREE

ABSENCE
OF THE
KINGDOM

10

ROOTS OF WAR
(PART I)

In Germany they came first for the Communists, and I didn't speak up because I wasn't a Communist. Then they came for the Jews, and I didn't speak up because I wasn't a Jew. Then they came for the trade unionists, and I didn't speak up because I wasn't a trade unionist. Then they came for the Catholics, and I didn't speak up because I was a Protestant. Then they came for me, and by that time no one was left to speak up.

MARTIN NIEMOLLER

One match flared, illuminating a single face above the collar of a brown shirt. He was a middle-aged man with a paunch and a face scarred by innumerable street battles.[1]

The man held the match to a fuel-soaked torch, which leaped into flame. Quickly he held the torch to another and then another. In a matter of minutes hundreds were alight, their flickering red glare glazing the street crowded with men dressed in brown shirts and dark pants.

They formed into ranks and began their march through the city. Singing, shouting in triumph, swaggering as though they owned the world, thousands marched, filling the widest streets of Berlin and lighting its ancient walls with their smoking torches. They swept under the Brandenburg Gate and down the Wilhelmstrasse. When they passed the chancellery, they became strangely agitated. The tramping of their steps grew louder and the men strained their necks looking upward.

This account is based on historical records and quotations from the major figures. In an effort to recreate the historical environment, however, some dialogue has been invented, along with some minor characters. The main characters, their activities, and their views, are as accurate as it is possible to make them.

141

"Sieg Heil, Sieg Heil." Their cries echoed from the buildings at the sight of their leader.

Above them, at a window, Adolf Hitler fondly looked down. After years in the political wilderness, that very day, January 30, 1933, he had been named Chancellor of Germany.

FEBRUARY 1, 1933, BERLIN

A tall, blond young man, well-dressed and carrying himself with aloof self-confidence, stepped out of the heavy black car that had pulled up in front of the German Broadcasting Company on the busy Potsdamerstrasse. As he entered the building, a younger man in a neat but frayed jacket hustled up to greet him enthusiastically.

"Dr. Bonhoeffer! Please come in. Let me take your coat. It is indeed a pleasure for the former student to welcome his professor. You have your script?"

Dietrich Bonhoeffer tapped his chest. "It is here."

"You have it memorized?" the younger asked, his eyes widening. "Are you sure? This is a live broadcast, you know."

Bonhoeffer's cold, patrician face broke into an amused smile. "No, Herr Schmidt, I have the script here, in my pocket." He reached inside his suit coat and pulled out a sheaf of typed pages.

"Oh, excuse me, Doctor." Schmidt murmured with a look of embarrassed pleasure. "I know you are brilliant, but ... one can be too brilliant."

"You know the time limit," the younger man added as he led Bonhoeffer upstairs to the broadcast room. "I'm sure I don't have to tell you it is very strict." Bonhoeffer nodded. He had worked out the length of his speech with his usual precision.

Schmidt took a seat before the microphone and glanced at his watch. "We have a little time," he said. "Would you like to smoke?" Bonhoeffer declined.

Then, with an effort at casualness, Schmidt said, "I hope you won't mind if I say that I was quite surprised at your choice of the subject, 'The Younger Generation's Changed View of the Concept of Fuehrer.' Most of the theologians who come here speak on very dry material. But you have chosen just the topic people want to discuss. Tell me, were you inspired by the parade in the Wilhelmstrasse last night?"

"Inspired?" Bonhoeffer seemed suddenly to notice the younger man. "What do you mean, 'inspired'?"

At this invitation, the words poured out of Schmidt. "People say that Hitler is just one more politician, but I don't think so. Somehow, Dr. Bonhoeffer, I feel he is a different kind of man, a man who knows the soul of Germany. I am sure you must know what I mean. The old people cannot stop living in the past. But they will learn. This man may be the leader we in the younger generation have been seeking. That is what I meant by 'inspired.' That march seemed to signal that he had touched some secret chord in our hearts."

Bonhoeffer appeared aloof, almost bored, when in fact he was intensely interested. "What do you think he will do now that he has power, Herr Schmidt? He has been very evasive in laying out his plans."

"But that is exactly what I mean! He is not just another politician, with one promise or another. He offers himself. We have had so many years of these weak politicians. They act as though Germany's defeat and betrayal is simply a fact that must be accepted. If that is realism, we should get rid of realism! We don't need just another political program; we need a complete transformation of the nation. You can only get that from a leader you trust completely. Our soul was meant to be forged into unity! Don't you think so?"

"I doubt Hitler will last long in power," said Bonhoeffer coolly. "He seems strong because he has not had to be responsible. Now he will have to make the usual compromises." As he spoke, Bonhoeffer fingered a signet ring on his left hand. "Nor, Herr Schmidt, do I completely agree with you about the need for a leader. It is, of course, a very appealing idea. We are so tired of politics. We would naturally like to give it all over to a leader in the way that a child can turn over some difficult struggle to his father. But we cannot just hand over authority to our leaders and consider that the end of our responsibility. I think that is what Herr Hitler would like us to do. But the government can only do, and should only be called on to do certain things. It cannot replace God."

Schmidt was silent for a few moments. When he spoke, he weighed his words carefully. "For years godless Communists have had the run of the streets. You have seen the fights, real battles, as though Berlin were in a war zone. The national economy is devastated. People lack food, jobs. Money has become worthless. Nobody goes to church any more. Now Herr Hitler has at last barred the Communists from meeting, something none of our 'leaders' had the courage to do. He will save us from Bolshevism. This is leadership. This will lead the German people to greatness."

"Be careful that such leadership does not lead you to disaster," Bonhoeffer said quietly.

Schmidt stood up. "Did you bring the extra copy of your script, Dr. Bonhoeffer? I should take it to the director now."

"Why does he need it?"

"It's a new directive. Everything should go across his desk."

Bonhoeffer reached into his suit-coat pocket and pulled out a second copy of his script. Schmidt took it away. Shortly after he returned, Bonhoeffer went on the air.

Bonhoeffer, who spoke rapidly in normal conversation, delivered his radio address slowly and deliberately. He described the development of Adolf Hitler's "Führerprinzip," or "leadership principle," through which discipline and dignity would be restored by vesting authority in a single leader. This idea was tremendously attractive to young Germans who had known only the chaos of the last fifteen years. At many points in his address it seemed that Bonhoeffer was embracing the Fuehrer principle. But at the end his words grew ominous as he warned against placing blind faith in any authority.

"For should the leader allow himself to succumb to the wishes of those he leads, who will always seek to turn him into an idol," he concluded, "then the leader will gradually become the image of 'misleader.' This is the leader who makes an idol of himself and his office, thus mocking God."

When he finished, Bonhoeffer glanced at his watch, stood and shook hands with Schmidt, and left the broadcasting room. As he was putting on his overcoat on the ground floor, Schmidt came down the stairs hurriedly.

"Dr. Bonhoeffer," he called. "Just a moment. . . . The director said I ought to tell you . . . just so you would not be surprised . . . that unfortunately the last few sentences of your address were not broadcast. It seems you went slightly over the time allotted."

Bonhoeffer's blue eyes were icy behind his rimless glasses. "What do you mean? They turned off the microphone?"

Schmidt smiled. "I'm so sorry, Doctor. But you know radio is very precise."

FEBRUARY 27, 1933

While at a party in his honor at the apartment of Joseph Goebbels, Adolf Hitler received a call telling him that the ornate, gilded Reichstag building was in flames. The Reichstag was the historic German parliament building. "It's the Communists!" the Führer shouted. Then he stalked out into the frigid night where the buildings were silhouetted against an orange sky.

Shortly thereafter, Hitler convened a meeting in Hermann Göring's nearby office. Cabinet ministers filed in, talking excitedly. Finally Rudolf Diels, head of the Secret Police, was ushered in to report on the initial investigation. Diels said that a Dutchman named van der Lubbe had been arrested and had confessed to lighting the fire as a protest.

Both Göring and Hitler began shouting simultaneously. "This is the beginning of a Communist uprising! Now we'll show them! Anyone who stands in our way will be mowed down!"

Diels interrupted them. The idea of an uprising was nonsense; his spies all said no Communist move was coming. Undoubtedly van der Lubbe had acted alone.

Hitler ignored Diels. "This is a cunning and well-prepared plot! But they have reckoned without us and without the German people! In their rat holes, from which they are now trying to crawl, they cannot hear the jubilation of the masses!" He ranted until Diels and everyone else fell silent.

By morning truckloads of hurriedly deputized brown shirts were breaking down doors and arresting Communists throughout the nation. Four thousand suspects were sent to newly organized concentration camps. Hitler, claiming a national emergency and demanding instantaneous action, convinced the government to suspend all constitutional rights. News broadcasts proclaimed that Hitler had miraculously saved Germany from a Communist insurrection.

In this frenzied atmosphere Adolf Hitler won his first bare majority in the March 5 elections.*

APRIL 1, 1933

The first splash of morning light struck the front door of the small hardware store as three young "Brown Shirts," laughing and joking, began fixing a large poster to the front window. The proprietor, who was sweeping the sidewalk, came over to ask what they were doing. After a short, noisy argument

---

*It is generally accepted now that the fire was set by the Nazis to give them pretext for destroying the Communist political organization.

he retreated into his store. He could be seen from time to time peering out the door.

The sign announced, in six-inch letters visible from across the street, that the proprietor was a Jew and requested that shoppers not patronize his business. A few curious passersby gathered on the sidewalk and watched the storm troopers post the signs on several other storefronts.

A man dressed in dark blue working clothes came down the sidewalk and walked up to the door of the hardware store, not noticing the signs or the small crowd. Before he could enter the store, one of the Brown Shirts politely stopped him and explained that a national boycott of all Jewish businesses had been called by Adolf Hitler. The man looked up and around, startled to see the spectators, and hurried off. The crowd chuckled.

After three days the boycott ended. Hitler had learned what he wanted to know: no one would stand up for the Jews.

On the same day the boycott was launched, a group known as the German Christians held their first national rally. Included in their number were some widely respected theologians and church leaders. Their chosen name, which placed more emphasis on *German* than *Christian*, expressed their belief that German experiences and culture had given them a unique understanding of God.

The German Christians wanted to harmonize the church in Germany with Hitler's political movement, which was, to them, more than politics; it was the revival of hope and the force of destiny for their nation. Many of them believed the Germans were God's chosen people and Hitler the new messiah. The national revival was more vital than anything they had ever found in their faith.

JULY 1933

In six months Hitler had accomplished an almost unbelievable consolidation of power. He had, thanks to the Reichstag fire, imprisoned all known Communists. He had convinced the members of the Reichstag parliament to virtually suspend its own powers. He had outlawed all significant opposition parties and imprisoned many of their leaders. He had taken over, by force, all labor unions and removed all Jews from the civil service.

More significantly, however, he had done all this without arousing any substantial resistance. In January he had been head of a minority party, little liked or trusted. By July, thanks to his skillful manipulation, the majority of German citizens had fallen under his spell. Germans talked excitedly of the renewal of their country. It was no longer only his swaggering, heel-clicking Brown Shirts who cheered Hitler to the skies. Ordinary men and women, laborers and tradesmen, businessmen and housewives went into hysterical chants of "Heil Hitler!" when he passed through the streets, his motorcade swathed in red and black Nazi flags. He had given them hope again.

William Shirer, an American correspondent in Berlin, wrote in his diary: "I'm beginning to comprehend, I think, some of the reasons for Hitler's astounding success. Borrowing a chapter from the Roman church, he is restoring pageantry and color and mysticism to the drab lives of twentieth-century Germans. This morning's opening meeting … had something of the mysticism and religious fervor of an Easter or Christmas Mass in a great Gothic cathedral."

The pageant Shirer had viewed was played dozens of times in every part of Germany: an immense hall packed with citizens and soldiers … a sea of red and black Nazi standards swaying overhead … a giant golden eagle glaring down from an upper balcony … an orchestra playing solemn symphonic music.

The orchestra stops. A hush falls over the strangely orderly crowd and thousands of people crane their necks to see. Then a stately patriotic anthem begins and from far in the back, walking slowly down the wide central aisle, comes the Führer.

Thousands of arms snap stiffly out in salute. Thousands of eyes focus on Hitler's pale, grave face. Behind him march his closest aides—faces and names that will go down in history, recorded in blood—Göring, Goebbels, Hess, Himmler. They take their places on the raised dais under huge lights. Above them is the huge Nazi Blood Flag, stained with the blood of Nazis killed in the Munich Beer Hall Putsch.

Finally the Fuehrer himself rises to speak. Beginning in a low, velvety voice, which makes the audience unconsciously lean forward to hear, he speaks of his love for Germany and his long struggle to restore its dignity. He describes his own humble beginnings, his injuries as a foot soldier in World War I, and the terrible injuries Germany has suffered as a result of that war. Gradually his pitch increases until he reaches a screaming crescendo. But his audience does not think his rasping shouts excessive. They are screaming with him.

JULY 14, 1933

By now Hitler had only one significant source of opposition. Not the journalists, political parties, universities, or labor unions; all these he had almost completely converted to Nazism in less than six months. Instead, opposition came from a most unexpected source: the church.

Two thirds of the German population — 45,000,000 people — were Protestants, primarily Lutherans, who traditionally kept their noses entirely out of politics. As a group, they were known as the German Evangelical Church. They were conservative, rural, and patriotic, and had Hitler been content to leave them alone, they undoubtedly would have supported him almost unanimously at this stage. But Hitler would allow no independent source of authority in his resurrected Germany. Everyone must answer to a single leader, the Fuehrer. Every institution must serve the aims of the Fatherland, including the church.

Publicly, in the beginning, Hitler gave the appearance of being a religious man. A nominal Catholic, he sometimes displayed a tattered Bible and spoke of its inspiration in his life. Officially, his party platform called, rather ambiguously, for religious freedom and supported "positive Christianity." In private, however, he expressed his utter contempt for the church, particularly for the Protestants. He expected their pastors to knuckle under easily to his schemes for remolding the church, his main source of opposition. "They will betray anything for the sake of their miserable little jobs and incomes."

Early on he had negotiated an agreement with Rome that removed Roman Catholic opposition to his regime. Eager to support the spirit of the times, the twenty-eight main Protestant denominations voluntarily began work on a new constitution that would unite them under one leader according to the "Fuehrer principle."

But Hitler was impatient; he did not want to wait for the church bureaucracy. He decided to push an obscure, obsequious naval chaplain, Ludwig Müller, into leadership of the newly united Protestant church. Despite the Führer's prestigious support, however, Müller was defeated in a May 27 election.

Hitler refused to meet the elected bishop. Instead, radio and press propaganda poured out favorable material about Müller. Then in late June Nazi government officials invaded church offices, forcibly taking over administrative positions. Müller proclaimed himself national bishop-elect.

The new officials ordered services of praise and thanksgiving for this takeover. Every church in Germany was to be decorated with Nazi flags and a proclamation read from the pulpit, stating that "all those who are concerned ... feel deeply thankful that the state should have assumed, in addition to all its tremendous tasks, the great load and burden of reorganizing the church."

But while all Germany was being wooed to Hitler, a stubborn resistance was taking root within the church itself: the Young Reformation Movement. Martin Niemoller, Hans Jacobi, and Dietrich Bonhoeffer were among its first members. They were apolitical, and their meetings often included a resolution of loyalty to the government and, sometimes, to Adolf Hitler. But they also valued the church's independence and rejected any attempt to blend a religion of Germany with the religion of Jesus Christ.

On July 14, 1933, Hitler surprised everyone by calling a special church election to be held nine days later on July 23. The German Christians were given complete access to the state-run radio and newspapers; the Young Reformation hastily organized a slate of candidates and began feverish campaigning. Over the weekend leaflets were written and duplicated.

On Monday, July 17, the Gestapo invaded the Young Reformation offices and confiscated all 620,000 campaign leaflets.

JULY 17, 1933

The cramped offices of the Young Reformers, which just two days earlier had been a hive of activity, were ominously silent. Martin Niemoller, whose rounded face and cleft chin gave him the appearance of perpetual boyhood, paced around Bonhoeffer, Jacobi, and a young man wearing the brown shirt and Nazi armband of the SA.

"I don't see any point in appealing to underlings," Niemoller said stubbornly. "You might as well appeal to the stones in the street. I would rather go directly to Hitler. If he knew what was being done, he would put a stop to it. But I am sure they all lie to him."

"How do we get to Hitler?" Jacobi asked..

"Perhaps through President Hindenburg," said Niemoller. "We have contacts there, and he has always been sympathetic."

Bonhoeffer's impatience would have been invisible to anyone who did not recognize his mannerism of fiddling with the ring on his left hand.

"That is a fine idea, Martin," he said, "but the elections are Sunday. If we have no literature we might as well go home. What else can we do, stand in the street and yell our slogans? We must go to the Gestapo now!"

The discussion seesawed until Niemoller shrugged his large shoulders and smiled. "All right, go then," he said. "But at least take Henke with you." He pointed to the young storm trooper, a hybrid rare but not unknown — a staunch Nazi who was also a Young Reformer. "They may respect his uniform more than they respect yours."

Jacobi vetoed this. "Martin, I think not. Maybe these will count as much as Henke's swastikas." He indicated the two Iron Crosses he wore, won in World War I. "At any rate, for every SA member we can produce, the German Christians can show fifty."

At Gestapo headquarters on the Albrechtstrasse, Jacobi and Bonhoeffer's demand to see Rudolf Diels, the Gestapo chief, met with opposition by several underlings. They persisted. Finally a rude, overbearing officer ushered them into Diels's presence.

To their surprise, the Gestapo chief politely invited them to sit down and said that he certainly hoped he could be of help to them. It was really not his department, but he would do what he could. He noticed Jacobi's decorations and asked about his service in the war.

But the initial cordiality was mere display. When he heard their complaint, Diels did not budge an inch.

"It seems clear to me, Pastors, that you are in the wrong. You have published scurrilous literature. You have taken a slogan that cannot be proper, 'The Program of the Evangelical Church.' You are fortunate not to have been arrested yourselves." He stood up and held out his hand, as though that closed the matter.

Neither Bonhoeffer nor Jacobi moved.

"The Führer made the explicit promise that this election would be free and secret," Bonhoeffer said. "He wanted to settle the political quarrels of our church through a fair election. Do you think confiscating all of one party's literature can be considered fair treatment? It is certainly a violation of the Führer's words."

Diels slowly took his seat again.

"Pastor, I have heard the Führer's words. He appointed me to safeguard them. He did not give you that responsibility. My officers have been very lenient with you. If it were up to me I would send you to the concentration camp now. In fact I am thinking of it. Why don't you simply leave now and go prepare your next sermon?"

"You have not answered my question," Bonhoeffer pressed him. "The state has promised a free election. How can this be considered free?"

The Gestapo leader leaned back in his chair and looked Bonhoeffer over while absentmindedly brushing off his jacket. He forced a smile. "You do not really have much respect for the state, do you, Pastor?"

"I have enough respect for the state to protest when it does wrong," Bonhoeffer snapped back.

After another silence, Diels asked, "What do you want me to do? There is a court injunction against you. Do you want me to ignore it? That would be contrary to the law."

Jacobi spoke up. "The injunction is against our slogan, not against our literature."

"But the slogan is all over your literature."

"Not all of it."

Diels agreed, finally, to let them have their literature back. The pastors, in turn, agreed to change their slogan from "Evangelical Church" to "Gospel and Church."

The parting was stiff and unfriendly; no one was satisfied.

"I assure you, Pastors," Diels said, "that I am still considering whether you are safe outside this building or whether you would be better off in the KZ.* If a single pamphlet appears, under your names or anyone else's, that insults the German Christians or that uses some slogan similar to the one you have agreed to discard, I will certainly send for you. Do not think that I lack the power to put you anywhere I want to, or that I will hesitate again."

That weekend Hitler was in Bayreuth for the annual Wagner Festival. During an interval in the program, he broadcast a message calling for the German people, in support of all he had done, to elect those forces that "as exemplified by the German Christians, have deliberately chosen to take their stand within the National Socialist State."

For Martin Niemoller that address was a lightning bolt. As a former U-boat captain from World War I and an ardent German patriot, he had supported Hitler. Now he heard, in disbelief, a state official telling the church whom to elect as their spiritual representatives. Niemoller would never trust Hitler again.

---

*Concentration camps.

For others, however, the address proved that as popular as Hitler was, he could sway most church members to support anything he wanted. When the votes were tallied the next day, the German Christians had over 70 percent. Even in Niemoller's parish they took half the vote. Now, by "legal" means, the Nazis took over key positions in the church.

SEPTEMBER 1933

In September the new governing body of the German Evangelical Church met. It became known as the Brown Synod because most of the delegates wore the brown shirts of the SA. They elected Hitler's man, Müller, their bishop and passed the much-debated Aryan Paragraph, outlawing all Jews or persons married to Jews from church office. They also passed a ruling that all pastors take a loyalty oath to Hitler and his government.

Dietrich Bonhoeffer urged vehemently that all dissenting pastors resign from the church. Instead, protest formed under a new organization, the Pastors' Emergency League, led by the tireless Martin Niemoller. Within a week 2,300 pastors had signed its pledge to be bound in their preaching "only by Holy Scripture and the Confessions of the Reformation." By the end of the year members would total 6,000, approximately the same number as the German Christians.

OCTOBER 17, 1933, LONDON

Dietrich Bonhoeffer stood at the window of his new London vicarage, thoughtfully smoking a cigarette. Though located in the south London suburb of Forest Hill, the large Victorian house was surrounded by a forest of trees. He watched the dying leaves being whipped away by a strong wind and shivered in the wet English air. The room behind him, one of two he would occupy, was bare and inhospitable; clearly mice had been its most frequent residents. His furniture and his piano had yet to arrive from Germany.

Bonhoeffer had come to London to pastor two tiny German-speaking congregations and to place some distance between himself and the church struggle in Germany. Still under thirty years of age, yet often consulted for his wisdom, Bonhoeffer needed time to think and pray. He was deeply concerned with the Jewish question, and he was frustrated by the gap between his own uncompromising stand and the views of others who still thought accommodation with Hitler possible.*

Just three days before Hitler had announced that Germany was resigning from the League of Nations. Germans, for whom the League was a symbol of their World War I defeat, had rejoiced as though at a stunning martial victory. Even Martin Niemoller, to Bonhoeffer's horror, had sent Hitler a congratulatory telegram.

The Germany he had left rang with the marching and singing of tanned, fit bands of children, the Hitler Youth. Hitler was obviously preparing to violate the Versailles Treaty, which limited the size and armaments of Germany's army. Yet few Germans, including his comrades in the church struggle, saw any danger. They were stirred by their love for their nation and their faith in its God-given destiny.

Sadly, the people in England were equally unaware of the danger. They did not understand the degree to which Hitler had transformed the German nation, particularly the young people, into passionate believers. They wanted Bonhoeffer to explain what was happening in Germany, but their attention span was short. The Christians he had spoken with could not even distinguish between the German Christians and those who opposed them.

London was to give Bonhoeffer a chance to develop perspective from a distance. Yet he longed for the battle he had deliberately left. He spent hours on the phone and found excuses for returning to Berlin frequently.

NOVEMBER 12, 1933, BERLIN

Martin Niemoller was a popular preacher and the services in his newly built church in the affluent suburb of Dahlem were generally full. But this Sunday many people, including the usual Gestapo plainclothesmen, came early and waited with particular expectation. Yesterday church officials had informed Niemoller and two other leaders of the Pastors' Emergency League that they were suspended from their pastorates. Later in the day the suspension had been cancelled; some said because Hitler had ordered it.

Niemoller was very different from the introspective Bonhoeffer. Blunt to a fault, he never kept his thoughts to himself. His critics called him unreasonable and unbending.

---

*Often in his meditations in those days he turned to the Sermon on the Mount. A few years later his thoughts would coalesce into his book *The Cost of Discipleship*.

This Sunday marked the four-hundred-and-fiftieth anniversary of Martin Luther's birth. The German Christians claimed Luther as their hero. To them the bluff, courageous, uncompromising reformer embodied the true German character. What would Niemoller say to that?

He began by welcoming this "1933 picture of Luther, which represents him as a fighter." Clearly battle lines were being drawn in the German church today. It was proper to ask, which side of the battle would Luther be on if he were here?

Niemoller acknowledged with a warm smile that behind all the German Christians' discussion of the "Luther spirit" lay a genuine admiration for Luther's "naïve unconcern, for his intrepid courage, for his tenacious steadfastness, for his straightforward and unflinching will, for his profound tenderness." Many Germans felt, said Niemoller, that Germany and its church desperately needed more of this Luther spirit if they were to renew themselves.

"But here is a grave error," Niemoller said, his clear voice ringing over the quiet congregation, "the substitution of a human hero for the message God sent through him. What a strange paradox it would be if the Devil used Luther's four hundred and fiftieth birthday to fill German minds with the delusion that they needed not the grace of God, but the courage of Martin Luther! Luther's message was always that no human qualities or human works could bring salvation—only the goodness of God."

Now Niemoller applied this to practical political issues. "One can even hear that our whole nation would do the will of God if only it had purified its species and its race!" Luther himself, Niemoller said, would certainly have fought such ideas.

"There is absolutely no sense in talking of Luther and celebrating his memory within the Protestant church if we stop at Luther's image and do not look at Him to whom Luther pointed." And Luther pointed, Niemoller reminded his listeners, to a Jew, the rabbi of Nazareth.

The next evening, as though in confirmation of Niemoller's words, 20,000 German Christians, including bishops and church officials in full regalia, gathered in the Berlin Sports Palace, a massive new building, symbolic of the Nazi resurgence in its raw modernistic architecture.

Joachim Hossenfelder, head of the German Christians and a Berlin pastor, presided in his Nazi uniform. After the usual parade of swastika-bedecked flags, a fanfare of trumpets and throaty chorus of "Now Thank We All Our God," Hossenfelder announced that in his diocese the Aryan paragraph, dismissing all Jews from church office, was being put into effect immediately. He also announced that Niemoller and other leaders of the Pastors' Emergency League would be suspended, since their activities were entirely foreign to the true spirit of Germany. At each announcement the crowd erupted into a resounding cheer.

The main speaker of the evening was a senior Nazi official who demanded that everything un-German be purged from the church. His final admonition was that the Bible be reexamined for non-German elements: "liberation from the Old Testament, with its Jewish money morality and these stories of cattle-dealers and pimps." It also meant purging the New Testament of its Jewish elements, especially the unheroic theology of the apostle Paul with his "inferiority complex." A proud, heroic Jesus must replace the model of a "suffering servant."

His speech was interrupted again and again by applause. Not one of the bishops or church leaders stood to disagree. Instead, when the speaker had finished, resolutions were enthusiastically passed supporting his words and calling for Jewish Christians to be forced into "ghetto churches."

In the days that followed, the reports in the press of the Sports Palace rally shocked many. The Emergency League printed a protest to be read from their pulpits the next Sunday, but the proclamation was confiscated and fifty pastors who read it were dismissed from their churches.

Bishop Müller, terrified that he might lose his position as head of the national church, resigned from the German Christians. He also rescinded the Aryan paragraph. At the same time, he published volleys of orders, some illegal, some self-contradictory. He secretly arranged for the transfer of all church youth work to the leadership of the Hitler Youth. He then reinstated the Aryan paragraph and published the Muzzling Decrees, which forbade the discussion of all church issues by pastors, on pain of dismissal. Most church leaders lost all confidence in him.

In January Hitler intervened. He had hoped that Müller would unite the entire church behind the Nazi program, but Müller had failed. Now the Führer himself would meet with the leadership of the German Evangelical Church.

JANUARY 25, 1934, BERLIN

Martin Niemoller and a group of his fellow bishops waited quietly in the Reich Chancellery watching the black-uniformed SS officers marching back and forth. One of the bishops nudged Niemoller as a Nazi official passed carrying a scarlet briefcase under his arm. Niemoller recognized fat, baby-faced Hermann Göring. Truly they were near the seat of power!

Finally they were ushered into the Führer's office. Hitler rose from behind his desk and came forward to greet them. Seen closely, he was less than superhuman. He was not tall; his complexion was pale, his face almost undernourished. Only his frigid blue eyes betrayed the real man.

Hitler was about to begin the discussion when Göring burst into the room. He clicked his heels, gave the Nazi salute, and breathlessly launched into a diatribe accusing Bishop Niemoller of conspiring against Hitler. As Göring read from a paper, Niemoller recognized some of his own words, a direct quote from an innocent jest he had made less than an hour before in a telephone conversation with one of his fellow pastors from the Emergency League. The slightly garbled version presented by Göring made it sound as though Niemoller had been gloating about political maneuverings that would outsmart Hitler, the master politician.

Hitler's face flushed and he began to lecture the pastors angrily, pacing the room while they stood before him. Hitler's entire manner made them feel like criminals.

"Do you think you can pull such outrageous, backstairs politics with me? You underestimate me if you do. I am sick of being treated this way, by the church leaders of all people. What have I done to you? Only tried to make peace between all your warring factions. Peace in the church and peace with the state! And this is my reward! You obstruct me at every point and sabotage every move!"

Hitler raved on. The bishops were dumbfounded and Niemoller was horrified. The thought of a treason trial crossed his mind. How would he answer these complaints? *If only Hitler would stop his horrid tirade*, Niemoller thought. *Dear God, let him stop.*

When Hitler finally did stop, Niemoller stepped to the front of the group and tried to explain calmly that the comments had been made during a private conversation with his secretary and were a perfectly innocent joke. Niemoller went on to explain that the struggle for the church was by no means aimed against the Third Reich; it was for the sake of the nation. As a pastor his concern was that the people of Germany not be deluded or led astray.

"I will protect the German people," Hitler shouted. "You take care of the church. You pastors should worry about getting people to heaven and leave this world to me."

The shaken clergymen timidly tried to soothe Hitler's temper, assuring him that isolated expressions of political discontent indicated no overall disloyalty. They suggested that Bishop Müller simply lacked the mature qualities that a national bishop needed. For their part they were tremendously grateful for the Führer's efforts to make peace in the church. The reason for their concern was the possibility of mixing false doctrines with the true gospel.

At this the German Christian representatives spoke up and said that as far as they were concerned the whole controversy was purely church politics.

Hitler listened to their wrangling without apparent interest. He had already stated in his original tirade that he would not remove Müller.

Surprisingly, in light of his anger, Hitler did shake hands with the churchmen when they left. As he came to Niemoller, the pastor looked into the Führer's face and spoke directly and carefully. "A moment ago, Herr Hitler, you told us that you would take care of the German people. But as Christians and men of the church we too have a responsibility for the German people, laid upon us by God. Neither you nor anyone else can take that away from us."

For a moment Hitler stared at him. Then he touched Niemoller's hand and moved on without a word.

Outside, several of the clergymen accosted Niemoller. "How could you speak that way to the Führer? Don't you see that you have ruined it all?"

On the Monday after their meeting with Hitler, the Protestant bishops of Germany gathered for a meeting with National Bishop Müller. Shocked and frightened by Niemoller's behavior, they completely capitulated. They issued a statement of unconditional support for Hitler, the Third Reich, and Bishop Müller, and vowed to carry out any measures and directives he ordered.

Alarmed by Niemoller's radical leadership, two thousand members of the Pastor's Emergency League—almost a third of the group—resigned. Encouraged by this victory, Bishop Müller became more aggressive and dictatorial. He published a series of disciplinary measures, suspensions, dismissals, and retirements. He declared that from then on the church would not be governed by useless synods but by a centralized bureaucracy. He appointed a Nazi lawyer with lapsed church ties to head this administration.

MARCH 13, 1934

Seeing Müller's tactics, several church leaders who had pledged loyalty began to backtrack. Two key bishops, Wurm and Meiser, met with Hitler to complain. This time Hitler was sharply belligerent.

"Christianity will disappear from Germany just as it has in Russia," he told them. "The German race existed without Christianity for thousands of years before Christ and will continue to exist after Christianity has disappeared.

"The church must get used to the teachings about blood and race. Just as the Catholic Church couldn't prevent the earth from going around the sun, so the churches today cannot get rid of the indisputable facts connected with blood and race. If they can't recognize these, history will simply leave them behind."

Other Nazi leaders had expressed such views, but never the publicly pious Hitler. Shaken, the two bishops said if this was his view they could only look forward to being his most loyal opposition. Hitler flew into a rage.

"You are not my most loyal opposition, but traitors to the people, enemies of the Fatherland and the destroyers of Germany."

MAY 29, 1934, BARMEN, GERMANY

They met in a large church in a modern industrial town: 139 delegates in all—half pastors, half laymen—representing eighteen different German denominations. A few wore Nazi uniforms; some were state officials. Some were frightened, others elated about the statement of faith they were about to draw up as the charter of the church's resistance.

The Barmen Declaration was not a political document, and it said not a word about Hitler or Müller. Rather, it set out the theological foundations of the church for which they were prepared to suffer, and it spoke strongly and directly against the false teachings of the German Christians. The clear implication was that Hitler's elevation of the German race was anti-Christian. God had not specially revealed Himself through the German nation, blood, race, or even Hitler.

Barmen also spelled out an understanding of church and state:

> The Bible tells us that according to divine arrangement the state has the responsibility to provide for justice and peace in the yet unredeemed world, in which the church also stands...
>
> We repudiate the false teaching that the state can and should expand beyond its special responsibility to become the single and total order of human life, and also thereby fulfill the commission of the church.
>
> We repudiate the false teaching that the church can and should expand beyond its special responsibilities to take on the characteristics, functions and dignities of the state, and thereby become itself an organ of the state.
>
> The commission of the church, in which her freedom is founded, consists in this: in place of Christ and thus in the service of His own word and work, to extend through word and sacrament the message of the free grace of God to all people.

For their expression of faith, some of those present would lose their livelihood, be imprisoned or exiled. Others would lose their lives. A great many others, however, would fail the test.

One of the results of the Barmen meeting was the organization of a group that called themselves the Confessing Church. They represented the large number of Christians within the badly divided German Evangelical Church who most opposed the policies of Hitler. Among their numbers were Niemoller and Bonhoeffer.

A month after Barmen, Hitler murdered hundreds of militant, dissident Nazis in a bloody slaughter that became known as the Röhm Purge. Even the Confessing Church made no public protest—not even Niemoller. Most members expressed thankfulness that Hitler had restrained the more violent elements among his followers.

NOVEMBER 28, 1934, LONDON

Winston Churchill stood before Parliament. He was an old man, a defanged lion, regarded sometimes with pity in the House of Commons. Even his own party would not give him a cabinet position. Still, the old lion could roar.

Today his deep growl was asserting that "the strength of our national defenses, and especially of our air defense, is no longer adequate to secure … peace, safety, and freedom." Germany's air force, which according to the Versailles Treaty should not exist, "is rapidly approaching equality with our own" and would be fifty percent stronger by the end of 1936.

The MPs settled back into their seats with relief when Prime Minister Stanley Baldwin, another old but more amiable man, far better liked than Churchill, flatly contradicted him. Few noticed that Baldwin carefully hedged his cheery assessment of the future with the condition, "If Germany continues to execute her air program without acceleration." And while it was true that Churchill had exaggerated, it was also true that the Secret Service had told Baldwin of Hitler's plans to surpass Britain's air force by the fall of 1936.

MARCH 10, 1935, BERLIN

Outside a cold March wind swept the sky, but inside the old brick house the coal fire burned hot. Niemoller, his collar loosened, held his youngest son, Martin, on his knee. From the kitchen came the sounds of his wife washing dishes. Two of his older children were curled in chairs by a window, reading. Niemoller's eyes began to droop.

In the midst of this sleepy Sunday afternoon a knock came at the door. When the maid answered it, Niemoller heard a voice he did not recognize. She ushered in a slim, dark man in a heavy overcoat, who introduced himself as Pastor Schollen from a small church in the countryside about fifty miles from Berlin.

Schollen seemed frightened. He declined a cup of tea and sat fidgeting and glancing around nervously until Niemoller said impatiently, "Get on with it, man! What did you come about?"

Schollen fished in his wallet and brought out a small red card, which he tried to hand to Niemoller. Niemoller waved it away, smiling. He recognized it as the membership card for the Confessing Church.

"Yes, I knew you had joined, Pastor Schollen. I recognize your name."

"I came for counsel, Brother Niemoller. Did you read the statement aloud today?"

"Yes, of course. We had a meeting with the entire congregation in the parish hall. I not only read it, I demanded that everyone make clear where they stand. We took a vote and it was passed overwhelmingly."

Schollen fidgeted, looked down at his feet, then said, "I didn't read the statement this morning because the chief of police is in my congregation. He warned me against it, told me I could lose my position. And I did not feel certain that the tactics were correct." As an afterthought he added, "None of the pastors in my valley will read it. But I told them I would go and talk to you."

Niemoller's sleepiness was gone. "Pastor Schollen, you are not the only one lacking courage. But many pastors were not afraid this morning. They read the statement and hundreds more will read it next week."

"You don't think it is too severe?" Schollen asked. "Some of the pastors thought a more reasonable tone would be more honoring to those with different views. I mean, calling it 'a new religion making idols of blood, race, nation, honor, eternal Germany.' That's quite strong."

"It is nothing less than a new religion," Niemoller said. "A new religion with a different God. Do you know what they are teaching the Hitler Youth now? They are saying that just as Jesus went through three days in the grave, Hitler spent a year in prison. But Hitler's resurrection did not take him away from earth; he stayed here to save the German people. They are teaching that to our children now! Don't you know that?"

"One hears all kinds of things. But how do you know that it is the whole picture?"

"By the time you know the whole picture they will have taken down our crosses and put up swastikas. And you and I will be in the KZ!"

A tremor shook Schollen's body. Quietly he said, "They have already put Hitler's picture next to the crucifixes in our Catholic schoolrooms. One of the teachers told me."

"You see?" Niemoller said, striding to the window. "What is there to discuss?"

"But even Bodelschwingh, your old mentor, says we should wait," Schollen said. "They are talking to Hitler, and soon they will reach a reasonable solution. We are good Germans. We are thankful for what the government has done. Is it proper to be making proclamations against the government when discussions are continuing on a daily basis? I ask myself, how could I justify this to the Führer?"

"Justify yourself to the Lord Jesus!" Niemoller shouted.

"I will tell you something," Niemoller added in a lower tone. "Hitler is a coward, a coward and a bully. He will terrify you so long as you are willing to be terrified. We must stand up to him for the church of Jesus Christ. I beg of you!...Bodelschwingh, Meiser, Wurm...they think they will work out some sort of agreement with the beast. But the beast will swallow them up."

"I really must go, Pastor Niemoller," Schollen said stiffly. He had heard what he needed to hear to make up his mind. He left quickly, not looking back.

That week seven hundred pastors were arrested before they went to church to read the statement passed by the Prussian synod, which was a regional faction of the Confessing Church. German Christians were dispatched to lead the services in those churches. In some Berlin churches the congregations walked out on these substitutes after singing "A Mighty Fortress Is Our God."

Niemoller was one of those arrested. The police were polite and released him after two days. From then on, Niemoller's prayers from the pulpit included prayers for pastors in prison, in concentration camps, or under house arrest. The Gestapo came and took notes.

On the same Sunday as the arrests, the most massive military parade in decades marched through Berlin, viewed by cheering, jubilant throngs estimated at half a million. Hitler had announced that all young men would be conscripted into the growing army.

SEPTEMBER 15, 1935, NUREMBURG

Every September in the Third Reich thousands gathered at the ancient city of Nuremburg for the Nazi Party convention. From all over the nation they came, the best and most loyal Nazi farmers, students, and workers. They stayed in carefully regimented tent camps and marched in precise formations to the vast field where rallies were held. The gigantic assemblies were masterpieces of emotional orchestration, building up to the moment each night when Hitler arrived.

The tiny specks of humanity in the darkened stadium welcomed their Führer in a frenzy of awe and worship. During his two years in office, unemployment, inflation, and poverty had magically disappeared. Germans now had clean streets, orderly cities, disciplined and enthusiastic young people. They remembered the disorder and decadence of only a few years ago and were grateful. Part of their pride was in the resurgent German army; it meant the shame of World War I was erased. Germany was strong and independent again.

When the wild cheering had quieted, Hitler began to speak in his quiet, fatherly tone. This year he had reassuring words for Christians: the Nazis would never intervene against Christianity or against either the Roman Catholic or Protestant churches. This came on top of his formation, two months before, of a new government department, the Ministry of Church Affairs.

Then Hitler's voice changed to a snarl as he turned to the subject of his most implacable hatred. He had summoned the Reichstag, the almost useless Parliament, to Nuremburg just for this. He asked them to unanimously pass two laws against Jews. One took away all their rights of German citizenship. The other forbade marriages between Germans and Jews. From now on, Jews had no rights in Germany.

SEPTEMBER 23, 1935

"I can see no purpose in self-inflicted martyrdom," Bishop Meiser said to Martin Niemoller. The two men sat facing each other in a small hotel room, heatedly discussing the agenda for the gathering of the Free Synod at the Berlin-Steglitz church. This was the same body that had passed a strong anti-heathenism resolution in March, but now they were greatly divided in spirit.

The radicals, led by Martin Niemoller, did not want to compromise with Hitler's new church ministry nor to approve the Nuremburg laws. Many others, such as Meiser, counseled moderation and conciliation.

"We are trying to bring peace to the church," said Meiser, "and this Jewish question can only make us seem like the greatest troublemakers in Germany."

"What does it matter how we look in Germany compared with how we look in heaven?" Niemoller replied forcefully. "We pray for our pastors when they are imprisoned. Why has no one prayed for the Jews?"

"But the business of a synod is the church. We cannot pronounce judgment on all the ills of society. Most especially we ought not to single out the one issue that the government is so sensitive about, with the foreign criticism filling the air. First things first."

"And what is the first thing you are referring to?" Niemoller asked.

"The very existence of a church free from interference!" Meiser said.

"And how are we free if we cannot pronounce judgment on the ills of society?" Niemoller asked wearily. "Tell me that."

The Free Synod ended with nothing resolved. True they had, over Bishop Meiser's opposition, asserted that everyone, including Jews, should be offered salvation. They had strongly censured congregations that refused baptism to Jews. But the matter of the general condition of Jews in Germany had been referred to a committee. The majority of pastors thought laws about Jews were a state matter. So long as the Jews' position in the church remained unrestricted, the church should not interfere.

Bonhoeffer was depressed. Back in Germany now and heading a new seminary for the Confessing Church, he had come to the conference along with several of his students, who were bitter. They were becoming an embattled minority within an embattled minority — the radical faction of the Confessing Church in a Germany that cared little about the disputes of a handful of pastors and bishops.

Only Niemoller still had fire in his eyes. As he looked out over the delegates, he issued a solemn warning: "We shall be obliged to say more," he said, "and it may be that our mouths will only be really opened when we have to undergo suffering ourselves."

DECEMBER 1935

Hans Kerrl, the new government minister heading Hitler's Ministry of Church Affairs, had set up a church committee to resolve the disputes within the German Evangelical Church. He persuaded a widely reputed clergyman to chair it, and some of the foremost leaders of the Confessing Church agreed to cooperate — against Niemoller's adamant disapproval.

Kerrl declared all organizations of the Confessing Church illegal and gradually, firmly, began to tighten the noose around the necks of those who would not cooperate with his new committee. Pastors who belonged to an illegal organization were not paid their state-supported salaries. Seminarians from Bonhoeffer's seminary could not get pastoral appointments. Kerrl's bureaucratic harassment so blurred the issues — they were arguing not doctrine now but salaries and pensions and appointments — that most of the Confessing Church pastors found cooperation easier than defiance.

In the following months the great energetic unity of Barmen began to crack into a thousand fragments.

MARCH 7, 1936, NORFOLK, ENGLAND

Lord Lothian's twelve guests gathered around the radio after dinner to listen to the BBC. Among them were the Astors — Waldorf, one of the richest men in the world, and his witty, beautiful wife, Nancy, who would later become the first woman to sit in Parliament; Thomas Jones, secretary to the British cabinet and a close friend of the prime minister; Thomas Inskip, a cabinet minister; and Arnold Toynbee, the famous historian. Their host, Lord Lothian, was himself one of the most eloquent and renowned statesmen in Britain.

All were weekending in the beauty and luxury of Lothian's ancient rose-red brick castle, Blickling Hall, with its deer park at one end and acres of grass and woodland at the other.

Tonight, however, their pleasure was interrupted by the dry authoritative tones of the newscaster announcing that earlier that day German troops had moved into the Rhineland. Hitler had offered twenty-five years of peace based on disarmament of both sides of the border. The peace proposal was, according to the French ambassador to Germany, "as though Hitler struck his adversary across the face and said, 'I bring you proposals for peace!'"

Lord Lothian, a broad-chested, handsome man in his fifties, flicked off the radio, loosened his tie, and sat back in a heavy leather chair. "I never thought I'd hear this group so quiet," he said. "Do you think war has begun?"

"If this means war," Nancy Astor said, "it will be because of the French, not the Germans. If the Germans want to march into their own backyard, I wish them well."

"What nonsense!" said someone from the other end of the room.

"I have a suggestion," said Thomas Jones with a twinkle in his eye. "We'll form a shadow cabinet and draw up a list of suggestions. I'll call up the prime minister tomorrow morning and tell him what we think."

Toynbee enthusiastically supported the idea. He himself had recently returned from a long meeting with Hitler. "I suppose that this may well be the only drawing room in all Britain containing two men who have had a long conversation with Herr Hitler," he said. "Lord Lothian, it seems to me that the essential question is one of motive. Do you think, based on your conversation with the man, as well as with Göring, Ribbentrop, and so on, that Hitler is merely making the first of a series of expansionist movements? Or are you convinced as I am that Hitler really has no evil intentions? He certainly convinced me that he wants peace."

"Why don't we call up Winston and ask him to help us on that point?" Jones jested.

"Heavens, no!" Nancy Astor retorted. "If the real cabinet won't have him, why should the shadow?"

"Hear, hear!" said Lothian. "We can easily refer to Churchill's views on the Germans without his presence. To him the Germans are the Devil incarnate.

"Speaking of the German motives," said Lothian, folding his arms across his chest, "I would state firmly that the Germans are not fundamentally aggressive. They have been goaded into aggression by the Versailles Treaty and by the French policy of encirclement. A great nation with an ancient culture and history cannot reasonably be denied a position of equality in Europe. Yet the view of the French government, and incidentally some elements in our Foreign Office, is that they are a group of gangsters the likes of which the world has never seen."

"If we don't give them what they deserve," said Nancy Astor, "we'll have war, and we'll be the ones to blame when the entire continent is Bolshevik."

The debate carried late into the night, for this mannered, richly dressed crowd loved talking politics more than almost anything. In the morning, Jones telephoned Prime Minister Baldwin with their resolutions: the group "welcomed Hitler's declaration wholeheartedly" and thought he wanted "above all to be accepted by England as respectable"; therefore, the militarization of the Rhineland was to be treated as relatively insignificant. The chief thing was to seize on Hitler's peace proposals.

Nobody mentioned the military fact that was to be reinforced so strikingly in years to come. The Rhineland had been demilitarized at Versailles deliberately to make Germany vulnerable; without it, France and Britain lost any leverage short of war—for which the under-armed British and disorganized French were clearly unprepared.

In permitting the German troops to march into the Rhineland, both countries were betting that reason alone would persuade the Germans to behave in a civilized manner. And the elegant men and women at Blickling Hall believed in the power of reason.

AUGUST 3, 1936, BERLIN

They sat in a circle, sober-faced and quiet. In the distance they could hear the popping of fireworks and the low murmur of sound from a crowd of happy Berliners enjoying the festivities of the Olympic Games. Those sounds came from a different world than the one facing these leaders of the Confessing Church.

Bonhoeffer was there, as well as Niemoller and Jacobi — the young and the middle-aged, but not one of the older bishops.

Bonhoeffer was depressed. He was thinking of yesterday, spent at the games in Olympic Stadium. He had been happy and excited.

Warm summer sun had bathed the tanned, happy crowds surrounding him. Children, their hair bleached white from hours in the sun, clutched their parents' hands and tried to see everything. *I do love my country*, Bonhoeffer had thought, *in spite of everything.*

Berlin was decorated and scrubbed clean for the games. White Olympic flags and red Nazi pennants hung from every lamppost. The ugly signs warning shoppers away from Jewish shops had disappeared overnight. Uniformed, heel-clicking troops still filled the streets, but they seemed like part of the parade.

With Bonhoeffer had been a seminarian named Schultz. Ordinarily a serious and rather dull fellow, the young man bubbled with enthusiasm. But his pleasure had turned to sadness during their parting conversation at the end of the day.

"Dr. Bonhoeffer ... I must tell you," the young man had begun haltingly, "I am taking a parish in Hamburg. I could not refuse."

For a moment Bonhoeffer had been speechless. "Leaving the Confessing Church?"

"No, Dr. Bonhoeffer, please understand my deep respect and admiration for all that you stand for. I only think that I am called to be a pastor and there are no pastorates for those of us who will not cooperate. What is the good in preaching if you have no congregation? Where will this noncooperation lead us? We are no longer a recognized body; we have no government assistance; we cannot care for the souls in the armed forces or give religion lessons in the schools. What will become of the church if that continues? A heap of rubble!"

"Those are not your words," Bonhoeffer had instantly accused.

"No, you are right. They are Riehl's. He has convinced me that we must for the sake of Jesus Christ make use of the great opportunities the government is offering us rather than sticking to a path so narrow there is only space for one at a time."

Bonhoeffer had stared disbelievingly at him. "If you board the wrong train, Schultz, it is no use running along the corridor in the opposite direction."

Schultz's words had been like a knife. So all the teaching and all the community they had practiced at the seminary had been wasted on this man! And, Bonhoeffer wondered, on how many others? That was the question that pounded in him as he sat in the meeting. How many others?

Suddenly his reverie about the day before was broken by the words of Niemoller—"Why not read the whole memorandum, just as we sent it to Hitler?"

"We will certainly lose Meiser and others if we do that, Martin," said Jacobi. "They will say we should stick to the issues of the church and leave the politics to the state."

"The Jews are our issue!" Niemoller shot back. "And the concentration camps! We had the courage to write to Hitler. Why not read it to our congregations?"

Someone asked Bonhoeffer what he thought. He had difficulty raising himself out of his gloom.

"I think," he said slowly after a few moments of silence, "I think we must not worry what people think. We must be the church and speak as Christ. And the words of Proverbs, which some have quoted so often, remain relevant, 'Open your mouth for the dumb.'"

On August 23 only a few hundred pastors, out of perhaps 18,000, read the proclamation. The uncompromising Confessing Church was now very small.

JULY 1, 1937, BERLIN

The symbol of defiant resistance to Hitler crouched on the floor in his bathrobe, pushing a toy car. His son, Martin, only a toddler, yelped with glee.

Niemoller had arrived home late the night before, exhausted from a tour of church meetings. His eyes and gaunt face showed the strain. The screws had tightened on the Confessing Church. In the past three weeks many of the resisting leaders had been arrested. But with every arrest Niemoller's drive seemed to grow.

Downstairs the doorbell rang. The maid came to tell him that two Gestapo agents were waiting in the living room. It had become a familiar routine.

Niemoller dressed hurriedly and went downstairs. The officers shook hands politely. They had a few questions to ask him. Would he please accompany them?

A trace of sadness crossed Niemoller's face. This once, on a Saturday, he would have liked to play with his son and talk to his wife. He went to tell Else what was happening. "They say it will be brief," he said. "But only God knows, my love."

Once he was seated in the black police van, he did not bother to look out the window. He knew too well the route to police headquarters. Exhaustion settled over him and he nearly slept.

At the Alexanderplatz they took him to a large room and left him. Several hours passed inside the bustling headquarters before a tall captain entered, called Niemoller's name, and coldly told him to follow.

The officer did not take the familiar route up the stairs to the interrogation rooms. Instead, he turned in the opposite direction and led the pastor outside to a black police van.

"Are you sure?" Niemoller asked the officer. "No one has talked to me yet."

The captain just nodded. Now Niemoller was strangely afraid, and this time he looked out the window. They were not retracing the route.

Eventually they reached Moabit prison, its ancient dark walls fringed with barbed wire. *You do not come here for questions,* Niemoller thought. *You come to stay.*

When they heard of Niemoller's imprisonment, many pastors felt ill-disguised satisfaction. They had, after all, warned him. Perhaps now he would not disturb them with his uncompromising speeches.

An earnest chaplain, visiting the Moabit prisoners, happened upon Niemoller. Somehow this chaplain had not heard the news of his arrest.

"But brother!" he said in shock, "What brings you here? Why are you in prison?"

"And, brother, why are you not in prison?" Niemoller replied.

In succeeding months seven hundred pastors were arrested. Most were released after a few days or weeks behind bars. Some were sent to concentration camps. Yet the vast majority of the 18,000 German Evangelical Church pastors stayed well out of trouble. The reputable Bishop Marahrens issued a statement: "The National Socialist conception of life is the national and political teaching that determines and characterizes German manhood. As such, it is obligatory upon German Christians also."

MARCH 2, 1938, MOABIT PRISON, BERLIN

It was the final day of Martin Niemoller's trial. He sat in the courtroom, awaiting the judges' verdict, dressed neatly in a dark suit, conservative wing collar, and black tie. He had lost weight but not spirit. In the front row sat his Else and his eldest daughter, Brigette. They had been apart for eight months. How wonderful even to see their faces. Perhaps tonight they would be together again.

He had been charged with "malicious and provocative criticism of the minister of Propaganda and Public Enlightenment, Dr. Goebbels, of the Minister of Education, Dr. Rust, and of the Minister of Justice, Dr. Gurtner, of a kind calculated to undermine the confidence of the people in their political leaders." Another charge dealt with his reading from the pulpit names of people the government had imprisoned.

Yet the prosecution had failed to bring out any convincing evidence of his guilt. Instead, a series of witnesses had endorsed him as a man of sterling character. Niemoller's spirits, so grim at the beginning of the trial, had been rising. Waiting for the judges to enter, he could not keep a smile from his face. He chatted and joked with his attorney and kept glancing at his wife's shining, hopeful face.

The presiding judge began to read, slowly. They had found him guilty!

As the fifteen typed pages of the judgment unfolded, however, it became clear that the conviction was merely a slap. Niemoller, the judge read, had been inspired by "completely honorable motives." He was a man of "unquestionable veracity, the type of person who has nothing whatsoever of the traitor in him." Nonetheless, he has violated the letter of the law and must be found guilty. He would be imprisoned for seven months and fined 2,000 marks. The eight months he had already served would apply, so he could be freed today. As the implication came home to him, Niemoller beamed. It was as good a verdict as he could have possibly hoped for—as good as an acquittal. So there were still honest men in Germany!

At last the judges were finished and he was able to grasp his wife's hand. "Pack our trunks," he said in her ear. "We'll have a holiday together."

"Will they really let you go?" Else asked, still uncertain of their good fortune.

"Pack our bags!" he said, looking into her eyes. "I'll be home in an hour or two."

Hitler had arranged to hear the Niemoller verdict immediately. He was furious. He remembered well meeting the pastor two years before when Niemoller had spoken so impudently.

Calling an immediate cabinet meeting, Hitler demanded a resolution that Niemoller be placed in a concentration camp.

"This man is my personal prisoner," Hitler shouted. "And that is the end of it!"

In the early hours of the morning, Martin Niemoller passed through the barbed wire of Sachsenhausen, a concentration camp of 30,000 prisoners.

ROOTS OF WAR
(PART II)

For any government deliberately to deny to their people what must be their plainest and simplest right [to live in peace and happiness without the nightmare of war] would be to betray their trust, and to call down upon their heads the condemnation of all mankind.

I do not believe that such a government anywhere exists among civilized peoples. I am convinced that the aim of every statesman worthy of the name, to whatever country he belongs, must be the happiness of the people for whom and to whom he is responsible, and in that faith I am sure that a way can and will be found to free the world from the curse of armaments and the fears that give rise to them, and to open up a happier, and a wiser future for mankind.

PRIME MINISTER NEVILLE CHAMBERLAIN,
November 1937

MARCH 11, 1938,
NO. 10 DOWNING STREET, LONDON

Prime Minister Neville Chamberlain gave no impression of bending to his nearly seventy years. He was a tall, hawk-like man with a luxuriant mustache and a rather high opinion of himself. Perhaps he was entitled. No one in government worked harder than he.[1]

Chamberlain came from a peculiar background for a prime minister. Unlike a great many members of his cabinet, he had made a success of himself — first in running a hard-headed, family-owned manufacturing firm and later in politics — without benefit of a huge inheritance or elegant title. A further drawback might have been his religious affiliation. His family had long been Unitarians, who, because they rejected the deity of Christ, were ostracized from semi-official Church of England channels. Yet it was that very affiliation that contributed so strongly to the Chamberlain family's dedication to public service; both his father and older brother were prominent in politics. Government was a natural vocation for those raised in Unitarian tradition, with its belief in the universal goodness of all men, growing out of a sense of duty to mankind and a deep-seated belief that reasonable, fair-minded men could work together to solve any difficulty.

Chamberlain had reached the pinnacle of power in his country, succeeding Stanley Baldwin without a struggle because no one else was comparably qualified. Now, well into his first year as Prime Minister, he was warming to his task with all sorts of ambitious improvements in mind. If only he could keep the German issue in its proper perspective and not let the war-lovers in either country gain too much momentum.

The latter concern was on his mind today as he greeted the German ambassador, Joachim von Ribbentrop, whom he had invited to this farewell luncheon in the spacious inner rooms of his residence. Ribbentrop was a ridiculous, strutting ninny with cotton for a brain, but he was closely connected with Hitler. What a pity, Chamberlain thought, that a great nation is governed by such irrational men, driven by such illogic. If he could only make them see sense!

Chamberlain, a private man whom most thought cold and arrogant, tried to make small talk as he escorted the German ambassador among the clusters of men he was hosting; most were chatting informally and shaking hands with an easy, confident charm, as well they might. They were on the whole the most powerful men of the most powerful empire in the history of the world.

Feeling the pull of the leonine presence, Chamberlain looked over at Churchill sprawled in a chair at the other end of the table. The prime minister could never help feeling a little scornful of the man who had never made the top rank despite his long career in government and his rhetorical gift. They had worked together on previous cabinets, but he would never let Churchill serve under him. The man was too emotional, drank too much, and his tirades took up precious time. He rarely had his facts straight. Churchill, Chamberlain thought, would gladly fight Germany tomorrow, if only to give himself a chance to make saber-rattling speeches in the House.

The lunch went well, Chamberlain thought. With elaborately feigned politeness, Ribbentrop raised the issue of Chamberlain's "White Paper on Defense" given to the House five days before.

"Why do you talk of fighting?" Ribbentrop asked. "You say that you want peace and then you talk of fighting. The Führer is a man of peace, but he is also a man of strength, and this talk of fighting for democracy he can only see as pure aggressiveness."

Only a German could have read his talk as aggressive, Chamberlain groaned inwardly. But he answered patiently and logically that his policy had always been based on a willingness to defend his nation were it necessary. "I assume that Germany's policy is the same; that is the only legitimate reason for keeping armies and navies. You may remember that I also spoke of our earnest hopes for appeasement and then disarmament."

He was not sure his words made any impression on Ribbentrop, who immediately began speaking at great length on what a peace-loving man Hitler was. Fortunately Churchill held his tongue.

After lunch Chamberlain and Ribbentrop spent another twenty minutes together as the prime minister tried to drive home his one point: he wanted to solve any difficulties Germany might face as the result of the Versailles Treaty. If he repeated that message often enough it might make its way back to Berlin.

Yet Ribbentrop persisted in babbling on about the astonishing transformation of Germany, a miracle to those who had known the bad years. "It is preposterous that the British public remains so utterly ill-informed," he complained peevishly. "Yesterday I met a mob of people shouting the most intolerable insults about Pastor Niemoller's imprisonment. I am sure they would be astonished to learn that there are twice as many people in church today as there were five years before, when Hitler came to power."

At last Chamberlain smilingly withdrew and returned to the drawing room where the other guests lingered. He was handed some telegrams to read and stopped short, bristling in disbelief. The telegrams informed him that Hitler, that morning, had delivered an ultimatum to the Austrian Chancellor. Schuschnigg was to resign his office by 2:00 P.M. and turn over the government to Seyss-Inquart, the Nazi Hitler had forced into the government just a month before. Hitler's troops were massed on the border, ready to march if Schuschnigg refused. Schuschnigg begged the British government for advice. All this had happened while he was chatting pleasantly about peace with Ribbentrop.

Chamberlain quietly asked the German ambassador for "a private word" in his office downstairs, along with Lord Halifax, England's foreign secretary. Any attempts at friendliness had disappeared into British frost as he read out the telegrams and stiffly demanded an explanation. "I want you to understand that this has the most serious implications for our relations."

Ribbentrop smiled and said he personally knew nothing about these negotiations. "Do you have any confirmation of these reports? Because I know for a fact that the Chancellor's discussions with Schuschnigg were conducted in a tremendously friendly atmosphere. I was there personally. I must say that I would think Schuschnigg's resignation would be a very positive development and a hopeful sign for a peaceful solution."

"This is intolerable behavior in a civilized nation," Halifax said, his voice loud and threatening. He called it naked aggression.

Chamberlain admitted graciously that they had no definite proof of aggression but said they had ample reasons for deep concern. "All we can ask is that you convey to Herr Hitler our sincere and ardent wish that he hold back from any rash act that would imperil our chances for a negotiated settlement."

After Ribbentrop left, Chamberlain sank into a wing chair and cut short the overexcited Halifax. "If you must, go and talk to Ribbentrop at the embassy."

Then he dictated a response to Schuschnigg, which Halifax accepted with a pinched, reluctant expression. "His Majesty's Government cannot take responsibility of advising the chancellor to take any course of action that might expose his country to dangers against which His Majesty's Government are unable to guarantee protection."

Afterward Chamberlain sat alone in his study with his dark thoughts. He would not get off to the country for a rest this weekend. His plans were spoiled. His carefully drafted message to Hitler would be buried under the necessary protests. It meant more work for him — not positive work, but preventive. Seeing Halifax in a rage had only reinforced the prime minister's conviction that he was the only one cool enough to abide the Germans' irrational behavior and make them see reason.

Late that afternoon the Austrian government, finding support from no other country, capitulated, and the German army marched unopposed across Austria's border.

Chamberlain wrote his sisters, his closest confidantes, that he took comfort in the fact that the *Anschluss* had taken place without any loss of life.

MARCH 25, 1938, CLIVEDEN

The house rose up ahead of them like a tiered wedding cake, more of a monument than a home—Cliveden, where for years Nancy Astor had gathered the wittiest and wealthiest men and women in Britain for weekend parties. Hardly anyone of significance failed to turn up at Cliveden, even the king and Gandhi. George Bernard Shaw was a frequent guest, although he usually stayed in his room, writing.

Cliveden was a comfortable weekend retreat for Prime Minister Chamberlain. Many of his cabinet spent time there, and the ceaseless political talk was so reliably conservative that the press had seized on the idea of a "Cliveden set" that was supposed to be darkly pro-German. Chamberlain found the idea amusing; as though any Cliveden set determined *his* foreign policy.

Today Nancy Astor, a short woman with a high-cheeked face that had once been beautiful, met Chamberlain and his wife at the door with one of her usual greetings. "Hello, you old windbag. Your speech was so exquisitely balanced that no one had the slightest idea where you stood."

"Thank you," he said with a smile. "I intended that."

"If you were truly part of the Cliveden set you would let Herr Hitler know where you stand by singing 'Deutschland Uber Alles' to the House."

"I'll leave that to you, Nancy, in your next speech."

"No, no, those Nazis are not my friends. If they would stop locking up Christian Scientists they might be."

Nancy Astor was a devout Christian Scientist who always had Christian Science lecturers at her weekend gatherings. Lord Astor and Lord Lothian were Christian Scientists too. Their sympathetic view of Germany was strengthened by the Christian Science doctrine that man is good, that there is no evil that the mind cannot overcome. This Chamberlain was inclined to agree with, though he was quite irreligious himself.

As they bantered, waiting for the servants—there were dozens of them at Cliveden—to hustle in the Chamberlains' luggage, other guests began drifting into the vast dark paneled entrance hall with its elaborately carved wooden columns, suits of armor, and tapestries. Chamberlain knew most of the guests, except for an American couple and an odd-looking man whom he supposed was one of Nancy's ever-present Christian Science lecturers. Several people thanked him for the speech he had given in the House on Thursday. Sir Alexander Cadogan, his undersecretary of state for foreign affairs, took him aside and said that the nation had breathed a sigh of relief at stepping back from the brink.

"I don't believe we stepped back," Chamberlain said dryly. "I wanted us to avoid stepping over." He had declined before the House of Commons to guarantee that Britain would come to Czechoslovakia's aid if Germany invaded. Since Austria had been adopted into the Reich, Czechoslovakia was now vulnerable, half-surrounded by German armies.

"Yes, I liked what you said," Cadogan admitted, "about not letting others determine when we would fight."

"I have the sense," said Chamberlain, "that to draw a line in the dust is to dare Herr Hitler to cross it. I am not anxious to enter matches of daring with him. I want to convince him that he can get all that Germany is entitled to without having to fight."

The next morning Chamberlain rose early and went into the dining room where breakfast was laid out as a self-service buffet. Nancy Astor always provided every luxury and pleasure imaginable—except liquor; she was an absolute teetotaler. Nancy herself, as usual, would not join her guests until nearly noon; she was alone in her bedroom reading her Bible.

A light mist was falling as Chamberlain strolled out across the formal garden, past pieces of Italian statuary, and into one of the long lanes that led through Cliveden's forest, with views over the Thames. A solitary person, Chamberlain loved to walk. Often after a session of Parliament he would walk as many as six miles to calm himself.

He mused as he walked about the state of affairs with Germany. The subject nagged at him as though there were some detail he had neglected. Yet really things were going well. The whole country stood behind him.

But he saw clearly enough that this support might not last. Europe was an unstable mass, like snow on the mountains that even a loud shout might turn into an avalanche. He had to find the way to create stability, with little time to do it. He had to discover precisely what Germany wanted and how to get it for them. *If only we could sit down and reason together*, he thought. *I am sure we could ease the tensions overnight.*

His thoughts grew darker, for the future was so unknown and he was a man who liked to make tidy plans.

Churchill had made one of his magnificent bursts of oratory in response to Thursday's speech. Chamberlain could still hear that deep, robust voice booming out the warning like Pompeii's town crier.

"I have watched this famous island descending incontinently, fecklessly, the stairway which leads to a dark gulf. It is a fine broad stairway at the beginning, but after a bit the carpet ends. A little farther on there are only flagstones, and a little farther on still these break beneath your feet...."

Yes, Chamberlain thought, *the warning is just. Except Winston's warmongering is likely to speed our journey down.*

On his return to the house he walked through a little cemetery. Cliveden had served as a hospital during the Great War, and those who had died of their wounds were buried here under a Union Jack. It was a beautiful, melancholy spot, all moss and shadows. Standing there, he thought of his cousin Norman, the only man he had ever been truly attached to, buried in France in a much vaster cemetery than this. Nothing matters more, he thought, than avoiding war; another generation of Normans must not die.

Suddenly his melancholy lifted. He would find a way to make a lasting peace.

SEPTEMBER 12, 1938, LONDON

Chamberlain sat by a large radio cabinet at No. 10 Downing listening fretfully to the man who held the world in the palm of his hand. It was the end of the greatest Nuremburg Party Congress yet — the first to celebrate the new, expanded Germany. Now, at the climax of the week, endless squadrons of Hitler Youth, Hitler Workers, SS, army, navy, and air force had converged to hear their Fuehrer. All over the world, in Czechoslovakia, in France, in England, and in America, men and women listened in rapt fear to the crowd's roars of "Sieg Heil!"

Chamberlain was not afraid. He was distressed. The world held its breath waiting for the words of a lunatic! How foolish. How utterly mad! How could the lives of hundreds of millions, as well as his own reputation, hang on this?

He had written his sister: "I fully realize that if eventually things go wrong ... there will be many, including Winston, who will say that the British government must bear the responsibility and that if only they had had the courage to tell Hitler now that, if he used force, we would at once declare war, that would have stopped him."

Now, as the prime minister listened, Hitler began his assault on Czechoslovakia, working himself into his usual snarling frenzy. Thousands standing before him responded wildly. They were primed for battle, ready to die for the honor of Germany.

The world waited, expecting Hitler to declare war. But instead, he veered onto another subject.

Listening to the distant roar, Chamberlain let out an involuntary sigh. "Not so bad as I feared," he said to himself. "Distasteful, though."

SEPTEMBER 24, 1938

Chamberlain was leaving Germany after his second visit with Adolf Hitler in ten days. On September 15 he had arrived at Hitler's Berghof headquarters for his first face-to-face encounter with the man who was shaking the world. At that time he had learned of Hitler's plans to proceed against Czechoslovakia.

Shocked at first, he had left feeling he had made an impression on the Fuehrer. His only problem was convincing his own nation and France — as well as Czechoslovakia — to simply cede a large portion of Czechoslovakia to Nazi Germany, a portion that held large numbers of Czechs as well as Germans and also contained most of the border defenses that made Czechoslovakia a significant, if overmatched opponent for the invading German army. Chamberlain had already made up his mind that such a price was worth paying for peace.

Now the prime minister felt betrayed. He had risked his political career for the proposals given at Berchtesgaden a few days earlier. He could not understand why the Fuehrer, when he would receive all the territory he wanted through peaceful means, insisted on using force. An immediate takeover of Czechoslovakia by German troops would be looked on as sheer aggression. All this he had said to the Fuehrer, but Hitler was adamant.

Now that he was setting off for London, however, the prime minister had recovered some of his equilibrium. The situation did not look so utterly hopeless. He was beginning to adjust to Hitler's demands. The immediate occupation would offend democratic sensibilities, but was it worth fighting a war over?

Back in London at 5:30 that afternoon Chamberlain spoke to the cabinet.

He spoke of Hitler's anxiousness to develop better relations with Great Britain, stressing that Czechoslovakia was the last territorial claim the Fuehrer would make. "It would be a great tragedy if we lost this opportunity of reaching an understanding with Germany. I have now established an influence with Herr Hitler. I believe he trusts me and is willing to work with me."

But the cabinet raised so many objections that Chamberlain backed off on his recommendation that they advise the Czechs to accept Hitler's plans.

A few days later the Czechs, who were given the German demands without any recommendations, rejected them in ringing terms.

SEPTEMBER 26, 1938, CLIVEDEN

Charles Lindbergh, the brave, dashing pilot who ten years before had challenged the Atlantic and won, was one of the most famous men in the world. Tall, firm, resolute, he never doubted himself for a moment. Full of his own importance in a tortured way, he hated yet needed adulation.

But Lindbergh was more than a great pilot; he had become a high priest of a new technological era. People listened to him, particularly of late.

He had spent several weeks in Germany, warmly welcomed by the Nazis, even given a medal, and had come away tremendously impressed. The democracies seemed to him tired and decadent; in Germany he found a virile masculinity and spirited commitment that resonated in his own soul.

He had also been impressed by the German air force; so much so that wherever he went he preached that no one could stand against it.*

After the terrible kidnapping and death of their son, the Lindberghs had fled America for England; today they were guests at Nancy Astor's Cliveden

---

*Lindbergh was wrong in his estimates of German air dominance. London was at the very limit of bomber range from Germany. Without bases in Holland or France it is doubtful the German air force could have done significant damage.

weekend. Anne, Lindbergh's shy and intelligent wife, soon faded into the background when Charles and the others held forth on the possibility of war.

"I am afraid this is the beginning of the end for England," Lindbergh said sternly. "The old instincts are being summoned up for war. People are talking about 'dishonorable peace,' and so on. Nobody seems to realize that England is in no condition to fight a war."

"It's madness," Nancy Astor said in one of her wild, stabbing protests. "War will destroy Western civilization. Europe will be destroyed. Then certainly Communism will spread, for it always feeds on death like a vulture."

Lord Astor and Thomas Jones came into the room looking glum and depressed; they too had been discussing war. Jones's Welsh twinkle was gone; he looked old and haggard. "I understand that Chamberlain has sent two messages to Hitler to be delivered before he speaks tonight. The first is a last plea for more negotiations on the terms they had previously agreed on. If Hitler rejects that, he will be given the second message, a warning that if he marches into Czechoslovakia England will go to war."

"It's madness," Lady Astor said. "To destroy our civilization with our eyes open to all that we are doing."

"There are some things that are worth more than life," Jones said stiffly.

"Unquestionably!" said Lindbergh. "But that is not the case now. We would not be fighting to preserve something. Unless war is averted now there will be no one left who knows the meaning of the words *right* and *wrong*. This is no longer an affair of national pride and laws of right and wrong. It is a case of our whole civilization going under."

"I must disagree with you," Lord Astor said, his back to the fireplace. "I have supported all the prime minister has done to appease the Germans. But by now we can see that they are bent on war. We shall have to fight them, and I think it would be better to stop them now before they grow any stronger."

"Your logic may be sound, but it ought to lead you in the opposite direction," said Lindbergh, pouncing eagerly. "If we must fight—and I am not so certain as you seem to be that Hitler is bent on war—then by all means buy as much time as possible. At the moment England's defenses are so weak as to be utterly incapable of defending the nation, let alone punishing Hitler."

Astor looked around him with sad, kind eyes, but the way he gripped the fireplace betrayed his tension. "I think you have it wrong. Germany is already arming at full speed; it would be years before we could even reach her pace. So every day we wait to fight, Germany grows stronger. Furthermore, if we keep backing down to every threat Hitler makes, we will soon have no friends to fight with us."

"But don't you think that before you go to war you must have some idea of victory? You cannot separate political decision from military strategy."

"Would you simply have us surrender?" Astor asked.

"No, but avoid war at any cost!" said Lindbergh.

There was an awkward pause. Jones glanced at his watch. "The speech is about to begin," he said. "Unfortunately, the decision may be out of our hands."

The small troop gathered by the radio in the parlor included two German boys summering in England. Lady Astor had asked them to translate the speech.

Lord Astor turned on the radio and almost immediately the angry roar of the mob could be heard. It was a terrifying sound: animalistic, threatening, violent. First Goebbels spoke, his high, ranting voice interrupted by cheers, chants, and shouts. The German boys scribbled on pads of paper and shouted out brief summaries during the roaring of the crowd.

Then Hitler spoke, beginning with his usual calm and slowly catching fire as never before. His voice snarled, ripped, rasped, and cut. He returned repeatedly to "Benes." The Czech head of state, his name spoken like a curse, had become the fountain of all the hurt and harm that Germany had ever suffered.

"My patience is at an end," Hitler concluded. "The decision now lies in his hands. Peace or war ... I have never been a coward. Now I go before my people as its first soldier. And behind me—this the world should know—there marches a different people from that of 1918. We are determined!"

Hitler had never spoken with such demonic fury. The crowd roared on and on into a single furious will, delirious with the delight of hatred.

"A terrifying speech," said Jones. "But no declaration of war. He spoke gratefully of the prime minister's efforts on behalf of peace. He also said that there would be no more territorial demands after this one."

"We have a little more time," Lindbergh said solemnly. "And with every extra day there is a little more hope."

Jones and Astor, more at ease now, were gradually swayed by Lindbergh's argument. If he was right, it would be necessary to face facts and avoid war at all costs. They agreed before they went to bed that they would dedicate the next few days to escorting Lindbergh into the highest governmental circles they could reach. And those at Cliveden had access to some very high circles indeed.

SEPTEMBER 28, 1938, LONDON

A darkness hung over London. Trenches were being dug in every park. Children were being herded into trains, evacuating the city that everyone expected would be annihilated in flames within the next twenty-four hours. Outside Parliament a grim, quiet crowd gathered. Hitler's deadline for Czechoslovakia to accept his ultimatum had been 2:00. It was 2:50 when Chamberlain began his speech to the House of Commons where the narrow benches were jammed.

There was not a wearier, more discouraged man in England than the prime minister. He had not given up trying. He had sent fresh appeals to Mussolini and Hitler, suggesting a five-party conference. But little hope now existed.

Last night he had addressed the nation on the BBC, his voice filled with despairing resignation, yet still incredulous that his efforts had been in vain and that death would soon rain down on his beloved nation.

"How horrible, fantastic, incredible it is that we should be digging trenches and trying on gas masks here because of a quarrel in a faraway country between people of whom we know nothing...

"I have done all that one man can do to compose this quarrel.... I shall not give up the hope of a peaceful solution or abandon my efforts for peace as long as any chance for peace remains.... But at this moment I see nothing further that I can usefully do."

Wearily, dryly, he told the whole story in careful chronological detail: of all the British government had done, of the moments of apparent hope and the dashing of hopes, of last-minute appeals. He spoke for over an hour, building to only one conclusion. The certainty of war.

Then, with hardly anyone noticing, a piece of paper was handed into the House. It moved to several ministers before John Simon, the Chancellor of the Exchequer, waved it at Chamberlain. Deeply involved in his speech, the prime minister did not immediately notice.

Simon finally got his attention and Chamberlain quickly scanned the paper. He hesitated for a moment, then whispered to Simon, "Shall I tell them now?" Simon vigorously nodded yes.

When Chamberlain spoke again, life had flooded into his voice. "I have now been informed by Herr Hitler that he invites me to meet him at Munich tomorrow morning. He has also invited Signor Mussolini and Monsieur Daladier. . . . I need not say what my answer will be."

Someone in the back of the hall shouted, "Thank God for the prime minister."

Chamberlain continued. "We are all patriots and there can be no honorable member of this House who did not feel his heart leap that the crisis has been once more postponed to give us once more an opportunity to try what reason and goodwill and discussion will do to settle a problem which is already within sight of settlement. . . ."

Again from the back a voice boomed out, "Thank God for the prime minister." Then all were on their feet, applauding, cheering, crying, throwing papers into the air. The great fear that had gripped them all was ecstatically released.

No one, or practically no one, thought about the fact that although Hitler had invited Italy, France, and Britain to meet with him, he had not invited Czechoslovakia.

SEPTEMBER 30, 1938

"What is that noise?" Chamberlain asked.

It was morning. They had signed the agreement at 1:30 A.M., and after that he had had to endure the conference with the Czechoslovakians, who had wept.

William Strang, a top foreign office representative, strode to the window of the Regina Palace and looked out. "The street is full of people," he said. "They want to see you. Why don't you step out onto the balcony for a moment?"

Chamberlain did and found himself bathed in a warm ovation. Leaving the hotel a few minutes later, he had to press through the large, happy crowd, bronzed by the sun and still in summer clothing. He could not help smiling.

Chamberlain sat in a flowered armchair in the same apartment where Hitler, unknown to the prime minister, had only the day before vilified him to Mussolini. Today Hitler was gracious, though pale and subdued. They talked in generalities, and nothing the prime minister could say would make the Fuehrer disagree with him.

"I trust that the Czechs will not be mad enough to reject our agreement," Chamberlain said. "But in case they do, I hope that you will do nothing which would diminish the high opinion in which you will be held throughout the world in consequence of yesterday's proceedings." Chamberlain glanced at Hitler while the translator interpreted his words. Seeing no resistance, he pressed on. "That is to say, I trust that there will be no bombardment of Prague or killing of women and children by attacks from the air."

Hitler smiled and raised his hand. "As a matter of principle," he said, "I intend to limit air action to frontline zones. I will always try to spare the civilian population and confine myself to military objectives. I hate the thought of little babies being killed by gas bombs."

Returning to the hotel, Chamberlain's car could only creep through the crowds. Men and women pressed forward from all directions, trying to shake his hand. Children threw flowers. Some women wept. All cheered.

Sitting down to lunch with Strang at the hotel, the prime minister proudly patted his breast pocket. "I've got it," he said, a visionary gleam in his narrow eyes. "It" was a brief communiqué that Hitler had agreed to sign. The central paragraph read, "We regard the agreement signed last night ... as symbolic of the desire of our two peoples never to go to war with one another again."

He had the same scrap of paper in his hands when he stood, exhausted and elated, at a large open window at No. 10 Downing Street. The street below could not take another body; the cheering made it impossible to hear another sound.

All day he had been cheered—in Germany, then arriving back in England at Heston airport, and on the road all the way to Buckingham Palace where he had met with the king to accept his congratulations. Now he raised his hands until the crowd quieted enough for him to be heard.

Waving the communiqué, he said, "My good friends, this is the second time in our history that there has come back from Germany to Downing Street peace with honor."

The crowd roared its approval at the historic phrase that the famous statesman Disraeli had used at *his* hero's welcome sixty years before.

"I believe it is peace for our time," he concluded.

OCTOBER 5, 1938, LONDON

Winston Churchill was one of the few in all of England who understood that government's first duty was not to avoid confrontations with evil but to restrain it. As a result he was an outcast, going against the tide of opinion. He stood solemnly before the House of Commons, knowing full well the immense enthusiasm supporting Chamberlain. Nevertheless, his deep bass reverberated, full of doom.

"All is over.... Silent, mournful, abandoned, broken, Czechoslovakia recedes into the darkness. I do not begrudge our loyal, brave people ... the natural, spontaneous outburst of joy and relief when they learned that the hard ordeal would no longer be required of them at the moment.... But they should know the truth. They should know that there has been gross neglect and deficiency in our defenses. They should know that we have sustained a great defeat without a war, the consequences of which will travel far with us.... They should know that we have passed an awful milestone in our history ... the terrible words have for the time being been pronounced against the Western democracies: 'Thou art weighed in the balance and found wanting.' And do not suppose that this is the end. This is only the beginning of the reckoning."

NOVEMBER 9, 1938, CRYSTAL NIGHT

It was late afternoon when the truck lurched to a stop in front of the synagogue in the small German town. About thirty men got out, some in uniforms, others in street clothing. A red can of paint appeared and one of them began painting a huge red star on the synagogue. The others shouted insults.

A passerby, a woman carrying a bulging shopping bag, asked what the problem was. A uniformed officer explained. "The diplomat Rath, the one the Jews shot in Paris, has died. We are expressing our outrage. This is to happen all over Germany."

Just then two of the men who had run inside emerged dragging a man in a skull cap. "There's more in there," they shouted. "Go get them out." Others raced into the building. From inside came angry cries and the sharp sound of breaking glass. Shards of crystal rained down on the street from a second-story window.

The dozen or so men who still stood in the street were shouting insults at the Jewish man. Two of them held him on his knees, pressing his nose into the cobblestones. A small silent crowd had gathered, standing cautiously at a distance.

Eight more Jews were herded out, five men, one woman, and two young girls. The jeers of the men grew louder as these too were forced to kneel on the pavement. One of the men struggled against his captors. They lifted his head by the hair and banged it down on the stones. Once, twice, three times. Blood oozed between the cracks in the stones.

The woman with the shopping bag approached the knot of men holding the two girls. "Why don't you let me take these two away. They're just children."

"No, Fräulein, these are not children," one said. "They're Jews."

"What's the difference?" the woman demanded.

The man hesitated a moment. Then he pointed his chin down to the road. "You go away if you don't want to watch this. Those who interfere will only be hurt. You go away now."

When the woman hesitated, he spat out, "So you're a Jew-lover?"

She turned and crossed the street, where she continued to watch.

The Jews were formed into a rough circle; then the men took turns kicking them, yanking their hair, slapping their faces. The victims stared at their tormentors silently. They had stopped crying for mercy. One of their number already lay on the pavement, blood flowing from one of his ears.

From one of the broken windows above, a thread of smoke wandered skyward. One man pointed it out to the others. "It's burning," he cried with excitement. He seized the hair of the woman and whirled her violently around, jerking her head back. "Look you bloodsucker!" he screamed. "You Christ-killer, your synagogue is burning!"

Similar scenes were played out in almost every town in Germany.

NOVEMBER 10, 1938

The world was shaken from its post-Munich bliss. The night, which became known as Crystal Night because of the broken glass, sparked foreign protest. In Germany, however, the government announced that the extensive damage would be repaid by appropriating Jewish bank accounts. The Jews, after all, had provoked the spontaneous reaction.

Chamberlain was annoyed. He would probably have to make a statement in the House; someone was certain to raise the matter. This could well disrupt further negotiations. But he did not refer to it in his public speech that night in which he said, "Political conditions in Europe are now settling down to quieter times."

Charles Lindbergh wrote with bewilderment in his diary: "They have undoubtedly had a difficult Jewish problem, but why is it necessary to handle it so unreasonably?"

In Germany the official church said not a word. Only a tiny minority of Christians were brave enough to offer public sympathy. One lonely Catholic priest, Father Lichtenberg, led his Berlin congregation in prayer for the persecuted non-Aryans. He was imprisoned and eventually died in confinement. In Württemberg, Pastor von Jan used his sermon to warn against such violent hatred, which he said condemned the German people in the sight of God. He called for contrition, lest God allow Germany to reap the harvest they had sown. Eleven days later a screaming mob of about five hundred men dragged him from a home Bible study and beat him for two hours. He was then imprisoned.

Dietrich Bonhoeffer found himself staring again and again at Psalm 74. He underlined verse 8: "They burned every place where God was worshiped in the land," and in the margin beside it wrote, "Nov. 11, 1938." Then he underlined the verse that followed, putting an exclamation mark beside it: "We are given no miraculous signs; no prophets are left, and none of us knows how long this will be."

MARCH 15, 1939

In the frozen dawn Hitler's armed column probed its way through the thick fog that lay on the Czechoslovakian border. The proud Czech border guards did not resist, but stood and watched the tanks rumble by. Just a few hours before they had received orders from Prague not to fight.

Hitler had, through a series of manipulations and ultimatums, convinced a fractured government not to put up a pointless and bloody battle against his invasion.

In London Chamberlain was stunned. Less than a month before he had written to his sisters: "I myself am going about with a lighter heart than I have had for many a long day. All the information I get seems to point in the direction of peace.... I believe we have at last got on top of the dictators."

The British cabinet, meeting in emergency session, decided to offer no military aid to the nation they had "guaranteed" at Munich. Chamberlain held sway when he said that although he did "bitterly regret what has now occurred," the country should not "on that account be deflected from our course.... The aim of this government is now, as it always has been, to substitute the method of discussion for the method of force in the settlement of differences."

Yet they could not keep this blindfold on much longer. A few days later Chamberlain reversed himself completely, speaking long and bitterly about Hitler's broken promises. Wearily he spoke of the implications he had just begun to see and wondered aloud, "Is this, in fact, a step in the direction of an attempt to dominate the world by force?"

JULY 7, 1939, NEW YORK

Dietrich Bonhoeffer leaned on the railing of the ship looking at the jagged silhouette of Manhattan skyscrapers against the night sky. Tomorrow at 12:30, they would sail. He had been in New York for nearly a month — a month filled with frustration, anxiety, and uncertainty.

He smiled to himself and thought of how he must have confused his American hosts. Ostensibly he had come to the United States at the invitation of several professors who had made hasty arrangements under the mistaken impression that he was about to be thrown into a concentration camp. But his entire stay had been a struggle to determine why he was there. Had he fled the coming struggle in Germany? Was he afraid of what he had to do? His hosts had tried so hard to help, had welcomed him so warmly, and all he had done was smoke an endless chain of cigarettes, speak obscure and contradicting pronouncements, and scribble illegible notes to himself.

A few days ago, while still wavering, he had written in his journal: "Today I read by chance in 2 Timothy 4, 'Make every effort to come before winter,' Paul's petition to Timothy. 'Come before winter' — otherwise it might be too late. That has been in my mind all day.... We cannot get away from it any more. Not because we are necessary, or because we are useful (to God?), but simply because that is where our life is.... It is nothing pious, more like some vital urge. But God acts not only by means of pious incentives, but also through such vital stimuli. 'Come before winter' — it is no misuse of Scripture, if I accept that as having been said to me. If God gives me grace for it."

Now, at last, on the verge of returning to the darkest corner of the earth, his mind was at ease. He had not known how deeply he loved Germany and loved the church in Germany until now.

SEPTEMBER 1, 1939,
BORDER BETWEEN POLAND AND GERMANY

The early morning darkness was warm and beautiful, the clear sky filled with clusters of stars. On the roads from Berlin long convoys of trucks, troop transports, tanks, and artillery moved slowly toward Poland. But here at the border nothing moved.

Suddenly a flare of light flickered through the trees; almost immediately the boom of an artillery piece followed. As if in reply, hundreds of guns up and down the border began to thunder.

The invasion of Poland was launched. World War II had begun.

AFTERWORD

When Germany invaded Holland and France in May 1940, Chamberlain's government collapsed in ignominy. Churchill became prime minister promising "blood, toil, tears and sweat." Exhausted and sick, Chamberlain died that same year. A besieged Britain was the only democracy left in Europe.

During the war, pressure eased somewhat on the Confessing Church in Germany; the government had other worries. Besides, the most troublesome pastors were either in the army or in concentration camps. Only scattered individuals in the church protested against the wholesale annihilation of Jews, gypsies, and the mentally retarded.

Dietrich Bonhoeffer evaded the draft and continued secret activities in the resistance. In 1943 he was arrested and, just before the surrender of Germany in May 1945, was executed for his part in an attempted assassination of Adolf Hitler.

Martin Niemoller narrowly escaped execution and emerged from seven years in the concentration camps to play a significant role in the reconstruction of Germany.

It would be an overstatement to suggest that Chamberlain's inability or unwillingness to see the nature of Hitler's evil was the cause of World War II. Like all major events of history, the war was the result of a combination of powerful forces. But it is unarguable that Chamberlain and many in Britain grossly misjudged the situation on the continent. Why?

First of all, there was great revulsion in England over the senseless butchery of trench warfare in the First World War. The country had little stomach to fight again. Chamberlain himself had lost a cousin, perhaps his closest friend, in France. He never stopped grieving.

A second factor was Chamberlain himself. He had grown up in a tight-knit Unitarian family. They rejected the Christian belief in man's innate sinfulness, preferring to place faith in the innate goodness and "reasonableness" of man. Influential Britons of all backgrounds were infected by such thinking. Faith in the social sciences, in intellectual solutions to moral problems, had never been higher than in the thirties. The flourishing of Christian Science within Nancy Astor's influential circle at Cliveden was symptomatic; Christian Scientists believe that all evil is an illusion that can be eliminated by the exercise of the mind. Chamberlain, who was close to many of the Cliveden group, lived among people to whom the harshness of human evil had ceased to seem real. Hitler gave Chamberlain more than adequate evidence that he was evil, unreasonable, and bent on war. Yet the prime minister could not, would not, see it. Well-meaning, honorable, quoting Shakespeare all the way, he earned a dreadful epitaph: "He could have stopped Hitler."

And finally, the church in England failed to provide an independent moral voice for the country. They too had difficulty discerning evil except in "outmoded" policies. Much of the clergy seized on the peace issue and promoted forums like the League of Nations with such indiscriminate fervor that they seemed to believe that God Himself spoke exclusively through international gatherings. Led by Bishop William Temple, they put more faith in progressive politics and economics than in God. Churchmen were so enamored with the fledgling ecumenical movement that, to Bonhoeffer's disgust, they refused to censure the German church even after German Christians had taken control. Though a few individuals were well informed about Germany, most Christian leaders in Britain failed to see the critical moral issues unfolding there. Even though men like Dietrich Bonhoeffer made a point of appealing to them, they failed to understand what the church struggle in Germany represented and thus failed to warn against it. The church, representing the Kingdom of God, was caught up in the trendy issues of the time, surrendering its influence as an independent moral voice.

This failure of both the state and the church contributed to the disaster that befell the world. Had they acted sooner to discharge their respective duties, the Holocaust might well have been avoided.

On the continent the circumstances were reversed. A power-hungry maniac who masterfully played upon the passions of the masses seized the German government. From the start Hitler was determined to exceed government's ordained and delegated role. For him the state was everything, and he was its god. The Communists and the Jews, his hated targets, could offer little organized resistance, and no one spoke in their defense. In the face of Hitler's enormous popularity, all the trusted institutions of modern society utterly failed to resist. The trade unions, the Parliament, the political parties, the universities, the associations of medical doctors, scientists, and intellectuals—all were completely under Hitler's power within six months. Only the church had the independence and the institutional power to stand between Hitler and absolute totalitarianism.

Oddly, the story of the German church struggle has all but disappeared from modern historical accounts. But in contemporary writings it was cited as the single outstanding example of resistance to Hitler. The *New York Times*, for instance, filed approximately 1000 separate news accounts of the

German church struggle from 1933 to 1937. Martin Niemoller's name was a household word.

Nazi files clearly record that the church struggle was a constant thorn in the flesh to Hitler and his aides during their early years in power. This was hardly due to the church's political vision or sophistication; rather it was a credit to the church's reliance on an ultimate authority and vision quite apart from the political order to resist Hitler's blasphemous claims, even when his political popularity was soaring. The church's authority, deeply rooted in the lives of the German people, could not be erased by a simple directive from Berlin. It was the only institution in Germany that offered any enduring or meaningful resistance.

But it was not enough. Eventually alone, divided from within, with large numbers of its membership capitulating and even supporting Hitler's schemes, the church failed to hold the state to account.

The roots of World War II were in a sense theological. In England and in Germany, the state and the church failed to fulfill their God-ordained mandates. And whenever that happens, evil triumphs.

12

YEAR ZERO

*What will we do as the earth is set loose
from its sun?*

FRIEDRICH NIETZSCHE

Six years after Hitler's troops marched into Poland, much of Europe lay in ruins. London, victim of German air power in the early years of the war, had been bombed incessantly; France, Italy, and the Netherlands had faced the cruelty of enemy occupation. But it was Japan that had borne the full brunt of modern warfare: the atom bomb. Her will to fight was incinerated in the mushroom clouds that devastated Hiroshima and Nagasaki.

Sunday, September 2, 1945, as the sun climbed in the sky over Tokyo Bay, the decks of the battleship USS *Missouri* grew hot. The massive hulk of steel, the length of a football field, was the site of the formal surrender ceremony of the Axis powers to the Allies.[1]

General Jonathan Wainwright, commander of the American forces defeated in the Philippines, had been liberated only four days earlier after three years in a Manchurian prison camp; he and Arthur Percival, the British general who had surrendered Singapore, flanked General Douglas MacArthur, now supreme commander for the Allied powers. Fanning out behind them on either side were Allied admirals and generals from England, Canada, Australia, New Zealand, Russia, China, the Netherlands, and America.

In the center of the rows of khaki, medals, and ribbons stood a microphone, an old mess table covered with a thick green cloth, and two straight chairs. Surrounding them was the network of scaffolding erected for war correspondents and cameramen, now clinging to their perches, checking camera angles, and scribbling notes. The gun turrets and decks overhead were lined with sailors in sparkling white. Many held Kodaks, straining for a shot of General MacArthur.

High above it all, the Stars and Stripes snapped in the breeze, the same flag that had flown over the U.S. Capitol on the morning of December 7, 1941, when the Japanese had destroyed much of the American fleet in Pearl Harbor.

At 9:00 A.M., Commander Horace Byrd, the *Missouri's* gunnery officer, cupped his hands to his mouth and shouted, "Attention all hands." The jubilant buzz of conversation quieted as the Japanese delegation approached the *Missouri*.

Eleven Japanese officials, wearing silk hats, ascots, and cutaways, climbed the ship's stairway, their faces expressionless. Several had been forced to participate in the ceremonies by the emperor himself; they had vowed to commit hara-kiri, as many of their fellow officers already had, upon their return to Tokyo.

The ceremony began with an invocation by the ship's chaplain, then the "Star Spangled Banner" blared over the public-address system. General MacArthur, wearing his familiar sun glasses and visored cap, walked briskly to the microphone. He stood erect and confident, though his hand trembled slightly as he held the sheet of notes before him.

"We are gathered here, representative of the major warring powers," he said in a strong voice, "to conclude a solemn agreement whereby peace may be restored.... It is my earnest hope and indeed the hope of all mankind that from this solemn occasion a better world shall emerge out of the blood and carnage of the past—a world founded upon faith and understanding—a world dedicated to the dignity of man and the fulfillment of his most cherished wish—for freedom, tolerance and justice."

Two copies of the surrender agreement lay on the table, one bound in leather for the Allies, the other bound in canvas for the Japanese. Cameras clicked everywhere as the signing began. Foreign Minister Shigemitsu sat down and fumbled with his hat and gloves, obviously bewildered. MacArthur's chief of staff showed him where to sign. Then the other Japanese officials signed the agreement, as did the nine representatives of the Allied powers. At eight minutes past nine, MacArthur sat at the table and affixed his signature to the document.

"Let us pray that peace be now restored to the world and that God will preserve it always," he announced. At that moment a steady drone in the clouds above the ship became a deafening roar, and an aerial pageant of 400

B–29s and 1,500 carrier planes swept across the sky and disappeared in the mists of Mount Fuji to the southwest.

World War II had ended.

At that dramatic moment General Douglas MacArthur spoke the first words of peace to a waiting world.

"Today the guns are silent … the skies no longer rain death … the seas bear only commerce … men everywhere walk upright in the sunlight. The entire world is quietly at peace. …

"A new era is upon us. Even the lesson of victory itself brings with it profound concern both for our future security and the survival of civilization. The destructiveness of the war potential, through progressive advances in scientific discovery, has in fact now reached a point which revises the traditional concept of war. …

"Men since the beginning of time have sought peace, [but] military alliances, balance of power, leagues of nations, all in turn failed, leaving the only path to be by way of the crucible of war.

"*We have had our last chance. If we do not now devise some greater and more equitable system, Armageddon will be at our door. The problem is basically theological and involves a spiritual recrudescence and improvement of human character. It must be of the spirit if we are to save the flesh.*"

Nineteen forty-five, "Year Zero," as one historian labeled it,* was the year of promise. Old mistakes were not to be repeated.

Douglas MacArthur was one of the few to fully understand that the challenge of this new beginning was not primarily political, military, or economic, but spiritual. The crisis was not one of organization or technology, but of character and ideas. He issued his prophetic challenge in light of two events that had already occurred, ominous portents that would shape the post-war world: the atom bomb and the accession to Stalin's demands.

---

*John Lukacs in his book *1945: Year Zero* (Garden City: Doubleday, 1978). Lukacs explains: "Nineteen forty-five was both Year Zero and Year One. Year Zero, Jahr Null—this is what a generation of Germans called the year 1945. Year One, Year I of the Atomic Age, this is how certain intellectuals, editorialists, scientists kept referring to that year, at least for awhile." Lukacs contends that the end of a united Germany (which would not be reunited until 1990—45 years later) was a much more important event in 1945 than the atomic bomb.

The bomb MacArthur had seen. He knew that the devastating power of the atom bomb would forever change the rules of war, international politics, and the universe. Hiroshima's blackened ruins testified to the possibility of global annihilation and the ultimate destructive power of man over nature and humanity. The mushroom cloud of Armageddon would haunt future generations.

Catholic novelist Georges Bernanos, author of *The Diary of a Country Priest*, called the use of the bomb the "triumph of technique over reason."[2] Questions of justice, prudence, responsibility, and consequences were set aside in pursuit of a technique to win the war. Though the bomb hastened the end of the war, it would shape civilization's values for the remainder of the century. Just as technique had triumphed over reason, so expediency would triumph over morality.

The second event to significantly shape the post-World War II world was the Allied decision to accede to Soviet demands for the return of all Russian nationals. The West was amazingly compliant; the singular goal was victory and that meant keeping Stalin happy. In 1944 hundreds of thousands who had come under Allied control during the liberation of Europe were sent back to the Soviet Union.

Sir Patrick Dean, legal advisor for the British foreign office, advised his superiors: "This is purely a question for the Soviet authorities and does not concern His Majesty's government. In due course, all those with whom the Soviet authorities desire to deal must be handed over to them, and we are not concerned with the fact that they may be shot or otherwise more harshly dealt with than they might be under English law."[3]

Again, technique superseded reason and principle at the price of an estimated one and a half million people. The forced repatriation served as Stalin's death warrant on Croats, Cossacks, and the other Russians who had hoped to escape Communist rule.

MacArthur realized the peril the post-war world faced. But his stirring words of warning that day in Tokyo Bay were washed away in the waves of euphoric relief that swept over victor and vanquished alike. Instead of seeking spiritual renewal, which might have established a healthy balance between the religious and the political, the post-war generation was left to thrash about in a vacuum of values.

For at that point the modern mind had already been seized by the powerful ideas of an odd prophet—a syphilitic and eventually insane nineteenth-century German who could see into the soul of the future.

In 1889 Friedrich Nietzsche told a parable:

Have you not heard of the madman who lit a lamp in the bright morning and went to the marketplace crying ceaselessly, "I seek God! I seek God!" There were many among those standing there who didn't believe in God so he made them laugh. "Is God lost?" one of them said. "Has he gone astray like a child?" said another. "Or is he hiding? Has he gone on board ship and emigrated?" So they laughed and shouted to one another. The man sprang into their midst and looked daggers at them. "Where is God?" he cried. "I will tell you. We have killed him — you and I. We are all his killers! But how have we done this? How could we swallow up the sea? Who gave us the sponge to wipe away the horizon? What will we do as the earth is set loose from its sun?"[4]

Nietzsche's point was not that God does not exist, but that God has become irrelevant. Men and women may assert that God exists or that He does not, but it makes little difference either way. God is dead not because He doesn't exist, but because we live, play, procreate, govern, and die as though He doesn't.

The effect of this widespread notion can be seen in the despair that followed World War I, in the void that gave rise to fascism, in the militant atheism that has claimed countless lives in Russia and China, and in modern Western culture. The death of God has profound implications for individuals as well as for society and politics because it is the philosophic context in which modern governments operate.

In Western civilization God had traditionally played the role of legitimizing government. In classical and Christian political philosophy He was the author of natural law — that body of just and reasonable standards that guided human rulers and by which the ruled were bound to respect and obey those given charge over them. Even atheistic political philosophy acknowledged that the idea of God was useful: a little dose of religion would keep the masses quiet. As Napoleon said, "Religion is what keeps the poor from murdering the rich."[5]

But Nietzsche's atheism was the most radical the world had yet seen. While the old atheism had acknowledged the need for religion, the new atheism was political, activist, and jealous. One scholar observed that "atheism has become militant … insisting it must be believed. Atheism has felt the need to impose its views, to forbid competing visions."[6]

Nietzsche himself predicted the result of this new atheism on politics. "I am not man, I am dynamite ... my truth is fearful; it is that in the past we called lies the truth—the devaluation of all values.... The concept of politics is completely taken up in a war of the spirits, all the structures of power are blown up into the air, for they are based on the lie. There will be wars of a kind that have never happened on the earth."[7]

"The devaluation of all values" is what the death of God has meant to politics. Distinctions between right and wrong, justice and injustice have become meaningless. No objective guide is left to choose between "all men are created equal" and "the weak to the wall."

In Year Zero no one could have predicted the consequences that the void at the heart of the nations would produce. But philosopher Blaise Pascal had foreseen, three centuries earlier, the chilling consequences. He argued that in a spiritual vacuum, men can pursue only two options: first, to imagine that they are gods themselves, or second, to seek satisfaction in their senses. Unknowingly, he predicted the routes that would be followed in the East and West in the aftermath of World War II.

On the surface, however, when the USS *Missouri* sailed out of Tokyo Bay, there seemed every reason for hope. Plans were being laid for a great council of nations dedicated to the dignity of man and the end of war. It would be a brave new world in which the nations of the globe could unite to seek peace and justice.

The United Nations complex sits on sixteen acres of New York City's choicest real estate, bordering the East River and Manhattan. The lean, immense Secretariat building rises into the sky, the sun reflecting off its window walls. Bright flags of the nations of the world fly in the breezes off the river; the most prominent is the blue and white UN flag, its two white reeds of olive branches surrounding the world.

A visitor is immediately struck by the grandeur of the building, and stirred by the sight of dignitaries stepping out of black limousines to cross the massive plaza. He realizes that if this place represents the powers of the world, one might well want to see the place of worship, where the nations bow before the One under whose rule they govern.

The information personnel are bemused. "The chapel? We don't have a chapel. If there is one, I believe it's across the street."

The visitor darts across the thoroughfare, dodging New York's taxis, and successfully arrives at the opposite building's security-clearance desk.

"Well, there's a chapel here," responds the officer, "but it's not associated with the UN." He thumbs through a directory. "Oh, I see, all right, here it is. It's across the street—and tell them you're looking for the meditation room."

Again the visitor dashes across the pavement. An attendant tells him that the room is not open to the public; it's a "nonessential area," and there has been a personnel cutback. But a security guard will escort the visitor through long, crowded hallways and swinging glass doors. Again, there is the pervasive sense of weighty matters being discussed in the noble pursuit of world peace.

The guide pauses at an unmarked door. He unlocks it and gingerly pushes it open. The small room is devoid of people or decoration. The walls are stark white. There are no windows. A few wicker stools surround a large square rock at the center of the room. It is very quiet. But there is no altar, rug, vase, candle, or symbol of any type of religious worship.

Lights in the ceiling create bright spots of illumination on the front wall. One focuses on a piece of modern art: steel squares and ovals. Beyond the abstract shapes, there is nothing in those bright circles of light. They are focused on a void. And it is in that void that the visitor suddenly sees the soul of the brave new world.

The conversion of chapels to meditation rooms was only a symptom and a warning. Aggressive secularists in American and Western life have zealously endeavored to scrub every last vestige of religious influence out of public life. In their view, it's fine to pray in the privacy of one's home, or listen quietly to sermons (as long as the minister doesn't say anything too controversial). But there is no longer any room in the public square for religion. This was recently evidenced by a judge's extraordinary decision to shut down Prison Fellowship's InnerChange Freedom Initiative, now operating in five prisons.

InnerChange is an innovative in-prison program, begun in 1997, that teaches prisoners moral values. It requires prisoners to rise at dawn for a long day of hard work, classes, and interaction with volunteers from the surrounding community. A Texas warden described it as one of the toughest ways to do time — and it works. A study of Prison Fellowship's InnerChange Freedom Initiative by the University of Pennsylvania proved that inmates who graduate from the program have a dramatically lower recidivism rate than do comparable inmates — eight percent versus 65 percent.[8]

Most people applauded this news — including President George W. Bush, who met InnerChange graduates at the White House. But the fact that IFI was a proven success was too much for Barry Lynn of Americans United for Separation of Church and State. The group sued Prison Fellowship, IFI, and the state of Iowa, claiming IFI was unconstitutional. Not true: The program is open to prisoners of all faiths or no faith, and is entirely voluntary. Prisoners know from the start that the program is taught from a Christ-centered, biblical perspective. The small amount of money spent in relationship to IFI is for non-religious purposes such as computer training.

But in June of 2006, U.S. District Judge Robert Pratt declared IFI an unconstitutional "establishment of religion." Incredibly, the judge devoted a dozen pages to analyzing evangelicalism and Prison Fellowship's statement of faith, apparently determined to separate evangelicals from other Christians. Evangelicalism, he wrote, is "quite distinct from other self-described Christian faiths," such as Roman Catholicism, Mormonism, and Greek Orthodoxy." It is also "distinct from other ... Christian denominations, such as Lutheran, United Methodist, Episcopalian, and Presbyterian."[9]

Evangelicals, he found, tend to be "anti-sacramental," downplaying "baptism, holy communion or Eucharist, marriage, and ordination" as "appropriate ways to interact or meet with God." (The charge of downplaying baptism probably surprised my 20 million fellow Baptists.) The belief held by evangelicals and Prison Fellowship in the "substitutionary and atoning death of Jesus" reflects "a legalistic understanding of the sacrifice of Jesus, [which] is not shared by many Christians." So much for the central tenet of every historic creed and confession of the Christian church. Moreover, evangelicals are "contemptuous" of Roman Catholic practices, a conclusion that likely amused my colleagues with Evangelicals and Catholics Together.[10]

To sum up: Evangelicals are a fringe cult inherently discriminatory, coercive, and antagonistic to other Christians. The judge ordered that the program be shut down (a decision he stayed pending the outcome of PF's appeal) and that IFI and Prison Fellowship pay back the state of Iowa $1.5 million, money the state had paid to IFI under a valid contract and which had already been spent providing services to prisoners.

Ironically, just days after the judge's decision, the Commission on Safety and Abuse in America's Prisons reported a desperate need in prisons for "highly structured programs which reduce misconduct in correctional facilities and lower recidivism rates after release."[11]

The commission understood the urgency of these programs, because every year, some 600,000 prisoners are released. Within three years, more than two-thirds will be re-arrested. Why? Because merely warehousing prisoners leaves them unprepared to re-enter society as productive citizens. Indeed, it makes them worse.

Bad enough that the judge ordered closed a program that has proven successful. Even worse, he expanded the Supreme Court precedent in *Lemon v. Kurtzman*, thus imperiling thousands of faith-based programs. A careful reading of his opinion leads to the conclusion that even if state funds are not involved, any close government cooperation with "pervasively sectarian" groups is unconstitutional. Such a broad standard could easily be applied to church services or evangelistic events not only in prisons, but also in hospitals, military bases, or any government facility.

But the most alarming question is why the judge chose to write a hostile sociological analysis of evangelicalism. And why would he so inaccurately characterize evangelicals as a fringe cult? After all, we make up between 33 and 40 percent of the American population, drawing from scores of denominations made up of Asians, whites, Hispanics, and blacks, as well as many millions of Catholics.

By distinguishing evangelicals from all other Christian groups, Judge Pratt supported his findings that we discriminate and coerce conversions — despite the fact that every inmate testifying in the trial denied any coercion. (Inmates can drop out of IFI at any time, and many participants are not Christians.)

Think of the consequences if this judgment survives on appeal — enshrining in federal law a definition of evangelicals as a narrow, mean-spirited minority. What will prevent a court from deciding what is and is not legitimate theology, according to the trendiest, most politically correct standards?

Prison Fellowship is appealing Judge Pratt's decision all the way to the Supreme Court, if necessary, because we want to see a level playing field for religious Americans. People of faith should not be excluded from providing services in the public square to those who have volunteered to receive them—indeed, who desperately need them. We want prisoners to be able to take part in a program—yes, even a Christ-centered one—that will help them change their lives for the better if they desire to do so. Americans United, on the other hand, wants religion forced out of every aspect of public life, including prisons—regardless of the consequences for those prisoners who wish to participate.

Hostility toward religion caused Americans United for Separation of Church and State to sue Prison Fellowship at the very moment studies emerged proving how dramatically IFI transforms lives. Tragically, they are undermining prisoners' hopes for a law-abiding, God-fearing life—and helping to usher in a frightening future in which religious freedoms—once steadfastly protected—lie in ruins.

13

MARXISM AND
THE KINGDOM OF GOD

*If you will not have God (and He is a jealous God), you should pay
your respects to Hitler and Stalin.*

T. S. ELIOT

"God remains dead," wrote Nietzsche. "How shall we, the murderers of all
murderers, comfort ourselves? Must not we ourselves become gods simply
to seem worthy of it?"[1] With these words Nietzsche was at once echoing
Pascal's first option that "men become gods themselves" and heralding the
creation of a new type of man—a heroic individualist no longer bound to a
traditional "slave" morality, but creating his own rules. Such a "superman"
would exercise the "will to power."

The history of the twentieth century is littered with such "supermen"
who exercised the will to power. The first monstrous tyranny was carried
out by the Nazis; tens of millions died as a result. A second tyranny, Marxist
Leninism, would continue to kill and destroy for decades more.

During the 1980s, one-third of the world's population lived in the vise-
like grip of states run by gangster-statesmen. The goal of these massive bureaucracies was to preside over the death of God; their system for achieving
it was most often called Marxist Leninism.* They carried out their policies with surgical efficiency, as millions of Christians and Jews who passed
through Communist gulags would testify—if they could. But sometimes

---

*The Soviet Union set the course that virtually all Marxist governments followed. Before
the 1917 revolution 83.4 percent of the people living in what is now the Soviet Union were
identified as Christians—three quarters of them Russian Orthodox. Orthodox, Catholic,
and Protestant Christians have suffered violent persecution since the revolution, except for
a brief period during World War II when the regime needed the support of the churches.
Between 1917 and the disintegration of the Soviet Union, some 60 million Soviet citizens

the system performed with comic clumsiness, as I witnessed one night in Leningrad, many years ago.

In February 1973 President Nixon had sent me to the Soviet Union for follow-up negotiations to the trade agreements Nixon and Leonid Brezhnev had announced at their 1973 summit. My real job, however, was to pressure the Soviets into allowing more Jews to emigrate. Their refusal to do so was imperiling trade legislation in the U.S. Congress.

After our official meetings in Moscow, my wife, Patty, and I were escorted on a three-day visit to St. Petersburg (then called Leningrad), Russia's showcase city for Western visitors.

St. Petersburg takes on an eerie beauty in the filtered light of the northern winter, its sprawling skyline a dazzling mix of gilded, traditional onion domes and the rich blue and pastel hues of French and Italian provincial architecture. This splendid city is the place where East and West have traditionally met—and divided.

Like all Western visitors, Patty and I eagerly walked the treasure-laden corridors of the Hermitage, one of the world's greatest art repositories; saw the famed Peter and Paul fortress, within whose massive walls have been enacted many of the turbulent events of Russian history; explored the palaces where czars of the Imperial era lived in unrivaled splendor; and visited the cathedrals of Leningrad, which reflect the Russian culture. The ecclesiastical façade of one, the Peter and Paul Lutheran Church, had been preserved, but the interior had been converted into a gigantic public swimming pool. Another, the spectacular Cathedral of Our Lady, was now a state museum exhibiting the history of religion and atheism.

The Soviet Foreign Ministry capped our visit with an evening at the Kirov Ballet for a performance of Tchaikovsky's *Swan Lake*. The Kirov was the crown jewel of St. Petersburg. The Soviets spared nothing to repair the heavy damage the building suffered during World War II, restoring its nineteenth-century elegance. During the renovation, completed in 1970, nearly nine hundred pounds of gold were used to gild the interior walls where five

---

were killed and 66 million sent to labor camps or imprisoned. At least half of these were Christians.

Activist theologian Reinhold Niebuhr once described Communism as "an organized evil which spreads terror and cruelty through the world." And Aleksandr Solzhenitsyn, the great writer who came to faith while in prison, explains why Communists were so determined to destroy Christianity: "They flee from Christ like devils from the sign of the cross."

tiers of balconies sweep around the huge horseshoe-shaped hall like elegant ivory and gold rings, glistening in the blaze of massive crystal chandeliers. The sight took our breath away.

Our escort, a veteran U.S. Consulate officer, seemed pleased as we were shown to our orchestra center seats — thick, plush, sapphire-velvet chairs.

"This is very good for protocol," he whispered.

"Good for watching great ballet too," I replied.

His smile vanished. "Of course we may not see *Swan Lake*," he said.

I thought he was joking. "Why not?" I asked, prepared for a quip.

"Well, we know the Soviets respect your high rank because you got these seats," he said. "And often when American VIPs come they pull a switch at the last minute and put on a dreadful atheistic propaganda piece called *Creation of the World*. I've seen it six times."

"But these people," I said, gesturing at the audience. "They're here to see *Swan Lake*. They'll be in an uproar."

"No, they won't," the consular officer replied with a smile. "This is Russia."

Sure enough, when the lights dimmed and the velvet curtain rose, it was not the opening strains of Tchaikovsky's masterpiece we heard, but the strident chords of *Creation of the World*. I watched the faces of the surrounding audience. Not a murmur, not a single expression of displeasure. Seventeen hundred people sat stoically in their seats.

It was a dreary evening indeed. The ballet was a parody of the Garden of Eden, with a buffoon-like character, God, contesting with a vital, vigorous figure, Satan, for the soul of man. In the closing scene God retreated lamely, vanquished, leaving self-sufficient man living happily ever after in his earthly paradise.

The architect of this earthly paradise was Vladimir Ilyich Ulyanov, the son of Christian parents, known to history as Lenin.

Lenin, a single-minded radical, became the most successful revolutionary of the twentieth century. With the "will to power," he pursued and eliminated his enemies ruthlessly — liberals and socialists, rival Marxists, reluctant peasants and skeptical military officers, monarchists and capitalists, Jews and various other "class enemies." Above all, Lenin pursued and murdered Christians. He hated them. "There can be nothing more abominable than religion," he wrote.[2]

Lenin particularly hated seriously committed Christians. Weak Christians he could manage, but serious Christians meant nothing but trouble for a Marxist-Leninist regime. They owed allegiance to the one power greater than the totalitarian Communist state. History has borne Lenin out on this point, if not on others.

The pattern of Communist persecution of Jews and Christians was (and still is) remarkably ecumenical. It has fallen on orthodox believers in Russia, Romania, Bulgaria, and the Ukraine; Roman Catholics in the Baltic Republics, Poland, Hungary, Cuba, Vietnam, and Nicaragua. It has fallen on Lutherans in East Germany (now part of the Federal Republic of Germany), Czechoslovakia (now the Czech Republic and Slovakia), Reformed Christians in Hungary and Czechoslovakia; Pentecostals, Baptists, and other evangelicals in Eastern Europe, Latin America, and Asia; it has fallen on Christians belonging to underground house churches in China.

In 1980, twenty-eight Marxist regimes around the world were committed to a policy of atheism, repressing and persecuting Christianity to some degree. These nations contained approximately 250 million Christians — almost one of every five Christians in the world. In Vietnam, evangelical pastors were jailed and hundreds of churches closed. In Hungary, Czechoslovakia and the Soviet Union, police cracked down on Christians for meeting for prayer and Bible study. In Nicaragua, dozens of Monrovian pastors were imprisoned and killed.

Today — twenty-seven years later — the vast Soviet empire is no more. Its godless pretensions are nothing more than a hideous joke. But we dare not forget what happened during those years of rampant Communism.

For the battle against the Kingdom of God continues. Hitler is dead, Stalin is dead, Mao is dead, Communism is a spent force, but others carry on in the fight against God and his people. The persecution of Christians goes on — in North Korea, in Islamic nations, in China, and in many other countries.

Consider just a few representative reports of that persecution around the world:

- In Saudi Arabia, on July 19, 2001, the Saudi religious police burst into the home of Christian missionaries Isaac and Sucilla Prabhu, confiscated religious books and Bibles, interrogated the couple, and took Isaac to prison, where he was repeatedly tortured to reveal the names of other Christians. While the Saudi government claims to allow non-Muslims to worship in private, in reality, the Saudis regularly arrest Christians, imprison, and torture them.[3]

- From North Korea come stories reminiscent of the horrors of Auschwitz. Kwon Hyuk, who defected from North Korea a few years ago, told a British journalist what it was like to work at Camp 22, North Korea's infamous concentration camp. As Hyuk recalled, "I witnessed a whole family being tested on suffocating gas and dying in the gas chamber. The parents were vomiting and dying, but till the very last moment they tried to save the kids by doing mouth-to-mouth breathing."[4] Above the gas chamber, scientists were calmly observing and taking notes, just like the Nazis did sixty years ago when *they* conducted medical experiments on children. Whole families are sent to the gulags for the most trivial of reasons—such as listening to South Korean radio broadcasts—or simply for their Christian faith. North Korea has been described as one of the world's worst persecutors of religious believers.

- In China, 30 to 60 million people belong to illegal house churches. Their pastors have been tortured, murdered, and imprisoned. Many Christians are imprisoned in the Laogai, China's slave-labor system, where they are forced to make toys and other products destined for American homes. The *Washington Post* ran an op-ed about a certain Pastor Wong, who ran forty evangelical churches in Wuhan, China. Wong—who'd been imprisoned four times for the crime of spreading the Gospel—had his fingers broken by his captors with pliers.[5]

- In Sri Lanka, Buddhist terrorists have taken part in hundreds of attacks in recent years toward religious minorities. The Sri Lankan government refuses to charge or punish terrorists who attack Christians and other religious minorities. According to Dr. Richard Land of the Southern Baptist Convention, "The government's toleration of violence against religious minorities has encouraged radical Buddhists to propose anti-conversion bills in Parliament, which would punish religious minorities with up to seven years in prison for the crime of 'attempted conversion.'"[6]

- In Indonesia, Muslim jihadists have murdered some 10,000 Christians and burned down over a thousand churches. On October 29, 2005, Muslim terrorists beheaded three girls on their way to school, and threatened to murder "one hundred more Christian teenagers."[7]

- In Iran, President Mahmoud Ahmadinejad announced, "I will stop Christianity in this country." Christian leaders have been arrested, imprisoned, and murdered there, and young Christian girls are forced into marriage with Muslim men.[8]

So while the Soviet Union fell and communism has largely shattered, the persecution of Christians goes on. Tragically, a Regent University study showed that worldwide, more Christians are being martyred in the modern era than were murdered in the first century.[9]

Today, the great dialectic of the twenty-first century is the clash of civilizations between Islam and western democracy, which Samuel Huntington foresaw in *The Clash of Civilizations*. Islamo-fascist radicals threaten to destroy the West through terrorism—a relentless slaughter of innocents the world over. Their favored victims will be—as they always have been—Christians and Jews.

The struggle that took place in the second half of the twentieth century with communism is instructive. One of the greatest stories of modern history is the way in which, in the latter days of the 1980s, some of these tyrannies finally began to fall.

I witnessed much of the long tumble. In 1991 I was in Moscow with plans to visit an infamous concentration camp for political prisoners known as Perm Camps 135. (A fuller discussion of this trip occurs in Chapter 20) Everywhere I went I asked dissidents why the system was collapsing. Their answer was: President Reagan, fax machines, and the Church. Reagan, of course, upped the ante by forcing the Soviets to try to compete with the United States in weapons advancements. The West beat them economically, but fax machines were also crucially important (as they are among persecuted and oppressed peoples today, throughout the Middle East and elsewhere). The Internet also plays a great role these days in spreading information. Oppressed peoples are discovering the glory of free minds in free nations—and history reminds us that they will remain oppressed only for so long. As we witnessed in Tiananmen Square in 1989, they will literally stand in the path of tanks, willing to give their lives for freedom.

Even though communism has lost much of its force in the world, it is vitally important we not forget the lessons we learned during the long years in which we were engaged in battling it.

The seeds of the overthrow of Communism started with Cardinal Joseph Mindszenty, the primate of Hungary. In late January, 1949, Cardinal Mindszenty stood naked in his chilly cell in the secret-police headquarters at 60 Andrassy Street in Budapest, trembling with fear and cold as a furious agent of the state advanced on him with a rubber truncheon in one hand and a long knife in the other.

"I'll kill you," the man snarled, lashing the truncheon across the cardinal's back. "By morning I'll tear you to pieces and throw the remains of your corpse into the canal. We are the masters here now."

Cardinal Mindszenty had been enduring such tortures since his arrest the day after Christmas. Every night his Communist interrogators demanded that he confess to crimes against the state. Every night Cardinal Mindszenty refused to sign the confession.

"I was being made to feel in my soul, my body, my nerves, and my bones the power of bolshevism which was taking over the country," he later wrote.

Although his jailers may not have known it, Cardinal Mindszenty embodied, in a sense, the sufferings of an entire nation. The events that led to his imprisonment paralleled the ideological imprisonment of the Hungarian churches. The Communists had consolidated their power the summer before, in 1948, and their first target had been the churches. Two days after the new regime took control, they secularized the nation's religious schools. Party boss Matyas Rakosi pressed church leaders to submit to government control over church affairs, including requirements that priests and ministers publicly support government policies.

The chief obstacle to the Communists' plans, however, was Cardinal Mindszenty. As Catholic primate, he was the leader of the largest denomination in Hungary, a stubborn man with a record of fierce opposition to tyrants. The Nazis had jailed him during World War II. Later, as Communist power grew in Hungary, he constantly protested their abuses of human rights.

Cardinal Mindszenty was especially offended by the government's demands that the church sign a formal treaty with the state. He had watched Lenin and Stalin subdue the Orthodox Church in the Soviet Union through a campaign of terrorism, judicial persecution, and subversion. He vowed that he would not allow the same thing to happen in Hungary.

The church-state agreement in the Soviet Union gave the state control over religious instruction, seminary education, and appointment of bishops. Bishops were called upon to give public support to government policies when their Communist masters wanted it, and all priests had to swear allegiance to the Communist government.

Significantly, the party ruthlessly forbade the church to evangelize or to provide services to the poor, elderly, sick, and needy. Thus, the church was barred from conducting any activities that would publicly testify to its members' allegiance to another King.

Party Chief Rakosi wanted to make the church in Hungary a puppet church like the one in the Soviet Union. Cardinal Mindszenty would have none of it. After months of bickering with the recalcitrant cardinal, Rakosi and his henchmen moved against the church leader.

The day after Christmas 1948, police occupied the cardinal's offices in Esztergom. Officers carrying submachine guns led Cardinal Mindszenty to a car and drove him to secret-police headquarters in Budapest. There he was subjected to torture. Thirty-nine days after his arrest—beaten, confused, plagued with despair, and racked with fear and anxiety—the cardinal signed the confession the authorities wanted.

The Cardinal later told the harrowing account of those weeks of torture in his memoirs.[10] The mental and psychological pain were far worse than the physical deprivations and beatings, he wrote, and he was certain that the police had used drugs on him. He candidly admitted that the Communist torturers had shattered his personality, reducing him to a state where even the regime's most absurd charges began to seem plausible.

Certainly the man whom the Communists put on public trial for treason in February 1949 looked like a drugged, programmed shell, reciting the lines of a memorized script. He was found guilty of treason and sentenced to life in prison.

Soon after Cardinal Mindszenty's trial, the government suppressed the Catholic Church in Hungary. Religious schools were abolished, religious instruction was outlawed, and religious orders were dissolved.

Eventually the regime got the agreement it wanted. The bishops agreed to support the government and to tolerate state supervision of seminary training, clerical appointments, and other internal matters. In return, the government allowed the church to open eight schools and put the clergy on the state payroll.

The Reformed Church submitted to a similar agreement.

Thus the Communist rulers in Hungary achieved what they consider "normal" relations with the church. Church authorities cleared key appointments in advance with the government. Troublesome clerics were reassigned to the provinces. Bishops made regular expressions of support to the regime. When needed, priests and ministers read from their pulpits pastoral letters composed by the government Bureau of Religious Affairs.

Why was the conflict between the Christian church and the Marxist state so fundamental, ceaseless, and protracted?

Many in the secularized West were offended by terms like "mortal enemies," preferring to see Communists as a particularly enthusiastic band of social reformers and the church as one of the many social institutions that must adapt to changing political circumstances. History, however, teaches a different lesson. Communism and Christianity have always been at odds for very good reasons.

First, Christianity and Communism are irreconcilable in their basic premises. The Christian believes that the dynamic of all history is spiritual, that its unfolding reveals God's dealings with men, that Jesus Christ is God in the flesh, and that at the end of history, He will reign over all the nations.

For Marxists, the material realm is all there is. God and the spiritual order are illusions. Mankind swims in the current of history, which progresses by economic forces from the decline of capitalism, through the dictatorship of the proletariat, to the earthly paradise of the classless society. Communists are materialists and determinists; individuals count for nothing, the collective or state for everything.

Lenin thought that those who believed in God were worse than fools. "Every man who occupies himself with the construction of a god, or merely even agrees to it, prostitutes himself in the worst way," he wrote. "For he occupies himself not with activity, but with self-contemplation and self-reflection, and tries thereby to deify his most unclean, most stupid, and most servile features and pettinesses."[11] Consequently, anyone who believes in God is not simply in error; he is mentally deranged. This is why believers in the Soviet Union were frequently judged insane and committed to mental institutions.

Second, Communism and Christianity clash because each is a religion and each is inherently expansive and evangelistic.

Marxists claim that their system is scientific, in contrast to the "superstition" of Christianity. But anyone who ever visited a Communist county knows better. Before the disintegration of the Soviet Union, Marxist Leninism functioned as a religion in the lives of the faithful. Communist "saints" and martyrs were revered, their utterances preserved in books and studied carefully. May Day marches and other public ceremonies were atheistic liturgies whereby unbelievers worship the superiority of unbelief.

Philosophically, Marxism is certainly a religion. It offers a comprehensive explanation of reality and claims to put adherents in touch with higher powers—namely, the inexorable laws of history. Its eschatology is millennial. At the end of the class struggle against capitalism lies the classless society where exploiters are banished, the state withers away, and man's natural goodness flows forth unobstructed. The laws of history will bring justice to the oppressed and wipe away every tear. It's a system that an atheist can put his faith in.

Lenin, Stalin, and Rakosi recognized that a renewed and purified Christianity was the only force that could move the masses as powerfully as the Marxist ideal could. They attacked it as the enemy that it was—and is.

Trotsky, Tito, Mao, Ho Chi Minh, Castro, and the Sandinistas of the eighties—all the tyrants who followed Marx have believed substantially the same thing about Christianity. The greatest obstacle to the Marxist ideal of total control was the Christian faith, which is not simply a set of intellectual beliefs or weekly worship services, but involves personal submission to a King whose culture was and is incompatible with Lenin's. The Christian church and the Marxist state may have worked out an accommodation for a time, but they were always adversaries. The very nature of each made any lasting accommodation impossible.

The people of Jaworzyna had had enough. For years they had petitioned the party authorities in the Silesia region of Poland for permission to build a church. Their repeated applications were denied. The men on the church-building committee tried pulling strings with higher party officials in Crakow and Warsaw. No luck. When they angrily protested the refusal, the petty bureaucrats turned a deaf ear. Now, other measures were required.

Months before, the authorities had issued a permit to build an auto-repair garage on a site near a highway. Now workers moved onto the site, erected a tall fence, and began to build the garage. The building progressed slowly over a period of two years, but no one paid much attention. The party authorities in Jaworzyna were busy men.

Then, on Sunday, February 5, 1978, the fence came down and the garage turned out to be a new church — its wide portals adorned with a picture of Our Lady of Czêstochowa, the protector of Poland. Masses were celebrated until late in the evening; thousands of people came to worship and rejoice.

That spring, Cardinal Karol Wojtlya of Crakow came to Jaworzyna to dedicate the church. Soon afterward the authorities tried to close it, but hundreds of angry Poles organized a twenty-four-hour guard. The church building committee was taken to court and fined. Their clever lawyers tied the case up in procedural disputes.

Just before the May Day celebrations of the glorious triumph of Communism in Poland, the party authorities attempted to hide the church from the nearby highway by surrounding it with giant billboards bearing propaganda. The next morning the billboards lay on the ground, their messages celebrating the revolution ripped and shredded, their supports smashed. Even the cement footings had been ripped from the ground.

The wreckage lay outside the church for months. Many in Jaworzyna took it as a graphic symbol of the conflict in Poland between the church, which bears authority, and the state, which merely has power.

Joseph Stalin, who murdered millions during his twenty-nine-year reign as perhaps the most ruthless tyrant in history, once scoffed at a colleague who warned that the pope was likely to denounce one of Stalin's barbaric plans. "The pope!" sneered Stalin. "How many divisions does the pope have?"[12]

The pope's divisions were on display to the entire world in June 1979 when the former Cardinal Karol Wojtlya of Crakow, now John Paul II, visited his homeland. Ecstatic crowds gathered everywhere he went — 200,000 in Warsaw, 500,000 at the shrine of the Black Madonna at Czêstochowa, 1,000,000 in Crakow. Similar throngs were present at Gniezno, the first capital of Poland; at Wadowice, the pope's birthplace; and at Auschwitz and Birkenau, the sites of the infamous Nazi extermination camps. The world saw that the church possessed the soul of the Polish people and embodied the essence of Polish nationhood. By contrast, the Polish Communists who operated the machinery of the state were alien usurpers who did the bidding of Russian masters. Though he went out of his way to avoid a direct confrontation with the Communist regime, John Paul's message was widely understood by the restive Polish masses, and he lit a fuse during his triumphant nine-day visit to his homeland.

"Christ would never approve that man be considered merely as a means of production," he told workers in his old archdiocese in Mogila.[13]

At Czêstochowa, he urged the government to honor "the cause of fundamental human rights, including the right to religious liberty."[14]

At Novy Targ, he told Poles to set a Christian example "even if it means risking danger."[15]

The long fuse that the pope lit exploded in July 1980 when workers at the Lenin shipyards at Gdansk went out on strike. Under the leadership of a Catholic electrician named Lech Walesa, the workers seized the shipyards and made a radical demand of the authorities: the right to organize free labor unions. Workers throughout the country walked off their jobs in sympathy. The Communist regime, discredited and despised, lost control.

By 1981 the Polish government was desperate. Millions of Poles, including many members of the Communist party, had joined the Solidarity movement. Lech Walesa became a household name around the world. Labor unrest spread from the cities to the rural areas. The economy was a shambles. The Red army maneuvered on Poland's eastern border. No one doubted that Soviet party boss Leonid Brezhnev would use his divisions if the pope's couldn't be curbed.

John Paul II announced that if Soviet tanks moved, he would return to stand with his countrymen. In desperation the government did the only thing it could do: it turned to the church. Cardinal Stefan Wyszynski, the primate of Poland, skillfully negotiated a deal among church, state, and Solidarity. The state would allow Solidarity freedom to organize and would loosen censorship in return for labor peace and an end to attacks on the fundamental legitimacy of the regime. The church would guarantee the arrangement.

That June, shortly after negotiating the agreement, Cardinal Wyszynski died at the age of eighty. He had been imprisoned by the Communist regime from 1953 to 1956. Now he received a state funeral that rivaled the funerals of Winston Churchill and Charles de Gaulle for national pomp. The president of Poland and three deputy prime ministers came to the funeral to honor the cardinal. They stood with a quarter million other Poles in Victory Square in Warsaw under a forty-three-foot-high wooden cross that proclaimed the triumph of Christianity.

Later that year, in December 1981, a reorganized Polish government imposed martial law and drove the Solidarity movement underground. That Solidarity was a religious movement no one, least of all the Soviets, could deny. In November 1981, *Pravda* denounced "religious fanaticism" as a grave challenge to socialism; failure to contain it, *Pravda* said, was at the root of the problems in Poland.[16]

Among those who symbolized the religious nature of the uprising against the Soviet oppressors was Father Jerzy Popieluszko. Father Jerzy's lifelong hero, Maximilian Kolbe, had given his life for another inmate at Auschwitz during World War II. Now, as I describe in detail in *Being the Body*, Father Jerzy felt a call to lay down his own life for his brothers.

Soon after the birth of Solidarity, Father Jerzy preached among the striking workers in Warsaw's huge steel works. He showed them how alcoholism contributed to their oppression: If their drinking caused absenteeism or mistakes at work, it could be used to blackmail them. After that, alcoholism dropped dramatically.

Not long after martial law was imposed, Father Jerzy instituted a monthly "Mass for the Homeland," dedicated to all victims of the repressive regime. Eventually, thousands, then tens of thousands, attended these services at St. Stanislaw Kostka, with Father Jerzy ministering from a balcony and the people fanned out in the courtyard and streets below.

The pale, gaunt priest spoke without flair or passion. Yet his words themselves were filled with power.

"A man who bears witness to the truth can be free even though he might be in prison ... The essential thing in the process of liberating man and the nation is to overcome fear ... We fear suffering, we fear losing material good, we fear losing freedom or our work. And then we act contrary to our consciences, thus muzzling the truth. We can overcome fear only if we accept suffering in the name of a greater value. If the truth becomes for us a value worthy of suffering and risk, then we shall overcome fear—the direct reason for our enslavement.

"*A Christian must be a sign of contradiction in the world ... A Christian is one who all his life chooses between good and evil, lies and truth, love and hatred, God and Satan ... Today more than ever there is a need for our light to shine, so that through us, through our deeds, through our choices, people can see the Father who is in Heaven.*"

Father Jerzy's influence did not escape the notice of the authorities. The secret police followed him everywhere. On the first anniversary of martial law, a pipe bomb sailed through the front window of his small flat, exploding in his sitting room.

Then, on October 19, 1984, while driving back to Warsaw from Bydgoszcz where he had celebrated a special mass and delivered a homily called "Overcome Evil with Good," Father Jerzy disappeared.

Thousands prayed for him in churches all over Poland. The steelworkers stopped their work in order to pray and threatened a national strike if their priest was not returned to them. The universities smoldered with unrest.

On the last Sunday of October, as fifty thousand people filled St. Stanislaw Kostka in an emotional Mass for the Homeland and listened in tears to a tape of Father Jerzy's final Sermon, Father Antoni Lewek, one of the thirty priests at the altar, received word: "Just a moment ago it was announced on television that Father Jerzy's body has been found in the Vistula River."

"I shall never forget what happened," Father Lewek said later. "In a second people went down on their knees, crying and shouting; what we had feared most, the worst, had happened...

"And then something very moving happened. This crying crowd managed to show that they could forgive. Three times they repeated after the priest: 'And forgive us our trespasses as we forgive them that trespass against us.' It was a Christian answer to the unchristian deed of the murderers."

On November 2, the day of Father Jerzy's funeral, people marched the streets past the secret-police headquarters bearing banners reading, "We forgive."

Regardless of their expertise in murdering the body, the executioners could not kill the soul. Father Jerzy had taught his people well.

By the end of the eighties, Poland's problems, including a $38.9 billion debt and continuous consumer shortages, had driven the government to desperation. As a result, the authorities did the unthinkable: They opened avenues for discussion with their longtime opponents.

Solidarity representatives who had spent time in jail during martial law now found themselves being wooed by party members offering to reinstate the union and give it a share of parliamentary power—if Solidarity would, in turn, assure the government's continued control of the parliament.

In June of 1989, Poland's elections made it clear that Solidarity had won everywhere. Many leading Communists, running unopposed, had failed to get enough votes to win. The power struggle continued through the summer, however, since the party still controlled a portion of the government. But by August 19, President Jaruzelski had appointed Tadeusz Mazowiecki as prime minister of Poland.

Mazowiecki, a journalist, a devout Roman Catholic, and an advisor to Solidarity leader Lech Walesa, had the heady distinction of being the first non-Communist to head a government in Eastern Europe since Stalin had imposed his Soviet-style Communism there after World War II.

In Hungary that September, Hungarian troops tore down their barbed-wire fences and watchtowers on the border with Austria. Since early 1988 the Hungarians had been able to travel more freely, but this physical opening of the border crossing meant that it was now possible to walk from Hungary into Austria—and on into Western Germany.[17]

And at midnight on September 13, 1989, the Hungarians went further, formally suspending their agreement with East Germany and officially opening their western border. Within three days, fifteen thousand East Germans had headed for freedom.

As more and more special trains were added to the freedom railroad from east to west, the hundreds of thousands who chose to remain in East Germany took to the churches and the streets. In Leipzig, Dresden, Halle, Weimar, and Wittenberg, churches were filled. Monday evening prayer services at St. Nikolai's in Leipzig overflowed, and after the services, the people spilled outside to march for freedom.

Fifteen hundred people crowded into Leipzig's Evangelical Reformed Church on Monday evenings, though the building seated only 550. Meanwhile, people were spilling out of the doors of the larger churches in the city centers. The huge Church of the Cross in Dresden was packed, as was Gethsemane Church in East Berlin.

Clearly, the people of East Germany had had enough of slavery, and Communism's triumphal forty-year anniversary celebration on October 7 was not quite the event the Party had planned. In East Berlin, Lutheran bishops boycotted the affair, and riot police broke up a peaceful candlelight vigil of some fifteen hundred protesters.

On October 9, after the usual Monday night prayer meeting at Leipzig's Nikolai church, 150,000 people took to the streets.

"We are the people!" they shouted.

State security forces and riot police stood by with live ammunition, but this time, at least, blood was not shed.

On October 19, Bishop Leich arrived at the party offices for his scheduled meeting with Communist leader Erich Honecker. After the mass demonstrations of October 9 and the averting of disaster, Honecker had sent for the bishop to discuss the church's role in the protests erupting all over East Germany. Instead of meeting with Honecker, however, Bishop Leich found himself the first official visitor of a new prime minister.

Secretly, the day before, the man who had been the leader of the East German Communist establishment for eighteen years had fallen from power, but not before replacing himself with his protégé, Egon Krenz.

Krenz hastened to present himself as a younger, more sophisticated leader, aware of the people's discontent. Within a day or two, however, angry citizens were bold enough to shout down the East German party chief.

"You are finished!" they cried. "Give us free elections!"

On November 9, work crews in Germany embarked on a deconstruction project the people had awaited for twenty-eight years. Several days earlier the entire Communist cabinet of the German Democratic Republic had resigned — and today, the Berlin Wall was coming down.

It turned into a celebration the world would never forget.

The people of Czechoslovakia were also on the road to freedom. During the third week of November, 1989, all of Czechoslovakia seemed to be in the streets, shouting for change and demanding the resignation of Milos Jakes, Czechoslovakia's hard-line Communist leader.

Those not crowding Wenceslas Square watched in fascination as the rallies unfolded on television. There was playwright and freedom fighter Vaclav Havel, with hundreds of thousands cheering him madly. A worker named Honza Lexa, interviewed by a reporter, was saying openly that she thought the government had been lying. "What is the government afraid of?" she asked.

Suddenly their screens went black. The voice of an announcer soon came on, explaining that some unidentified television workers had disagreed with Lexa's statement. Thirty-five minutes later the broadcast was reinstated and the people heard the strong voice of Father Vaclav Maly from Wenceslas Square.

"There can be no confidence in the leadership of a state that refuses to tell people the truth," shouted Maly, a Catholic priest whose propensity for truth-telling had annoyed the government for years. Long barred from performing priestly duties, Maly was reading from an open letter from Cardinal Frantisek Tomasek, who had prayed for the day when the people would no longer accept lies.

Maly had prayed for this day as well. Not for his own advancement, but for the proclamation of gospel truth against the government's lies. After his clerical license had been revoked in 1979, he had cleaned toilets in the Prague subways and worked as a coal stoker in a hotel.

Maly knew the police listened in on his conversations through a microphone hidden in a ceiling light fixture; he hoped they paid special attention when he prayed aloud to God for his nation.

In a demonstration along the Letna Plain, the huge riverfront park bordering the northern edge of downtown Prague, Father Maly had an unexpected opportunity to practice the faith he had learned from years of sacrifice.

As Maly was speaking before a crowd of half a million demonstrators, a young police officer pushed his way forward, climbed the steps to the podium, and explained to the shocked crowd that he had been among the police officers who had beaten a group of student protesters several weeks earlier. "I am sorry," he stammered. "Please forgive me."

Maly put his arm around the weeping officer, then spoke firmly to the crowd about the Christian duty to forgive. "Let us pray," he shouted.

And in a voice five hundred thousand strong, they affirmed the faith the Communists had not been able to steal: "Our Father, who art in heaven ... Thy will be done on earth, as it is in heaven ... forgive us our trespasses, as we forgive those who trespass against us."

Soon after, the people received the news that Czechoslovakia's Communist party leadership had resigned. The nation's long-ago springtime dreams were finally coming to harvest.

The people of Romania could not believe that such changes might possibly come to their own land. Nicolae Ceausescu was too powerful, his Securitate too insidiously pervasive.

Nevertheless, believers in Timisoura spent hours in prayer. Lying prostrate on the cold floors of their small flats, they were warmed by a spiritual passion that caused them to thunder a bold and unlikely prayer: "Lord, help our nation. Turn your face to our land. Bring revival to Romania—and bring it through Timisoara!"

God answered that prayer. And help for Romania did indeed begin in Timisoara.

On December 15, 1989, government agents came to the home of Laszlo Tokes, the dangerously influential, anti-communist pastor of the Hungarian Reformed Church. Protesters from his church blockaded the door. Their numbers swelled, and soon thousands of citizens filled Timisoara's central square. Christians from all over the city rallied and prayed that this might be the beginning of the end of the godless tyranny of Ceausescu's regime.

Some believers held back from the protest demonstrations at first. Was this their answer to prayer? Surely they would give their lives for Christ and the cause of the gospel—but was this that time? Or was it merely a political situation? They were ready, but they wanted to be wise.

As they prayed for wisdom, they also brought tea and soup and blankets to warm the people in the square. As they did so, they believed God was leading them to join these demonstrators against a dictator who had despised His name.

Meanwhile, in Bucharest, Ceausescu convened a meeting of the Political Executive Committee of the Romanian Communist party, furious that the military had yet to open fire on the Timisoura demonstrators. He gave orders to warn the demonstrators—and shoot all who resisted.

Supposing the situation resolved, Ceausescu left for a three-day trip to Iran, leaving his army and faithful Securitat agents to carry out his violent measures. What he didn't realize was that his army was not entirely with him.

Marius Miron was on the streets of Timisoara on the evening of December 17 after Ceausescu had given his order to shoot. Near Laszlo Toke's church he saw tear gas canisters and water cannons. On the city square a huge bonfire raged in front of a bookshop: People had broken the windows and were dragging out books by and about the Ceausescus, throwing them into the flames. Near the opera house he saw soldiers firing their guns into the air; he heard the sounds of breaking glass and people shouting slogans.

He was at the corner of Liberty Square and Karl Marx Street when he saw a group of ten people shot down by soldiers. Miron, a trained medical assistant, ran and bent over the man closest to him; the man's femoral artery had been severed by a bullet, and he was bleeding to death.

When Miron stood up to take off his belt to make a tourniquet, he saw a soldier take deliberate aim at him and fire. He felt no pain. His leg just suddenly blew up. He hit the ground, his limb shattered, and began to drag himself backward by his elbows until someone picked him up and took him to the hospital. The shooting continued.

Gradually, hundreds, then thousands, of people flooded the streets, making their way toward Timisoara's main square, carrying signs and banners.

"Liberty," they shouted. "Freedom!"

In nearby Arad, Nellie Iovin knew about the drama being played out in Timisoara. Then Arad's own uprising began as a hundred thousand people gathered in Arad's main square in front of the city hall, where they were soon ringed by tanks and soldiers.

As Nellie and other Christians approached the square, they had to pass these tanks and a line of soldiers. Would they shoot? Fearful but determined, Nellie and the others knelt in front of the guns and began to pray; the soldiers let them pass.

Here, as in Timisoara, the Christians in the crowd shouted slogans reflecting their defiance of forty-five years of attempted communist brainwashing. A hundred thousand people shouted as one, "God exists! God is with us!"

Across the street from city hall, Baptist pastor Mihai Gongola was given a microphone. His main theme was the people's slogan: "God is with us!"

Pastor Doru Popua preached to the crowd, as well. "Finally we are free," he shouted. "But some of us were free already: We had been made free by God." He gestured toward the Communist headquarters.

"We will write on this building three words," he said. "*Via, veritas, vita*: the way, the truth, the life."

On December 21, with Romania on the verge of total upheaval, Ceausescu staged a rally in Bucharest. Appearing on a balcony high above the people, Ceausescu intoned with unintended irony, "I would like to extend to you ... warm revolutionary greetings."

Suddenly, there was a movement in the crowd. Undistinguished shouts. A sense of confusion. Then a faint cry began: "Timisoara!" "Timisoura!"

Several people unfurled a banner they had hidden under their coats: "Down with Ceausescu!" A group of people began singing "Romanians, Awake," the same song the crowd had sung outside the church of Laszlo Tokes.

As Ceausescu tried once more to speak to the crowds, his once docile people booed and threw their shoes at him. Furious, the ugly little man turned back into the Central Committee building and ordered the army to fire.

By this time, however, many members of the army had defected to the people. Vasile Milea, minister of defense, refused to give the firing order to his troops. When a crowd stormed the Central Committee building, Ceausescu, his wife, and a few aides fled by helicopter from the roof.

Just as the news of Ceausescu's flight reached Timisoara, Pastor Peter Dugulescu was poised to speak to the two hundred thousand people assembled in the city square. On this night, just hours before Christmas, people in the crowd had requested that a pastor come to preach to them.

Dugulescu took the microphone. "I'm Pastor Peter Dugulescu from the First Baptist Church, Timisoara," he began. "I have come to speak to you in the name of God, as you wanted. For almost forty-five years — my age, unfortunately — we have been told there is no God. The Communists wanted to take God away from our hearts, from our minds, from our families, from our schools. I want to speak to you in the name of this God."

Cheers interrupted him periodically as he continued for a few minutes, then asked the people to pray with him. "This is a historic moment. Let us turn our hearts to God. Please follow me in the Lord's Prayer."

As far as Dugulescu he could see, a tidal wave of people knelt on the pavement and began to pray.

As Christmas dawn crept across the land of Romania, the church bells rang for the first time in forty years. Christians who had not sung carols in public during their lifetimes sang out the good news of Christ's coming: "Immanuel, God with us!"

Ceausescu and his wife were captured almost immediately after their flight from Bucharest. After being tried by a military tribunal for crimes against the people, they were convicted of genocide and executed.

The bells ringing in Romania rang across the rest of Eastern Europe as the people gathered in the streets, hugging each other and weeping for joy, singing Christmas carols with the fervor of newfound freedom.

Meanwhile, in the West, who did reporters give the credit to? Mikhail Gorbachev.

They missed the biggest story of century. Surely bad politics and dismal economics played their part in fueling the unrest over Eastern Europe. But man does not live by bread alone, and in Eastern Europe, the people were marching for far more than bread. They were marching for a freedom that transcends the physical—the freedom of the human spirit.

As *Time* magazine celebrated Gorbachev as the "Man of the Decade," Vaclav Havel—now president of Czechoslovakia—adjusted his glasses and began his New Year's Day address to his people.

"Our first [pre-Communist] president wrote, 'Jesus and not Caesar' ... This idea has once again been reawakened in us."

Christ or Caesar? This was the choice made all across Eastern Europe. And what began in Nowa Huta with the raising of the cross in the public square came to its denouement three decades later in, of all places, the heart of the Communist behemoth.

It was May Day, 1990. The place: Moscow's Red Square.

"Is it straight, Father?" one Orthodox priest asked another, shifting the heavy, eight-foot crucifix on his shoulder.

"Yes," said the other, "It is straight."

Together the two priests, along with a group of parishioners holding ropes that steadied the beams of the huge cross, walked the parade route. Before them had passed the official might of the Union of Soviet Socialist Republics: the usual May Day procession of tanks, missiles, troops, and salutes to the Communist party elite.

As the throng passed directly in front of the Soviet leader standing in his place of honor, the priests hoisted their heavy burden toward the sky. The cross emerged from the crowd. As it did, the figure of Jesus Christ obscured the giant poster faces of Karl Marx, Friedrich Engles, and Vladimir Lenin that provided the backdrop for Gorbachev's reviewing stand.

"Mikhail Sergeyevich!" one of the priests shouted. "Mikhail Sergeyevich! Christ is risen!"

A few months later, the Soviet Union was officially dissolved.

Each uprising of the Polish people against their government and its Russian masters was triggered by Christian outrage over the brutality of the regime, its indifference to human needs, its suppression of fundamental rights, and its incessant lying. Christianity possessed the hearts of the people and shaped Polish culture. This was evidenced at the height of the Gdansk strike when Western newspapers published front-page photos showing strikers in the Gdansk shipyards kneeling to receive communion. Such a sight was a shock to jaded, secularized eyes. Union workers in other industrialized countries are often part of the anticlerical left. In Poland the Christian workers are loyal to the church against the state.

Why, during that critical time in history, was the church so much stronger in Poland than almost anywhere else in the world? Why was it so much stronger than in Hungary and elsewhere in Eastern Europe?

The election of a Polish pope was surely a factor. So was the fact that Christianity had been firmly established in Poland for a thousand years. But a primary reason was the church's long tradition of resistance to secular power.

From 1795 to 1918 the Polish nation was divided among the Prussian, Austrian, and Russian empires, and church authorities resisted all three. In 1874 the archbishop of Poznan was imprisoned for opposing Bismarck's program of requiring religious instruction in German. The czar's plans for forced Russification in eastern Poland ran into similar opposition. From 1918 to 1939, during the period of the First Republic, the church remained independent from the Polish republic. The church also resisted the Nazi regime and suffered greatly for it. A third of the Catholic clergy in Poland were executed by the Germans or died in concentration camps.

When the Communists imprisoned him in 1953, Cardinal Wyszynski reflected that of his seventeen seminary classmates, only he had thus far escaped being sent to German or Russian concentration camps. Cardinal Wyszynski confided a somewhat wry reflection to his diary: "Most of the priests and bishops with whom I worked had experienced prisons. Something would have been wrong if I had not experienced imprisonment."[18]

A church with such a history, led by such tough-minded men, was ready for anything the new totalitarian state could devise. The Polish church was one of the few in Eastern Europe to have avoided entanglement with the state. Many other church bodies allowed themselves to become closely identified with secular authorities, and in doing so, the official church in these countries lost the people. They became mere puppets of their Communist ruler.

The late French philosopher Jacques Ellul points out this lesson, one that the church around the world must always remember: "Collaboration with power, whether Communist or not, is always ruinous for the church. If the church exists, if it is to have legitimacy in the eyes of the people, it must always stand erect as a counter-power to political power."[19]

Cardinal Wyszynski understood this. In prison in 1953, alone but supremely confident, he wrote a prophetic comment in his diary: "Any form of government, no matter how ruthless, will slowly cool and wane as it runs up against difficulties that the bureaucrat cannot resolve without cooperation from the people. Somehow the people must be taken into account."[20]

When the time came to reach the people, the Polish state found the church already there. It had been there for centuries.

The struggle between church and state has lasted for hundreds of years in Poland. In Nicaragua it began in the early seventies when the Catholic Church opposed the right-wing tyranny of the dictator Anastasio Somoza.

Jimmy Hassan wasn't surprised when the police came for him in October 1985. He had become national director of Campus Crusade for Christ in Nicaragua in 1982, when the revolutionary Sandinista government started serious persecution of evangelicals. An officer at the security police headquarters held up a copy of Campus Crusade's basic literature, a small booklet called "The Four Spiritual Laws."

"Is this yours?" he snarled.

Hassan admitted it was. The officer ripped it up. Several agents shoved him in a car and drove him to Campus Crusade's Managua headquarters. There they confiscated about 2000 "Four Spiritual Laws" booklets and hundreds of books, including Bibles.

The police then locked Hassan alone in a room at the Interior Ministry. Hassan thought of his wife and three children. He thought of the Moravian pastors in the remote Atlantic provinces of Nicaragua who had been murdered by Sandinista gangs. He thought of his evangelistic work and the churches that were growing. People were being saved despite the persecution. It gave him satisfaction to know he was being held because the Marxist authorities hated Campus Crusade's success. But he wondered whether he would ever see his family again.

The security forces released him in late afternoon, and Hassan went home. At 11:00 P.M. the agents returned with a summons to report back to the Interior Ministry the next morning.

The interrogators threatened him with prison. They said he would be beaten if he did not confess. Hassan took these threats seriously, but he would not budge. Then a tall man came into the room, took out a pistol, and held it to Hassan's head.

"You have one more chance to confess," one of the agents said. "Do it now. You are a paid American agent. Tell us about it. If you don't, you'll be killed."

"My only activity is to preach the gospel," Hassan replied.

The tall man pressed the pistol against Hassan's forehead. Hassan could feel the pressure increase as the man pressed his finger on the trigger. Harder. He pulled the trigger.

Hassan heard a click.... The gun was empty.

Hassan was released later that day with threats that he would be killed the next time they had to deal with him. Just before Christmas that year, the Hassan family escaped to Mexico. In exile, Jimmy spoke for other evangelicals of his country: "No matter what the threat, no matter what the conditions, no matter what the persecution, we will not stop preaching the gospel to the people of Nicaragua."[21]

In 1982, the year Jimmy Hassan took over Campus Crusade, Nicaragua's evangelicals were a minority in a Catholic country. Traditionally, they avoided politics. That meant the Protestants had little leverage in high places; most didn't know what was coming when a Marxist regime began to consolidate its power.[22]

In May the authorities began to confiscate evangelical churches, many of them in remote Atlantic provinces far from the capital and the inconvenient scrutiny of the Western press.

In August Interior Minister Borge told a mob that Protestants were collaborating with the CIA and the defeated Somoza regime.

"Que se vayan, que se vayan." "Get them out. Get them out," chanted a mob of militants. They seized more Protestant churches.

At the same time the Sandinista government moved against the Catholic Church, which claimed the loyalty of 80 percent of the Nicaraguan people. They pressured the Catholic schools, replacing loyal Catholic teachers with Cuban-trained personnel indoctrinated in Marxist ideology. The schools were forced to adopt a new curriculum featuring crude Marxist propaganda.

The visit of Pope John Paul II in 1983 was marked by open hostility between the Sandinista regime and the Catholic Church. Government officials lined the ramp when the pope descended from his plane on his arrival in Managua. Ernesto Cardenal, a Catholic priest who continued to serve as a member of the revolutionary government despite a papal ruling that he step down, knelt to kiss the pope's ring. John Paul II angrily snatched it away, thus making dramatically clear to those watching his disapproval of priests serving in the Sandinista government.

The climax of the pope's visit came when he celebrated Mass in a public square in the center of Managua. The pope stood alone on a platform while Sandinista officials held back the huge, friendly crowd. Then they took over the front seats and for the benefit of the grinding television cameras, shook their fists and screamed at the pope. Each time they did so he lifted his crucifix higher over his head.

The Sandinista officials were genuinely angry. John Paul II, a remarkable linguist, was conducting the Mass in the language of the Miskito Indians. Symbolically he was conveying a powerful truth: God offers grace to the people you killed. He was also indicting the Sandinistas. The crowd cheered; the protesters howled with rage.

Most Christians, including the Catholic bishops, welcomed the 1979 revolution that toppled the corrupt regime of Anastasio Somoza. Archbishop Miguel Obando y Bravo had been a persistent and effective critic of Somoza for a decade. In fact, the revolution probably would not have triumphed without the active support of the bishops and the great mass of clergy and lay leaders.

The Marxist Sandinistas were a minority in the broad coalition that made up the revolutionary government that took over in 1979. By 1980, however, the Sandinistas had forced most of their democratic colleagues out of the governing junta by using time-honored Marxist techniques: control of the army and ruthless, single-minded pursuit of their goals, unhampered by democratic procedure. But the Sandinistas could not subdue the church. It had wisely kept a distance from the state before the Sandinistas came to power. The people were with the church.

So a new strategy emerged: the Sandinistas dressed the Communist program in Christian language and raised the tactics of Lenin and Hungary's Rakosi to new heights.

During the 1980s four Catholic priests held cabinet office in the Sandinista government. Sandinista officials spoke of the "Kingdom of God" coming through the revolution, and many Sandinistas passionately regarded themselves as members of *la iglesia popular* (the people's church) and follow-ers of *el Dios de los pobres* (the God of the Poor). Protestant sympathizers with the Sandinista regime acted through the Center for Promotion and Development. One of its leaders declared in 1982 that "it is required that we as Christians understand that biblical faith is inseparable from political militancy."[23]

The strategy was expounded by Daniel Ortega, the junta leader, in his address at Managua airport welcoming Pope John Paul II. The true Christ-ians in Nicaragua, he said, were "basing themselves on faith corresponding to the revolution."[24]

The vehicle for this congruence of Christianity and revolutionary politics was liberation theology, a movement that equated partisan political involve-ment with Christian commitment. As the Protestant liberation theologian Jose Miguez Bonino noted, "Latin American theology becomes a militant theology—a partisan theology, perhaps."[25]

"Our only solution is Marxism," said Fr. Ernesto Cardenal, the Nicara-guan minister of culture in the eighties and one of the four priests in the government. "The revolution and the Kingdom of heaven mentioned in the gospel are the same thing. A Christian should embrace Marxism if he wants to be with God and all men."[26] Or as a revolutionary poster put it, "Faith without revolution is dead."[27]

This line of thinking guts the gospel. If a Christian must embrace Marx-ism and revolution to do God's will, then something was lacking in the atonement and revelation of Jesus Christ.

The paradoxical end to this hall of mirrors is the bizarre conclusion that Christians need Marxists far more than Marxists need Christians.

Despite co-opting and oppression, however, Catholic as well as Protestant churches continued to resist the Sandinistas. For years, church authorities had denounced and opposed the tyranny of the right. During the eighties, they denounced and opposed the tyranny of the left. They resisted pres-sures to do the conservatives' bidding for the sake of "order, stability, and tradition," and resisted the left's demands to identify the gospel with "equal-ity, justice, and peace." They demonstrated the first law of survival for the church under pressure from secular authorities: Do not legitimize tyranny. Remain aloof from the enticements and threats of the secular authority. Be faithful to God alone.

In 1990, after a twelve-year rule, the Sandinistas were voted out of office. But in 2006, the Nicaraguan people once again voted in Daniel Ortega (and a second Sandinista government). Ortega had managed to persuade enough Nicaraguans that the former leader of the Soviet-backed Communist regime was now more Catholic than the Pope. The future of Nicaragua remains uncertain.

These stories of the church in Eastern Europe and Nicaragua are just a part of the picture. They are, however, representative of the raging conflict in the latter half of the twentieth century. With rare exceptions, the church was driven underground or made a puppet of the state in Marxist-dominated countries. At no other time in human history did so much of the world come under the dark cloud of an oppressive regime consciously determined to eliminate religious influence from culture.

But we can be grateful that the Kingdom of God does not depend on the structures of man. Though much of the world still lives under tyranny, the Kingdom of God remains visible. It is visible when leaders like Jimmy Hassan and John Paul II take their stand. It is visible when ordinary people refuse to compromise what is most precious in their lives.

That was the case in the little town of Garwolin, Poland, in March 1984.[28]

The government of Polish Prime Minister Jaruzelski had ordered crucifixes removed from classroom walls, just as they had been banned in factories, hospitals, and other public institutions. Catholic bishops attacked the ban that had stirred waves of anger and resentment all across Poland. Ultimately the government relented, insisting that the law remain on the books, but agreeing not to press for removal of the crucifixes, particularly in the schoolrooms.

But one zealous Communist school administrator in Garwolin decided that the law was the law. So one evening he had seven large crucifixes removed from lecture halls where they had hung since the school's founding in the twenties.

Days later, a group of parents entered the school and hung more crosses. The administrator promptly had these taken down as well.

The next day two-thirds of the school's six hundred students staged a sit-in. When heavily armed riot police arrived, the students were forced into the streets. Then they marched, crucifixes held high, to a nearby church where they were joined by twenty-five hundred other students from nearby schools for a morning of prayer in support of the protest. Soldiers surrounded the church. But the pictures from inside of students holding crosses high above their heads flashed around the world. So did the words of the priest who delivered the message to the weeping congregation that morning.

"There is no Poland without a cross."

The story of the long battle between the followers of Communism and the followers of Christ is a parable for believers living in the twenty-first century: It reveals the power of the Church to bring down the most oppressive earthly power. It's an instructive lesson today, as the world wages what will surely be a decades-long battle to preserve civilization against inroads by the fanatical followers of radical Islam.

The standoff with Islamo-fascists raises many of the same questions faced squarely by Communism's victims: Are people willing to live without freedom, without human rights? Are they willing to be forced out of their homeland, as is happening to the Chaldean Christians of Iraq? Are they willing to live under oppressive *sharia* law in Saudi Arabia, Afghanistan, Pakistan, Iran, and the rest of the Muslim world—governments that send the religious police to hunt down, torture, and kill Christians and all others who defy those who abuse them in the name of Islam?

Just as fax machines helped bring down communism and brought freedom to the people of Eastern Europe, the Internet threatens to bring down radical Islam. Just as the Communist era represented a battle between two religious views—aggressive humanism on the one hand and Christianity and Judaism on the other—so, too, is the struggle today a religious battle: It's a clash between two very different worldviews regarding the nature of God and the nature of man.

The conflict we face today is, at its heart, no different from the conflict we faced during the latter half of the twentieth century. Islamo-fascism is something Hitler would have recognized and approved of: The leaders of radical Islam take their inspiration from some of the same thinkers that roused the future Fuehrer.

As we enter this, the latest chapter in the clash of civilizations, will we remember the hard-won lessons of the past?

14

CONFLICT
AND COMPROMISE
IN THE WEST

It is bad to live under a prince who permits nothing, but much worse to live under one who permits everything.

JOHN CALVIN

Before the War of the Crosses erupted in the streets of Poland in 1984, a similar battle had already been lost in the U.S. In 1980 the Supreme Court declared unconstitutional a Kentucky law requiring that the Ten Commandments be posted in public-school classrooms.[1]

In Poland the outcry against removal of the crucifixes led to mass defiance. The crucifixes were reinstated. But in Kentucky, when the offending commandments were taken down, the few holdouts, threatened with court action, soon capitulated.

What a repressive government could not force upon Poland was quietly accepted in an indifferent West. The Kentucky case is less important on its own merits than as a symbol of a growing movement in the courts that is narrowing the influence of religion in American life. Of the many cases, none has been more revealing—and bizarre—than one originating in the quiet Oklahoma town of Collinsville.

"Welcome to Collinsville," proclaims the sign marking the city limits where State Highway 20 slices through this small Oklahoma town and slows down to fit the lifestyles of its three thousand citizens. Many of them are retired, enjoying Collinsville's grid of neat streets, restaurants, theaters. During the 1980s, when this case was fought, residents could choose from five feed-and-seed stores, eleven grocery stores, two funeral homes, and twenty-nine churches.

Collinsville's teenagers hold a somewhat dimmer view of its charms. "There's nothin' to do but get drunk and drag Main," said a young waitress at the Tastee Freez.

But in 1984 Collinsville became the focus of a national media spotlight when one of its citizens, thirty-six-year-old nurse Marian Guinn, sued her church for invasion of privacy.[2]

Marian Guinn was raised in Kansas as a Southern Baptist. She married at eighteen and had a child at nineteen. Three other children followed, then a divorce. Guinn wanted to start over. In 1974 she moved to Collinsville, about twenty-five miles north of Tulsa, to live with her sister, Sue Hibbard.

Sue was active at the Collinsville Church of Christ, and Marian began attending the 110-member church with her sister. The members welcomed her. They baby-sat her children while she attended a high-school equivalency class; they provided food, clothing, and Christmas presents after Guinn moved into her own small rented house; the elders drove her to the hospital when her daughter had pneumonia. Later the church gave Guinn a car.

Guinn joined the church and was baptized. She eventually enrolled in college, then nursing school, and seemed to be getting her life together. But after a few years Marian Guinn's church attendance began to slip. Perhaps it was her school schedule; or maybe it was her romance with Pat Sharpe, part owner of Howland and Sharpe Pharmacy and former mayor of Collinsville.

Sharpe, like Marian Guinn, was divorced, and neighbors began to notice his blue-and-white Cadillac parked in her driveway late at night. In Collinsville their relationship was the juicy gossip item it might not have been in New York or Los Angeles. But to the Church of Christ leadership it was a spiritual problem. The elders felt that Guinn's relationship with Sharpe and lack of participation in the church were evidence of spiritual wavering. During the course of a conversation with one of the elders on an unrelated matter, Pat Sharpe admitted he and Marian were sleeping together.

In spite of the later assertion of Guinn's lawyer that "he was a single man. She was a single lady. And this is America," the Collinsville Church of Christ adhered to a different standard: the biblical law from the Old and New Testaments stating that sexual relations outside of marriage — fornication — is sin. They also abided by the biblical mandate that the church has a distinct responsibility "not to associate with sexually immoral people"[3] and that rebuking their sin must be public "so that the others may take warning."[4]

Church elders Ron Witten, Ted Moody, and Allen Cash met with Marian Guinn three times, praying with her and asking her to break off her relationship with Sharpe and return to the church's fellowship. Guinn tearfully refused. The elders said they would give her time to reconsider, but after a certain date they must make a public announcement urging the congregation to withdraw fellowship from her because of her lack of repentance. This was in accordance with the mandates of Matthew 18:15–17 and with the practices of the church.

At this point Guinn, a slight woman with large dark eyes, was angry and embarrassed. She scribbled a letter to the elders: "I do not want my name mentioned before the church except to tell them that I withdraw my membership immediately!" she wrote furiously. "I have never fully adopted your doctrine and never will!... You have no right to get up and say anything against me in church.... I have no choice but for all of us [herself and her children] to attend another church—another denomination where men do not set themselves up as judges for God. He does His own judging."

The elders maintained that the church was not some sort of club. Guinn had agreed to abide by its doctrine and adhere to scriptural mandates. She knew, or should have known, the consequences of her actions.

At the end of the Sunday-morning service on October 4, 1983, elder Ted Moody read a short letter to the congregation: "After much time spent in counseling, exhorting, encouraging, and prayer, we the elders of the Collinsville Church of Christ have no alternative but to lead in the withdrawing of fellowship from our sister in Christ, Marian Guinn."

Guinn accused the elders of libel. But to be libelous, the things being said have to be untrue, and Guinn acknowledged in court depositions that she was having an affair. She was content, therefore, to file a $1.3 million civil lawsuit against the church and its elders for invasion of privacy and emotional distress.

A Tulsa court took jurisdiction over the case, and in March 1984, a twelve-member jury sided with Guinn and awarded her $390,000 for her distress. One juror summed up their reasoning: "I don't see what right the church has to tell people how to live."

This is the kind of case that makes everyone mad.

Christians see within it a takeover of the church's realm by the state. After all, people don't join a church blindly, not knowing what is expected of them. And if the church can't hold its members to a biblical standard, what is it allowed to do? Become a Sunday-morning hymn-singing club? What right does the government have to prevent a church from maintaining standards of holiness, one of its primary purposes?

Meanwhile, many secularists view the elders' actions as the worst type of backwoods inquisition. Guinn's colorful Tulsa lawyer, Tommy Frasier, called the elders a "goon squad" and "the ayatollahs of Collinsville."

"It doesn't matter if she was fornicating up and down the street," Frasier declared angrily. "It doesn't give [the church] the right to stick their noses in."

One doubts that the citizens of Collinsville would agree that Guinn or anyone else has an inherent right to fornicate up and down Highway 20. But Frasier's words reflect what has become a cardinal rule of American life: the right to personal autonomy.

The Guinn ruling pushes the privatization of religion to the extreme, allowing government to restrict religion to an internal matter bearing no relationship to one's behavior. It also says that the church has lost its right to define its own rules for membership.* And as Richard Neuhaus has written, "When an institution that is voluntary in membership cannot define the conditions of belonging, that institution in fact ceases to exist."[5]

But the church's principal task, as we have seen earlier, is a spiritual one —to proclaim the Good News and to cultivate holy living among its members. If a church cannot do this, it no longer has a purpose for existing.

The Guinn case was one of the earlier assaults in the present conflict between Christians and the state that have narrowed the influence of religion in American life. Others have dealt with equally sensitive issues, like religious activity on public property. The Evansville, Indiana, case is one.

At the Harper Elementary School in Evansville, teacher's aide Mary May and several Christian co-workers had met before classes every Tuesday morning since early 1981 for prayer, Bible reading, and discussion. Students were not allowed to participate. But in 1983 the principal told May and her seven fellow Christians that there were to be no more Tuesday-morning meetings—or they would all be fired. Mary May eventually sued the board of education and the superintendent of schools, claiming that the school

---

*The government has consistently held that people not discriminate even in private organizations; but if a policy applies equally to all, it is nondiscriminatory. The Church of Christ rules applied equally to all. Guinn willingly surrendered her right to privacy when she joined the church. And while in some churches she might have been allowed to quietly resign, the particular doctrine of the Church of Christ, to which Guinn subscribed, does not permit resignation.

board had violated her First Amendment rights to free speech, free association, and the free exercise of religion. She also argued that other teachers and aides discussed politics, economics, and sports over their morning coffee before school; why couldn't she and her friends talk about God?

A school-board representative replied that impressionable elementary-school kids might see "her carry a Bible to and from a meeting in their school, even if it is before classes. To children, teachers are very strong authority figures." And, he added, school officials would be forced to make sure that no Bibles or other religious materials were left behind. "We don't want the children exposed to them," he concluded ominously.[6]

Even the right of religious organizations to insist that their employees adhere to their beliefs has been challenged, as in the much-publicized 1986 case of the Dayton Christian School. The Court ruled that it was "unlawful discriminatory practice" for any employer to refuse to hire an employee because of the religion or sex of that person.[7] By this ruling, notes constitutional lawyer William Ball, St. John's Church, a Lutheran congregation could not, solely on the basis of the applicant's religion, refuse to hire a pastor who was of some other religious faith; nor could St. Mary's Seminary, a Roman Catholic seminary, refuse to hire a woman as an instructor solely on the ground of her sex — in spite of the Canon Law of the Catholic Church that would forbid use of female instructors within the seminary.*

A number of zoning cases have affected the right of worship in private homes. In Colorado Springs, minister Richard Blanche has been repeatedly cited for holding religious meetings in his home in violation of a city zoning ordinance. In Fairhaven, Massachusetts, local zoning officials ruled that Bible studies were home occupations and therefore prohibited under the

---

Ohio Civil Rights Commission v. Dayton Schools has not been overruled, but the following year the Supreme Court handed down *Corp. of the Presiding Bishop v. Amos*, which upheld a federal law stating that religious organizations don't have to comply with the part of Title VII that prohibits religious discrimination in employment. In that case, a religion employer (a gym run by the LDS church) fired an employee (a maintenance worker) for his religious beliefs. The employee sued for discrimination, but the Supreme Court ruled in favor of the church, upholding Title VII's special exemption for religious organizations. While *Amos* is not directly on point, it demonstrates a much more reasonable approach on the part of the courts to religious employment disputes, one not entangled with the procedural and jurisdictional issues that muddied the waters in *Dayton*. Fortunately, several recent lower court opinions have also reinforced the right of religious organizations to use religious criteria in employment decisions: *Petruska v. Gannon University* (Third Circuit, 2006), and *Tomic. V. Catholic Diocese of Peoria* (Seventh Circuit, 2006).

town's property-use ordinances. In Los Angeles, officials ruled that home-occupancy regulations forbade orthodox Jews from holding prayer meetings in their homes.* As civil-liberties lawyers could not help but note in a Stratford, Connecticut, case, prayer in home Bible studies is penalized while Tupperware parties enjoy the full protection of the Constitution.

In 2001, Congress passed the Religious Land Use and Institutionalized Persons Act (RLUIPA), which protects the rights of houses of worship in zoning disputes. This has given churches some much-needed protection in zoning disputes, but unfortunately, local governments around the country are still all too happy to unlawfully restrict religious worship through zoning laws. A notable RLUIPA case is *Murphy v. New Milford*, in which a local town prohibited weekly Bible studies in a family home. The lower court got it right and protected the Murphys; however, the Second Circuit threw it out on questionable procedural grounds.

America's Founders regarded religion as a positive good—something so foundational that they placed it first in the Bill of Rights. Today we see an almost complete reversal. Recent Supreme Court cases seem to reflect a determination to strip even the thin veneer of religious signs and symbols from culture.

For example, in 1986, Daniel Weisman objected to what he considered an overtly religious invocation at his daughter Merith's high school graduation ceremony, which included a prayer by a Jewish rabbi. He requested a temporary restraining order, which the Rhode Island district court denied. The Weismans attended Merith's graduation (and managed to survive hearing the invocation), but continued litigation. The First Circuit sided with them, and so did the U.S. Supreme Court when the school district appealed. What the Court implied in *Lee v. Weisman* was that adolescents must be protected from being asked to listen politely to even the briefest, blandest, non-coercive, To-Whom-It-May-Concern graduation prayer.

Once again, Justice Kennedy wrote the majority opinion, and once again, Justice Scalia dissented, writing that the Court had laid "waste to a tradition that is as old as public school graduation ceremonies themselves, and that is

---

*In 2005, the Eleventh Circuit ruled on *Konikov v. Orange County*, in which a local government prohibited Orthodox Jews from holding regular prayer meetings in homes but permitted Boy Scouts and other groups to meet in private homes, even if those meetings included the same number of people and occurred with the same frequency as the prayer meetings. In this case, the court came to its senses and ruled in favor of Rabbi Konikov under RLUIPA.

a component of an even more longstanding American tradition of nonsectarian prayer to God at public celebrations generally. As its instrument of destruction, the bulldozer of social engineering, the Court invents a boundless, and boundlessly, manipulable, test of psychological coercion . . ."*

The same year Merith Weisman's father was objecting to his daughter having to hear an invocation, the Almighty was being banished from high school graduation ceremonies all over Los Angeles.

During the spring of 1986 a last-minute decision by the Los Angeles Board of Education took God off the programs of area high school commencements. A lawsuit filed by an area atheist successfully barred prayers, invocations, or religious observances from graduation ceremonies. Even as local schools made sure that offending prayers were removed from the programs, one principal noted, however, that students will, God forbid, occasionally mention Him during a speech. "If you happen to get a kid who's religious, they frequently thank God. That's all right. I'm not going to censor the kids' speeches."[8]

We can be grateful for that, at least—or we could until 2006. That's the year Brittany McComb, an eighteen-year-old valedictorian at Foothill High School in Las Vegas, tried to thank Jesus in her commencement address. But as soon as she said the words, "God is so great that he gave his only Son up," school officials pulled the plug on her microphone, preventing the audience from hearing the rest of her speech. In response, Brittany's 400 fellow graduates and their parents stood and applauded while some shouted "Let her speak!" Brittany, helped by the Rutherford Institute, is suing school officials for violating her rights to religious freedom and free speech.

Good for her. As Rutherford president John Whitehead puts it, if you check your history books for the kind of countries that encourage bureaucrats to pull the plug on religious and political speech, you find, not bastions of freedom, but regimes like Nazi Germany.

---

*American communities also continue to be battered by lawsuits brought by those who object to the public posting of the Ten Commandments. Among recent cases are McCreary County v. ACLU and Van Orden v. Perry, which the Supreme Court handed down on the same day in 2005, and which came to different conclusions. Courts around the country are still trying to sort out these two decisions. And then there are the endless Pledge of Allegiance cases. In 2002, the Ninth Circuit, in Elk Grove Unified School District v. Newdow, threw out the Pledge. The Supreme Court vacated this decision on procedural grounds in 2004. Newdow has since re-filed, and in 2005, a U.S. District Court once again threw out the Pledge. That case is currently on appeal to the Ninth Circuit; oral arguments will likely take place in 2007.

The height of anti-religious hysteria was reached in the mid-eighties in a conflict involving the city seal of Zion, Illinois, which since 1902 had included a cross, dove, crown, scepter, and the words *God Reigns*. The emblem appeared on the city's water tower, badges worn by public officials, and city vehicles.

Robert Sherman, director of the Illinois chapter of the American Atheists, though not a resident of Zion, was so offended by the seal on the water tower that he threatened to sue if it wasn't removed, describing the seal as the "most blatant abuse of religious symbols by a governmental unit in the history of mankind.[9] (Evidently, Sherman had managed to get through his entire life without once seeing any U.S. coins—all of which are engraved with the words "In God We Trust.") The Federal Appeals Court in Chicago agreed that the seal was unconstitutional.*

But where religious symbols have been spared, it has been on grounds that offer little solace to the religious. The celebrated Pawtucket crèche decision is a case in point.

For forty years, one of the highlights for Pawtucket's predominantly Catholic citizenry was the annual Christmas display that included something for everyone: Santa Claus, reindeer, Christmas trees, and a crèche scene with baby Jesus, Mary and Joseph, and assorted barn animals.

The crèche was challenged, however, because it was paid for ($1,365, with another $20 a year to maintain it) by tax money; this was said to be an infringement on the separation of church and state.

In 1984 the Supreme Court, in a 5–4 decision, upheld the city's right to display the crèche—because, as Chief Justice Warren Burger expressed it, the crèche served a "legitimate secular purpose." After all, he noted, the crèche was merely "a neutral harbinger of the holiday season, useful for commercial purposes, but devoid of any inherent meaning."[10]

Burger's words are significant beyond the Pawtucket case: religion "devoid of any inherent meaning" defines that which is legally and culturally acceptable in contemporary culture.†

---

* In *Weinbaum v. City of Las Cruces*, equally silly citizens sued the town of Las Cruces, New Mexico, for including three crosses on its seal.

† A few years ago, the ACLU sued Jersey City, New Jersey, for a seasonal display that included both a crèche and a menorah in recognition of both holidays. This was not enough for the ACLU, which sued to have the display ruled unconstitutional. Several years and multiple court rulings later, the Third Circuit finally approved the display—but only if it included additional non-religious symbols such as a Santa, a tree, and a Kwanzaa symbol, along with an explanatory sign.

A torrent of church-state cases, which have with rare exception been decided against the church, was unleashed by the landmark 1963 school-prayer case, *Abington School District v. Schempp*. Contrary to popular opinion, the most radical import of this case was not that public Bible reading or organized prayer could not be held in public schools, but the grounds on which the court made its decision. While acknowledging as historical fact that religion had been a crucial aspect of human experience, it for the first time held as conscious policy that the state must be indifferent toward all religion in any form.*

This was a dramatic turnabout from the 1954 *Zorach v. Clauson* case, in which Justice William O. Douglas, a civil libertarian, explicitly upheld what had been the law from the nation's beginning. Douglas refused to "find in the Constitution a requirement that the government show a callous indifference to religious groups. That would be preferring those who believe in no religion over those who do believe."[11]

Two dissenting justices in *Abington* warned that "unilateral devotion to the concept of neutrality can lead to ... not simply noninterference and noninvolvement with the religious which the Constitution commands, but a brooding and pervasive devotion to the secular and a passive, or even active, hostility to the religious."[12]

The dissenters were prophets. No phrase could more aptly summarize public life of the last two decades than this "brooding and pervasive devotion to the secular." Seven years after *Abington* the Court redefined religion. What had been in 1931 "obedience to the will of God" was now defined as "a sincere and meaningful belief which occupies in the life of its possessor a place parallel to that filled by God."[13] Thus by 1970 religious belief

---

*The Supreme Court has been more friendly to religion in recent years, particularly in funding cases, but continues to create trouble in cases involving public display of religious symbols and religious activity in public schools (although *Rosenberger v. Rector and Visitors of UVA*, (1995), *Lamb's Chapel v. Center Moriches* (1993) and *Good News Club v. Milford Central School District* (2001) all uphold private religious activity in public schools.

There is also the disastrous 1990 decision, *Employment Division v. Smith*, in which the Supreme Court ruled that the Free Exercise clause does not protect believers from neutral, generally applicable laws. Up until 1990, laws that burdened religion had to pass the most stringent legal test (strict scrutiny) or else create exemptions for the religious activity burdened by the law (*Sherbert v. Verner*, 1963). *Smith* prompted Congress to pass the Religious Freedom Restoration Act (RFRA), which restored the old standard. The Supreme Court proceeded to strike down RFRA in 1997. Congress then passed RLUIPA in 2001; the Supreme Court upheld that more narrow protection (at least, regarding its prisoner provisions) in 2005.

had become a belief in whatever one might fancy — from the Rockettes to Ramtha.

Then in 1973 came the case that aroused the deepest passions of all, *Roe v. Wade.*

Could *Roe v. Wade* — or the entire abortion rights movement — have been imagined without the dominance of a "passive, or even active, hostility to the religious"? The right to life, guaranteed by the Constitution, had always been understood as a sacred right, a right that pre-existed all governments, grounded in the relationship of the Creator with His creation. But as Richard Neuhaus observed, "for the first time ... it was explicitly stated that it is possible to address these issues of ultimate importance without any reference to Judeo-Christian tradition.... For the first time in American jurisprudence, the Supreme Court explicitly excluded philosophy, ethics and religion as factors in its deliberation."[14]

And in *Roe v. Wade*, the Court replaced the right to life and its transcendent origins with a new right, the right to privacy or individual autonomy — regardless of the terrible cost.

Since *Roe*, a series of cases has advanced the right of the individual to make his own moral choices apart from any transcendent value or transcendent interest of the State to protect human life. In 1992, in *Casey v. Planned Parenthood*, the high court affirmed the "central holding" of *Roe*. (Then, as now, the best case that could be made for *Roe* was "respect for precedent:" *Roe* had been on the books for a long time, so women had come to "rely" on the availability of legalized abortion, the justices decreed.) This was the case in which Justice Kennedy famously (and absurdly) wrote, "At the heart of liberty is the right to define one's own concept of existence, of meaning, of the universe, and of the mystery of human life." This was a sweeping definition of liberty as the right of a person to determine for himself the meaning of life. Many feared this definition could embrace anything.

Sure enough, it did.

In 1995 the Court struck down a democratically enacted state referendum in Colorado denying special civil rights based on sexual orientation. Kennedy wrote the opinion, *Romer v. Evans*, saying the vote of the people demonstrated "animus," that is bigotry, against homosexuals.

Then in 2003, in *Lawrence v. Texas*, the Supreme Court struck down a Texas law banning sodomy. Again Justice Kennedy, who could have used a very simple Fourteenth Amendment guarantee argument, resorted instead to his holding in *Casey* and in *Romer v. Evans*. By legislating against homo-sexual behavior, the state was guilty of bigotry or prejudice.

Justice Scalia delivered a blistering dissent to *Lawrence*. "Today's opinion," he said, "dismantles the structure of constitutional law that has permitted the distinction to be made between heterosexual and homosexual unions ..." He went on to charge that the case meant the end to the possibility of all legislation concerning morality.

Scalia is right. Who can say the common good demands the preserva-tion of traditional marriage when personal choice is exalted to the *summum bonum* of society and is constitutionally protected?

Decisions like these assume that government's sole purpose is to protect individual, personal values. Kennedy's "mystery passage"—the assertion that the individual's right to make any decision about his life trumps the right to life itself—is now the law of the land.

The Court not only expunged religious influence, which is bad enough. It set asunder the traditional roles held by government, individuals, and religion. Historically, the job of government has been to enforce the com-mon good.

At the beginning of modern government, people gave up arms in ex-change for giving government the right to defend them. The preservation and protection of life became central to the bargain between individuals and modern government. And throughout the Middle Ages the role of gov-ernment was to enforce the moral code, to take the religious consensus embraced by the people and by the Church, and to see that it was carried out in laws and acts of government.

Today, thanks to the Supreme Court, we have almost a complete role reversal. Although it started with *Roe*, the pivot point was in 1992, with the language of *Casey*. Now, the job of government is to protect the in-dividual from the imposition of any moral values of any kind—or even from what society might determine to be the common good (assuming, in today's relativistic environment, we could ever agree on what *is* the com-mon good).

Why such a radical reversal—from a court explicitly approving religion's crucial public role to one committed to its total privatization—in just a few years' time? The dramatic change has been nothing short of a judicial revolution, but the reasons for the revolution are not so much legal as politi-cal and cultural. Judges, after all, don't live in cocoons—they go to church, listen to television, read magazines, belong to clubs, and talk to their families over the breakfast table.

To understand this cultural backdrop, however, we must go back to 1945, Year Zero. After enduring the Great Depression, World War II, unemployment and rationing, Americans were determined to make up for lost time—and as the years went on, times were good.

The nation's nuclear monopoly seemed to assure security; for the first time in history nearly everyone could afford his own home; millions of returning veterans went to college on the GI bill; business boomed. Eisenhower's 1956 reelection theme, "Peace, Progress, and Prosperity," captured the mood of the nation.

Admittedly, there were undercurrents of discontent. The Korean War had not been lost, but it hadn't been won either. The "beats," led by Jack Kerouac and Allen Ginsberg, had already "dropped out" of society. In *The Lonely Crowd*, sociologist David Riesman described how self-discipline and self-motivation were being replaced by peer pressure as the primary determinant of American character. And though church attendance was up, religion was, in the words of an eminent historian, "so empty and contentless, so conformist, so utilitarian, so sentimental, so individualistic, and so self-righteous."[15]

On the surface, however, these were the best of times. The sixties began with the same confidence. A handsome young president expressed America's bravado and promised the moon. "Let every nation know, whether it wishes us well or ill, that we shall pay any price, bear any burden, meet any hardship, support any friend, oppose any foe to assure the survival and the success of liberty."[16] The future held only opportunity.

Five years later a rapid-fire series of historical events had shaken Americans' faith in their political institutions. Our vigorous young heroes were dead with the assassinations of John Kennedy, Robert Kennedy, and Martin Luther King, Jr. Streets across the country reeked of pot and tear gas as a new generation bombed buildings, did drugs, and dodged the draft. Once again society was adrift.

An unending war in Vietnam took thousands of lives—and network television brought the carnage into American living rooms each evening. A once-popular and powerful president was forced to give up his reelection bid. Just a few years later, a White House scandal shook the confidence of the nation—and caused a disgraced president to resign in ignominy.

At the same time, a destructive philosophic trend had gripped American intellectuals. The long fuse lit by the ideas of Nietzsche, Freud, and Darwin finally set off an explosion of relativism. All moral distinctions were equally valid and equally invalid since all were equally subjective.

A bland civil religion was no match for these powerful trends. Millions felt betrayed by their leaders and resentful that the establishment had any more claim to truth than they did. Sociologist Daniel Bell argues that "the ultimate support for any social system is the acceptance by the population of a moral justification of authority."[17] Now this support was removed and all authority questioned.

These developments were most obvious in the universities, which became both centers of political activism and defenders of relativism. But just as the influence of the university was expanding, it suddenly had very little to teach. The very idea of truth had been called into question as early as 1940, when Reinhold Niebuhr warned that America was a victim of "an education adrift in relativity that doubted all values, and a degraded science that shirked the spiritual issues."[18]

Universities responded by simply changing the goal of education. Whereas once the object of learning had been the discovery of truth, now each student must be allowed to decide truth for himself. Dogma, not ignorance, became the enemy.

The youth culture of the universities took what they were taught to heart, developing what scholar James Hitchcock calls "a visceral sense that all forms of established authority, all rules, all demands for obedience, were inherently illegitimate."[19]

Influenced by existential writers such as Jean-Paul Sartre and Albert Camus, the generation of the sixties made autonomy its god and sought meaning in the pleasures of easy sex and hard drugs. The consequences were felt not only in private standards of morality, but in the literature and art of the times. Take for example the work of Andy Warhol, who on his death in early 1987 was hailed by *Newsweek* as "the most famous American artist of our time."[20] Warhol was responsible for the rise of "pop art" in the early sixties, gaining international fame for his two hundred Campbell soup cans, an oil painting of row after row of those familiar red and white labels.

Inspired by the mass production techniques of industrial societies, pop art deliberately denied the distinctions between high culture and popular culture. Implicitly and explicitly it asserted relativism's principal tenet that all values are equal: The distinction between bad taste and good taste is elitist; all notions of bad and good are merely one class's way of snubbing another. There are no lasting values, no timeless truths, only artifacts of the moment.

Within such an aesthetic vision there can be no room for the eternal. Shortly before his death, Warhol remarked that he always thought his tombstone should be blank. Then as an afterthought he added, "Well, actually I'd like it to say 'figment.' "[21]

In place of MacArthur's spiritual renewal, the post-war generation created figments: images devoid of meaning in place of objective truth. These figments set the stage for the "me decade" of the seventies and the acquisitive yuppie-ism of the eighties captured in one popular T-shirt and bumpersticker slogan, "He who dies with the most toys wins."

Pascal's second option has thus become the route of western experience: Separated from God, men seek satisfaction in their senses. This is more than mindless hedonism; it is a world view in which, according to professor Allen Bloom, "the self has become the modern substitute for the soul."[22]

A 1985 study titled *Habits of the Heart* calls this attitude "utilitarian individualism," arguing that the two primary ways Americans attempt to order their lives are through "the dream of personal success" and "vivid personal feeling."[23] This was reinforced as those interviewed consistently defined their ultimate goals in terms of self-fulfillment or self-realization. Marriage was seen as an opportunity for personal development, work as a method of personal advancement, church as a means of personal fulfillment.

What this study reflects is simply the inevitable consequences of four decades of the steady erosion of absolute values. As a result we live with a massive case of schizophrenia. Outwardly, we are a religious people, but inwardly our religious beliefs make no difference in how we live. We are obsessed with self; we live, raise families, govern, and die as though God does not exist, just as Nietzsche predicted a century ago.

This cultural revolution, rendering God irrelevant, has permeated the Western media, the instrument that not only reflects, but often shapes societal attitudes. God is tolerated in the media only when He is bland enough to pose no threat. One national columnist, annoyed by what she regarded as religious zealots, wrote longingly of ancient Rome, where "the people regarded all the modes of worship as equally true, the intellectuals regarded them as equally false, and the politicians regarded them as equally useful.

What a well-blessed time.... I think we could try to emulate the laid-back spirit it reveals."[24]

More often, however, the media reflect something less than this laid-back spirit and at times even seems infected with a "brooding and pervasive devotion to the secular—and ... hostility to the religious," a view confining religion to a "neutral status, devoid of any inherent meaning."

One illustration was the coverage of the so-called Monkey Trial II, the December 1981 challenge to the Arkansas statute requiring that creationism be taught in schools alongside evolution. The following description of the two parties involved appeared on the front page of the December 21, 1981, *Washington Post*.[25] "The ACLU and the New York firm of Skadden Arps attacked the Arkansas law with a powerful case. Their brief is so good that there is talk of publishing it. Their witnesses gave brilliant little summaries of several fields of science, history of sciences, history and religious philosophy." Such was the enlightened plaintiff.

The witnesses defending creationism, however, were "impassioned believers, rebellious educators and scientific oddities. All but one of the creation scientists came from obscure colleges or Bible schools. The one who didn't said he believed diseases dropped from space, that evolution caused Nazism, and that insects may be more intelligent than humans but are hiding their abilities."

With whom were uninformed readers going to align themselves? The firm of Skadden Arps with its brilliant summaries or the backwoods idiots from no-name colleges who probably still make live animal sacrifices up in the hills when nobody is looking?

Though such a negative slant within news coverage appears regularly, the more common tactic is to ignore religion altogether. For instance, when the late theologian Francis Schaeffer approached PBS to air *How Shall We Then Live*, his film series presenting a view of history, creation, and the universe framed in the Judeo-Christian tradition. He was turned down cold; his series was "too religious."

In a slick manifesto called *Cosmos*, Carl Sagan artfully packaged his own creed: "The Cosmos is all there is, or was, or ever will be."[26] The Supreme Court's working definition of religion, "A sincere and meaningful belief which occupies in the life of its possessor a place parallel to that filled by God," would seem to identify Sagan's video treatment of the Cosmos (which he religiously capitalizes) as religious. But PBS and public-school classrooms regularly air *Cosmos*, while they shun Schaeffer's or any similar work.*

I've often encountered the same attitude in interviewers who suggest, just before we go on the air, that we steer away from religious topics. "Some people take offense, you know," said one. Another advised me it was against station policy to discuss religion on the air. Others say nothing; once we begin they simply steer the questions to the comparatively safer ground of prisons, criminal justice, or politics. They usually appear aghast when I bring the answers back to my experiences with Jesus Christ.

The print medium does the same thing. Over the years since I became a Christian, I have always deliberately explained that I have "accepted Jesus Christ." These words are invariably translated into "Colson's professed religious experience." I discovered that one major U.S. daily, as a matter of policy, will not print the two words *Jesus Christ* together; when combined, the editor says, it represents an editorial judgment.

Such reporting is not always a matter of hostility; it often reflects the reporter's lack of knowledge in spiritual matters. It can also be the result of the very nature of news itself. By definition, the media report events that are out of the ordinary — the bizarre, the hostile, the aberrant; otherwise news is not news. Thus, coverage of Christianity, when it occurs at all, is most often the outlandish exception rather than the norm practiced by millions of Christians daily.

Consider the sensational coverage in early 1987 of Rev. Carl Thitchener, a minister who distributed condoms to his congregation to dramatize the AIDS crisis. Camera crews obligingly descended on his church; evening news broadcasts featured Thitchener's parishioners braying the word *condoms* as he somberly challenged them to repeat it after him. The ludicrous scene made for an entertaining close-out to the evening news, featured as a current event in the church.

---

*In fairness it should be noted that some viewers believe there is a significant quality difference between the two film series. Still, that was not the basis of PBS's rejection of the Schaeffer series. In recent years, PBS has aired more "faith-friendly" programs such as "The Question of God: Sigmund Freud and C.S. Lewis, with Dr. Armand Nicholi," and "The Jesus Factor," which has aired several times on *Frontline*. While ostensibly about the faith of President George W. Bush, this program was an exploration of evangelicalism in the larger sense and provided viewers with resources to better understand evangelicalism. Was it critical at times? Yes — a bit. But critical is not incompatible with respectful. These days, the disrespect toward religion and the religious is infinitely more likely to come from commercial networks.

What the media failed to distinguish, however, is that as a Unitarian Universalist, Thitchener is not a Christian minister. His church rejects the divinity of Christ. The media also overlooked several small details about Thitchener's life and character. Consider, for example, his police record: "Subject: male, Caucasian, 54. . . . Pled guilty to second degree assault, 1957. Convicted of exposing himself, 1958. Convicted of drunk driving, 1975. Convicted of 'Parading naked in front of Brownies,' 1982. Convicted of drunk driving, 1984."[27]

Such selective media focus is not the result of a conscious antireligious policy but is indicative of a pervasive cultural attitude, what G. K. Chesterton described as "a taboo of tact or convention, whereby we are free to say that a man does this or that because of his nationality, or his profession, or his place of residence, or his hobby, but not because of his creed about the very cosmos in which he lives."[28]

Harvard psychiatrist Robert Coles gives a poignant illustration of this taboo. He found he could write about almost any human motivation without having its authenticity questioned. But when he once wrote about a civil rights worker who risked his life "out of love for Jesus," people around him considered the worker, and maybe Coles himself, to be phony.[29]*

The same disposition to dismiss religious influence pervades the field of education.

Paul Vitz, professor of psychology at New York University, examined sixty social-studies textbooks used by 87 percent of the nation's elementary-school children in a study done under the auspices of the U.S. Department of Education.[30] He looked for "primary" references to religious activity such as prayer, church attendance, or participation in religious ceremonies, as well as "secondary" references, such as citing the date when a church was built. What Vitz discovered was a "total absence of any primary religious text about typical contemporary American religious life"[31] and only a few secondary pictures and passages touching upon the religious. The few direct references to historic religion centered on Amish, Catholic, Jewish, and Mormon faiths, leaving a "very curious" deletion of characteristic Protestant religious life.[32]

Religion appeared to be relevant only in remote points in history. Pictures of the Pilgrims and the first Thanksgiving were bountiful—without

---

*In short, orthodox faith is treated the way homosexuality once was: it is tolerated as long as it is practiced only by consenting adults and isn't flaunted in public.

any mention of to whom thanks was being given. One mother told Vitz that her son's social studies book made no mention of religion as part of the Pilgrims' life. Her son told her that "Thanksgiving was when the Pilgrims gave thanks to the Indians." When the mother called the principal of her son's suburban New York City school to point out that Thanksgiving originated when the Pilgrims thanked God, the principal responded, "That's your opinion." He continued by saying that the schools could only teach what was in the books.[33]

Vitz concluded that the study suggests "a psychological motive behind the obvious censorship of religion present in these books. Those responsible for these books appear to have a deep-seated fear of any form of active contemporary Christianity, especially serious, committed Protestantism. This fear could have led the authors to deny and repress the importance of this kind of religion in American life."[34]*

This elimination of the transcendent from serious public discussion is merely a reflection of an underlying cultural revolution that has eliminated absolute values from public consciousness, thus ushering in an age of relativism. This has inevitably affected public policy, as in the court decisions discussed earlier, and it has turned our traditional notion of pluralism on its head.

Historically pluralism meant that conflicting and firmly held values could be voiced in public debate, and from such debates might emerge a consensus of values by which a community would be governed. But relativism, which insists that there are no objective truths, drives all values out of public debate, since in a pluralistic society they are "divisive." In an attempt to be neutral, we ignore all values. Columnist Joseph Sobran writes, "The prevailing notion is that the state should be neutral as to religion, and furthermore, that the best way to be neutral about it is to avoid all mention of it. By this

---

*In the midst of the controversy aroused by the Vitz study, Doubleday, a major publisher, announced its decision to write God back into school textbooks. "We made a decision long before Judge Hand's decision in Alabama that you can't leave religion out of textbooks," said Herb Adams, then-president of Doubleday's Laidlaw Educational Publishing division, which ranks among the nation's top textbook publishers. "The allegation that religion has been soft-pedaled in textbooks is true," he added. Doubleday has since prepared a supplementary book that discusses the role of religion in the development of the country. It was designed to go along with existing history and social-studies books. Many other textbooks will be fully rewritten and revised, said Adams, but it will be a "long, long process." Adams added that the reason religion had been omitted from textbooks in the past was that publishers wanted to "avoid controversy." Evangelical Press News Service (February 6, 1987).

sort of logic, nudism is the best compromise among different styles of dress. The secularist version of 'pluralism' amounts to theological nudism."[35]

This modern vision of pluralism has infiltrated nearly every branch and level of government, progressively institutionalizing the privatization of religious values. The absurd extreme to which this has taken us is illustrated by the 1982 New York law outlawing the use of children in pornography.[36] In its preamble the statute specifically states that it is not based on any moral or religious considerations. Only by making such a disclaimer did the bill's drafters believe it could withstand a court challenge that it was "religiously" motivated and thus unconstitutional.

Former Congressman Henry Hyde offers a personal perspective of what it means to run afoul of the secular need for control. In 1976 Congress passed the Hyde Amendment, which barred federal funding for abortion in the Medicaid program. Planned Parenthood, the American Civil Liberties Union, and other groups challenged the amendment's constitutionality, claiming that it "used the fist of government to smash the wall of separation between church and state by imposing a peculiarly religious view of when a human life begins." To prove their theory, the lawyers for these organizations asked to review Hyde's mail for expressions of religious sentiment. They also hired a private investigator who followed Hyde to a Mass for the unborn and took notes as the congressman read Scripture, took communion, and prayed. The investigator even recorded in his notebook the inscription on the cathedral's statue of St. Thomas More: "I die the king's good servant, but God's first."

In an affidavit, the plaintiffs presented these observations to the court as proof of a religious conspiracy. They claimed that Hyde, as a devout Catholic, could not separate his religion from his politics and that the amendment was therefore unconstitutional. The judge threw out the affidavit, and Planned Parenthood and the ACLU finally lost their case in 1980 when the Supreme Court affirmed the amendment's constitutionality.

Though victorious, Hyde was infuriated by his opponents' tactics. "The anger I felt when they tried to disenfranchise me because of my religion stayed with me. These are dangerous people who make dangerous arguments. Some powerful members of the cultural elite in our country are so paralyzed by the fear that theistic notions might reassert themselves into the official activities of government that they will go to Gestapo lengths to inhibit such expression."[37]

This stripping away of religious import is not limited to the U.S. Europe has become a post-Christian culture in which the principal religious influence is visible in art treasures and cathedrals filled with tourists rather than worshipers. A 2000 study by the World Values Survey revealed just how low church attendance is in Western democracies. The number of people who say they never, or practically never, attend church is at 60 percent in France, 48 percent in the Netherlands, 46 percent in Sweden and Belgium, and 33 percent in Spain. And in England, site of the great nineteenth-century awakening and home of missionary movements, more people worship in mosques than in the Church of England today. Some 55 percent of the population never attends church.[38]

In fact, resistance to Christian influence has become overt. Donald Bloesch cites an official on ecclesiastic affairs in Sweden who boasted some years ago, "We are dismantling the church bit by bit and where necessary we are using economic means to do so."

And when economic means fail, the state uses the threat of prison. In 2005, a Swedish pastor faced a jail sentence for committing a "hate crime": preaching the biblical view on homosexual behavior. Pastor Ake Green was sentenced by a district court to one month's imprisonment, but the Gota Court of Appeals overturned his conviction. The prosecutor, egged on by homosexual activists, has appealed the ruling to the Swedish Supreme Court.

Other countries are using the same coercive tactics. In February of 2006, Belgian police questioned twenty-nine Americans with the Assemblies of God Church for possibly violating a work permit law. Four were detained and later deported on charges of being "illegal workers" — despite the fact that they were volunteers.

In Canada, a Christian mayor in London, Ontario, was fined $10,000 for refusing to proclaim "Gay Pride Day." In England, Christian groups have been banished from college campuses because their biblical stance on homosexuality is equated with hate; similar attacks on Christian organizations have begun to occur on American campuses. In 2006, police in Wales arrested a man for passing out leaflets containing Bible verses pertaining to homosexuality. As the arrested man put it, "I am astonished that South Wales Police have a special unit dedicated to silencing those who disagree with homosexuality."

Perhaps one of the most fitting images of Western spiritual apathy was captured in Italian filmmaker Federico Fellini's award-winning film *La Dolce*

Vita. The movie opens with a panorama of Rome's magnificent skyline, the grand dome of St. Peter's in the center. A helicopter carrying a large object appears in the distance. The camera zooms in; the object is a statue of Christ being hauled away from a downtown square. The camera then focuses on a group of young sunbathers who, distracted from their pleasure by the whirring blades, laugh mockingly. Why shouldn't Jesus take the bus like everyone else? The helicopter flies on to discard its outdated cargo on a trash pile, and the youngsters return to their sun worship.

Fellini filmed his blasphemous scene in 1959, but it has proved prophetic.

Many believe that religious values and liberties have fallen victim to some sinister conspiracy in which the ACLU, humanist educators, the media, and gay rights groups meet in darkened corridors of CBS headquarters to plot the demise of religion in America. Admittedly, the ACLU has a powerful lobby and the media are unsympathetic. Skeptics and radical gays dominate college campuses. But even if such forces were organized to consciously eradicate religious values they could do little to wipe out real Christianity.

Christian values are in retreat in the West today, primarily, I believe, because of the church itself. If Christianity has failed to stem the rising tides of relativism it is because the church in many instances has lost the convicting force of the gospel message. Earlier we argued that while humanists did not understand humans, Christians did not understand Christianity. This is surely evident in post–World-War-II Christianity, which has become a religion of private comfort and blessing that fills up whatever small holes in life that pleasure, money, and success have left open, what Bonhoeffer called a "god of the gaps."[39]

Television's emergence as the dominant medium of communication gave birth to the slickly marketed health-wealth-and-success gospel rampant in today's church. As Donald Bloesch notes, "I believe that technology can be harnessed in the service of the gospel, but I recognize that such a venture entails the risk of accommodating the Christian message to technological values. Utility, i.e., practical efficacy and tangible results, rather than fidelity to truth then becomes the criterion for evaluating the program of the church."[40] When asked about his affluent lifestyle in the face of a needy world, one prominent evangelist explained, "I live in one of the finest homes. I drive one of the finest, safest cars, and if a newer, safer one were to pull up in front of my door, I'd go out and say, 'I want it,' ... God designed life for believers to be an abundant life ... God designed for you to live in the overflow."[41]

One of the top-selling books of recent years was a repackaging of that horror of the 1980s, the prosperity gospel. This message is now being peddled by purveyors who smile benignly from the television cameras and the covers of their name-it-and-claim-it books to tell us that we can have everything with Jesus.

In addition to succumbing to this arrogant heresy, the church has allowed itself to become dangerously polarized into two camps: politicized and privatized views of faith. The problem is, neither view has anything to do with historic Christianity.

The politicization of the church in the sixties was largely the work of liberal mainline denominations whose bureaucracies issued weekly policy papers on social issues. They became so absorbed in social causes that they neglected the church's first mission and in the process suffered declining membership.* Just as their influence was waning, the political polarity was reversed, and the Christian New Right emerged as a potent force in American politics. They made the same mistake — equating the gospel with a particular partisan agenda. Even today, many conservative Christians appear ready to make politics the ultimate goal, putting political agendas ahead of spirituality.

Politicized religion simply reinforces the tendency toward civil religion, which was perhaps best articulated by Dwight Eisenhower, who once said that American government makes no sense "unless it is founded in a deeply felt religious faith — and I don't care what it is."[42] What Eisenhower was referring to was nothing more than a generic religion — any brand will do, no-name is the best — to encourage civic duty.

---

*As James Wall observed in the liberal *Christian Century*:

> Mainline religion ... has failed to convince the public that there is a link between its politics and its theology because, perhaps unwittingly, it has allowed religion to be confined to what David Tracy has perceptively termed the "reservation of the spirit."
>
> ... the political left has had a morbid fear of religion encroaching on the secular realm. This fear leads, at its extreme, to legal action if a crèche shows up on city property. Such expressions of cultural religion hardly pose a threat to the separation of church and state, but the doctrine of the left is that "religion" must not lead the public debate. Instead, it must be on call to serve only when commanded by secular leaders.
>
> Ironically, this view of religion imposes as rigid an attitude toward societal solutions as that found on the political right. Mainline religion has for too long taken this "closed" attitude for fear of appearing to impose religious solutions in a pluralistic culture.

On the other side is privatized faith, which divorces religious and spiritual beliefs from public actions. Like its politicized counterpart, privatized faith has a mixed heritage theologically and politically. In the nineteenth century, conservative evangelicals led the abolition campaign and progressive social reforms; in the early twentieth century, they abandoned this commitment in reaction against modernism and the so-called social gospel. Fundamentalists separated from the mainstream, leaving the world's concerns behind so they could preach the good news among the faithful.

All of this dramatically changed by the late seventies when Jerry Falwell led a fundamentalist stampede back to center stage. Ironically, liberals who had been so socially concerned were now, in reaction perhaps, arguing that faith is a private matter. Perhaps it depends on which issues are identified at any given moment as religious and moral.

This would seem the case in the 1984 presidential campaign. Democratic challenger Walter Mondale attacked President Reagan's public statements that "without God, democracy will not and cannot long endure" as "moral McCarthyism."[43]

Mondale's running mate, Geraldine Ferraro, added, "Personal religious convictions have no place in political campaigns or in dictating public policy."[44] In an interview with the *New York Times*, Ms. Ferraro asserted that her faith was "very, very private."[45]

Governor Mario Cuomo of New York made the most eloquent defense of this privately engaging but publicly irrelevant faith during his much-publicized speech at the University of Notre Dame in 1984. As a practicing Catholic, he said, he subscribed to his church's teachings on the question of abortion. But as an office holder in a secular society he could not impose his views on anyone else. So far, so good.

Cuomo then went on to say that he was under no obligation to advocate the views of his church or to seek a public consensus based on those views (which he confesses to be the truth of God) until there is what he calls a "prudential judgment" that could justify such a course.[46] In other words, one is under no obligation to provide leadership on moral issues. Thus, Cuomo carried privatized faith to its ultimate conclusion when he asserted that he could, while agreeing with his church, nonetheless tolerate or even support abortion legislation. This clever-sounding but dangerous argument gives sophistry a bad name.

I debated Cuomo long distance through an exchange of mail and letters to the editors of newspapers. The debate, I'm glad to say, had the effect of pulling Cuomo off his pedestal. But disturbingly, the Cuomo defense, considered scandalous in the eighties, is shared by virtually everyone today. (Democratic presidential candidate John Kerry, a Catholic, recycled this bogus argument in 2004 on the same hot-button subject: abortion.) The result is to make one's private faith of absolutely no relevance beyond what it might do for one personally. No wonder fewer and fewer people take Christianity seriously.

Those who fear the encroachment of religion in public life can relax. Neither politicized civil religion nor privatized religion is likely to impose itself on our governmental or social institutions, for in either case there is nothing to impose. The one holds the gospel hostage to a particular political agenda while the other is so private it refuses to have any impact on daily life in the public arena. Thus is the divided church impotent to reverse the tides of secularism.

In 1896 the Victorian-minded planners of St. John the Divine in New York City envisioned a great Episcopal cathedral that would bring glory to God. More than a century later, the church is being used in ways that its planners might well have regarded with dismay.[47]

St. John's Thanksgiving service has featured Japanese Shinto priests; Muslim Sufis are welcomed guests; Lenten services have focused on the ecological "passion of the earth" (one gathers that Christ's passion is passé). The cathedral has featured "Christa," a huge crucifix with a female Christ, and St. John's pulpit has welcomed everyone from the Rev. Jesse Jackson to Norman Mailer, rabbis, imams, Buddhist monks, secular politicians, and atheist scientists. The only guest to cause a stir in recent years was the visit by Amina Wadud, a female professor of Islamic studies at Virginia Commonwealth University, who led an Islamic prayer service while men were present. (The protests, needless to say, came not from Christians, but by Muslim men, whom police forcibly restrained from entering the cathedral.) During one memorable feast of St. Francis, an ark-load of animals received blessings from the high altar, including a llama, an elephant, and a goose.

Logistical questions such as curbing your elephant within the cathedral notwithstanding, St. John the Divine seems to have ceased to be a house of the one God of the Scriptures, and has become instead a house of many gods. Novelist Kurt Vonnegut Jr. wrote for the cathedral's centennial brochure that "the Cathedral is to this atheist ... a suitable monument to persons of all ages and classes. I go there often to be refreshed by a sense of nonsectarian community which has the best interests of the whole planet at heart."

Underneath the main altar are seven stone chambers housing the cathedral's artists-in-residence: painters, photographers, sculptors, poets, blacksmiths, and, at one time, a high-wire performer. I suppose every church should have its own trapeze artist.

Opposition to the menagerie (both human and animal) is not unknown. Some Episcopalians are concerned about the menorah, Islamic prayer rug, and Shinto vases that adorn the sanctuary altar along with the crucifix. But as former dean James Morton once responded, "This cathedral is a place for birth Episcopalians like me who feel constricted by the notion of excluding others. What happens here — the Sufi dances, the Buddhist prayers — are serious spiritual experiences. We make God a Minnie Mouse in stature when we say these experiences profane a Christian church."

As *Newsweek* observed admiringly, "The eclectic dean of St. John's seems to be reaching for a theology as high and wide as the cathedral he serves."

Maybe so. Or perhaps his grand cathedral, like the United Nations meditation room, is a monument to no god at all — and thus, a fitting icon of late twentieth-century and early twenty-first century Western culture.

15

THE NAKED
PUBLIC SQUARE

The greatest question of our time is not communism versus individualism, not Europe versus America, not even the East versus the West; it is whether men can live without God.

WILL DURANT

A 1987 *Time* magazine cover story titled "Ethics" raised many disturbing issues: "What's wrong? Hypocrisy, betrayal and greed unsettle the nation's soul.... At a time of moral disarray, America seeks to rebuild a structure of values."[1]

Yet even in the midst of this long-overdue national soul-searching, the authors still hedged the issue. "Who is to decide what are the 'right' values?" wrote a professor of education. "Does ultimate moral authority lie with institutions such as church and state to codify and impose? Or, in a free society, are these matters of private conscience, with final choice belonging to the individual?"[2]

What such experts do not see is that by raising such questions, they are pointing to the answer. We live in a society in which all transcendent values have been removed and thus there is no moral standard by which anyone can say right is right and wrong is wrong. What we live in is, in the memorable image of Richard Neuhaus, a naked public square.

On the surface, a value-free society sounds liberal, progressive, and enlightened. It certainly sounded that way to the generations of the sixties and early seventies—probably many of the same people now wringing their hands on the pages of *Time*. But when the public square is naked, truth and values drift with the winds of public favor and there is nothing objective to govern how we are to live together. Why should we be shocked, then, by the inevitable consequences; why should we be surprised to discover that society yields what is planted?

Why are we surprised that crime soars steadily among juveniles when parents fail to set standards of right behavior in the home, when school teachers will not offer a moral opinion in the classroom, either out of fear of litigation or because they cannot "come from a position of what is right and wrong," as one New Jersey teacher put it?[3]

Why are we horrified at the growing consequences of sexual promiscuity—including a life-threatening epidemic—when sex is treated as casually as going out for a Frosty at Wendy's?

Why are we shocked at disclosures of religious leaders bilking their ministries of millions when they've been preaching a get-rich-quick gospel all along?

Why the wonderment over the fact that, for enough dollars or sexual favors, government employees and military personnel sell out their nation's secrets? As C. S. Lewis wrote forty years ago, "We laugh at honor and are shocked to find traitors in our midst."[4]

Why is it so surprising that Wall Street yuppies make fast millions on insider information or tax fraud? Without objective values, the community or one's neighbor has no superior claim over one's own desires.

Whether we like to hear it or not, we are reaping the consequences of the decades since World War II when we have, in Solzhenitsyn's words, "forgotten God." What we have left is the reign of relativism.

As discussed in an earlier chapter, humanity cannot survive without some form of law. "The truly naked public square is at best a transitional phenomenon," wrote Richard John Neuhaus. "It is a vacuum begging to be filled."[5] Excise belief in God and you are left with only two principals: the individual and the state. In this situation, however, there is no mediating structure to generate moral values and, therefore, no counterbalance to the inevitable ambitions of the state. "The naked public square cannot remain naked, the direction is toward the state-as-church, toward totalitarianism."[6]

As we have seen, this occurred in Marxist nations where the death of God created a new form of messiah—the all-powerful state whose political ideology acquires the force of religion. The same is true, though not as extreme, in the West where traditional religious influences have been excluded from public debates either by law or by G. K. Chesterton's "taboo of tact or convention." As a result, government is free to make its own ultimate judgments. Hence government ideology acquires the force of religion.

The removal of the transcendent sucks meaning from the law. Without an absolute standard of moral judgment backing government "morality," where is the protection for the minorities and the powerless? "When in our public life no legal prohibition can be articulated with a force of transcendent authority, then there are no rules rooted in ultimacies that can protect the poor, the powerless and the marginal, as indeed there are now no rules protecting the unborn, and only fragile inhibitions surrounding the aged and defective."[7]

With no ultimate reference point supporting it—no just cause for obedience—law can only be enforced by the bayonet. So the state seeks more and more coercive power.

But the most dangerous consequence of the naked public square is the loss of community.

A community is a gathering of people around shared values, a commitment to one another and to common ideals and aspirations that cannot be created by government. As Arthur Schlesinger observed, "We have forgotten that constitutions work only as they reflect an actual sense of community."[8]

Without commitment to community, individual responsibility quickly erodes. One vivid illustration of this was a Princeton student's protest after President Jimmy Carter proposed reinstating the draft registration in 1977. Newspapers across the country showed the young man defiantly carrying a placard proclaiming: "Nothing is worth dying for."

To many, these words seemed an affirmation of life, the ultimate assertion of individual worth. What they fail to reckon with, however, is the reverse of that slogan: if nothing is worth dying for, is anything worth living for? A society that has no reference points beyond itself "increasingly becomes a merely contractual arrangement," says sociologist Peter Berger. The problem with that, he continues, is that human beings will not die for a social contract. And "unless people are prepared, if necessary, to die for it," a society cannot long survive."[9]

We are sailing uncharted waters. Never before in the history of Western civilization has the public square been so devoid of transcendent values.

The notion of law rooted in transcendent truth, in God Himself, is not the invention of Christian fundamentalists calling naïvely for America to return to its Christian roots. The roots of American law are as much in the works of Cicero and Plato as in the Bible. If fundamentalists are guilty of distorting American history, their critics are guilty of distorting the whole history of Western civilization.

Plato, in terms as religious as Moses or David, claimed that transcendent norms were the true foundations for civil law and order. He taught that "there exist divine moral laws, not easy to apprehend, but operating upon all mankind." He refuted the argument of some Sophists that there was no distinction between virtue and vice, and he affirmed that "God, not man, is the measure of all things."[10]

Cicero, to whom the American Founding Fathers looked for guidance, maintained that religion is indispensable to private morals and public order and that it alone provided the concord by which people could live together.[11] "True law," wrote Cicero, "is right reason in agreement with Nature; it is of universal application and everlasting; it summons to duty by its commands, and averts from wrong-doing by its prohibitions."

Augustine wrote *The City of God* to defend the role of Christianity as the essential element in preserving society, stating that what the pagans "did not have the strength to do out of love of country, the Christian God demands of [citizens] out of love of Himself. Thus, in a general breakdown of morality and of civic virtues, divine Authority intervened to impose frugal living, continence, friendship, justice and concord among citizens."[12] Augustine contended that without true justice emanating from a sovereign God there could never be the concord of which Cicero wrote.

At the time of the French Revolution, Edmund Burke contended that the attempt to build a secularized state was not so much irreverent as irrational. "We know, and it is our pride to know, that man is by his constitution a religious animal; that atheism is against, not only our reason, but our instincts; and that it cannot prevail long."[13]

Religion has always been a decisive factor in the shaping of the American experience According to one modern scholar, it was the Founding Fathers' conviction that "republican government depends for its health on values that over the not-so-long run must come from religion."[14]

John Adams believed that the *moral* order of the new nation depended on biblical religion. "If I were an atheist ... I should believe that chance had ordered the Jews to preserve and propagate to all mankind the doctrine of a supreme, intelligent, wise, almighty sovereign of the universe, which I believe to be the great essential principle of all morality, and consequently of all civilization."[15]

Alexis de Tocqueville, the shrewd observer of American democracy, maintained that "religion in America takes no direct part in the government of society, but it must be regarded as the first of their political institutions.... How is it possible that society should escape destruction if the moral tie is not strengthened in proportion as the political tie is relaxed? And what can be done with a people who are their own masters if they are not submissive to the Deity?"[16]

In considering such lessons from the past, historians Will and Ariel Durant cited the agnostic Joseph Renan, who in 1866 wrote, "What would we do without [Christianity]?... If rationalism wishes to govern the world without regard to the religious needs of the soul, the experience of the French Revolution is there to teach us the consequences of such a blunder." The Durants concluded, "There is no significant example in history before our time, of a society successfully maintaining moral life without the aid of religion."[17]

The supreme irony of our century is that in those nations that still enjoy the greatest human freedoms, this traditional role of religion is denigrated; while in nations that have fallen under the oppressor's yoke, the longing for the spiritual is keenest. In the West intellectuals widely disdain religion; in the Soviet Union they cry out for its return.

Three popular contemporary Soviet writers, Vasily Bykov, Viktor Astafyev, and Chinghiz Aytmatov, have blamed Russia's moral degradation on the decline of religion. "Who extinguished the light of goodness in our soul? Who blew out the lamp of our conscience, toppled it into a dark, deep pit in which we are groping, trying to find the bottom, a support and some kind of guiding light to the future?" asks Astafyev, a Christian, in *Our Contemporary*, a popular Moscow journal.[18] Though a Muslim, Aytmatov centers his writings on Christ, whom he admires as a greater influence than Mohammed. He and his fellow writers have boldly attacked Communism for creating "an all-encompassing belief" that has plunged the Russian people into a moral abyss. Bykov, winner of every Soviet literary award, declares there can be no morality without faith.[19]

Yet our twentieth century has set itself apart as the first to explicitly reject the wisdom of the ages that religion is indispensable to the concord and justice of society.

Mankind now has three choices: to remain divorced from the transcendent; to construct a rational order to preserve society without recourse to real or imagined gods; or to establish the viable influence of the Kingdom of God in the kingdoms of man.

The first option invites chaos and tyranny, as the bloodshed, repression, and nihilism of this century testify. We are then left with the second and third choices. These opposing arguments were well presented by two of the great thinkers of the twentieth century: the eminent journalist, Walter Lippmann, and the Nobel laureate, Aleksandr Solzhenitsyn.

Before writing A Preface to Morals, Lippmann concluded that modern man could no longer embrace a simple religious faith. For Lippmann, the goal was to create a humanistic view in which "mankind, deprived of the great fictions, is to come to terms with the needs which created those fictions." For himself, Lippmann came to a rather fatalistic conclusion: "I take the humanistic view because, in the kind of world I happen to live in, I can do no other."[20] Lippmann thus set about to extract the ethical ideals of religious figures from their theological and historical context. Man in his own rational interest, he believed, could sustain a man-made religion. Some religion, even if it was a religion that denied religion, had to be followed.

On the other side of the spectrum from this religion of humanism stands Aleksandr Solzhenitsyn, a lonely and often outspoken prophet. In his 1978 Harvard commencement address, Solzhenitsyn listed a litany of woes facing the West: the loss of courage and will, the addiction to comfort, the abuse of freedom, the capitulation of intellectuals to fashionable ideas, the attitude of appeasement with evil.

The cause for all this was the humanistic view Lippmann had embraced. "The humanistic way of thinking," thundered Solzhenitsyn, "which had proclaimed itself as our guide, did not admit the existence of evil in man, nor did it see any task higher than the attainment of happiness on earth. It started modern western civilization on the dangerous trend of worshiping man and his material needs ... gaps were left open for evil, and its drafts blow freely today."

In American democracy, said Solzhenitsyn, rights "were granted on the ground that man is God's creature. That is, freedom was given to the individual conditionally, in the assumption of his constant religious responsibility."

Solzhenitsyn lamented that two hundred years ago, as the Constitution was being written, or even fifty years ago, when Walter Lippmann was trying to preserve the husk of Western virtue, "it would have seemed quite impossible ... that an individual be granted boundless freedom with no purpose, simply for the satisfaction of his whims.... The West has finally achieved the rights of man, and even to excess, but man's sense of responsibility to God and society has grown dimmer and dimmer."[21] Like General Douglas MacArthur, Solzhenitsyn was saying that nothing less than spiritual renewal could save Western civilization.

If we reject the nihilism that denies all meaning and hope, we must believe human society has purpose. We are forced to choose, therefore, belief in man, faith in faith, hope in hope, and the love of love; or we must look for a point beyond ourselves to steady our balance.

The view that man in his own rational interest can sustain a man-made religion is voiced regularly on op-ed pages, on television specials, even from church pulpits. It remains fashionable because it offers a positive view of human nature, filled with hopeful optimism about man's capacities. But it ignores the ringing testimony of a century filled with terror and depravity.

If the real benefits of the Judeo-Christian ethic and influence in secular society were understood, it would be anxiously sought out, even by those who *repudiate* the Christian faith. The influence of the Kingdom of God in the public arena is good for society as a whole.

PART FOUR

PRESENCE
OF THE
KINGDOM

16

BENEFITS
OF THE KINGDOM

*Although church and state stand separate, the political order can-
not be renewed without theological virtues working upon it.... It
is from the church that we receive our fundamental postulates of
order, justice and freedom, applying them to our civil society.*

RUSSELL KIRK

If Solzhenitsyn, MacArthur, and many of the great political philosophers since Cicero are right that society cannot survive without a vital religious influence, then where does this leave us? Will any religion or belief do?

No. As expressed earlier, I believe as a matter of faith *and* intellect that the Judeo-Christian religion must be that transcendent base. But—and I cannot emphasize this too strongly—even if I did not, I would still argue that Christianity is the only religious system that provides for *both* individual concerns and the ordering of a society with liberty and justice for all. A creed alone is not enough, nor is some external law code.

If Christianity were merely another creed, it would have no superior claim over Hinduism and Buddhism, for example. Or if it were merely another prescriptive order for society, it would have no advantage over Islam. Instead, Christianity alone, as taught in Scripture and announced in the Kingdom context by Jesus Christ, provides both a transcendent moral influence and a transcendent ordering of society without the repressive theocratic system of Islam.[1]

Many Christians tend to see their faith as merely a belief system or a religious palliative for all life's ills. Secularists see it, most often, through the pejorative pen or the selective lens of the media, which portray the Christian activist as a Bible-thumping bigot condemning everyone, expounding simplistically on everything from evolution to gun control, and pushing

267

heatedly to take over the government to cram his narrow-minded agenda down society's unwilling throat. Sadly, many in the church have perpetuated this stereotype with thoughtless rhetoric and posturing.

Yet none of this bears any resemblance to true Christianity. The Kingdom of God provides unique moral imperatives that can cause men and women to rise above their natural egoism to serve the greater good. God intends His people to do this; furthermore, He commands them to influence the world through their obedience to Him, not by taking over the world.

No one can be coerced into true faith, and the last people who even ought to try to coerce others are Christians. As the Westminster Confession states, "God alone is Lord of conscience."[2] This conviction lies at the heart of the agreement reached by America's Founding Fathers. For them, secularists and believers alike, freedom of conscience was the first liberty guaranteed by the Constitution. This means religious liberty for all—Jew, Muslim, Christian, Hindu, Buddhist, atheist, or neo-pagan earth worshipper.

The Christian, knowing that the will of the majority cannot determine truth, seeks no preferential favor for his religion from government. His confidence, instead, is that truth is found in Christ alone—and this is so no matter how many people believe it, no matter whether those in power believe it. While this may sound exclusivistic, it is this very assurance that makes (or should make, when properly understood) the Christian the most vigorous defender of human liberty. And those who resent the exclusive claims of Christianity are practicing the same intolerance they profess to resent. The essence of pluralism is, after all, that each person respects the other's right to believe in an exclusive claim to truth.

If society's well-being depends on the presence of a healthy religious influence, then, it is crucial that Christians understand their responsibilities in the kingdoms of man as mandated by the Kingdom of God. It is equally imperative that the rest of society realize the benefits those responsibilities, when properly carried out, offer them.

We are a benefit-driven society. How will this move benefit us? we ask. What benefits come with this plan? What benefits does this company offer if I take the job? It should come as welcome news to the pragmatists of the world that the Kingdom of God offers benefits no society can afford to be without.

When I was serving time for my part in the Watergate conspiracy, Al Quie, a senior congressman, offered to serve the remainder of my prison sentence if authorities would release me so I could be with my then-troubled family. Al, who later became governor of Minnesota, was a respected political leader; I was a member of the disgraced Nixon staff and a convicted felon. Al and I had not even been friends until a few months earlier when we met in a prayer group. Why would a man like Al Quie make such an offer?

The answer? Al took seriously Jesus' words: "As I have loved you, so you must love one another."[3] This commandment is a central law of the Kingdom, and Al Quie was my first encounter with it.

This law of the Kingdom motivates Christians to serve the good of society. Certainly it motivated Christians of the nineteenth century when they spearheaded most of our nation's significant works of mercy and moral betterment. They founded hospitals, colleges, and schools; they organized welfare assistance and fed the hungry; they campaigned to end abuses ranging from dueling to slavery. Though much of this work has now been taken over by government agencies, Christians provided the original impetus.

Today, Christians still contribute the bulk of resources for private charities of compassion — something even some liberals now acknowledge. Arthur C. Brooks, director of nonprofit studies for Syracuse University's Maxwell School of Citizenship and Public Affairs, wrote a book titled *Who Really Cares: The Surprising Truth About Compassionate Conservatism* in which he concludes (to his own astonishment) that conservative Christians are far more generous than liberals. Conservatives not only donate more money, they contribute a higher percentage of their incomes — even though liberal families average 6 percent higher incomes than conservatives. "For too long, liberals have been claiming they are the most virtuous members of American society. Although they usually give less to charity, they have nevertheless lambasted conservatives for their callousness in the face of social injustice," Brooks writes. By contrast, secular liberals who are devout believers in government entitlement programs are far more reluctant to open their own wallets than are Christians. Even when government underfunds worthy charities, secular liberals are averse to writing their own checks.

Religious conservatives are also more likely than liberals to *do* good. According to Brooks, they're more likely to volunteer their time, donate blood, and sacrifice for their loved one. They're more than twice as likely as liberals to help the poor.

This is not to say that all good deeds are done by Christians or that all Christians do good deeds. Sacrificial deeds are often done for other than religious motives, of course. But in those instances the actions depend on an individual's personal reasons. Motive is crucial. In one instance it is an individual choice—a choice that often wavers or falters. For the Christian it is a matter of obedience to God's commandments; it is not choice, but necessity.

It is, in fact, their dual citizenship that should, as Augustine believed, make Christians the best of citizens. Not because they are more patriotic or civic-minded, but because they do out of obedience to God that which others do only if they choose or if they are forced. And their very presence in society means the presence of a community of people who live by the Law behind the law.

Even as unreligious a figure as modern educator John Dewey recognized that "the church-going classes, those who have come under the influence of evangelical Christianity ... form the backbone of philanthropic and social interest, of social reform through political action, of passivism, of popular education. They embody and express the spirit of kindly good will towards [those] in economic disadvantage." [4]

A Gallup poll confirms Dewey's (and Brooks's) observations. Forty-six percent of those in the United States who describe themselves as "highly spiritually committed" work among the poor, the infirm, or the elderly—twice as many as those describing themselves as "highly uncommitted" spiritually. [5]

To accomplish works of mercy and justice, however, Christians do not rely on government, but on their own penetration of society as "salt and light." This, too, is in obedience to a command of God that orders them to be the "salt of the earth" and "the light of the world" [6]—the great cultural commission of the Kingdom.* In Hebrew times salt was rubbed into meat to prevent it from spoiling. In the same way the citizen of the Kingdom is "rubbed in" to society as its preservative.

---

*The Great Commission is Jesus' command to *preach the gospel.* "Therefore go and make disciples of all nations, baptizing them in the name of the Father and of the Son and of the Holy Spirit" (Matt. 28:19). The cultural commission, as I've called it, is to *do the gospel.* That is, to be salt and light, letting "your light shine before men, that they may see your good deeds and praise your Father in heaven" (Matt. 5:16). As I've written in *How Now Shall We Live?*, the scriptural justification for culture building starts with Genesis. Until the sixth day, God did the work of creation directly. But then he created the first humans and ordered them to carry on where he left off. They are to reflect his image and have dominion (Gen. 1:26). From then on, the development of the creation will be primarily social and cultural: It will be the work of humans as they obey God's command

Citizens of the Kingdom, therefore, form what Edmund Burke called "the little platoons," mediating structures between the individual and government that carry out works of justice, mercy, and charity.[7]

The presence of Christians in society also helps break the endless cycle of evil and violence in the world. For example, the conflicts in the Middle East, which have been going on for thousands of years, thrive on hatred and bigotry, the basest of human instincts—which in turn beget violence, which begets more violence. Only forgiveness and love can break this cycle, and only the Kingdom of God orders its citizens to take such radical steps. God commands His people to forgive those who hurt or wrong them and to love their enemies.

Though "turning the other cheek" may sound like weakness or impractical idealism, in reality it takes raw courage and is the most powerful weapon for restoring civil tranquility—far surpassing any bayonet or legislation. No conquering army can destroy evil; at best it can suppress it. But as we will see dramatically illustrated in a later chapter, whenever men and women are reconciled by the Law of the Kingdom, evil is defeated.

In this and many other ways, the moral standards demanded of the citizen of the Kingdom of God inevitably affect the moral standards of the kingdoms of man. This is not well understood today because of the widespread view that private moral values have no bearing on public conduct. Scripture and history indicate otherwise, as do our own life experiences.[8]

Whether a politician cheats on his wife, for example, should have no bearing on his fitness for office, many say. But a broken vow is a broken vow and reveals a weakness of character. If a man or woman cannot be trusted with private moral decisions, how can he or she be trusted with moral decisions affecting the whole of society?

During the debate in the nineties over the Monica Lewinsky scandal, President Clinton's defenders said what he did in private had no public

---

to fill and subdue the earth (Gen. 1:28). The same command is still binding on us today. Though the Fall introduced sin and evil into human history, it did not erase the cultural mandate. Sin introduces a destructive power into God's created order, but it does not obliterate that order. And when we are redeemed, we are not only freed from the sinful motivations that drive us but also restored to fulfill our original purpose, empowered to do what we were created to do: build societies and create culture—and, in so doing, to restore the created order. It's my belief that the Lord's cultural commission is inseparable from the Great Commission. Salvation does not consist simply of freedom from sin; salvation also means being restored to the task we were given in the beginning—the job of creating culture.

consequences—that he should not be impeached for telling a lie because the lie was "only" about a personal matter. Advocates of this point of view never tired of telling us about former presidents whose marital infidelities did not prevent them from attaining political greatness, and that our country's Founders would have been dismayed at our making a man's private conduct the basis for judging his fitness for office.

The Founders themselves would not have agreed; they did not make the distinction between private and public conduct that so many do today. In his book, *On Two Wings*, theologian Michael Novak tells the story of a prominent Boston doctor, Benjamin Church, Jr. Church's fellow Bostonians thought him to be a patriot and were subsequently shocked to learn that he had been selling his services to the British. In a letter to James Warren, Samuel Adams offered an explanation that would be incomprehensible to many contemporary Americans: He linked the doctor's treason to his reputation as an adulterer.

Adams wrote: "He who is void of virtuous attachments in private life, is, or very soon will be, void of all Regard for his country." He added that "there is seldom an instance of a man guilty of betraying his Country, who had not before lost the feeling of moral obligations in his private connections ..." In other words, if a man or a woman won't honor private obligations, why should we believe that he or she will honor his public ones? They won't, as was made abundantly clear by the end of the Clinton presidency. Scandal followed scandal literally up to his final day in office, when—for self-serving reasons (his wife's Senate campaign)—Clinton pardoned 140 criminals including a cocaine trafficker, fugitive financier Marc Rich, his brother Roger, and 16 members of a Puerto Rican terrorist group that had exploded 120 bombs in New York and Chicago. The release of these terrorists was condemned by both the Senate and the House of Representatives, the FBI, members of Congress, and the Fraternal Order of Police. Victims of the terrorists were horrified.

The personal moral failings of American presidents—not just Clinton and my friend and former boss Richard Nixon, but others whose sins remained hidden while they were in office—undoubtedly affects their public trustworthiness and the respect they enjoy abroad. The truth of this came home to me when I attended a black-tie dinner in England just prior to the president's impeachment. As is the custom of the British, the host stood at the dinner's conclusion, raised his glass and said, "To the Queen." The rest of the diners echoed, "To the Queen." The senior American present then stood and said, "To the President of the United States." The crowd's response? Snickers and outright laughter.

Clearly, the White House stood in a shadow of shame. The scandals would affect Clinton's dealings with China, the Middle East, and a myriad of problems on the international stage—such as the growing threat of Islamic terrorism. For the sake of the country he claimed to serve, President Clinton—like President Nixon—should have resigned. A nation that does not demand high standards of character in its leaders will end up being a nation of barbarians. Anyone who doubts that ought to accompany me into prison one day.

If the link between private and public virtue is hard to understand, the problem lies with us, not our Founders. Our culture has forgotten what the Founders knew: The American experiment is a moral, not just a political, exercise. And as such, it assumes certain things to be true about human nature and about the authority of the God of the Bible.

Moral values do affect character, and the influence of individual character has an impact on society. Not just with public officials, but in the lives of ordinary citizens. Nowhere is this more evident than in the area of criminal behavior.

Though for years conventional wisdom held that racial discrimination, economic deprivation, and environment were the chief causes of crime, leading criminologists and psychiatrists are now concluding that personal character is the single greatest determining factor in criminal behavior.

James Q. Wilson, Harvard social scientist, after surveying American history and comparing religious activity with crime data during specified periods, discovered a startling correlation. In the middle of the nineteenth century when rapid urbanization would normally lead one to expect increased crime, the level of crime actually fell. Interestingly, it was during that same period that a great spiritual awakening occurred. Thus, Wilson explains, morality took hold just as industrialization began. From the mid–1800s to 1920, despite environmental, economic, and social pressures that should have made it rise, the crime rate decreased.

Conversely, during the "good" economic years of the twenties, crime began to rise. Because, says Wilson, "the educated classes began to repudiate moral uplift, and Freud's psychological theories came into vogue." People no longer believed in restraining a child's sinful impulses; they wanted to develop his "naturally good" personality.[9]

Even more surprising, crime did not rise, as sociologists expected, during the Great Depression when, it is estimated, 34 million men, women, and children were without any income at all — 28 percent of the population.[10] Tough times seem to develop strength of character and a tendency for the populace to pull together, whereas good times leave people free to seek self-interest and satisfaction, legally or otherwise. If this correlation is valid, the soaring crime rates in today's affluent, egocentric Western culture are altogether understandable.

Correlation between religious values and public order was dramatically evident during a religious revival early in the last century. The revival began in small Methodist churches in Wales and quickly spilled out into society. During New Year's week in 1905, for the first time ever there was not a single arrest for drunkenness in Swansea County, the police announced. In Cardiff the authorities reported a 40 percent decrease in the jail population while the tavern trade fell off dramatically. Prayer meetings sprang up in coal mines; stores reported stocks of Bibles sold out; dockets were cleared in criminal courts; and many police were unemployed. Stolen goods were returned to shocked store owners. One historian reported, "Cursing and profanity were so diminished that ... a strike was provoked in the coal mines ... so many men had given up using foul language that the pit ponies dragging the coal trucks in the mine tunnels did not understand what was being said to them and stood still, confused."[11] The revival soon spread throughout the British Isles and much of the English-speaking world. Church attendance rose, and in many areas, as in Wales, public morality was dramatically affected.

Men and women who profess allegiance to the Kingdom of God become models for the rest of society. The role of the City of God, as Augustine said, is "to inspire men and women to organize their communities in the image and likeness of the heavenly city."[12]

In the Kingdom of God, God is King and Lawgiver for all. This does not mean that the Old Testament's civic code should be passed by modern governments. What it does mean, as Plato and Cicero recognized, is that there are moral absolutes that must govern human behavior; there is a law rooted in truth upon which the laws of human society are based.

The presence of the Kingdom of God in society means the presence of a community of people whose lives testify to this Law behind the law. They eschew relativism, believe that some things are right, some are wrong, and adhere to universal ethical norms. The presence of such people in society, therefore, is a powerful bulwark to legal sanity.

But the Kingdom of God is more than just a model. It actually operates as a restraint on the kingdoms of man through its individuals and through its most visible manifestation, the church. For in our society the church is the chief institution with the moral authority to mediate between individuals and the government, to hold the state to account for its obligations to its citizens.

The American government was established with the understanding that such transcendent values would affect what otherwise is simply a social contract. When the state forgets or denies those values that were original conditions of the contract, in essence it abrogates its contract with its citizens. It is then that the church must take the initiative and call the state to account, for as Richard Neuhaus writes, the church is "the particular society within society that bears institutional witness to the transcendent purpose to which the society is held accountable."[13]

This is the point at which the conflict between the two kingdoms often becomes the greatest. Government by nature seeks power and will always attempt to generate its own moral legitimacy for its decisions. Inevitably, it resents any group that attempts to act as its conscience.

But as history demonstrates, and as we have already discussed, the result of government attempting to impose its own moral vision upon society or acting without the restraint of an independent conscience is tyranny. Contrary to today's popular illusion, the job of propagating moral vision belongs not to government but to other institutions of society, most notably the church. When the state oversteps the bounds of its authority, the church becomes, as we saw during Poland's fight to overthrow communism, the one effective source of moral resistance. The church does this not for its own ends as an earthly institution, but for the common good.

This may well be the area most perplexing to Christians and secularists alike, for both sides are frequently confused about the right, and indeed in some cases the duty, of the church, as well as individuals within the church, to confront the state.

To understand, we must first examine what citizenship in the Kingdom really means. What must citizens of the Kingdom do to be true to their allegiances and bring the healthiest influence of the Kingdom of God to bear on the kingdoms of this world—to be true patriots in the best sense of the word?

17

CHRISTIAN PATRIOTISM

Whatever makes men good Christians,
makes them good citizens.
DANIEL WEBSTER

In the kingdoms of man, young people learn the basics of good citizenship in high-school civics courses. Legal immigrants attend special classes to learn their new country's laws and their civic responsibilities; they must pass a test to prove they understand their new citizenship and then must swear their allegiance. Good citizenship requires such basic duties as paying taxes, voting, serving in the military and on juries, and obeying the laws of the land.

In the Kingdom of God one learns the obligations of citizenship from the Scriptures, the ultimate source of basic Christian truth. Unfortunately, many people, churched or unchurched, are woefully ignorant in this area. A 2005 report issued by the Bible Literacy Project suggests that American youth know almost nothing about the Bible. For instance, the report found that eight percent of American teens believe Moses is one of the Twelve Apostles. Another report reveals that while the average American household contains three Bibles, their owners are apparently not reading them. Fewer than half of Americans can identify the first book of the Bible, according to a Gallup Poll, just one-third of respondents know who delivered the Sermon on the Mount (quite a few think Billy Graham did), and a full one quarter have no idea what we celebrate on Easter Sunday. A 1995 Barna poll revealed that 12 percent of Christians think Joan of Arc was Noah's wife.

If the average churchgoer is uninformed, however, one does not have to look far to understand why. Church leaders have treated us to a smorgasbord of trendy theologies, pop philosophies, and religious variants of egocentric cultural values.

276

Some years ago, for example, a group of church scholars met to discuss which of Christ's words in the gospels could be accepted as authentic. Their modern critical analysis was carried out by ballot. Slips of colored paper were distributed to the group: a red slip meant the statement was authentic; pink meant probably authentic; gray meant probably not; and black meant not authentic. After intense discussion of each of Jesus' statements, participants cast their votes with the appropriate card. The Beatitudes and the Sermon on the Mount took a beating in the balloting. "Blessed are the peacemakers" was voted down; "blessed are the meek" garnered a paltry six red and pinks out of thirty votes. In the end only three of the twelve assorted woes and blessings from Matthew and Luke survived.

Such theological tomfoolery might be dismissed as too ludicrous to worry about except that this pink-slip mentality pervades the church. Orthodoxy— adherence to the historic tenets of Christianity—is under intense assault. This has been true since the Enlightenment, of course, but not until the last century have so many in the church seriously argued that truth can be determined by majority vote or that the gospel should accommodate the whims of culture.

I have heard it said that reinterpreting the gospel in the context of modern culture is enlightened and progressive. Maybe some find that so, but Joseph Sobran better expresses my feelings: "It can be exalting to belong to a church that is five hundred years behind the times and sublimely indifferent to fashion; it is mortifying to belong to a church that is five minutes behind the times, huffing and puffing to catch up."[1]

Christianity rests on the belief that God is the source of truth and that He does not alter it according to the spirit of the times. When Christians sever their ties to absolute truth, relativism reigns, and the church becomes merely a religious adaptation of the culture.

Theologian Donald Bloesch maintains that modern "secularism is preparing the way for a new collectivism." He points to a historical precedent we have already looked at in some detail, the church in Germany. It was the confessing orthodox church in Germany that rose up in resistance to Hitler while "the church most infiltrated by the liberal ideology, the Enlightenment, was quickest to succumb to the beguilement of national societies."[2] Enticed by secular ideology, they saw the state as a vehicle for advancing the church.

Bloesch also points to an illustration from the days of apartheid in South Africa. It can be shown, he writes, "that of the three Reformed churches the most liberal theologically is the most illiberal in racial attitudes, whereas the most consciously Calvinist is the most courageous in speaking out against racial injustice."[3]

The effect of preaching a false theology can be disastrous. Many readers will remember the much celebrated fall of televangelists Jim and Tammy Bakker (and later, Jimmy Swaggert). Most attribute the Bakkers' fall to greed, sexual indiscretion, and the corruption of power. These were, of course, serious contributing factors. But the root cause of their downfall was that for years the Bakkers had preached a false gospel of material advancement: If people would only trust God, He would shower blessings upon them and indulge them with all the material desires of their hearts—a religious adaptation of the prevailing "what's in it for me" mentality. Tragically, the Bakkers deluded themselves into believing their own false message. Taking a two-million-dollar-a-year salary, living in splendor, and indulging their every whim didn't seem wrong; it was "God's blessing." And millions of followers continued to support them, even after their fall, because they, too, wanted such blessings.

The first responsibility for the citizen of the Kingdom, then, is to understand historic Christian truth: to know Scripture and the classic fundamentals of the faith. This is not to say that Christians are to mindlessly accept whatever they are told is an orthodox creed. Honest inquiry and thoughtful examination of the evidence, I believe, are healthy and should be encouraged, for these invariably lead to firmer belief in the truth of God's revelation interpreted by the great theologians through the ages. As Chesterton said, "Dogma does not mean the absence of thought but the end [result] of thought."[4]

When Christians either lack knowledge or are insecure about what they believe, as is the case with many today, they forfeit their place in contending for theological truth, and secularism advances. This is why James Schall implores Christians "to regain their confidence in their own dogmas.... These are not idle speculations," he writes, "but the order of reality out of which a right order in human things alone can flow."[5] Such confidence is essential if Christians are to contend for values in culture and restore a sense of the transcendent to secular thought.

The problem is, as literary critic Harry Blamires states flatly, "there is no Christian mind."[6] By this he means that Christians have their own set of beliefs but, lacking confidence, keep them to themselves. As long as they are in a secular context, they act by secular values. When they return to the privacy of their religious enclaves where they can safely think and act in Christian terms, they do so. As a result their most fundamental beliefs never penetrate the culture. The late Jacques Ellul reminds us that the only way theological truth reaches the world is through the actions of laypeople in the marketplace.[7]

It is this first step of Christian citizenship in the Kingdom of God—knowledge and confidence in classical Christian truth—that enables the Christian to be a good citizen in the kingdoms of man. And it is in Scripture and classical doctrine that he or she finds the clearest expression of an individual's responsibility to both kingdoms.

On the one hand Scripture commands civil obedience—that individuals respect and live in subjection to governing authorities and pray for those in authority.[8] On the other it commands that Christians maintain their ultimate allegiance to the Kingdom of God. If there is a conflict, they are to obey God, not man.[9] That may mean holding the state to moral account through civil disobedience. This dual citizenship requires a delicate balance.

Christians who are faithful to Scripture should be patriots in the best sense of that word. They are "the salvation of the commonwealth," said Augustine, for they fulfill the highest role of citizenship.[10] Not because they are forced to or even choose to, not out of any chauvinistic motivations or allegiance to a political leader, but because they love and obey the King who is above all temporal leaders. Out of that love and obedience they live in subjection to governing authorities, love their neighbors, and promote justice. Since the state cannot legislate love, Christian citizens bring a humanizing element to civic life, helping to produce the spirit by which people do good out of compassion, not compulsion.

But Christians, at least in the United States, have all too often been confused about their biblical mandates and have therefore always had trouble with the concept of patriotism. They have vacillated between two extremes—the God-and-country, wrap-the-flag-around-the-cross mentality and the simply-passing-through mindset.

The former was illustrated a century ago by the president of Amherst College who said that the nation had achieved the "true American union, that sort of union which makes every patriot a Christian and every Christian a patriot."[11] This form of civil religion has endured as a peculiar American phenomenon supported by politicians who welcome it as a prop for the state and by Christians who see it enshrining the fulfillment of the vision of the early pilgrims.

The passing-through mindset is represented by those who believe they are simply sojourners with loyalties only in the Kingdom beyond. They believe that faith is an entirely private matter, and that they are under no obligation to the community or country in which God has placed them.

These two extremes miss the kind of patriotism Augustine had in mind. He believed that while as Christians we are commanded to love the whole world, practically speaking we cannot do so. Since we are placed as if by "divine lot" in a particular nation state, it is God's calling that we "pay special regard" to those around us in that state. We love the world by loving the specific community in which we live.[12]

C. S. Lewis likened love of country to our love for the home and community in which we were raised. It is a natural love of the place where we grew up, he said, "love of old acquaintances, of familiar sights, sounds and smells." He also pointed out, however, that in love of country, as in love of family, we don't love our spouses only when they are good. Similarly, a patriot sees the flaws of his country, acknowledges them, weeps for them, but remains faithful in love.[13]

Dr. Martin Luther King, Jr., spoke of love for his country even as he attempted to change its laws. "Whom you would change, you must first love," he said.[14]

That's the kind of tough love Christians must have for their country. We are called to love the land faithfully, but not at the expense of suspending moral judgment. Indeed, it is the addition of that moral judgment that makes Christian patriotism responsible. "Loyalty to the civitas can safely be nurtured only if the civitas is not the object of highest loyalty," is the way Richard Neuhaus expresses it.[15]

The basic principle from Scripture is straightforward: Civil authorities are to be obeyed unless they set themselves in opposition to divine law. As Augustine put it, "An unjust law is no law at all."[16] This is the other side of Caesar's coin and can lead to civil disobedience. Practical application of this principle, however, raises perplexing questions, as we have witnessed in recent decades.

Since the sixties, civil disobedience has become a preferred method of protest. As unlikely as it may seem to some, this is an area where the Christian church has a major contribution to make in public discussion. After all, we've wrestled with this matter for two thousand years.

If Scripture does give clear principles on the matter, as I believe it does, then when is civil disobedience justified? And how is it to be carried out?

Civil disobedience is clearly justified when government attempts to take over the role of the church or allegiance due only to God. Then the Christian has not just the right but the duty to resist. The Bible gives a dramatic example of this in its account of three young Jewish exiles who were drafted into the Babylonian civil service.[17]

All citizens of Babylon were required to worship the statue of Nebuchadnezzar, the king; those who disobeyed were incinerated. Like many political leaders, King Nebuchadnezzar was not satisfied with power and authority; he wanted spiritual submission as well. Shadrach, Meshach, and Abednego, the young Hebrews, refused. To worship an earthly king would be the ultimate offense against their holy God.

"Our God will deliver us," they told the king when they were condemned to death for their disobedience. "But if not, we will still not worship you."[18] (It is significant to note, a point we will address later, that they were willing to pay the price for their disobedience.) The three young men were thrown into a blazing furnace. God did miraculously deliver them—something we can't always count on—and as a result the king began to worship the one true God.

Civil disobedience is also mandated when the state restricts freedom of conscience, as in the case of Peter and John, two of Jesus' disciples.

Peter and John were arrested for disturbing the peace. They were taken before the Sanhedrin, a religious body holding authority from the government of Rome, and ordered to stop preaching about Jesus. Peter and John refused.

"Judge for yourselves whether it is right in God's sight to obey you rather than God," they said. "We cannot help speaking about what we have seen and heard."[19]

Their first allegiance was to the commandment they had been given by the resurrected Christ: the Great Commission to preach the gospel first to Jerusalem, then to the rest of Judea, and then to the ends of the earth.

They could not permit the authority of the government-backed Sanhedrin to usurp the authority of God Himself.

This is a very real conflict for many Christians around the world—even in democracies. For example, in August of 2006, police took two pastors and five students from the Christian Education Institute in Katuwa in the Indian state of Jammu and Kashmir and charged them with "abetting conversions." In the southern Indian state of Karnataka, during the same month, Hindu extremists ordered Christians to leave their homes, slapped them, and took them to the village temple, where they were forced to bow down before Hindu gods and goddesses; watching police did nothing. In Saudi Arabia, Iran, and Pakistan, citizens can be put to death for converting to Christianity.

During a visit to the United States a few years ago, a pastor from Nepal told of his imprisonment in his own country for proselytizing. In conclusion he gave an excellent summary of Christian duty. "Of course I must obey my Lord and spread His Word," he said. "But even though we are persecuted, we who are Christians in Nepal pride ourselves on being the best citizens our king has. We try to be faithful to the fullest extent we can. We love our country—but we love our God more."[20]

The third justification for civil disobedience is probably the most difficult to call. It is applied when the state flagrantly ignores its divinely mandated responsibilities to preserve life and maintain order and justice. Those last words are key for Christians in deciding to disobey civil authority. Civil disobedience is never undertaken lightly or merely to create disorder. Replacing one bad situation with another is no solution, but when the state becomes an instrument of the very thing God has ordained it to restrain, the Christian must resist.

Inadequate though it was, the resistance of the German church to Hitler was a clear modern example of this necessity. In the fifties and sixties, this necessary resistance was modeled by those active in the American Civil Rights Movement. In the eighties and nineties, we saw necessary resistance modeled by those who took part in the Operation Rescue sit-ins at abortion clinics, where hundreds of nonviolent protestors were arrested for peaceful civil disobedience, particularly during the 1991 "Summer of Mercy" sit-ins in Wichita, Kansas. There, thousands of protesters were arrested at "rescues" at an abortion clinic run by infamous late-term abortionist George Tiller. For many years we also witnessed nonviolent resistance to apartheid in South Africa, which ended only when apartheid was outlawed in 1990.

When civil disobedience is justified, how is that disobedience to be carried out? When all recourse to civic obedience has been exhausted and the evil of the state is so entrenched as to be impenetrable, then the Christian may be justified (as discussed in a later chapter) in organizing to overthrow the state. First recourse, however, is always minimum resistance. Good citizens always avoid breaking just laws to protest unjust laws.

Daniel in the Old Testament exemplifies the use of the least resistance necessary to accomplish the result.

Daniel was another Jewish exile living in Babylon, a contemporary of Shadrach, Meshach, and Abednego. King Nebuchadnezzar was impressed with Daniel and enlisted his service. As a member of the king's court, Daniel was required to eat from the king's table. While such delicacies were tempting, Daniel did not want to be "defiled"; that is, he did not want to break God's strict dietary laws for His people.[21] He quietly sought his superior's permission not to eat the food, and permission was granted. Daniel could have launched a hunger strike, but it was not necessary. He achieved his objectives with minimum resistance.

Where peaceful means are available, force should be avoided. Clearly, at least in a democratic society, this should be the path civil disobedience takes. A person who, for example, feels the state's action in war is immoral has the right to pursue the matter of conscientious objection (although technically our government allows that preference only to those who practice pacifism at all times, not just for what they may perceive to be right or wrong wars).

Another important principle related to civil disobedience is illustrated by the apostles Peter and John as well as the three young Hebrews: though they disobeyed authority, they showed the appropriate respect for that authority by a willingness to accept their punishment. Those who practice civil disobedience must be prepared to pay the consequences of civil disobedience.

These general principles from Scripture are clear enough; but it is often another thing to apply them to specific circumstances, as the case of a zealous and deeply devout young woman illustrates.

Joan Andrews is a slight, soft-spoken Roman Catholic who on March 26, 1986, entered an abortion clinic and attempted to damage a suction machine used to perform abortions. She was charged and convicted of criminal mischief, burglary, and resisting arrest without violence. The prosecution asked for a one-year sentence. The judge gave her five.

Miss Andrews announced to the court, "The only way I can protest for unborn children now is by non-cooperation in jail." She then dropped to the courtroom floor and refused to cooperate with prison officials at any stage of her processing. Labeled a troublemaker, she was transferred to Broward Correctional Institute, a tough maximum-security women's prison where she was placed in solitary confinement.

On one level, Joan Andrews's sentence was severe. For example, the same day she was sentenced, two men convicted as accessories to murder were sentenced by the same judge to four years. Five years for Joan Andrews's crimes is disproportionately harsh.

On the other hand, in her protest against abortion, Miss Andrews violated several laws. Much like the civil rights activists who took part in lunch counter protests and pro-life activists who peacefully barricaded the doors to abortion clinics, Miss Andrews deliberately violated trespassing laws as a means of attracting public attention. In her case, the fear of doing nothing, of standing by while innocent lives were being taken, was greater than the fear of prison. But even if the cause is just, as I believe both civil rights and pro-life activism to be, are such means of opposition appropriate?

In a free or democratic society there are legal means available to express political opposition: we can picket, petition, vote, organize, advertise, or pressure political officials. Is it right to abandon our respect for the rule of law, the foundation for public order, simply to make statements that could be made legally in other forums? Can one break a just law in the name of protesting an unjust law? Few biblical precedents are set for us, and those that are clearly deal with laws that were themselves unjust. In our day, breaking laws to make a dramatic point is the ultimate logic of terrorism, not civil disobedience.

There may be situations, however, in which one has to respond to a higher law when life itself is at stake. Joan Andrews and Operation Rescue protestors justified their actions in those terms: by interrupting the abortion clinics' operations, they were saving lives. Many Jews and Christians during World War II refused to obey Nazi laws requiring registration of aliens. On the surface those might have seemed just laws, no different than alien registration laws on the books of most Western countries today. But the citizens disobeyed because they knew those laws were being used to identify individuals for extermination.

Rightly exercised, civil disobedience is divine obedience. But when Christians engage in such activities, it must always be to demonstrate their submissiveness to God, not their defiance of government.

Unfortunately, no neat formulas for civil disobedience exist. The citizen must seek wisdom in striking the fine balance between disobedience and respect for the law. The state, though ordained by God and thus deserving of respect, is not God. The true patriot, therefore, is not one who always obeys the law. If that were so, the sheriff enforcing Jim Crow laws or the Auschwitz guard would be the best of citizens. On the other hand, disobedience can never be undertaken lightly.

Many on both the political right and left seem all too eager to defy civil authority and disrupt order to make a point on the evening news. Their causes range from preventing military recruiters from entering college campuses, to sheltering illegal immigrants, to attacking churches that oppose same sex "marriage," to demanding that supermodels gain weight. Some seem temperamentally disposed to such protest, as if they get high on the thrill of civil disobedience. But as the late Harvard law professor Alexander Bickel warns, "Civil disobedience, like law itself, is habit-forming, and the habit it forms is destructive of law."

Good citizenship requires both discernment and courage — discernment to soberly assess the issues and to know when duty calls one to obey or disobey, and courage, in the case of the latter, to take a stand.

The citizens of the Kingdom of God should be patriots in the highest sense, loving the world by loving those in the nation in which they live because that government is ordained by God to preserve order and promote justice. Perhaps this is why John Adams wrote that a patriot must be "a religious man."[22] Christians understand the phrase "a nation under God" not as a license for blind nationalism or racial superiority but as a humbling acknowledgment that all people live under the judgment of God.

Christian patriots spend more time washing feet than waving flags. Ideally, flags should not even be thought of as symbols of military and economic might, but of the common good of the specific people a sovereign God has called them to serve.

18

LITTLE PLATOONS

The greatest thing is to be found at one's post as a child of God,
living each day as though it were our last, but planning as though
our world might last a hundred years.

C. S. LEWIS

For some three decades—ever since the entertainment industry decided that helping the needy was chic—the world has been treated to a billion-dollar bonanza of celebrity benefits. Band-Aid, a group of top British and Irish performers, put together a Christmas album to help starving children in Ethiopia in 1984. That started the aid wagons rolling. Then came Live Aid in 1985, a marathon rock concert simulcast from London and Philadelphia. This was followed by Fashion Aid, Farm Aid, and what can only be called AIDS Aid. Hands Across America linked up from Los Angeles to New York to raise $100 million for domestic homelessness and hunger, while the Freedom Festival raised money for Vietnam veterans.

And then there's my favorite: Sport Aid, which began with a runner leaving Ethiopia with a torch lighted from a refugee's campfire. He jogged through several European cities. Then this tireless athlete flew to New York, torch in hand (I wonder what he did when the "no smoking" sign came on?), where he lighted a flame in Manhattan's United Nations Plaza, signaling the start of simultaneous 10-kilometer runs around the world. The plan, said organizer Bob Geldof, also the mastermind of Live Aid, was to raise money to fight disease and hunger in Africa.

More recently, Bono, the lead singer of the Irish rock band U2, has invited the world to join him in fighting hunger and AIDS in Africa—not by purchasing a concert ticket, but by increasing America's foreign aid budget. And actor George Clooney has traveled the world bringing attention to the tragedy taking place in Darfur.

While few of us would deny that helping starving, homeless, and needy people is a good thing, this aid frenzy does raise some practical questions.

First, in an industry where publicity is the ticket to success, one may be excused for wondering if celebrity participation in compassion extravaganzas is altogether altruistic. The "We Are the World" video, which sold millions of copies and won several Grammies, reminds us less of starving children than of the great humanitarianism of its showcase of rock idols. The goals may be worthy, but such slickly publicized charity certainly recalls biblical warnings against hiring trumpeters—or camera crews—to record one's good deeds.

This point was made by the band Chumbawamba, which released a record called *Pictures of Starving Children Sell Records*. As one observer put it, Chumbawamba "viewed the Live Aid concert with cynicism, suggesting that performers were in it for themselves, as much as the people they were professing to help."

The late rock promoter Bill Graham said of celebrity aid, "It's an incredible power, knowing on any given day you can raise a million dollars."[1] Perhaps, as *Newsweek* observed, "that is why Live Aid and Farm Aid were such oddly upbeat exercises in self-congratulation. An industry was celebrating its power. Far from challenging the complacency of an audience, such mega-events reinforce it.... Now by watching a pop-music telethon and making a donation ... fans can enjoy vicariously a sense of moral commitment."[2]

We might put aside our suspicions as petty if only we knew that those in need were being helped. But are they?

In June of 2005, Fox News host Bill O'Reilly criticized Bob Geldof's oversight of the money raised for starving Ethiopians, pointing out that a substantial chunk of change ended up in the pockets of Ethiopian President Mengistu Haile Mariam, who was convicted of genocide in 2006. This is why relief organizations should control donations, O'Reilly declared—not corrupt governments.

Journalist Tim Russert made the same point while interviewing Bono on *Meet the Press*. Bono agreed, saying, "This is the number-one problem facing Africa: corruption. Not natural calamity, not the AIDS virus."

Even the best-laid plans sometimes succumb to squabbles over how money and food should be distributed, or stymied by machine-gun toting gangs who control the ports and food distribution centers of many developing countries.

Let's not kid ourselves. Just because the fans in London or Philadelphia go home satisfied does not mean that the hungry in Africa go home fed.*

The question of whether the money goes where it's intended came to mind when I watched Bono speak at the 2006 National Prayer Breakfast. Bono has given great visibility to the needs of suffering people, particularly Africans dying of AIDS. I have studied carefully what Bono has said and done, and while I approve of his efforts to give greater visibility to the needs of suffering people, I believe that his response to world poverty and hunger is too simplistic.

In his Prayer Breakfast address, Bono invited the audience — which included President Bush and many members of Congress — to increase the U.S. federal budget by one percent as a "tithe" to the developing world.

"America gives less than one percent now," Bono said. "We're asking for an extra one percent to change the world, to transform millions of lives."

Cheers and thunderous applause greeted his remarks, but I could not help thinking of the cynical comment of a Swiss banker I knew. He told me that every time we hand out large aid packages in Africa, there is a concurrent swelling of Zurich bank accounts belonging to African dictators.

While Bono's intentions are excellent, the problem is that we cannot get aid money to those who need it because it has to go through a system that is fundamentally corrupt. Without the rule of law and honest governments, no amount of money is going to solve the problems of poverty, hunger, and disease in the developing world.†

Despite all the ballyhoo, feeding the hungry did not originate with Live Aid. Christians have been doing it since the church began, not for T-shirts and pop albums, but in obedience to Christ's command to care for those in need. Organizations such as World Vision, Catholic Relief Services, the Salvation Army, and millions of local churches have for generations been feeding the hungry, housing the homeless, and clothing the needy without the glamorous carrot-and-stick razzle-dazzle so recently discovered by the rich and famous. This kind of Christian patriotism also benefits society as a whole.

---

*The answer, Bono says, is to "route the aid away from the governments and through the NGOs on the ground." But are celebrities equipped to pull this off?

†Bono's decision to launch, with Irish fashion designer Rogan Gergory, the clothing line EDUN, may ultimately prove more successful in helping peoples of the developing world. By encouraging investment in developing nations by using factories that pay workers fair wages and which practice good business ethics, Bono hopes to create a business model that will encourage investment in developing nations.

Jacques Ellul wrote that the answer to the big government illusion is small voluntary associations. As mentioned earlier, eighteenth-century statesman Edmund Burke described such voluntary groups as the "little platoons."[3] These are individuals or groups who perform works of mercy and oppose injustice. They are the salt and light of which Jesus spoke.

Culture is most profoundly changed not by the efforts of huge institutions but by individual people being changed. In the process, these citizens provide the main bulwark against government's insatiable appetite for power and control, and a safeguard against the sense of impotence fostered by today's overwhelming social problems. One person can make a difference.

A few months after Bob Geldof announced the success of the 1985 Live Aid concert, and while critics were still questioning whether food was actually arriving in the places of need, I went to Nairobi, Kenya, for a Prison Fellowship International conference. There I met a man who, though worthy of adulation, will never make the cover of *Rolling Stone*.

Pascal was a university professor when he was thrown into a Madagascar prison after a Marxist coup. While in prison he became a Christian.

After his release, Pascal began a small import-export company, but he kept returning to prison to preach the gospel to the men he had met there and others who had arrived since. During one such visit in early 1986, he walked past the infirmary and was shocked to see more than fifty naked corpses piled on the screened veranda, identification tags stuck between their toes.

Pascal went to the nurse. Had there been an epidemic, he asked. Of sorts, he was told. Prisoners were dying by the dozens of malnutrition.

Pascal left the prison in tears. He tried to get help to feed the starving inmates, but his own church was too poor, and there were no relief agencies to assist. So he began cooking food in his own kitchen and taking it to the prison.

Pascal and his wife fed prisoners every week, paying for the food out of the earnings from their small business. Without benefit of a government agency or even a theme song, this little platoon made all the difference for seven hundred prisoners in Madagascar.

There is no age limit for enlistment in America's little platoons. In December 1983, eleven-year-old Trevor Ferrell saw a television news report on

Philadelphia's inner-city homeless. The young boy couldn't believe people actually lived on the streets. When he questioned his parents, Frank and Janet reluctantly agreed to broaden their son's sheltered horizons — and their own. They left their home in an exclusive suburb and drove downtown.

A block past city hall, they spotted an emaciated figure crumpled on a sidewalk grate. While his parents watched a bit apprehensively, Trevor got out of the car and approached the man.

"Sir," he said, "here's a blanket for you." The man stared up at Trevor at first. Then, "Thank you," he said softly. "God bless you."

That encounter altered the Ferrells' lives forever. Night after night they drove downtown, trying in small ways to help the street people. They emptied their home of extra blankets and clothing, and made dozens of peanut-butter sandwiches. When others learned what they were doing, someone donated a van and volunteers charted nightly food distribution routes. To the Ferrells' surprise, "Trevor's Campaign" had begun.

Young Trevor found himself explaining what they were doing to local media, then to the nation. Merv Griffin, Mother Teresa, Ronald Reagan — all wanted to meet the small boy with the big mission. He told them simply, "It's Jesus inside of me that makes me want to do this."

But Trevor was a reluctant celebrity. He endured interviews with one eye on the door. He didn't know why people make such a fuss over him. Was it because helping the homeless was so unusual? In that case, said his father, the more who followed Trevor's example, the better.

For years, the blue van traveled the downtown streets of Philadelphia. It stopped first to deliver food to the residents of Trevor's Place, a ramshackle rooming house where some of the formerly homeless now lived. Then it proceeded to feed the hungry people gathered on sidewalk grates and street corners.

Asked how these handouts could make a difference in the complex business of helping the homeless, Frank Ferrell sighed. "We're trying to meet short-term needs and figure out ways to bring long-term changes to these people's lives. Sometimes it seems like just a band-aid. But this is how we build relationships. These people become our friends, and they trust us to help them in bigger ways."

Frank paused for a moment, looking at the landscape of broken bottles and bodies. "There are plenty of struggles. But I know one thing: *giving* has made all the difference in my Christian life. I used to just read the Scriptures. Now I feel like I'm living them."

The little platoon that began with a small boy's concern made a big difference to the homeless and hungry on the streets of Philadelphia—and to those who gave as well. Now in his thirties, married, and the father of two young girls, Trevor Ferrell is still helping the homeless and regularly speaking out on their behalf.

Thousands of miles from Trevor's Philadelphia home, some twenty years ago, a young Liberian woman began operating her own little platoon in Monrovia.

Lorince Taylor had a future in management as a claims supervisor for an insurance company, but her passion was for telling people about Christ. She wanted to do it full-time. When her husband encouraged her to follow her vision, Lorince resigned her job and in September 1985 began preaching in the city marketplace and in prisons and hospitals.

Although a number of people became Christians, Lorince soon realized that their problems went beyond the spiritual. She had to do more than tell them about Jesus. This became particularly evident one day when she visited a local mental hospital and, inadvertently, arrived during a staff strike.

The halls were littered with trash and dirty food trays. No doctors or nurses were in sight. The patients lay naked on the floors in their own filth, abandoned not only by their families but also by those paid to care for them.

Lorince Taylor left that building praying, "Lord, this is wrong. Help me do what I can to make it right."

Shortly thereafter Lorince went to the studios of ELTV, a national television station, and told them what she had found at the hospital. Reporters returned to the institution with her and filmed the shocking scenes of neglect. When the report aired, viewers were outraged. Public pressure not only got the hospital cleaned up, but brought forth donations of food and clothing for the patients.

Next Lorince went to the prostitutes of Monrovia. Many were receptive to her spiritual message; they became Christians and began studying the Bible with her. But sooner or later they returned to their old livelihood. Most had four or five children to support and had no other way to survive. Prostitution was all they had ever known.

"I believe," cried one young woman, "but I can't live the Christian life. I just can't climb out of the life I'm living."

It was then that Lorince envisioned a vocational center where the women could be trained in sewing, secretarial, and other skills. When a friend of mine last saw Lorince Taylor, a Liberian Christian had just donated a brand-new building to her ministry, and she had begun her center where former prostitutes and others in need can learn vocational skills.

Lorince Taylor's little platoon offered a ladder of escape to women trapped in a lifestyle that usually has no escape.

A little girl named Michelle learned the value of America's little platoons a few winters ago when a brutal storm nearly cost the child her life.

Michelle Schmitt had been on a waiting list for a liver transplant for two long, frustrating years. Finally the electrifying news came: A transplant was available. Michelle had just hours to fly from Louisville, Kentucky, to a hospital in Omaha, Nebraska.

Every minute counted. But heavy snows had shut down the entire city. If only Michelle could get to a county airfield, a helicopter ambulance service offered to pick her up and fly her to the Louisville airport, where a runway was being cleared.

But getting to the county airfield would eat up precious hours. That's when Southeast Christian Church came to the rescue. Church members had already helped raise money to cover the costs of the transplant operation. Now they had a brilliant thought: Let's not bring Michelle to the helicopter, let's bring the helicopter to Michelle. The aircraft could land on the church parking lot.

Members ran door to door, asking for help. Neighbors hurried to the church parking lot, shovels on their shoulders, to clear off a landing pad. Soon Michelle was on her way. The transplant operation was a complete success, and a little girl's life was saved.

Volunteerism is critical in ways we don't often think about: It fosters a distinctively American brand of civic responsibility.

America's founders did not believe governments could create virtue; government attempts to make people good are inherently coercive. In-stead, our Constitution rests on the premise that virtue comes from citizens themselves — acting through smaller groups such as the family, church, community, and voluntary associations.

These are what English statesman Edmund Burke called the "little platoons." They create the arena where virtue is best cultivated: both the disposition to be good and the impulse to do good. The little platoons are the roots of social order—schools in citizenship, where the art of self-government is practiced.

Historically, Americans have always impressed outsiders with their habit of volunteerism. In the nineteenth century, the French writer Alexis de Tocqueville marveled that Americans form associations for everything—to start libraries, send out missionaries, build hospitals and schools. By contrast, de Tocqueville remarked, in his own France there were not ten men doing what ordinary Americans do routinely.

As Christians we need to grasp the broad cultural impact of the ministries we devote our time to. Volunteerism is more than individual acts of justice and kindness, important though they are. When the members of Southeast Christian Church save the life of a little girl, or when you and I give up our Tuesday nights to visit a prisoner, in a very real sense we're helping to maintain the distinctive character of our society—to preserve America's richest heritage. We are strengthening the "little platoons" that foster virtue and are the bedrock of America's freedom.

An organization that began as a little platoon has exploded into a global enterprise, helping people like Jesse and Dora Garcia.

For years, the Garcias and their five children lived in a tent. They had no furniture, no bathroom. During every South Dakota wind storm, their patched-up tent nearly blew away.

Then the Garcias heard about Habitat for Humanity. Today the Garcias are sheltered from the wind in a sturdy four-bedroom home. And they're living proof of how Christians can transform a culture by living out the Gospel.

Habitat for Humanity was the brainchild of Millard Fuller. Three decades ago, building homes for the poor was the last thing on Fuller's mind. A millionaire by the time he was twenty-nine, Fuller thought he had it all: a successful law practice, a beautiful home, and a luxurious lifestyle. But his personal life was crumbling.

During this time of crisis, with his marriage collapsing, Fuller accepted Christ. And then he began searching for a way to put his newfound faith into practice. That's when he became aware of the tremendous need for decent housing for the poor. Soon, Habitat for Humanity was born.

Fuller's ministry brings together churches, businesses, and local governments to provide money, land, and lumber. They mobilize volunteers from local churches to do the actual building. And when a home is finished, it's sold at a modest price to a carefully chosen needy recipient. The new homeowners have to put in hundreds of hours of what Fuller calls "sweat equity": they swing a hammer or a paintbrush alongside the Habitat volunteers.

This remarkable ministry has earned kudos from liberals and conservatives alike. And over the years volunteers have built more than 200,000 homes around the world, providing decent housing for more than one million people.

I've personally witnessed what Habitat calls the "theology of the hammer." Twenty years ago I worked on a Habitat project on the west side of Chicago. About a hundred other volunteers, including men furloughed from prison, were there. So was former president Jimmy Carter. Together, we sawed boards, nailed studs, and put up drywall. We also prayed together and had devotions twice a day.

Habitat for Humanity illustrates the way faith in Christ leads to the right ordering of civil society. All too often, Christians are told to keep their faith private, out of the public realm. But Millard Fuller's example shows what happens when a man takes his faith into the street: Things happen. Poor people get decent homes.

Habitat for Humanity is faith in action. Without the theology of the cross, there would be no theology of the hammer.

John Perkins's little platoon dramatically illustrates a phenomenal restoration of community.

John grew up picking cotton in Mendenhall, Mississippi, for eight cents an hour. Early on, he grew frustrated with the injustice and endless cycle of poverty that fettered generations of black families in the rural south. He determined to escape.

Eventually, John beat the system by making it work for him. He and his wife, Vera May, left Mendenhall far behind for a successful business and comfortable lifestyle in California. But in 1957 John became a Christian and could no longer ignore those he had left behind. So in 1960 John and

Vera May returned to Mississippi with a vision of making the Kingdom of God visible there.

John had formulated a practical basis for change, what he now calls the three Rs of community development: relocation, reconciliation, and redistribution.

First, he saw that he couldn't help people from afar. Those who want to help the poor need to *relocate* and become part of their neighborhoods. Second, from his own experience, he realized that racial, social, and economic barriers created by racial hostility in the rural South of the sixties could be broken only by the forgiveness and healing that takes place through *reconciliation*; only the gospel of Christ truly provides this. And third, as he read his Bible, John saw that Christ presents a radical call for those who have, to share with those who do not. This means *redistribution* through sharing skills, technology, and educational resources.

As John, his family, and a growing platoon of individuals began to operate on these principles in Mendenhall, they formed what is now the Voice of Calvary Church. They soon began a store, a cooperative farm, nutritional and education programs. Meanwhile, the Christian community also came head to head with the injustice of racism dividing the South. In 1970 John and several others were jailed and nearly beaten to death by highway patrolmen and county sheriffs for their civil rights work. Once again, John struggled with bitterness in his own life—but he was able to forgive his tormentors.

Voice of Calvary expanded, adding organized tutoring and recreation programs, an adult education program, and a health center. By 1978 the Mendenhall work had become a model of Christian development in a rural community. In keeping with another of John's most passionate commitments, it was led by those who had been trained to lead in their own community.

In 1982 John and Vera May were ready for retirement. They returned to California, anticipating a quiet life of writing and traveling. Instead, the Perkinses decided to move into a crime-and-drug-infested neighborhood in otherwise peaceful and affluent Pasadena.

John knew the same principles that had given new life and dignity to people in rural Mendenhall would apply as well in the inner city. The result is the Harambee Center, a community of Christians helping their neighbors through education, employment, nutrition, neighborhood pride, and leadership training. Harambee, the Swahili word best translated "let's get together and push," evokes the Perkinses' commitment to working together with those who need help to help themselves.

John Perkins's little platoons model the values and hopes of the Kingdom of God for the kingdoms of man. Like Lorince Taylor's work, they are based in human dignity and a view of economics designed to equip people to climb out of their condition rather than manacling them to their poverty.

Sometimes the work of the little platoons mushrooms into a movement.

Another movement confronting widespread social evil is Mothers Against Drunk Driving (MADD). Started by a young mother whose teenage daughter was killed by a drunk driver, MADD has shattered complacency about alcohol and the carnage drunk drivers have created in our society. It offers services to victims through support groups and lobbies for legislatures to beef up drunk-driver laws. In a nation where a person is killed every half hour by a drunken driver, MADD has made a significant impact where government had made little progress.

Like the little platoons involved in MADD, who are committed to cracking down on a widespread social ill, millions of Americans have passionately campaigned against pornography. As one of the nation's least-regulated and most profitable industries, pornography recognizes few standards except the increasingly perverse tastes of its clientele. Yet it prospers, despite the FBI Academy's report convincingly tracing pornography's role in fantasies prior to sex-related murders, and such statistics as those from the Michigan State Police directly linking pornography to 40 percent of its assault cases.[4]

Pornography was not an area the government had ignored. In 1984 the attorney general appointed a panel to report on the issue. A year later the Commission on Pornography surfaced from the murky world of smut, and anti-pornography campaigners pinned great hopes on the panel's recommendations. Working through the leverage of big government seemed the most effective way to destroy such a widespread social cancer.

The commission, which included Focus on the Family's Dr. James Dobson, strongly believed there was a connection between some pornography and violent crimes. It recommended tougher prosecution, stronger federal laws, and more vigorous enforcement of existing obscenity laws.

Even if the panel's laudable proposals made it through the tough legislative process, however, they knew they could expect extended court challenges. As Barry Lynn of the American Civil Liberties Union boasted, "There are enough constitutional questions here [in the Meese report] to litigate for the next twenty years."[5]

As the commission was completing its report, the high-flying pornography industry suffered a major setback that caught everyone by surprise. It came from a little platoon.

When the late Jack Eckerd, founder of the Eckerd Drug chain, became a Christian in 1983, he called the company president and urged him to take *Playboy* and *Penthouse* magazines out of the Eckerd stores. The executive protested, telling him the magazines amounted to several million dollars a year in business. Jack Eckerd persisted. Eventually all 1,700 Eckerd drugstores stopped carrying *Playboy* and *Penthouse*. Eckerd then wrote to the directors of other retail stores and encouraged them to do the same. When his letters went unanswered, he wrote again.[6]

Meanwhile, the National Coalition Against Pornography was picketing and boycotting stores selling "adult" magazines. The pressure began to pay off. One by one Revco, People's, Rite Aid, Dart Drug, Gray Drug, and High's Dairy Stores pulled pornography from their shelves. And finally 7–11 removed these magazines from its 4,500 stores and recommended that its 3,600 franchises do the same.

Thus, without one debate before Congress or one case entangled in the courts, the shelves of nearly 12,000 retail stores were cleared of pornography!

Playboy's lawyers, shocked at their declining circulation, charged that a letter from the Meese Commission had put coercive pressure on the stores. Maybe so. But the real impetus came from the little platoons—thousands of individuals and one courageous man who put his faith into practice in his own business.

Not long ago someone brought to my attention a story in the Mobile, Alabama *Press-Register*. I was thrilled at the evidence that what I'm giving my life to is not a ministry but a movement.

The story was about Carolyn Morris, who runs a Christian bookstore in Atmore, Alabama. One day a story from my book, *Loving God*, caught her eye. It was about people in Jefferson County, Missouri who, upon visiting local prisons, discovered that families of inmates coming from out of town to visit did not have a place to stay. It wasn't unusual for them to sleep in their cars because they could not afford a motel room.

Touched by the story, Morris went to work in her own town. With the help of local churches, she bought and renovated a house. Volunteers painted it and added new carpeting and a roof. One room is fitted up with bunk beds, a crib, and high chair for younger guests. Many of the furnishings were donated by local churches and the community—right down to the bottles of shampoo saved from hotel visits. Each room contains a gentle reminder of why Morris has opened her home to such an unusual clientele: A Bible verse, or a picture of Jesus and his disciples.

Today, Morris lives in and directs Hospitality House, often befriending the women and children who stay there at little or no charge. Every weekend, Morris holds a garage sale to raise money to continue operating Hospitality House.

Morris got the idea for the name of the house from Romans 12:13: "Share with God's people who are in need. Practice hospitality." Few people are in greater need, or need hospitality more, than the mothers, wives and children of convicted criminals.

One of my favorite little platoons is a group of prison volunteers whose names I don't even know.

It was a rainy, dismal day in February when we arrived at the Maryland prison at Jessup, but the entry area was filled with the bright lights of television cameras. Reporters scribbled notes while Maryland officials greeted us warmly. Then-Governor Harry Hughes had even issued a proclamation for the occasion.

By the time we got to the prison chapel, it was on the verge of exploding with the excitement of more than 125 inmates and several dozen Prison Fellowship volunteers, all of whom had been participating in one of our in-prison seminars. With us was Wintley Phipps, the internationally known gospel singer who had sung only the day before for President Reagan at a prayer breakfast. When Wintley let loose in that cinder-block prison chapel, I thought the walls would come tumbling down.

Then, an African American inmate gave his testimony. This inmate had been converted while in a solitary-confinement cell. He had tremendous rapport with other inmates and his message was powerful, dramatic, and convicting.

The excitement continued as I challenged the men to accept Christ, then prayed with them. Afterward the inmates crowded around, hugging us and weeping.

The next day our instructor, Dick Robinson, was relieved to find all the inmates were back for the seminar's final session. He had thought the last day might be anticlimactic. Several inmates gave their impressions of the previous day.

"I really appreciated Chuck Colson's message," said one tall prisoner. "Wintley Phipps's singing stirred me beyond words, and [the African American inmate's] testimony reached me right where I was at. But frankly, those things really didn't impress me as much as what happened later.

"When the celebrities and TV cameras left," he continued, "the ladies among the volunteers went into the dining hall, with all the noise and confusion, and sat at the table to have a meal with us. That's what really got to me," he concluded, his voice choked.

Wintley's singing and Herman's testimony and my sermon were all appreciated. But the most powerful message came from the volunteers who went into the crowded, dingy dining hall to share prison food with the inmates.

Celebrities don't make the difference in society. The little platoons of ordinary people living extraordinary lives do.

At the height of the celebrity "feed the hungry" hoopla in the eighties, organizer Bob Geldof announced that his aid campaign's mission had been accomplished. "It's like a shooting star," he concluded. "For once ... something absolutely good and absolutely incorruptible came and went and worked."[7]

But shooting stars don't feed starving multitudes, and long after rockers have moved on to other causes, the hungry will remain.

Fortunately for the kingdoms of man, the little platoons march on.

THE PROBLEM
OF POWER

It is a magician's bargain: give up our souls, get power in return. But once our souls, that is, ourselves, have been given up, the power thus conferred will not belong to us. We shall in fact be slaves and puppets of that to which we have given our souls.

C. S. Lewis

John Naisbitt observed in *Megatrends* that significant movements begin from the bottom up, not the top down.[1] Truly important changes in culture begin not with officials or celebrities, but through ordinary people: the little platoons. Every person can—and should—seek to make a difference in his or her corner of the world by personally helping those in need.

Beyond this, some people, like William Wilberforce, are called to work through government structures and by political means to bring Christian influence into the culture. Those who do, however, need to be forewarned: the everyday business of politics is power, and power, as I know so well from my own experience, can be perilous for anyone.

My purpose here is not to deal exhaustively with the complex issue of power, nor could I. Entire books have been written on the subject. Yet no discussion of Christianity and politics would be complete without examining the dynamics of power, particularly as it affects the political arena and those who enter it.

The history of the last fifty years has validated Nietzsche's argument that man's desire to control his own destiny and to impose his will on others is the most basic human motivation. While I reject Nietzsche's atheistic cynicism, I do agree with his diagnosis of human nature. So did Christian psychiatrist Paul Tournier, who wrote, "We are moved without knowing it by an imperious will to power, which brooks no obstacles."[2]

Nietzsche's prophecy that the "will to power" would fill the twentieth-century's vacuum of values has been fulfilled. We see it on an individual level in the quest for autonomy and the shedding of all restraints. On a corporate level, it is dramatically evident in the rise of gangster leaders like Hitler, Stalin, and Mao, and evident as well in the bloated growth of Western governments.

The resultant illusion — that all power resides in large institutions — is the salient characteristic of modern politics. Power is often measured by one's prominence and ability to influence others. Politics is the most visible means to both in today's world.

Hunger for political power lures men and women from the comfort of their homes and jobs in the private sector and drives them to spend months, even years, traveling about their state or nation, subsisting on stale sandwiches, greasy chicken, and little sleep as they shout the same soul-stirring speech over and over until they are hoarse. Candidates for Congress spend several million dollars to fight for a job that pays $165,200 a year; others settle for lower-paying bureaucratic positions. Still others give huge political contributions in the hopes of acquiring even an obscure embassy appointment.

Certainly in every generation there are statesmen motivated by a genuine noblesse oblige, a sense of high calling to serve humanity. For the most part, though, Nietzsche's "will to power" fuels political passions in every culture.

I've seen it up close.

Even before I was invited to become part of the White House staff in 1969, I felt a sense of guilt that many of those I had worked with in the 1968 campaign joined the government at salaries far less than my own lucrative law-practice income. Duty to country had always weighed heavily with me, the flag-waving, ex-Marine, conservative political activist.

So when the offer came, I made the perfunctory protests about interrupting my career and burdening my family, but I was already packing up my office files. More than duty called me, of course. There was glamorous protocol, the possibility of shaping headlines and history, the enticement of being part of the inner circle surrounding the President of the United States. Deep down, though I wouldn't admit it, the White House represented the pinnacle of the power I had pursued all my life.

Joining the staff nine months into the new administration had some disadvantages. One of the first visible yardsticks of power is size and placement of office, and the best offices were already taken. I was given an inside suite a long way down the hall from the president's working office in the stately Old Executive Office Building (now called the Eisenhower Executive Office Building). Also, I reported not to the president, but to Bob Haldeman, his hard-nosed chief of staff. Not an auspicious beginning.

Within months, circumstances worked in my favor. An aide left, and everyone played musical offices. With a little fast footwork I maneuvered my way across the hall to an office commanding an impressive view of the South Lawn. From there I edged my way down the corridor toward the seat of power.

Within a short time my brusque get-it-done-at-all-costs approach won Nixon's favor, and I began to work directly with him. With that kind of clout I had little difficulty rearranging several Secret Service agents and secretaries so I could occupy the office immediately next to the president's.

Though the evidence of my change in status was visible in the attitude of my visitors when they realized that the president himself was just on the other side of the wall, the move was symbolic of something much more important. It meant I had passed an invisible divide. I was now *inside*. A *Newsweek* feature article heralded my arrival with the news that I was now on the top of every Washington hostess's guest list (ironic, since I never attended parties) and that the mere mention of my name "makes the tensions come in like sheet rain."[3] In Washington that means power.

In the political arena one of the most important attributes of power is its visibility. So we went to great lengths to protect our territory or prerogatives.

One Sunday in June 1971 the White House faced a sudden crisis: the *New York Times* published the "Pentagon Papers," the highly classified documents stolen by Daniel Ellsberg, a one-time Johnson-administration official turned antiwar activist. Mr. Nixon feared that our secret negotiations with the North Vietnamese would be exposed. For two days meetings went on around the clock, with the president, egged on by Henry Kissinger, barking angry orders to the Pentagon, the Justice Department, and his staff. (One such order led to my involvement in smearing Ellsberg, for which I later pleaded guilty and went to prison.)

At 8:00 on Tuesday evening the president phoned me with his latest instructions. "Chuck, I want you to call Lyndon Johnson. You explain to him that I'm taking all the heat for this. These are *his* administration's papers—

now, the least he can do is make some public statement supporting us. I mean, that will help us with the Democrats at least. You know what I mean? Now, just let Henry know and then you call Johnson. Understand?"

"Yes, sir," I replied.

"Good, good," said Nixon. "You get it done, and don't bother to call me back. I'm going to bed early."

Dutifully following orders, I called Kissinger first. The national security adviser, who admittedly had had a bad day, was outraged.

"If anyone is to call former President Johnson, it is me," he insisted, his accent thickening with his resolve.

Nothing I said made any difference, so I played my trump. "But the president ordered *me*, Henry," I said.

"Then I will call the president, and he will reverse that order," Kissinger replied.

In our power game Kissinger had checked me. The president had been up most of the night before; he needed sleep. Besides, he shouldn't have to bother with such squabbles. Kissinger knew this and he knew that I knew it. I hesitated a moment, then folded.

"Okay, Henry. Let's agree that neither of us will call until morning. Then we'll ask the president when we see him at the eight o'clock meeting."

"Good, Chuck. That is very good," he answered.

"But now you promise me," I added quickly, "that you won't bother him about it tonight."

"You have my word, Chuck," Kissinger said somberly.

The heat of our exchange left no doubt in my mind that the call to Johnson was important to Kissinger. Perhaps he feared that my making the call would indicate he was losing his influence or that I was taking responsibility for national security affairs. Whatever his thinking, I wasn't surprised at the White House operator's reply when I called ten minutes later to ask if anyone had phoned the president. "Oh, yes, sir," she replied. "Dr. Kissinger called him ten minutes ago."

Later that night Kissinger placed the call to Lyndon Johnson. Maintaining the appearance of power is also paramount, even when the reality is inconsequential.

On Nixon's last presidential trip abroad, in June 1974, he was accompanied by two senior aides, Al Haig and Ron Ziegler, both of whom were vying for top position. The trip, begun in the Soviet Union and including stops in Iran and Israel, was a vain last-ditch effort to divert attention away from the president's political crisis. By that time everyone knew Mr. Nixon couldn't survive the public clamor more than another month or two; his entire administration was about to collapse. Even so, the advance team was equipped with tape measures and meticulous instructions to insure that in all sleeping accommodations Mr. Ziegler's bed and General Haig's bed would be equidistant from the president's.

Those in office use their power to keep themselves in office. This is an accepted tradition in most Western democracies. In every American election since the forties the party in power has used grants and federal aid programs for political advantage. Truman won his upset victory in 1948 by doling out federal funds to struggling farmers and openly courting special-interest groups. Eisenhower judiciously announced grants in key states during the 1956 campaign. In the Kennedy and Johnson years a special White House office monitored election-year grants, and party fund-raisers notified defense contractors of impending contracts. Administrations since have adopted similar practices.

We were certainly not to be outdone in the Nixon years. I recall one incident from early 1972 when Bob Haldeman and I met with the president one morning to discuss reelection campaign strategy and schedules. We couldn't know at that point that Nixon would win in a record landslide. The polls showed him dead even with his expected opponent, Senator Edmund Muskie from Maine. Even though Nixon had only token primary opposition, I raised the question of visits to key primary states.

Haldeman chuckled. "No worry about the two big ones, New Hampshire and California. The Chinese and Russians will take care of those for us." Nixon laughed.

When I looked from one to the other in bewilderment, Haldeman delighted in detailing the tour de force he had arranged. Nixon's trip to China, he explained, was deliberately scheduled one week before the first primary in New Hampshire. Live coverage would dominate prime time for a week. Nixon would then receive a hero's welcome home, just days before New Hampshire voters went to the polls.

The summit in Moscow, Haldeman continued, would spotlight the first strategic-arms agreement ever signed on live television from inside the Kremlin. It was timed to transpire one week before the all-important California primary. The president would fly home on Air Force One, taking a helicopter from Andrews Air Force base to the Capitol. There he would address a joint session of Congress—all televised live on prime time, just four days before millions of Californians cast their votes. Haldeman had arranged which network reporters would be included. History had been scheduled according to the Nielsen ratings.

Nixon leaned back in his chair, took a long, deliberate puff on his Meerschaum pipe, and grinned. "Not bad, is it, Chuck? The Democrats won't even be able to buy time on TV."

"No, sir, not bad," I replied with open admiration. Even foreign policy was fair game.

These are not isolated examples, of course. All governments use the reality as well as the façade of power to maintain their own power. In democratic structures the process is somewhat subtle, but in regimes where there are few moral restraints, power is wielded shamelessly. We call it totalitarianism. George Orwell captured this in one of the most riveting scenes of his classic *1984*.

The book's central character, a hapless fellow named Winston, defies the state. He is eventually tracked down and tortured by the chief party functionary, O'Brien. As O'Brien administers massive electrical jolts to Winston's squirming body, he abandons all pretense and shrieks into Winston's ear, "The party seeks power entirely for its own sake ... we are interested only in power ... the object of power is power."[4]

Stalin rose to power by systematically murdering those who stood in his way; he then maintained his power by slaughtering millions. Hitler executed all potential threats to the Third Reich—even within his own SA—then consolidated his power grip on Germany with a regime of terror.* Mao Tsetung tormented millions in a never-ending cycle of public humiliation, beatings, torture and death, using terror and chaos to hold rivals at bay. More recent tyrants, such North Korea's Kim Jong-il and Iraq's Saddam Hussein, did the same thing.

One of the most startling commentaries on this century is the fact that millions more have died at the hands of their own governments than in wars with other nations—all to preserve someone's power.

---

*Hitler used a group of thugs to disrupt rival party meetings. The group became known as Hitler's brown shirted Strumabteilung or SA troopers.

In *The Masters*, British novelist C. P. Snow tells the story of a man who chooses not to be king but kingmaker, the ultimate achievement power affords.[5] Snow might well have been writing about me.

I entered government believing that public office was a trust, a duty. Gradually, imperceptibly, I began to view it as a holy crusade; the future of the republic, or so I rationalized, depended upon the president's continuation in office. But whether I acknowledged it or not, equally important was the fact that my own power depended on it.

While power may begin as a means to an end, it soon becomes, as O'Brien screamed in Winston's ear, the end itself. Having witnessed Watergate from the inside, I can attest to the wisdom of Lord Acton's well-known adage: Power corrupts; absolute power corrupts absolutely.

It is crucial to note, however, that it is power that corrupts, not power that is corrupt. It is like electricity. When properly handled, electricity provides light and energy; when mishandled it destroys. God has given power to the state to be used to restrain evil and maintain order. It is the use of power, whether for personal gain or for the state's ordained function, that is at issue.

The problem of power is not limited to public officials, of course. It affects all human relationships, from the domineering parent to the bullying boss to the manipulative spouse to the pastor who plays God. It is also wielded effectively by the seemingly weak who manipulate others to gain their own ends. The temptation to abuse power confronts everyone, including people in positions of spiritual authority.

The much-publicized corruption of some well-known evangelists can easily be traced to an inability to handle power. It's a heady business to run worldwide ministries, multimillion dollar television shows, or wealthy amphitheater churches. Leaders who rise to prominence in the religious world are placed on the precarious pedestal of Christian celebrity. When the celebrity is magnified a million times over by the electron tube, the dangers of falling increase dramatically.

At the time I was finishing the first edition of this book, Pat Robertson asked me if I would fill in for him on his daily broadcast. It was 1988, the year he made his ill-fated bid to win the Republican presidential nomination. The efficient staff of CBN was about as good as any I had encountered anywhere, including the White House. They arranged a home for Patty and me on Virginia Beach and sent a limousine to pick me up each morning to take me to the studio. In the dressing room, while they plastered me with powder and hair spray, aides busily ran in and out, handing me the latest dispatches off the wire services. Meanwhile, the producer was standing behind my chair, rapidly explaining what was expected of the program. Then, like a grand sultan surrounded by courtesans, I was swept from the makeup room, past all the wires and cameras and electronic controls, out to the stage. I heard the roar of the audience, which was watching this live telecast.

The first morning the whole business was a bit intimidating—frightening, in fact. The second morning I began to get accustomed to it. By the third morning I had really warmed to the task; I felt I could really teach listeners how to live Christianly. And by the fourth morning, I found myself almost liking all the attention. But at the beginning of the fifth day, I made a decision, which I announced at the conclusion of the broadcast. This was it: No more television hosting for me. Patty and I packed up and returned to Washington.

Admittedly, as I spoke into the camera, I felt, not only a sense of power, but *real* power. After all, every word I spoke was being heard by millions of people. In just one week I had discovered exactly why Jim and Tammy Bakker failed, and why Jimmy Swaggart fell so hard. Life in those studios is every bit as intoxicating as what I experienced in the White House. After my conversion I had vowed never to allow myself to be tempted by such power again. It is hugely seductive.

I witnessed the progress of this seduction with a man who became one of the country's most popular daytime television interviewers. The first time I was a guest on his show, before his popularity skyrocketed, he was humble, keenly interested in the subject, well-prepared and congenial. Two years later, when he had become the sensation of the television world, he breezed into the room flanked by obsequious aides, was woefully unconcerned with what his guests had to say, and was arrogant and rude on the air—to the delight of his studio audience.

For any Christian to believe that he or she is the worthy object of public worship is ludicrous; it would be like the donkey carrying Jesus into Jerusalem believing the crowds were cheering and laying down their garments for him. But the perks and public adoration accompanying television exposure are enough to inflate nearly anyone's ego. This leads to the self-indulgent use of power which reasons, "because I'm in this position, I have a right to do whatever I want," with total selfishness and disregard for others. Power is like saltwater; the more you drink the thirstier you get.

The lure of power can separate the most resolute of Christians from the true nature of Christian leadership, which is service to others. It's difficult to stand on a pedestal and wash the feet of those below.

It was this very temptation of power that led to the first sin. Eve was tempted to eat from the tree of knowledge to be like God and acquire power reserved for Him. "The sin of the Garden was the sin of power," says Quaker writer Richard Foster.[6]

Power has been one of Satan's most effective tools from the beginning, perhaps because he lusts for it so himself. Milton wrote of Lucifer in *Paradise Lost*, "To reign is worth ambition, though in hell. Better to reign in hell than serve in heaven."[7]

In the process of announcing the Kingdom and offering redemption from the Fall, Jesus Christ turned conventional views of power upside down. When His disciples argued over who was the greatest, Jesus rebuked them. "The greatest among you should be like the youngest, and the one who rules like the one who serves," He said.[8] Imagine the impact His statement would make in the back rooms of American politicians or in the carpeted board-rooms of big business—or, sadly, in some religious councils.

Jesus was as good as His words. He washed His own followers' dusty feet, a chore reserved for the lowliest servant of first-century Palestine. A king serving the mundane physical needs of His subjects? Incomprehensible. Yet servant leadership is the heart of Christ's teaching. "Whoever wants to be first must be slave of all."[9]

His was a revolutionary message to the class-conscious culture of the first-century. Position and privilege were entrenched, as evidenced by the Pharisees with their reserved seats in the synagogue, by masters ruling slaves, and by men dominating women. It is no less revolutionary today in the class-conscious cultures of the East and West where power, money, fame, and influence are idolized in various forms.

We see Jesus' attitude toward leadership modeled in the Old Testament as well. I love the tale of David when he was battling the Philistines. Enemy soldiers had surrounded David and trapped him in the cave of Adullan, which had to be a very dry and arid place.

David was desperately thirsty, and he said, "Oh, that someone would get me a drink of water from the well near the gate of Bethlehem."

Overhearing him, three of his soldiers got up, broke through the Philistine lines, drew water from the well near the gate of Bethlehem, and carried it back to David. But instead of drinking it, David dumped the water out on the ground. His men were astonished and probably outraged, but David said, "Far be it from me, O Lord, to do this. Shall I drink the blood of the men who went at the risk of their lives?"

David was saying, "Yes, I want that water badly, but I am not going to take it at the expense of the lives of my men." More than he wanted water, David wanted his men to know that he put their interests first, and that only the Lord was worthy of the sacrifice they had made. And so the water was poured out before the Lord.

There is a long tradition in the military that when an officer takes his troops into the field, the officer makes certain, always, that his troops are fed first. The same principle comes into play in the Navy when sailors are ordered to abandon ship: The captain is always the last man off.

These traditions follow directly from the story of King David. Leaders are to pour themselves out for those whom they serve. They do so with the authority that God has given them, to lead by being utterly selfless.

The Christian understanding of power is that it is found most often in weakness. This paradox has always been a thorn in the flesh of tyrants. The Judeo-Christian teaching that man is vulnerable to the temptations of power has also caused democracies and free nations to build restraints and balances of power into their structures.

Clearly, this is what motivated the revolutionaries in England to guarantee a Parliament independent of the monarchy. And in America the Founding Fathers, influenced by Judeo-Christian teaching about the vulnerability of man, wisely adopted the principle of the separation of powers. Within the government, power was diffused through a system of checks and balances so no one branch could dominate another. The Founders also assumed that religious values, evidenced through the separate institution of the church, would be the most powerful brake on the natural avarice of government. As Tocqueville observed, "Religion in America takes no direct part in the government or society but it must, nevertheless, be regarded as the foremost of the political institutions of that country."[10]

The most important restraint on power, however, is a healthy understanding of its true source. When power in the conventional sense is relinquished, one discovers a much deeper power.

Prisoners often discover this, as did Jerry Levin and Aleksandr Solzhenitsyn. In his memoirs of the gulag, Solzhenitsyn wrote that as long as he was trying to maintain some pitiful degree of worldly power in his situation—control of food, clothing, schedule—he was constantly under the heel of his captors. But after his conversion, when he accepted and surrendered to his utter powerlessness, then he became free of even his captors' power. Perhaps this is why Boris Pasternak once wrote that the only place one can be free in a communist society is in prison.

The apostle Paul said, "My power is made perfect in weakness," and concluded, "When I am weak, then I am strong."[11] And throughout Scripture God reveals a special compassion for the powerless: widows, orphans, prisoners, and aliens. Though the message of the Kingdom of God offers salvation for all who repent and believe, God does not conceal His disdain for those so enamored of their own power that they refuse to worship Him or to acknowledge His delight in the humble.

A culture that exalts power and celebrity, that worships success, dismisses such words as nonsense. Strong individuals rely on their own resources—which will never, ultimately speaking, be enough. But the so-called weak person knows his or her own limits and needs, and thus depends wholly on God. Perhaps this is why God so often confounds the wisdom of the world by accomplishing His purposes through the powerless and His most powerful work through human weakness.

I first learned this in prison myself. When the frustration of my helplessness seemed greatest, I discovered God's grace was more than sufficient. And after my imprisonment I could look back and see how God used my powerlessness for His purposes. What He has chosen for my most significant witness was not my triumphs or victories, but my defeat.

Similarly, Prison Fellowship's work in the prisons has been effective not because of any power we may have as an organization, but because of the powerlessness of those we serve. During an unforgettable trip to Peru in 1984, for example, I visited Lurigancho, the largest prison in the world. There seven thousand inmates, including a number of terrorists, were crowded in abysmal conditions; hatred, hostility, and despair seeped out of the cellblocks. Yet within the darkness of Lurigancho is a thriving Christian community—men who have found Christ and experienced renewed hearts and minds.

After visiting with these brothers, I went directly from the prison to meet with a number of government officials in downtown Lima. Covered with prison dust and marked with the sweaty embraces of Christian prisoners, I addressed these officials at the highest level of government—and they listened intently.

Had I gone to Peru specifically to meet with the key government leadership, I would have likely been stymied. They wanted to meet me not because of any power or influence I had, but because of our work in the prisons. They knew that in the chaos of Lurigancho, Prison Fellowship was doing something to bring healing and restoration. Therefore, they were eager to listen to our recommendations, and ready to discuss a biblical view of justice and imprisonment. Whatever authority I had in speaking to these powerful men came not from my power but from serving the powerless. I have experienced this in country after country. It is the paradox of real power.

The irony is that when I was released from prison I wanted nothing to do with politics. For the first twenty years of my ministry I devoted myself to going into the prisons and nothing else. But in the 1990s, more and more people in political life began asking me to come and speak to them. I probably visited more than half the state legislatures in America, talking about criminal justice reform. I continue to get requests and invitations from political groups and public office holders to talk not only about crime, but also about the moral breakdown in American life and the biblical understanding of reality.

Over the past few years I (along with other members of the Wilberforce Forum) have taught courses to Christian Congressmen about a biblical understanding of politics, truth, and Christian living—lectures often attended by fifty or sixty key members of Congress. This is influence, I hasten to add, that I have not sought or asked for. It represents the paradox of real power: To do what we are called to do, seeking nothing for ourselves. Then God can use us fully for His purposes.

Nothing distinguishes the kingdoms of man from the Kingdom of God more than their diametrically opposed views of the exercise of power. One seeks to control people, the other to serve people; one promotes self, the other prostrates self; one seeks prestige and position, the other lifts up the lowly and despised.

It is crucial for Christians to understand this difference. For through this upside-down view of power, the Kingdom of God can play a special role in the affairs of the world.

As citizens of the Kingdom today practice this view of power, they are setting an example for their neighbors by modeling servanthood and exposing the illusions power creates.

But how does this paradoxical view of power apply to the Christian who is in a position of influence and control? Sociologist Tony Campolo, drawing on the classic work of Max Weber, offers helpful guidance through the distinctions he draws between power and authority. Power involves the use of coercive force to make others yield to one's wishes even against their own will. Authority is achieved—or is conferred upon one—by virtue of character that others are motivated to follow willingly.[12]

Therefore, the citizen of the Kingdom should seek authority that comes from his or her own spiritual strength. Never for self-advantage, but for the benefit of others.

This does not mean that the Christian can't use power. In positions of leadership, especially in government institutions to which God has specifically granted the power of the sword, the Christian can do so in good conscience. But the Christian uses power with a different motive and in different ways: not to impose his or her personal will over others but to preserve God's plan for order and justice for all.

Those who accept the biblical view of servant leadership treat power as a humbling delegation from God, not as a right to control others.

Moses offers a great role model. Though he had awesome power and responsibility as the leader of two million Israelites, he was described in Scripture as "a very humble man, more humble than anyone else on the face of the earth."[13] He led by serving—intervening before God on his people's behalf, seeking God's forgiveness for their rebellion and caring for their needs above his own.

The challenge for the Christian in a position of influence is to follow the example of Moses rather than fulfill Nietzsche's prophecy concerning the will to power. In doing so the citizen of the Kingdom can offer light to a world often shrouded by the dark pretensions of power-mad tyrants.

20

CHRISTIANS IN POLITICS

Who's to say religion and politics shouldn't mix? Whose Bible are they reading anyway?

ARCHBISHOP DESMOND TUTU

Frequently I'm asked whether I would have participated in Watergate if I had been a Christian when I worked in the White House. The implication is that Christians are immune to corruption.

I'm always tempted to say, "Of course not." But that's self-righteous nonsense. While Christians know that their faith requires high standards of righteousness, they are human and often capitulate to the same temptations as anyone else. In fact, Christians may well face more problems than others when they become involved in the political process.

How does a Christian deal with the inherent divided loyalties: duty to God and duty to the national interest? Can a Christian successfully avoid the subtle snares of power? Can a Christian make the compromises necessary for the everyday business of politics?

What about the question of candor, for example? At times national security may well require not only concealing the truth, but lying. When I was in the White House, we went to elaborate lengths to conceal essential secret negotiations. Henry Kissinger had a bad cold when he visited Pakistan in 1971 — or so we told the press. Actually he had been flown to Beijing to conduct clandestine meetings in preparation for Mr. Nixon's historic visit to China.

Or take the day Nixon announced a major troop withdrawal in Vietnam. He immediately ordered Kissinger to bring Soviet Ambassador Dobrynin to a secret meeting room in the White House basement. "Henry," he roared, "You shake him up. Tell him not to believe these news stories. We're only pulling out a few troops—and if the Russians don't back off in sending supplies to Hanoi, we'll bomb the daylights out of that city. Tell him the president is uncontrollable, a madman—that he'll do anything. Let's keep them off balance." That such meetings took place was flatly denied in order to protect the lives of the withdrawing troops.

President Reagan did the same thing in 1983. When reporters asked about a rumored invasion of Grenada, official White House spokesmen dismissed such questions as "preposterous." Actually, troops were at that moment disembarking on the island's beaches. A "no comment" to the press, however, would have been tantamount to a "yes"—an admission that would have endangered lives.

In these days of delicate international tensions and the instant communications ability of an almost omnipresent press, such deceit is a common instrument of foreign policy. The press even accept it. In a 1987 *Newsweek* interview, ABC interviewer Ted Koppel acknowledged that government officials must be "prepared to mislead and ... sometimes even to lie."[1]

Deliberate lies, the corruption of power, compromise with ideological opponents, temptations on all sides—these appear to be the mechanisms of modern government. Should the Christian avoid the messy business of politics altogether?

The answer must be an emphatic no. As Robert L. Dabney wrote, "Every Christian ... whether law-maker or law executor or voter, should carry his Christian conscience, enlightened by God's Word, into his political duty. We must ask less what party caucuses and leaders dictate, and more what duty dictates."[2]

There are at least three compelling reasons Christians must be involved in politics and government. First, as citizens of the nation-state, Christians have the same civic duties all citizens have: to serve on juries, to pay taxes, to vote, to support candidates they think are best qualified. They are commanded to pray for and respect governing authorities. (For years many Christian fundamentalists shunned the "sinful" political process, even to the extent of not voting. Whatever else may be said about the much-maligned Moral Majority of the 1980s, it performed a valuable public service in bringing these citizens back into the mainstream. Although the Moral Majority no longer exists, other Christian groups have succeeded it—groups that advocate a responsible engagement with public policy on behalf of Christians.

Some [like their secular counterparts] have embraced heavy-handed tactics, but on the whole, they are to be commended.)

Second, as citizens of the Kingdom of God Christians are to bring God's standards of righteousness and justice to bear on the kingdoms of this world. This is the cultural commission discussed earlier. As former Michigan state senator and college professor Stephen Monsma says, Christian political involvement has the "potential to move the political system away from ... the brokering of the self-interest of powerful persons and groups into a renewed concern for the public interest."[3]

Third, Christians have an obligation to bring transcendent moral values into the public debate. All law implicitly involves morality; the popular idea that "you can't legislate morality" is a myth. Morality is legislated every day from the vantage point of one value system or another. The question is not whether we will legislate morality, but whose morality we will legislate.

Law is but a body of rules regulating human behavior; it establishes, from the view of the state, the rightness or wrongness of human behavior. Most laws, therefore, have moral implications. Statutes prohibiting murder, mandates for seat belts, or regulations for industrial safety are all designed to protect human life—a reflection of the particular moral view that values the dignity and worth of human life. And efficacy doesn't affect morality. If in America we have 16,000 deaths per year caused by drunk driving, it's not reason to repeal the laws making drinking and driving a crime.

The common argument against the legislation of morality is Prohibition, which conjures up such caricatures as Billy Sunday waving a chair over his head and Carrie Nation chopping up whiskey barrels. The church has taken an undeserved bad rap for this. No one entity imposed Prohibition; it was voted in by a clear majority after a lengthy national debate.

Admittedly, over the years of its existence Prohibition became increasingly difficult to enforce; it encouraged organized crime and ultimately led to widespread disrespect for the law. Eventually the costs outweighed the benefits.

But was it morally justified? Certainly one's personal decision to drink alcohol is a private matter. When millions do it to such excess that public safety is endangered, however, it becomes a public concern. That was the case in the pre-Prohibition era. Thousands reported to their factory jobs under the influence and were maimed or killed by the heavy industrial machines then being introduced in the American economy. The tavern trade spawned prostitution rings at a time when, as with AIDS today, there was no cure for the raging epidemic of venereal disease.

Though many write off Prohibition as a complete failure, the facts are that industrial safety improved dramatically as per capita drinking, particularly among working people, dropped precipitously, and the venereal disease epidemic slowed. Not until 1970 did per capita consumption of alcohol again reach pre-Prohibition levels.[4]

With one person being killed every half hour in the U.S. by a drunk driver and the majority of crimes being committed by people under the influence of drugs or alcohol, can anyone really argue realistically today that moral issues are not matters of public interest?

The real issue for Christians is not whether they should be involved in politics or contend for laws that affect moral behavior. The question is how.

Political involvement for the individual Christian entails not only voting and other basic responsibilities of citizenship, but dealing directly with political issues, particularly where justice and human dignity are at stake. A friend of mine, a prominent attorney in Ecuador, experienced this firsthand.

Dr. Jorge Crespo has always been an activist. For years he was an attorney for labor unions, fighting for justice and humane working conditions for Ecuador's laborers. Later he ran unsuccessfully for the presidency of his country. Then, after meeting with Prison Fellowship's South American regional director, Javier Bustamante, he agreed to consider prison ministry, even though he had always seen prisons as places where delinquents — and some clients — ended up.

But as soon as Dr. Crespo walked the cellblocks of a Quito prison, he felt "a deep sensation of pain, something like an echo of the pain of the prisoners. Since we are made in His image, we have been given His compassion toward our neighbor," he explained.

So Dr. Crespo became president of Prison Fellowship Ecuador. As he investigated prison conditions, he uncovered, to his horror, instances of cruelty, deprivation, and misery. In one prison twenty prisoners were wedged into a cell the size of a small bedroom. In another inmates received less care than animals; their food budget was less than that of the officers' guard dogs. In most women's prisons, children were incarcerated along with their mothers. In some cases they were being used as pawns in child prostitution rings to make profits for their parents, the prison guards, or both.

There were also reports of inhumane treatment. Some prisoners had confessed to crimes of which they were innocent in order to escape such measures.

Dr. Crespo and his colleagues documented their case, then began to educate the public through press, radio, and television. They sent letters to the prison wardens with copies to the minister of government; they met with ministers of social rehabilitation and justice. Their campaign was not without personal sacrifice and political risk.

Finally, they approached the tribunal overseeing constitutional enforcement, a governmental committee safeguarding Ecuador's provisions for human rights.

Crespo spent two hours testifying about the despicable prison conditions as well as the inhumane treatment of inmates and those who had been detained for crimes but not yet proven guilty.

The justices were shocked. Never before had such ugly topics been addressed in their ornate chambers. At the conclusion, the vice-president leaned forward to Dr. Crespo. "You have come here as Christians," he said, "and what you have done today is truly Christian."

As a result of Dr. Crespo's boldness, a series of reforms have been adopted in Ecuador. He has also organized a group of Christian police officers who are working to assure humane police investigation that does not rely on brutality.

Dr. Crespo has seen slow but deliberate progress in the prisons.

The political and personal risks have been worth it, he says. "To act as Christians we have to stand against injustice, and with prophetic voice talk courageously about truth, justice, fear, love. We ought not to bear infamy or atrocities. I believe a Christian who will remain silent is not a Christian."

Dr. Crespo took another step in the 1990s, when he started a Christian prison, taking over a wing of the notorious Garcia Moreno Prison, which once housed political prisoners subjected to brutal torture. Crespo's work is one of the most remarkable and convincing demonstrations of Christian love, transforming not only individuals, but also an entire community. Even in the midst of that dark prison hole, because of Crespo's leadership, we have seen a community of light arise — the kind of place where visitors linger, not wanting to leave.

The work begun by Crespo in Ecuador and by others in Brazil has now spread to the U.S. and even to England. This is the concept behind the InnerChange Freedom Initiative program, which is active in six American states as I write.

Activist Christians like Jorge Crespo who work as private citizens to address problems within the structures of government do so, as Stephen Monsma has written, "not as moral busybodies who are seeking to foist their morals onto all of society by the force of law, but as those who have a passion for justice, as those who respect all persons as unique image bearers of God and who therefore seek to treat them with justice."[5]

But many others are called to make a Christian witness from positions within government itself. As men like William Wilberforce or the great nineteenth-century social reformer, Lord Shaftesbury, clearly illustrate, Christians who are politicians can bear a biblical witness on political structures, just as other professionals do in medicine, law, business, labor, education, the arts, or any other walk of life. Augustine called God-fearing rulers "blessings bestowed ... upon mankind."[6] They exhibit this in their moral witness and in their willingness to stand up for unpopular causes, even if such causes benefit society more than their own political careers.

In the eighties there were two U.S. Senators, both strong Christians, who attended a Bible study on the topic of restitution as a biblical means of punishment. The two leaders later examined the federal statutes and discovered that restitution was only vaguely mentioned. Even though "lock 'em up" legislation was in political vogue, the two senators sponsored legislation to set new standards for sentencing: prison for dangerous offenders, but tax-dollar-saving alternative punishments, such as work and restitution programs, for nondangerous offenders. In 1983 the bill was adopted, after heated debate, as a resolution of the Congress and later was used as model legislation by several states.

Over the last twenty-five years I have repeatedly seen members of Congress, moved by their Christian convictions, take the lead in some of the great human-rights campaigns. For example, during the nineties, Congressmen Frank Wolf and Chris Smith were among the first members of Congress to get into Perm Camp 35 in the former Soviet Union. They arranged for me to go there in 1991 (along with Jack Eckerd and Justice Department officials) as the Soviet empire was crumbling. We traveled 800 miles east of Moscow, along rotted roads, into what turned out to be a primitive village called Perm. It was surrounded by snow banks; the facilities were sterile and forbidding. As we interviewed each inmate, a KGB officer stood staring and even tape recording comments. But the prisoners were not intimidated in the slightest. I spoke out against the monstrous gulag system they had been part of. Not long afterward, Perm 35 was closed.

Frank Wolf, Chris Smith, and later, Congressmen Joe Pitts and Sam Brownback have made a virtual crusade of human rights abuses. For instance, in 1998 Congressman Wolf traveled to Tibet, where he posed as an ordinary tourist. He eluded the tour guide by pretending to be ill, and then sneaked out to talk to Tibetans on the street to get the real story of Chinese repression. Another expedition took him to Sudan, a nation waging a religious war against its own citizens who are Christians or animists. Wolf has also investigated persecution in East Timor, El Salvador, Bosnia, and Ethiopia. Senator Brownback has also traveled to Sudan, and once spent a night in prison with the inmates; he said he wanted to experience what they were experiencing. Here is a man who really does "get it"; someone willing to put his faith on the line.

Christians can also bring mercy, compassion, and friendship to those in the cutthroat business of politics.

After his resignation Mr. Nixon withdrew to isolation behind the walls of his San Clemente compound. For nearly a year, as he struggled to recover from both the deep emotional wounds of Watergate and life-threatening phlebitis, Mr. Nixon saw only his family and a few close friends. No one, other than gloating reporters, tried to visit him.

No one, that is, except one man who had opposed Mr. Nixon as vigorously as anyone in the Senate. Without fanfare, Mark Hatfield, an evangelical Christian, traveled twice to San Clemente. His reason? Simply, as he told me later, "to let Mr. Nixon know that someone loved him."

Christians in public office should be motivated by something more than popularity or self-interest, something that frees them from being held hostage to political expediency. Their motivation to pursue what is right, in obedience to God, can give them a source of wisdom and confidence beyond their own abilities. The late Michael Alison, member of Parliament and Prime Minister Thatcher's senior parliamentary aide, offers a clear example.

After his Christian conversion at Oxford in the forties, Michael Alison initially planned to go into the ministry. But his keen interest in politics—and a desire to serve his nation—led him to change vocational directions. Elected to Parliament in 1964, he quietly earned his way from the back bench to leadership.

In 1979 Michael was named minister of state for Northern Ireland, a responsibility that included administration of Ulster's notorious prisons. Then, in the late fall of 1980, young Catholic terrorists in Belfast's Maze prison began to starve themselves to death in protest of British rule in Northern Ireland. By Christmas the first prisoner had gone nearly two months without food and was near death. Worldwide attention focused on Belfast. Would the British government allow this young inmate to die, or would they force-feed him once he slipped into a final coma?

The prison doctor came to Michael Alison for the decision. It was, of course, a Hobson's choice. To force-feed the protester would cause riots among the Irish Republican Army faithful; to let him die would be callous.

Michael had been praying for weeks for wisdom in the horrible situation. "Go to the prisoner's fellow hunger strikers," he told the doctor. "Ask them to make the decision." The other protesters could not have their brother's death on their consciences, but in the process of putting him on life-support equipment, they saw the inconsistency of their own position. The hunger strike ended, the crisis averted.*

But while being biblically motivated and informed may give wisdom, it does not necessarily assure political success. In this arena Christians in politics are often at a disadvantage.

In the self-aggrandizing world of politics, Michael Alison was an anomaly. He seemed more comfortable helping his adversary to his feet than cutting him down in debate. Though one of the most powerful men in British government, he had the unpolitical knack of blending into the background of any crowded political gathering.

His unconventional attitude began early in the day with his morning devotional. "If I was consumed with politics," he explained, "my first priority would be the morning newspapers, not the Bible." But Michael's first priority was not his political career; it was his relationship with God.

---

*By the time of a second IRA hunger strike several months later, the protesters hardened their resolve, and ten of their comrades starved to death.

Though Michael was conscientious in his work, his first ambition was not for the continued pursuit of position. He spurned political infighting and placed a higher premium on trust than power. Of his role as Prime Minister Thatcher's assistant, he said he was one of the few people she knew she could take for granted. "That's the highest compliment I could hope for in my role."

In 1993 I saw the fruits of the work of Michael and his associates first hand when I was in London to receive the Templeton Prize for Progress in Religion. At the home of then-minister of government Jonathan Aiken, just around the corner from Parliament, I met with sixty or seventy parliamentarians and media leaders, most of them Christians, and all of them organized into what was called the Tory Philosophy Society. This society—organized by Aiken, Alison, and several of their friends—was, in a small way, a replica of the Clapham Sect that Wilberforce and his friends had formed two centuries before. As we described in chapter eight, the members of the Clapham Sect came together regularly, sometimes for prayer and Bible study, sometimes to discuss public issues, but always looking at political life with a Christian or deeply traditional worldview.

When I addressed the Tory Philosophy Society that night, I found its members to be as formidable intellectually as they were spiritually. I also witnessed the incredible impact many of them had had on the Thatcher Revolution. It's worth noting that they exerted their influence in a very quiet way; it wasn't something they made a lot of fuss over. But they had a tremendous impact in shaping public policy in what most observers considered to be a very positive way. Thatcher, whatever else may be said about her, saved England; the island nation is a world power today. The members of the Tory Philosophy Society understood their role as public servants; mercifully missing was the arrogance of power one often sees in politics.

This servant-like attitude can easily be mistaken for weakness. In reality it gives a greater strength. The Christian in a position of power is not enslaved by his position—and thus the Christian has tremendous freedom to follow the dictates of conscience, not the fickle winds of self-interest.

But Christians are also exposed to greater struggles of conscience. They are honor bound to be the best statesmen they can be, as well as the best Christians they can be. These competing allegiances caused British writer Harry Blamires to conclude that perhaps "a good Christian [can] be a good politician ... but it is probably quite impossible for a good Christian to be a highly successful politician."[7]

Blamires may well have been referring to some of the dilemmas mentioned at the beginning of this chapter. Foremost is the issue of divided allegiances between God and the state. When there is a conflict of loyalty, the sincere Christian must obey God. Yet the politician's oath of office is to uphold the laws of the state.

The prevailing American view that faith is something private with no effect on public responsibility was first put forth by John Kennedy in a dramatic speech to the Houston Ministerial Association in the 1960 campaign. Protestants feared that Kennedy, a Catholic, would be bound by the dictates of the Roman church. So Kennedy pulled off a political masterstroke when he told the Texas ministers, mostly Baptists, that "whatever issue may come before me as president, if I'm elected ... I will make my decision in accordance ... with what my conscience tells me to be in the national interest, and without regard to outside religious pressure or dictate. And no power or threat of punishment could cause me to decide otherwise."[8]

Kennedy's message, which brought the house down, was a key to his election. But it set a precedent that has now become part of established American political wisdom: One's religious convictions must have no effect on one's public decisions.

But consider Kennedy's words: "No power ... could cause me to decide otherwise." Not God? Though Kennedy's approach was enormously popular, it was also a renunciation of any influence his religion might have. He subsumed his church responsibility under his patriotism—or his candidacy.*

What else can a public official do? you may ask. The officeholder in a free society cannot *impose* personal views on the electorate; the democratic process must be respected in a pluralistic society. That is true.

Some go on to conclude, however, that the Christian officeholder is thus free, in the name of political prudence, to support or accept the majority

---

*By contrast, Hilaire Belloc stood for election in 1906 in the British Parliament. As a Roman Catholic, he knew he would have to struggle to overcome religious prejudices, so he decided to confront the issue head-on. In his first campaign speech, he stood at the rostrum with a rosary in his hand and said, "I am a Catholic. As far as possible I go to Mass every day. As far as possible I kneel down and tell these beads every day. If you reject me on account of my religion, I shall thank God that He has spared me the indignity of being your representative." He was elected. From *The Little, Brown Book of Anecdotes* (Boston: Little, Brown, 1985), 50.

will when it is contrary to Christian teaching (a view eloquently espoused by Governor Mario Cuomo in his 1984 Notre Dame address). Religious conviction is thereby reduced to a private matter; the social implications of the gospel are simply ignored. And as we have seen, the results of such privatization can be dangerous to society as a whole.

Another position, often taken in reaction to the Kennedy-Cuomo view, is represented by the fictional President Hopkins of our prologue, who was prepared to thrust his own theological view on an unsuspecting nation. This view, articulated by some in political debate today, argues that a Christian politician should use his position to speak for God.

But such reasoning has no place in a pluralistic society and would, if carried out, make the frightening conclusion of Hopkins's fictional scenario entirely plausible. In his case the issue was not a conflict between human rights or human life and state policy, areas where a Christian leader must take a stand. Rather, it was a question of biblical prophecy, whose fulfillment is the responsibility of God, not man. Hopkins presumptuously, if unconsciously, played God.

Hopkins was also confused about the duty of government. As God's servant, his sworn task was to preserve order, promote justice, and restrain evil, which in this case meant acting decisively to prevent war in a volatile international situation. Richard Neuhaus writes, "To gain public office and take an oath before God to maintain the constitutional order, and then to use that office as a tool for advancing one's reading of Bible prophecy is an act of hubris, treachery, treason and deceit."[9]

Both views—privatized faith and using political power to play God—are deeply flawed. This brings us full circle: Is it possible for a devout Christian to serve in public office without compromising either his or her conscience or constituency?

It is possible. But only if the Christian officeholder understands several key truths. First, a government official must not play God; one's duty is to facilitate government's ordained role of preserving order and justice, not to use government to accomplish the goals of the church. Second, the Christian must respect the rights of all religious groups and insure that government protects every citizen's freedom of conscience.

There is an alternative to the imposition of religious values or the passive acceptance of majority opinion, a principle that pays both pluralism and conscience their due. Christian politicians must do all in their power to make clear, public arguments on issues of moral and political importance, to persuade rather than coerce. A recent Vatican statement put it this way: "Politicians must commit themselves through their interventions upon public opinion, to securing in society the widest possible consensus on ... essential points (matters concerning human rights, human life, or the institution of the family)."[10]

A third concern was posed at the outset of this chapter. What is the Christian responsibility in an age of terrorism where national leaders cannot be entirely candid in public pronouncements? Consider the dilemma posed by the Reagan administration's disinformation campaign designed to unsettle the government of Mohammar Khadaffi—a murderous tyrant imperiling any number of nations. Confronted with this question, Secretary of State George Shultz defended the government's actions by quoting Winston Churchill: "In times of war, the truth is so precious, it must be attended by a bodyguard of lies."[11]

Today the situation is even more tenuous because public pronouncements, particularly those having to do with how our government is fighting the war against Islamo-fascist terrorism, could tip off terrorists regarding how to avoid detection at airports, thwart efforts to listen into terrorists' conversations with fellow terrorists, or expose the fact that that terrorists' deadly plans are being monitored online. Counter-terrorism operations have to be kept completely secure in order for them to have any chance of being effective—and prevent another September 11 from happening.

The pressures of diplomacy in the age of terrorism create conscience-wrenching agony for sincere Christians who hold public office. During the MAD era (mutually assured destruction), there was always a chance of miscalculation. The situation for our leaders is even worse today, because we are not worrying about miscalculating the actions of rational people; we are concerned about the deliberate calculations of irrational fanatics—people who believe they will usher in the kingdom of God by destroying us.

Yet the Bible offers some surprising principles, citing Rahab, a prostitute, as one of the great heroes of the faith. Why? Rahab's place in history was established by the fact that she lied to protect Hebrew spies. Similarly, concentration-camp survivor Corrie ten Boom lied to the Nazis to protect the Jews she was hiding. Most Christians today would likely do the same, for in this cruel and complex world, a lesser evil may be required to prevent a greater one. A Christian in public office may be placed in a similar situation, say, to save the lives of hostages. If the situation forced the Christian to lie against his or her conscience, he or she should resign.

So far we have considered only laymen. But what about priests or ministers in public office, a question made timely by the presidential candidacies, in recent decades, of Pat Robertson and Jesse Jackson?

Before Constantine's Christianizing of the Roman Empire, all Christians were advised to avoid civil office because of the idolatrous emperor worship it demanded. (In some instances that concern is as relevant today as it was in ancient Rome.)

Even after Constantine, church policy restricted members of the clergy from holding office on the grounds that civil office would inevitably prevent their giving full attention to their ecclesiastical concerns.*

At one point in England's history, the government prohibited ordained ministers from holding office. The American colonists wrote similar prohibitions into several state constitutions, which remained in effect until 1978, when the U.S. Supreme Court struck down the Tennessee restrictions as a violation of a minister's First Amendment right.[12]

Despite the Tennessee case the tradition remains strong. Few clergy have held major offices in Western democracies.

In the Catholic Church, Pope John Paul's rejection of the tiara of temporal authority was a clear signal: ecclesiastical goals would not be sought through political means. Thus it was consistent that John Paul II in 1980 ordered priests out of secular office entirely. Five-term Congressman Robert Drinan, a Jesuit priest and outspoken liberal, quietly resigned.

In Nicaragua, however, three priests defied the papal order. This has been a major cause of the rift not only within the church, but it has compromised the integrity of the church. Those priests may say they are acting in a civil capacity but can they really disavow responsibility for the expulsion of missionaries and restrictions on the free press, including *Iglesia*, the official Catholic newspaper?

---

*There were few exceptions over the centuries; when they were made, it was to protect religious liberty, as, for example, when anti-Catholic legislation was being enacted in Hungary; the priests were released to engage in politics "for the sake of safeguarding religion or promoting the common good."

The cleric in public office can hardly avoid such double-mindedness. And presenting two faces to the world inevitably damages the work that should be of primary concern: the witness of the church.

Regardless of one's stand on abortion, for example, no one could seriously imagine the late Sister Agnes Mary Mansour as commissioner of Health and Welfare in Michigan in 1983, supervising state-funded abortions while in conscience maintaining her vows to a church that forbids abortion. Definitions of integrity have been stretched in recent years, but not that far. (Mansour resigned from her order rather than obey Pope John Paul II's order to resign as commissioner.)

Any priest or minister who feels called to seek public office should, as a citizen, be free to undertake that vocation. But doing so means that he must leave the pulpit, resigning all ecclesiastical functions. He must make it clear that he is acting as a private citizen seeking office to fulfill civic, not spiritual goals. (In many denominations, however, the priestly office cannot actually be resigned.)

But if the clergy should not hold office, should the institutional church be silent on political issues? This is perhaps the most sensitive question of all.

As we've noted earlier, the church acts as the conscience of society. Christopher Dawson notes that Christianity is "the soul of Western civilization. And when the soul is gone, the body putrefies."[13] So the church must address moral issues in society and measure public actions by biblical standards of justice and righteousness.

But there are pitfalls. One of the greatest is the tendency Christians have to believe that because the Bible is "on their side" they can speak with authority on every issue. Many church bureaucracies have succumbed to this temptation in recent decades, spewing out position papers on everything from public toilet facilities to nuclear war. Conservative Christians engaged in such excesses with their scorecards in the eighties and nineties, covering the gamut of issues from trade legislation to the Panama Canal. Even today, after some thirty years in the public square, Christian activists can still, on occasion, allow themselves to be ensnared by the uglier side of politics.

This was dramatically illustrated after President Bush was re-elected in 2004, and certain Christian leaders sent a letter demanding his support for an amendment banning gay "marriage." The letter contained a veiled threat that if the president did not support the marriage amendment, evangelicals would not support his Social Security program. I was offended by the letter—a fact I made known to the signatories, who happened to be good friends of mine.

First, I wasn't sure that the president's Social Security plan had anything to do with the biblical agenda. Yes, it represented good, conservative governing—but that was not something Christian activists should have been concerned with. Even worse, the signatories of this letter were using the political power they had gained (by virtue of the fact that millions of evangelicals had thrown their support behind conservative Christian groups) in a threatening manner.

This is not the way Christians should operate in the political arena. We should acknowledge that we will always be tempted to abuse whatever political power we accrue—as I know from personal experience, both before and after my conversion. It's what I experienced when I stood in for Pat Robertson on his television show for just one week. We begin to enjoy that power, and to think we are terribly important. And we attempt to flex our political muscles to achieve what are arguably good ends—but it is still wrong. We shoot ourselves in the foot—and then we become simply another political interest group, pontificating on matters about which we are often willfully uninformed.

When Christians use the broad brush, they become simply another political interest group, pontificating on matters about which they are often woefully uninformed.

A case in point was the U.S. Catholic bishops' position papers on the use of nuclear weapons during the Cold War. It hardly seems necessary to convene a conference to announce that it is a moral issue to unleash weapons that would annihilate millions. The bishops did, however, and they went on to conclude that the deterrent posture of the United States was unsatisfactory from a moral point of view.[14]

That could be true—particularly if one realizes that our missiles were, at that time, aimed at Soviet cities, just as Soviet missiles were aimed at U.S. cities. But deterrence itself is not immoral by definition; deterrence is impeding another nation's hostile act. The existence of a nuclear weapon (as with a policeman's gun) may prevent a much greater evil.

Any moral analysis must take into account the complexity of modern nuclear strategy and the actual efficacy of deterrence. To determine this, one cannot simply consider just numbers of bombs or throw-weight, but also targeting studies and the whole range of strategic options: what would remain after a surprise attack; what defenses neutralize attacking missiles; what the communications capacity would be like, and so on. Ironically, the country that renounces a first strike (the more moral position, as the bishops would no doubt have agreed) has need for a much larger deterrent capability (which the bishops decried as immoral). The logical consequences of their paper is a Catch–22.

While the bishops certainly could have commented on the immorality of unleashing nuclear war, they simply didn't have all the facts necessary to render an authoritative judgment beyond that. This was summed up by a University of Chicago professor who agreed personally with the bishops' position, but concluded that they could not determine whether deterrence was immoral because such judgment depended on facts "which are secret— and thus, unknown to the bishops."[15]

Russell Kirk, a Catholic layman himself, has described the delegates to such conferences as "utopians ... wondrously unaware of the limits of politics."[16] Certainly the heated controversy resulting from the bishops' attempt to formulate United States defense policy called their own competence into question far more than the government's. After attending a conference in which religious leaders addressed issues on every imaginable question of policy, most about which the church demonstrably lacked expertise, Kirk mused that he would "as soon go to a bartender for medical advice as to a church secretary for political wisdom."[17]

Those living under the most oppressive regime during the Cold War— Poland's Catholic's bishops—seem to have understood the need to stick to issues within their particular competence better perhaps than their U.S. counterparts. When, for instance, Poland's communist government engaged in one of its periodic purges of political dissidents in 1985, the bishops quickly condemned the persecution. A clear issue of human rights was at stake, and the moral question was unambiguous. They added, however, that "the Church is not and does not, want to be a political force [but it] has the right to give moral assessments, even in questions of political affairs when the basic rights of the individual or the salvation of the soul demands it."[18]

The Polish bishops understood the restraints imposed on the church when it speaks as the church. This is a crucial distinction. It is one thing for an individual Christian to address whatever issue his or her conscience dictates, but the church as a body, which purports to speak God's truth, should speak only to those matters in which fidelity to holy Scripture itself makes it necessary to speak out: issues where human life or dignity, religious liberty, or justice are involved. Even then, the church should claim no superior wisdom except in those areas where it is uniquely able to bring biblically informed truth to the debate.* An excellent example, one that stands in distinct contrast to the pastoral letter on nuclear policy, was the 2001 Vatican statement on the cloning of human embryos. It spoke forthrightly to a clear biblical issue on which the church has special competence and about which the secular world was grossly confused. It has helped clarify a moral question in the growing debate over reproductive technology.

Politics is not the church's first calling. Evangelism, administering the sacraments, providing discipleship, fellowship, teaching the Word, and exhorting its members to holy living are the heartbeat of the church. When it addresses political issues, the church must not do so at the risk of weakening its primary mission. As mainline churches discovered in the sixties, the faster they churned out partisan statements, the faster they emptied their pews.

And while Christian citizens can afford to be as partisan as they wish, Christian pastors cannot. If they are, they may soon discover they have compromised both their own witness and that of their church.

An extreme example was the case of the bishop who presided at the May 1987 funeral of former CIA Director William Casey. Because then-President Reagan, former President Nixon, and a host of other government officials were in the congregation, the Catholic bishop used the occasion to attack U.S. foreign policy in Central America, for which the deceased Mr. Casey was an outspoken proponent. It was in such deplorably bad taste that the

---

*Russell Kirk quotes Renee Divismay Williamson at length in Kirk's classic article, "Promises and Perils of 'Christian Politics,'" *Intercollegiate Review* (Fall/Winter 1982), 13, to clarify these difficult questions:

There are controversial issues in which the principle is unmistakable and the command of the hour comes through loud and clear. On these issues the church must make pronouncements....

But there are other general issues in which facts and motives are mixed, consequences contradict the principles involved and equally dedicated and knowledgeable Christians disagree. In these cases the church should remain silent, letting individual Christians and Christian groups decide for themselves what Christian witness means.... For the church to sponsor a political party, engage in lobbying, form coalitions with secular pressure groups and become entangled in the decisions of private business corporations, would be to take a position on precisely those issues in which the religious significance is unclear, ambiguous or non-existent.

incident, reported worldwide, resulted in an adverse reaction not against U.S. policy, but against the Church. Grieving families should receive spiritual comfort, not a political harangue against their loved one's views.

Admittedly a fine line exists here. It is clearly partisan for a pastor to stand in a pulpit and endorse a particular candidate, as some clergymen endorsed Jimmy Carter in 1980, and others endorsed Ronald Reagan in 1984. More recently the IRS has cracked down on churches it believed were violating their tax-exempt status by endorsing presidential candidates. In one well-known case, the IRS investigated All Saints Church in Pasadena over a sermon given by the Rev. George F. Regas two days before the 2004 presidential election. While Regas did not come right out and tell people to vote for John Kerry, he described an imaginary debate between Jesus, Kerry, and President Bush in which Jesus was deeply critical of the president's Iraq policy. According to the *Associated Press*, as of July of 2006, some forty churches were under investigation.

But what about Cardinal O'Connor's statement in the 1984 presidential campaign that a Catholic could not in conscience vote for a candidate who supported abortion? His remarks were reported as a partisan rebuke of the views of two of his New York parishioners, Governor Mario Cuomo and vice-presidential candidate Geraldine Ferraro. And during the 2004 presidential campaign, Oregon Bishop Robert Vasa told an interviewer that he agreed with Cardinal Joseph Ratzinger (now Pope Benedict XVI) that pro-abortion politicians must be refused Communion. If Senator John Kerry presented himself for Communion in his Baker City, Oregon, diocese, Bishop Vasa said, he would "absolutely" refuse to administer it.

Admittedly, the timing of Cardinal O'Conner's and Bishop Vasa's comments made them suspect, but they could also be regarded as no more than statements of elementary logic. Since the Catholic Church believes that the taking of unborn lives violates God's law, could a Catholic in conscience logically vote for one who willfully violated that law? While I believe an open pulpit endorsement of a candidate is improper, I also feel that—if made responsibly from the right motivations—a cleric's statement that Christians should not support candidates who reject basic human rights is justified.

In fact, Evangelicals and Catholics Together, chaired by Richard Neuhaus and myself, issued a statement in 2006 in which we said, "Those who take pro-choice positions are denying themselves the company of believers." There is a time-bomb paragraph in that statement which, to my amazement, the press has not picked up on. In essence, it supports the fact that people who work against the clear Christian imperative of the culture of life have taken themselves out of fellowship with us. It isn't that we are denying them the sacrament or benefits of church membership; it is that they are denying it to *themselves* by their actions, which are totally contrary to what Catholics call "The Gospel of Life," and which evangelical Protestants agree is an imperative for Christians.

Within these limits, then, we can conclude that Christians, both individually and institutionally, have a duty, for the good of society as a whole, to bring the values of the Kingdom of God to bear within the kingdoms of man.

It is fair to say, however, that Christians have not done a particularly good job at this task. Often they have terrified their secular neighbors, who see Christian political activists as either backwoods bigots or religious ayatollahs attempting to assault them with Bible verses or religious magisteriums. In a pluralistic society it is not only wrong but unwise for Christians to shake their Bibles and arrogantly assert that "God says …" That is the quickest way for Christians, a distinct minority in civil affairs, to lose their case altogether.

Instead, positions should be argued on their merits. If the case is sound, a majority can be persuaded; that's the way democracies and free nations are supposed to work.

I'm often asked to meet with government officials concerned with criminal-justice policies. They are frustrated. The more prisons are built — at great expense — the more the crime rate goes up. So whenever I suggest restitution as an inexpensive and effective alternative to prison for nonviolent offenders, politicians are receptive. But only after I have cited the facts of the position (for instance, only one tenth of the cost of incarceration is statistically effective in reducing recidivism) do I explain that the source of my thinking regarding restitution was God's law prescribed to Moses at Sinai.[19]

Christians are to do their duty as best they can. But even when they become disheartened — when they believe they are failing to bring Christian values to the public arena — success is not the criteria: Faithfulness is. For in the end, Christians have the assurance that even the most difficult political situations are in the hands of a sovereign God.

This assurance comes from the teaching of Christ. Jesus likened the Kingdom to the humble act of a farmer sowing seeds. The farmer tills the soil, but the seeds sprout and grow because of a power beyond the farmer's control.

Jesus is saying that Christians are to do their part, but the manifestation of the Kingdom comes through God's power, not theirs. I saw this firsthand over a six-year span in one of the toughest penitentiaries in America. It all began with one of the most frightening days I've spent in any prison.

21

SIGNS
OF THE KINGDOM

He also said, "This is what the kingdom of God is like. A man scatters seed on the ground. Night and day, whether he sleeps or gets up, the seed sprouts and grows, though he does not know how.... The kingdom of God is like ... a mustard seed, which is the smallest seed you plant in the ground. Yet when planted, it grows and becomes the largest of all garden plants."

MARK 4:26–27, 30–32

They called it the "Concrete Mama," the nearly one-hundred-year-old patchwork of brick and concrete surrounded by thirty-foot walls set amid the beautiful hilly country of Washington State. Mama wasn't beautiful inside, however—not on that October morning in 1979 when I first visited there.

The state penitentiary at Walla Walla, considered one of the toughest prisons in America, had been cited by an inspection report of the American Corrections Association (ACA) as overcrowded, filthy, and out of control. The inmates carried knives; homosexuals and drug pushers in silk shirts roamed the cellblocks; an inmate biker gang ran roughshod over underpaid and ill-trained guards as well as the other inmates. Walla Walla was, in the words of a longtime California warden, "Simply the worst prison in the U.S."

Four months before our visit a guard had been killed, and Walla Walla had been locked down ever since. That meant the prisoners were confined to their cells for twenty-three out of every twenty-four hours. Fifty-eight guards had gone on strike during the lockdown; most had subsequently been fired. Morale was miserable.

"When were the men released from lockdown?" I asked the officer at the gate, privately wondering who in my office had managed this kind of scheduling.

"Yesterday," he said, straightening his visored cap and squinting into the sun. "But don't worry. Riot police are standing by."

As I was digesting that heartwarming piece of information, the assistant warden, a former Jesuit priest, arrived at the gatehouse. "Glad you're here, Mr. Colson," he said cheerily. (I wasn't sure I was.)

"What's it like inside?" I asked.

He shrugged. "Tense, I guess. I don't really know. I don't get into the yard much. Whatever you can do I'm sure will help, though."

Unaccompanied by guards, we toured the concrete prison yard, and the cellblocks confirmed that the ACA had not exaggerated the conditions. The filth and overcrowding were incredible, and the tension in the air was as palpable as the concrete. The two thousand men in Walla Walla were angry.

At the moment their anger was directed at something that had happened during lockdown, senior chaplain Jerry Jacobson told me. The one relief from the sterile cement world inside the walls had been a grass playing field in the center of the compound. There, the inmates could lounge on the grass and play football. But when the men had been released from lockdown the day before, they discovered that their field had been covered by tons of concrete.

Officials said it had been done for security reasons; the men hid weapons in the grass. Valid or not, the fact was that the prison was now solid concrete. And to make it even worse, during the days the men had been locked in, the concrete pad had absorbed the heat of the hot autumn days. In every way Walla Walla was heated to the boiling point.

Chaplain Jacobson accompanied me on my tour, including a visit to the dungeon-like basement cellblock containing the more than ninety men in protective custody. These were inmates who could not be mixed with the rest of the prison population: informers, psychopaths, and sex offenders. As we completed the tour, a crackling loudspeaker invited all inmates to the auditorium to hear me speak immediately after lunch.

The auditorium was a cavernous room that seated a thousand men. The acoustics were terrible, but the only other meeting place was the chapel, and no one would attend if it was held there, since the chapel was used chiefly as a meeting place for homosexuals.

At 2:00 Jerry introduced me. In front of 850 empty chairs and 150 pairs of unresponsive eyes, I told how Prison Fellowship began, using lines that never failed to produce laughter. There was stony silence.

Two older inmates stared intently from the front row. Both sat erect, arms folded across their chests with an air of authority. I concentrated on them as I concluded my talk.

Later, as I walked across the yard to leave, consoling myself that at least there had been no trouble, I heard a gruff voice call my name. I turned and saw the two inmates from the front row. The first, a man in his forties with graying hair, stuck out his hand.

"I'm Don Dennis. We've been talking, and we believe you," he said without expression.

The other inmate slapped me on the back. "Yeah," he said, grinning, "you're one helluva guy."

"We'll do everything we can to help you guys," I said, grabbing their hands. I didn't realize then what that promise would mean.

The following week I asked George Soltau, Prison Fellowship's most experienced instructor, to conduct two Bible-study seminars at Walla Walla.

When George arrived at the penitentiary, the chief of security told him that he expected a blood bath any day. So George didn't know what to expect as he went to the private meeting that inmate Don Dennis had requested. With Dennis were six young prisoners who had long sentences, nothing to lose, and were ready, as Don put it, to "blow this place." George's palms were moist as he shook hands with each of the men.

From them George learned what we had not known the week before. After my sermon, inmate leaders had called off a riot they had planned. Six guards had been targeted for murder; there had even been talk of taking me hostage. Instead, the inmates had decided they could trust us and would seek our help in working out their grievances.

George was face-to-face with the kind of hatred and anger that leads men to kill. People's lives were in his hands. One misstep and the pent-up fury of the four-month lockdown would be unleashed.

George conducted a series of intense meetings with convict groups. When he learned that there had been no communication between inmates and prison officials for eighteen months, he approached the warden, who promised he would consider meeting with inmate leaders.

That promise at least bought time. When George returned to Walla Walla a week later, there was a glimmer of hope. The inmate power bases— the lifers, the bikers, the Native Americans, the Hispanics, and others— who were almost perpetually at war with each other were at least, for the moment, talking. Two men had become Christians in George's seminar, and they, along with Don Dennis, were gradually taking some leadership. Several guards who had been charged with brutality had been dismissed, and the warden was still promising to meet with the prisoners.

Over the next few months, George Soltau and Al Elliott, another Prison Fellowship staffer, shuttled in and out of Walla Walla, meeting with prison officials and convict leaders. Progress was slow, but violence was at a minimum. One night, however, frustrations erupted. Several men slashed their wrists and barricaded themselves in their cells to protest conditions.

Al Elliott was called to the scene. He stood alone outside the barricaded cells and pleaded with the men. Pools of blood gathered on the concrete floor. As Al talked, one man surrendered, then another, and finally the whole group. Medics rushed in with gurneys and plasma.

Later Al was in the mess hall when a chant began at several corner tables. The noise grew louder, echoing off the high ceilings. Al climbed on top of his table and shouted, trying to make himself heard above the clamor. Gradually the voices subsided.

"Don't blow this thing," he begged. "The politicians are beginning to listen, finally. But you'll lose it all if there's bloodshed. Chuck Colson has been asked to address the state legislature about the situation." At that, there was a loud roar of approval.

Two Christian politicians, Bob Utter, chief justice of the Washington State Supreme Court, and Skeeter Ellis, a newly elected Republican representative, had proposed that I speak to the Republican caucus committee about the conditions at the prison. When I laid out the hard facts of what I had seen at Walla Walla and what needed to be done, the legislators seemed interested, even receptive.

Later that day I gave the same message to an equally responsive Democratic caucus, and shortly thereafter the House passed a resolution vowing to deal with conditions at Walla Walla. This had no legal effect but signaled to the inmates that those in power were listening.

Justice Utter then organized a committee of prominent Christians to work with the legislators who were developing model legislation. My associate, attorney Dan Van Ness, now president of Justice Fellowship,* and a Christian attorney in Seattle named Skip Li proposed several significant amendments, which were incorporated in the reform package. After his election Governor John Spellman appointed Amos Reed, a committed Christian, to head the state corrections system. Amos immediately backed the proposed bill.

Meanwhile, a federal court was nearing a decision on an inmate lawsuit complaining of conditions at Walla Walla. Indications were that the case would go against the state.

These developments electrified the atmosphere at the prison. "Someone has finally heard us," an inmate told Al Elliott, choking back his tears.

During those months I also met with representatives from each of the ruling inmate gangs. Al warned me that they were a tough and unusual bunch of characters. *They can't be any more unusual than anyone else I've met in Walla Walla,* I thought. I was mistaken.

At the first meeting they were waiting for me, shoulder-to-shoulder in a tight semicircle, at the bikers' club headquarters, a small, bare-walled room with one barred window. One by one I greeted them, some of the toughest inmates I'd ever seen. Their leader, Bobby, had black hair hanging over a leather headstrap adorned with badges; a bushy beard flowed down the front of his leather jacket.

"Bobby," I said as I gripped his tattooed hand, "I'm here to help you."

His response was a nod and a grunt.

The next inmate wore elaborate eye makeup and deep red lipstick. He took my hand limply and said in a high-pitched voice, "Thank you, Mr. Colson." My eyes widened with shock; this was Bobby's cellmate, a transvestite and leader of the "Queens." Walla Walla had its own rules, its own code for survival. The inmates' hard eyes defied me to pass judgment.

---

*Justice Fellowship was incorporated in 1983 as the criminal justice affiliate of Prison Fellowship Ministries. As a national volunteer organization, Justice Fellowship works to make federal and state criminal justice systems more consistent with biblical teaching on justice and righteousness. It promotes restorative punishments, such as restitution and community service, based on the conviction that crime is primarily an offense against a victim rather than the state. For further information contact Justice Fellowship, 44180 Riverside Parkway, Lansdowne, VA 20176, or visit www.JusticeFellowship.org.

In May 1980 the U.S. District Court ruled that Walla Walla had violated the constitutional prohibition against "cruel and unusual punishment." Trial testimony had produced a litany of horrors: an inmate sodomized by a guard, another whose leg had to be amputated because gangrene was neglected, a third held naked in isolation for four days. But what proved decisive was the startlingly honest admission under oath of warden James Spaulding. His prison, he said, ought to be "closed down." It was simply beyond saving.

The inmates were jubilant. Help might finally be coming.

George and Al cut back their Walla Walla trips to once a month. Even the guards seemed to breathe easier as the court order transferred inmates to other prisons and relieved the overcrowding.

But the transferred inmates created dangerous overcrowding at the other prisons, and by the end of the year bloody riots erupted. One inmate was killed, twenty-five were injured, and there was $2 million in property damage. The tension affected the entire prison system, and officials imposed new restrictions at Walla Walla.

By early 1981, despite the best efforts of inmate leaders to prevent it, Walla Walla was again seething. A gang burned a prison office building. The warden threw the troublemakers, along with several inmate leaders who had had nothing to do with the riot, into segregation. The arbitrary order infuriated the inmates, who retaliated with a work strike. Their one demand was the removal of Warden Jim Spaulding.

Spaulding ordered another lockdown, and I returned to Walla Walla.

"Visit the hole," one inmate whispered to me. "But don't announce it. Just walk in." I followed his advice.

When the guards grudgingly swung open the heavy steel gate of B tier of segregation, I immediately stepped back. A foul mist hung in the air, giving an eerie glow to the dim overhead lights. Piles of rotting food and human excrement littered the floor. I had to force myself forward.

At the first cell the inmate rubbed his eyes. "You Colson?" he asked. Not even waiting for a reply, he continued listlessly, "What can you do?" as if my answer couldn't matter anyway. *Maybe he's right*, I thought.

I asked his name. It sounded familiar, I said.

"No." He shook his head. "You might have heard the name, but it's my brother. He hung himself in here last week. Just couldn't take no more after a year."

"A year!" I exclaimed.

"Man, that ain't nothin'." He shook his head again. "Some dudes been in here like two and three years."

Once outside I bent over, my hands on my knees, almost retching as I gulped the cold air of the prison yard. My face was hot, flushed with anger. How could human beings be allowed to live in such degradation? I made my way to Warden Spaulding's office.

Jim Spaulding was a decent and intelligent man, seemingly unflappable. But like his predecessors he had wrestled with the beast of Walla Walla and lost.

"Jim," I said, "you have to clean up segregation. Today. Use fire hoses or whatever it takes, but that swill has got to go."

"Wait a minute," he snapped. "What can I do? They throw everything at the officers. I can't order my men to clean it up."

"Have you been in that place?" I asked.

He shook his head.

The next day I held a press conference at which I described Walla Walla's segregation unit in detail. Spaulding fired back in the press, saying that the inmates "wouldn't let the staff clean the building." But soon thereafter, after a state investigation, Jim Spaulding was transferred.

Amos Reed, the corrections chief, began courting the Washington legislature to overhaul the criminal-justice system in the state. Justice Utter's committee continued to mobilize public support, and the court ruled in the inmates' favor and appointed a liaison to oversee the situation.

In the spring of 1981, almost two years after the Walla Walla lockdown began, the Washington state legislature passed the first in a series of reforms. A sentencing commission established a policy to put nonviolent offenders in alternative programs. Early-release plans relieved overcrowding, and several million dollars were allocated to clean up and refurbish Walla Walla.

Easter morning 1985 I returned to Walla Walla. From the road approaching the gatehouse, nothing seemed to have changed. Concrete Mama still loomed on the hilltop, as forbidding as it had looked nearly six years earlier.

The new warden, Larry Kinchloe, met us at the gate. "Wait until you see this place," he said enthusiastically.

Our first service was in the protective-custody wing. The floors were scrubbed clean, most of the cells newly painted, and recreation areas had been constructed in every block. It was still a prison, cold and sterile, but it had been miraculously — if that's a fair term to apply to a building — transformed. The prison population was stable, conditions were decent, and alternative programs were beginning. The reform legislation was working, and millions of state tax dollars were being saved.

The service for the maximum-security unit was held in the brand-new chapel, and I stood at the door greeting the men as they crowded in. I recognized some I had met years before as angry, hostile convicts; by their open faces and enthusiastic greetings, I realized they were now brothers in Christ.

Then came one vibrant, middle-aged inmate surrounded by a cluster of friends. "Remember me?" he grinned and grabbed my hand. I struggled for recognition. "Don't blame you," he laughed, stroking his clean-shaven chin. "I'm Bobby."

It was Bobby, the boss biker who had lived with the transvestite. He was a Christian now and sat through the service with a broad smile on his face, holding a well-worn Bible.

I watched in amazement, realizing that it was not just an institution that had been transformed. The story of Walla Walla was more than legislation and fresh prison paint, important as those changes were. It was the story of transformed lives.

One of the most extraordinary transformation stories involved Don Dennis, the tough inmate I'd met on my first visit to Walla Walla — a man once known as the most difficult prisoner in the Walla Walla prison system. Don lived his last years behind bars as a strong, committed Christian. He helped negotiate some of the problems at Walla Walla, which led to major changes in the prison system. Released in the late eighties, Don moved to Dallas and was mentored by Pastor George Soltan. He spent the last ten years of his life helping troubled teens on the streets of Dallas. Dennis's life represents one of the most miraculous stories of Christian conversion I have ever encountered — and one of the most extraordinary stories to emerge from Concrete Mama.

Easter weekend at Walla Walla ended with a fitting postscript, yet another sign of the Kingdom at work. Fred, a young man with a heroin habit and a robbery record, had done time at Walla Walla. The family of one of his robbery victims had prayed for him for years, visited him in prison, and eventually led him to Christ. During a subsequent parole hearing, Fred had confessed to additional crimes of which he had not been convicted, explaining to the startled parole board that as a Christian, he felt he could not do otherwise.

Fred's original conviction was overturned; he was released from prison and began to rebuild his life. He became active in a local church and got involved in a Christian ex-prisoner fellowship while awaiting his retrial.

As it happened, Fred's case was scheduled to be heard on Easter Monday. The Seattle Superior Court was filled with friends, family, and supporters who had already testified on his behalf. Fred had freely confessed his guilt; and now he told Judge Francis Holman that he was prepared to accept whatever punishment the judge deemed appropriate. For in any event, said Fred, "I am ready to go back to prison and serve Jesus Christ in there."

The judge leaned back in his tall leather chair and ticked off a long list of possible sentences. There was an awkward, drawn-out silence.

Then Judge Holman pounded his gavel. Ten years on each count of robbery—suspended. Fred would be free on probation, providing he would continue in a drug-treatment program and make restitution to his victims at 150 percent of their loss, or $2,200. He looked down at Fred again, his face still solemn: "We send you on your way with best wishes."

For a moment no one moved. Then Fred's pastor jumped to his feet and gestured to the packed courtroom. "Let's sing it!" he shouted.

A reporter for the *Seattle Times* captured what came next: "Everyone stood up, little old ladies in spring dresses, ex-cons, girls in jeans, men in business suits, a biker with his motorcycle jacket and helmet, prison guards—and they began to sing: 'Praise God from whom all blessings flow....'"[1]

Officials later said that it was the first time a Seattle Superior Court case had ever closed with the Doxology.

As I flew back home after that glorious Easter weekend in Washington State, I was exuberant. I have to confess I was thrilled at Prison Fellowship's involvement in the changes at Walla Walla, in the transformed lives of men like Bobby and Fred. Sending out a puffy fund-raising letter about the story was a tempting idea; the first lines were already beginning to form in my mind.

But as I started to put words on paper I was stopped by the sudden realization that I couldn't definitively say how the changes had come about at Walla Walla or who was responsible. Certainly George Soltau and Al Elliott had risked their lives going in there in the early days when the situation was red hot. Don Dennis, Bobby the Biker, and others played a vital role in convincing angry cons to talk with bitter guards and exhausted administrators. And then there was the work of Christian lawyers, legislators, and politicians: men like Amos Reed, Bob Utter, Skip Li, Skeeter Ellis, Dan Van Ness.

But the real transforming miracle at Walla Walla had been accomplished not by the efforts of all these people, but by the unseen work of the hand of God. I suddenly saw on the page before me the words of Christ — that the signs of the Kingdom of God are like a man planting seed. We do our part; but then God makes the seed — or the prison reform — grow.

And so I threw away my fund-raising letter, and the words of the Doxology from that Seattle courtroom filled my mind: "Praise God, from whom all blessings flow." For it is God who produces the signs of His Kingdom on this earth. We are merely the instruments.

We need to constantly be reminded that our efforts, vital as they are, will never bring utopia to this earth. Walla Walla, after all, is still bleak; it is still a prison filled with the angry, desperate, broken lives of those who seem unable to live in society. But it *has* changed. Because of God's power, not ours, Walla Walla is a "concrete" example of the Kingdom of God transforming places of hopelessness in the kingdoms of man. Justice and hope can now be found where there was once only inequity and despair.

Should Christians get involved in political issues and social reform?

Can anyone look at the story of Walla Walla and believe otherwise?

22

PERILS
OF POLITICS

Christian faith may work wonders if it moves the minds and hearts of an increasing number of men and women. But if professed Christians forsake heaven as their destination and come to fancy that the state ... may be converted into the terrestrial paradise — why they are less wise men than Marx.

RUSSELL KIRK

Christians in politics can make a difference — as Justice Utter, Skeeter Ellis, and others in Washington State illustrate. But these men were only part of the Walla Walla story. Private citizens, church groups, the courts, wardens, even inmates all had a hand in the process. Man planted, and God, using many people, brought in the crop.

But in recent years many Christians have urged a more direct approach for bringing needed social change: simply elect Christians to political office. One spokesman has even suggested a religious version of affirmative action; if, for example, 30 percent of the people call themselves evangelicals, then at least 30 percent of all office-holders should be evangelicals. Others have argued that Christians should "take dominion" over government, with those in public office speaking "for God as well as for the American people."[1]

On the surface this shortcut might seem an appealing answer to America's declining morality. It is, however, simplistic and dangerous triumphalism. To suggest that electing Christians to public office will solve all public ills is not only presumptuous and theologically questionable, it is also untrue.

Today's enthusiasm for political solutions to the moral problems of our culture arises from a distorted view of both politics and spirituality — too low a view of the power of a sovereign God and too high a view of the ability of man. The idea that human systems, reformed by Christian influence, pave

343

the road to the Kingdom—or at least, to revival—has the same utopian ring that one finds in Marxist literature. It also ignores the consistent lesson of history that laws are most often reformed as a result of powerful spiritual movements. I know of no case where a spiritual movement was achieved by passing laws.

In addition, history puts the lie to the notion that just because one is devout one will be a just and wise ruler. Take the nineteenth-century leader who forged a unified Germany from a cluster of minor states. Otto von Bismarck-Schönhausen was a committed Christian who regularly read the Bible, spoke openly of his devotion to God, and claimed divine guidance in response to prayer. "If I were no longer a Christian, I would not serve the king another hour," he once declared.[2]

Yet Bismarck was also the ruthless architect of *Deutschland Uber Alles* (Germany Over All), a chauvinistic worldview that laid the foundation for two world wars. Historians describe Bismarck as a Machiavellian master of political duplicity who specialized in blood and iron.

As we have said earlier, power can be just as corrupting—or confusing—to the Christian as to the non-Christian. (Just ask the ex-wives of Christian men who ran for Congress, won on a "family values" platform—and later divorced their wives to marry attractive young assistants.) And the results in some ways are more horrible when power corrupts men or women who believe they have a divine mandate. Their injustices are then committed in God's name. This is why an eminent conservative historian has suggested that "religious claims in politics should vary inversely with the power or prospects for power one has."[3]

It's a fair distinction: Prophets should make religious claims. Political leaders should not—otherwise they can become ayatollahs.

So the first test for public office should not be a spiritual one. The celebrated claim that "the ability to hear from God should be the number one qualification for the U.S. presidency"[4] is dangerously misguided.

Politicians, like those in any other specialized field, should be selected on the basis of their qualifications and abilities *as well as* on their moral character. Even in Israel's theocracy, Jethro advised Moses to select "capable men ... who fear God" to help in governing the Jewish nation.[5]

Jethro's advice makes sense. If terrorists were to take control of a grade school, would we want people who were merely devout Christians handling the crisis, or would we choose those who had specialized training in dealing with hostage rescue? Luther had it right when he said he would rather be ruled by a competent Turk than an incompetent Christian.

The triumphalist mindset also fails to make the crucial distinction between a Christian's function as a private citizen and as an officeholder. As private citizens, Christians are free to advocate their Christian view in any and every form. In America that is a fundamental constitutional right. Christian citizens should be activists about their faith, striving by their witness to "Christianize" their culture — not by the force of the sword, but by the force of their ideas.

But Christians elected to public office acquire a different set of responsibilities. Now they hold the power of the sword, which God has placed with government to preserve order and maintain justice. Now they act not for themselves but for all whom they serve. For this reason they cannot use their office to evangelistically "Christianize" their culture. Their duty is to ensure justice and religious liberty for all citizens of all beliefs.

This does not mean they can compromise their faith or their first allegiance to God; they should speak freely of their Christian faith and witness Christian values in their lives. But they cannot use their offices to seek a favored position for Christianity or the church.

A Christian writer has summed this up well: "The 'Christian state' is one that gives no special public privilege to Christian citizens but seeks justice for all as a matter of principle."[6]

At the turn of the century a towering Dutch theologian, Abraham Kuyper, was elected prime minister of the Netherlands. His opponents voiced fears of theocratic oppression. Instead, his administration was a model of tolerance and public pluralism as Kuyper affirmed proportional representation, that the legitimate rights of all be fully represented.[7]

If Christians today understood this distinction between the role of the private Christian citizen and the Christian in government, they might sound less like medieval crusaders. If secularists understood correctly the nature of Christian public duty they would not fear, but welcome responsible Christian political involvement.

But Christians should not unwarily plunge into the political marshlands, thinking they will drain the swamp.

There are traps. I know; I used to set them.

My first assignment as President Nixon's special counsel was to develop strategies for his 1972 reelection—a tough task. He had been elected by only a small margin in the three-way 1968 election against Hubert Humphrey and George Wallace. Not only was the Republican party a minority, but Nixon had inherited an unpopular war and a hostile press. Added to this, he himself projected something less than a charismatic presence for the television image-makers just beginning to dominate politics.

I studied the political classics, particularly the strategy devised by Clark Clifford for Harry Truman in the 1948 election. I learned that Clifford had curried the favor of disparate special-interest groups, one by one, assembling voting blocks into a surprise majority.

My first memorandum to the president outlined a similar strategy: write off the minorities, but reach out to traditional supporters in business and farm groups; pick off some conservative labor unions; cultivate Southern evangelicals; build a new coalition among Catholic, blue-collar voters of the Northeast and Midwest. I labeled it the "Middle America Plan," later dubbed the "Silent Majority Strategy." It was cynical, pragmatic, and good politics, designed to exploit whatever allies would let us cultivate them.

Nixon loved it. The memo was returned a few days later with his markings all over the margins: "Right.... Do it.... I agree." It became one of the key documents for the political strategy of Mr. Nixon's presidency.

Setting out to put it into practice, I began by inviting key leaders to the White House, following a scenario staged for maximum benefit.

First, they dined with me in the executive dining room located in the basement of the West Wing. I would escort my guests past saluting guards, down a long corridor lined with dramatic photographs of the president in action, then pause at the door to the dining room, pointing to another door to the right. "That's the situation room," I'd say in hushed tones. They all knew of the legendary super-secret national-security nerve center. The very words conjured up images of map-covered walls, whirring computers, and a bevy of generals studying the movements of Soviet aircraft. (Actually, it was then nothing more than a large, crowded office with some communications equipment and old charts on the wall; the real command centers had been moved to the Pentagon after World War II.)

The executive dining room was paneled in rich, hand-rubbed mahogany, lined with a waiting row of red-jacketed Navy stewards. Seated at the dozen tables, huddled in conversation, would be most of the cabinet and senior staff.

The dramatic effect overwhelmed even the staunchest adversary. One union leader, a lifelong Democrat who had never been to the White House before, blurted out during our first lunch together that he'd be available to help in any campaign. A Chicago alderman strong in the Polish neighborhoods signed up on the spot.

Those who needed more prodding were treated to a walk upstairs after lunch. If the president was out, I'd usher them reverently through the Oval Office; if Mr. Nixon was there, I'd ask if my visitor would like to meet the president. His chin would drop as I led him in the side door, cut almost unnoticeably into the wall, and remarked casually (always by prearrangement), "Oh, Mr. President. I was just having lunch with Jim here. Could we say hello?"

Nixon was a master at the game. He always gave his dazzled visitor gold-plated cuff links with the presidential seal. The person would be overwhelmed as he left, almost bowing, not more than sixty seconds later. It's not easy to resist the allure of the Oval Office.

I took all kinds of groups to see the president, from friendly cattlemen to sophisticated educators enraged over budget cuts or the Vietnam War. It was always the same. In the reception room they would rehearse their angry lines and reassure one another, "I'll tell him what's going on. He's got to do something."

When the aide came to escort us in, they'd set their jaws and march toward the door. But once it swung open, the aide announcing, "The president will see you," it was as if they had suddenly sniffed some intoxicating fragrance. Most became almost self-conscious about even stepping on the plush blue carpet on which was sculpted the Great Seal of the United States. And Mr. Nixon's voice and presence — like any president's — filled the room.

Invariably, the lions of the waiting room became the lambs of the Oval Office. No one ever showed outward hostility. Most, except the labor leaders, forgot their best-rehearsed lines. They nodded when the president spoke, and in those rare instances when they disagreed, they did so apologetically, assuring the president that they personally respected his opinion.

Ironically, none were more compliant than the religious leaders. Of all people, they should have been the most aware of the sinful nature of man and the least overwhelmed by pomp and protocol. But theological knowledge sometimes wilts in the face of worldly power.

I frequently scheduled meetings for evangelical groups, denominational councils, and individual religious leaders. Henry Kissinger's briefings in the Roosevelt Room across the hall from the Oval Office were always a big hit.

The weekly church services Nixon scheduled most Sundays for the East Room provided great opportunities as well. To select the preacher, we determined who would give us the greatest impact—politically, that is, not spiritually. At the time I was a nominal Christian at best and had no way to judge the spiritual. And there were always two hundred or more seats to be filled, tickets that were like keys to the political kingdom.

Then there were invitations to social functions and state dinners. I was allowed a quota for every event and filled it with those whose support we coveted most. It is difficult to resist the allure of that most regal of events, the state dinner, held in honor of visiting world leaders. Each of the twelve tables seated ten of the most influential people in America—Supreme Court justices, senators, ambassadors, film stars, cabinet members—and my targets for political support.

One instance I recall illustrates just how well the system works. We needed several electoral-rich Northeastern and Midwestern states to win the 1972 election—or so we thought. So one spring day I called a prominent Christian leader whose influence was particularly great in that region and invited him for a private dinner cruise with the president.

As we arrived at the Washington Navy Yard, sailors in white dress uniforms lined the gangway at attention and saluted as the three of us boarded the presidential yacht, *Sequoia*. Its mahogany sides and brass fittings sparkled as the grand old vessel eased away from its dock.

The Washington skyline faded into the distance, and the president escorted us to dinner in the main salon. White House china, silver, and crystal appointed the starched white tablecloth; stewards scurried back and forth serving chateaubriand and the vintage La Fête Rothschild.

The dinner discussion was as impressive as the food. When our guest mustered the courage to raise points of concern to the religious community, Mr. Nixon showed an amazing grasp of even the intricate details of those issues (as a dutiful aide, I had briefed him thoroughly that afternoon). Every now and then he would stop and say, "Chuck, I want this done. This man is right. You order the attorney general to take care of that tomorrow morning." Then he would resume the conversation.

It wasn't all sham, of course. The president meant what he said, and we even thought some of the things might be accomplished. But whatever else happened, that religious leader was convinced that Richard Nixon was on his side.

Before we arrived at Mount Vernon, the president led us to the foredeck and stood at attention as the colors were retired, his hand over his heart. Our guest did the same. When the bugle had faded, we docked; a waiting Marine helicopter took our new friend back to the airport, and another returned Mr. Nixon and me to the White House lawn.

It would be wrong to suggest that this leader was unduly influenced; but even such a wise, honorable, and religious man could not help but be impressed by the trappings of power. He got what he wanted — the president's ear on certain key issues. And we got what we wanted.

Nixon's prominent public friendship with this leader sent a powerful signal to millions of voters. That fall we carried more than 58 percent of the vote in many Northeastern and Midwestern precincts that had never before voted for a Republican.

This is not to suggest that the Nixon White House was engaged in a sinister conspiracy to corrupt the church. It is simply the way political systems work. People in power use power to keep themselves in power. Even if they are genuinely interested in a special-interest group's agenda — or naturally disposed to their position — they will work that relationship for everything they can get out of it.

In totalitarian regimes some officials are so unscrupulous as to feign religious interest simply to ensnare Christians. In Nicaragua, during the time the Sandinistas were in power, then-Interior Minister Thomas Borge Martinez maintained two offices. When he was receiving churchmen or American visitors, he sat in a Bible-laden office adorned with crucifixes. When he met with government officials or visitors from socialist nations, he occupied an office displaying Marxist slogans and pictures of such revolutionary heroes as Marx, Engels, and Lenin.

I'm not advocating that religious groups or leaders boycott the White House or the palaces and parliaments of the world. That's where the political action is, and Christians need to influence policies for justice and righteousness. That is in the best biblical tradition of Jeremiah, Amos, Micah, Daniel, and a host of others — though many prophets clearly preferred the desert to the palace.

But Christians (and others as well) need to do so with eyes open, aware of the snares. C. S. Lewis wrote that "the demon inherent in every [political] party is at all times ready enough to disguise himself as the Holy Ghost."[8] Tolstoy made a similar point: "Governments, to have a rational foundation for the control of the masses, are obliged to pretend that they are professing the highest religious teachings known to man."[9]

Consider several of the most dangerous pitfalls awaiting the unwary.

The first is that the church will become just another special-interest group.

When President Reagan was challenged by the press during the 1980 campaign for mixing religion and politics by attending a meeting of Religious Right activists, he responded that the church was like any other special-interest group, after all—like a union, for example."[10] Reagan was refreshingly candid, but dead wrong.

The church is not and must never allow itself to become just another special-interest group lined up at the public trough. For in doing so, as one contemporary scholar observes, it would "sacrifice its claim to objective ethical concern which [is the church's] chief political as well as moral resource."[11]

We've already come perilously close to letting this happen. After the 2004 election, the talking heads began buzzing about what the Christian vote for President Bush meant and what Christians believed they could expect for their efforts. "What are your demands?" they asked representatives of Christian groups.

The talking heads didn't seem to realize that evangelicals and conservative Catholics who turned out in great numbers to vote their moral values were not doing so in order to "get something" from the administration. Most did so because they'd agreed with the president for years and identified with who he was.

Christians should disassociate themselves from anyone who says "Now, we voted for you—it's payback time. Give us our due." We vote our conscience and what we believe is in the best general interest: That's called common grace. We also look for the godliest leader we can find, who is also able—as Jethro advised Moses.

We should always remember that our allegiance is to the kingdom of God. To behave as if the Church is just another special-interest group demeans the church and the Lord of the Church. The danger of the church aligning itself as another special-interest group has never been greater than today. Because of the death of truth in the relativistic era in which we live, the traditional ways in which we have come to form a moral consensus in society have been undermined. There is no standard of truth and so people are left to their own devices when deciding what is proper or not proper in political life. What has happened, as it inevitably does, is that the standards of truth governing society degenerates and political parties become controlled by rigid ideology. Ideology, after all, is the enemy of the Gospel because the Gospel is revealed truth while ideology is man-made.

This is why America is so rigidly divided into "red" and "blue" camps today. It's why so many people view evangelicals as an adjunct of the Republican Party. This is dead wrong. Representatives of the kingdom of God must never forget that the transcendence of God's justice must come before any political entanglement that marries Christianity to a political movement. It becomes easy to understand how this has happened because the Republican Party has been far more open and responsive to major concerns of America's Christian community—abortion, gay "marriage," human rights, embryo-destructive research, human cloning—than have Democrats. The Democratic Party, sadly in my mind, has almost excluded conservative Christians by its fanatical allegiance to the causes of abortion on demand (including late-term abortion) and, more recently, same-sex "marriage."

But while it's understandable that Christians turn to the Republicans who listen to their concerns rather than to the Democrats who often don't, our tendency to do so is both dangerous and unwise.

Tocqueville warned that if the church were to become a mere interest group, it would then be measured and honored according to political and not moral criteria.[12] The great strength of the American church, he believed, was that it was not linked to a partisan cause. By way of contrast, he pointed out that in Europe people "reject the clergy less because they are representatives of God than because they are friends of authority."[13]

A second danger is that politics can be like the proverbial tar baby. Christian leaders who are courted by political forces may soon begin to overestimate their own importance. The head of one large international relief agency mistakenly came to believe that heads of state welcomed him because of who he was rather than what he represented. It wasn't long before his work and his personal life failed to measure up to his delusions of power. He left his family and was eventually removed from his position—after doing great harm to the cause he had served for much of his life.

A side effect of this delusion is that rather than lose their access to political influence, some church leaders have surrendered their independence. "If I speak out against this policy," they reason, "I won't get invited to dinner and my chances to minister will be cut off." While such rationalizing is understandable, the result is exactly the opposite; they keep their place but lose their voice and thus any possibility of holding government to moral account.

In this way the gospel becomes hostage to the political fortunes of a particular movement. This is the third and perhaps most dangerous snare. Both liberals and conservatives have made this mistake of aligning their spiritual goals with a particular political agenda.

One conservative Christian leader, when asked what would happen if the Democrats won the 1988 U.S. election, said, "I don't know what will happen to us."[14] Religious leaders have made similar statements about every election. The danger, of course, is that we see the election as a vindication of our spiritual convictions, like the Methodist bishop who wrote, following the 1980 election, "The blame [for Reagan's victory] ought not to be placed on all the vigor of the Right, but maybe on the weakness of saints." A better day will come, he said, "If the people of faith will be strengthened by defeat and address themselves to the new agenda which is upon us."[15] The implication was clear: if you disagreed with the bishop's partisan politics, you were not among "the people of faith."

Nor are you if you support any of President Bush's policies, according to *Sojourners* founder Jim Wallis, who has attacked religious conservatives for being obsessed with abortion and gay "marriage," and for being indifferent to the plight of the poor. Unfortunately anyone who disagrees with Wallis's ideas on how we should go about fighting poverty — if they think, for instance, that faith-based initiatives do more to help those in need than simply throwing money at them — is dismissed as not caring about the poor.

A perhaps more self-serving instance of the "Support my agenda or you're a bad Christian" approach is Hillary Clinton, who, at a 2006 "Faith, Politics, and Policy" conference at Emory University, sneered at religious conservatives who supported cutting the federal budget: "I missed the Sunday school lesson about how we help the poor by giving tax cuts to the rich," she said sarcastically. Those who support Mrs. Clinton's own political agenda — increasing federal funding for Medicaid and housing vouchers, and raising taxes, are "faithful servants" of God who are "shining a light on the way people are trapped in poverty."

Several years ago a prominent leader of a large Christian mission visited a developing nation ruled by an authoritarian leader. The leader was friendly to the U.S. and held a regal dinner party at the palace honoring the mission executive. The awestruck visitor publicly and effusively praised the head of state. Months later when that head of state was deposed, the Christian's mission work in that country was deposed right along with him.

Inevitably, this kind of political alignment compromises the gospel.

Particularly in these days of a highly polarized and ideologically divided American society, Christians must use special discernment and great restraint. It isn't always easy. For instance, I consider myself to be a good friend of President and Mrs. George W. Bush. I have visited them may times and have found President Bush to be unfailingly sensitive to every major political issue I have discussed with him, whether it be partial-birth abortion, AIDS in Africa, slavery in Sudan, religious persecution in North Korea, prison rape, or international sex trafficking. But while I consider myself his friend and admire much of what he has accomplished, I still refrain from making any partisan endorsement or statement. I would have to challenge him if he took actions that were contrary to his own belief system.

After President Bush vetoed the stem-cell research bill in 2006, I congratulated him and told him that was an act of great courage. His response was that his veto had nothing to do with courage: it was a moral issue, and he had no choice but to act according to his conscience. (Or, as he put it in his speech, funding research that deliberately destroys healthy — and adoptable — human embryos "crosses a moral boundary.") I took the president's words as a healthy sign. Had he not vetoed this bill, I would not have hesitated to be critical. Having said that, I acknowledge that this is a tough issue for all of us.

The inherent danger of marrying religion to politics is summed up by James Schall, who writes, "All successful Christian social theory in the immediate future must be based on this truth: that religion be not made an instrument of political ideology."[16]

Because it tempts one to water down the truth of the gospel, ideological alignment, whether on the left or right, accelerates the church's secularization.[17] When the church aligns itself politically, it gives priority to the compromises and temporal successes of the political world rather than its

Christian confession of eternal truth. And when the church gives up its rightful place as the conscience of the culture, the consequences for society can be horrific.

As we've seen, many German churches in the thirties allied themselves with the new nationalistic movement. One churchman even described the Nazis as a "gift and miracle of God."[18] It was the *confessing* church, not the politically minded church, which retained its orthodoxy and thus resisted the evils of Hitler's state.

In the 1980s, liberation theologians, who were all the fashion at the time, fell into the same trap, putting ideology ahead of orthodoxy. It began, as did many Christian political movements, with noble intentions. Righteously outraged at injustices to the poor in so-called Christian cultures, priests and church workers began to organize communities for action. So far, so good.

But as those organizations failed to solve problems, frustrations grew; attacks on structures became more strident.

When Christians put economic issues ahead of spiritual salvation, they are embracing economic determinism; it is then but a short step to revolutionary politics and the fatal mistake of believing the Kingdom of God can be ushered in by political means. Ernesto Cardenal Martinez, a leftist Nicaraguan priest and government official under the Sandinistas, ominously illustrated this point when he said, "A world of perfect communism is the Kingdom of God on earth."[19] (Cardenal's activities earned him a stern rebuke from Pope John Paul II during his 1983 visit to Nicaragua.)

Does all of this mean that Christians cannot work with political groups? Certainly not. In fact, often Christians must work with coalitions of like-minded people who have different motivations. But as Donald Bloesch has pointed out, "In order to maintain their Christian identity they must inwardly detach themselves from the motivations and ultimate goals of their ideological colleagues."[20]

In World War II, for example, a devout Christian might have fought to stop the evil of Nazism and the Holocaust because he believed God commanded that the state is to restrain evil. Next to him in the same foxhole might have been a soldier fighting solely for national pride or honor. Both would have been shooting at the same enemy, but for different reasons.

Today Christians may find themselves suspect — I have experienced this myself — to the very people on whose side they are fighting. But that is the price they must pay to preserve their independence and not be beholden to any political ideological alignment.

Only a church free of any outside domination can be the conscience of society and, as Washington pastor Myron Augsburger has written, "hold government morally accountable before God to live up to its own claims."[21] And as the amazing events in the next chapter demonstrate, when the church faithfully fulfills this role, even the most determined of tyrants topple.

23

PEOPLE POWER

Justice without mercy is tyranny, and mercy without justice is weakness. Justice without love is pure socialism, and love without justice is baloney.

JAIME CARDINAL SIN,
speaking at a Prison Fellowship International
conference in Nairobi, Kenya, 1986

A small Filipino man with penetrating brown eyes stared, unbelievingly, at his prison door's cool, smooth surface. It was 1972. Moments before, the door had crashed shut on him with metallic finality. It felt like a bad dream. Never before had he been in a prison. In fact, until that day he had expected to become the next president of the Philippines.

It seemed impossible—ridiculous, really. Benigno Aquino was the boy wonder of Philippine politics—mayor of a large town at twenty-two, governor of a province at twenty-eight, at thirty-five elected senator, the youngest ever. Now he measured the entire extent of his freedom in two or three paces. He sat on his bunk and thought, and as the day passed into night he continued to sit there. For the first time in his life he had nothing else to do—nothing.

Son of a wealthy family, this charismatic, gregarious politician suddenly found himself stripped of everything that had propped up his ego. All his plans, his friends, his busy schedule, all his carefully cultivated followers were gone, replaced by the sheer loneliness and boredom of the prison cell and the venomous hostility of his guards. He kept waiting for Marcos to send for him, to offer a deal. Surely he could not simply leave him to rot in prison!

Half a year went by before Aquino was even questioned or confronted with any charges. Then a trumped-up murder case was brought, and a rigged military court condemned him to death. This too was a bad dream, for the real reason for his imprisonment was President Ferdinand Marcos's greed for power. With his two-term limit as president due to expire in 1973, Marcos had declared martial law, granting himself almost unlimited powers. He had thrown Aquino and other political opponents into prison. Marcos intended never to leave office—and so was determined never to let a popular Aquino out to challenge him.

Prison had, for Aquino, the same bewildering effect it has held for so many others. He lost all sense of direction and perspective. He became bitter not only at Marcos, but at the world, even at God. He hated everyone and his prison guards goaded him on. They sometimes put his dinner plate on the ground and let a mongrel dog wolf part of it down; then, kicking the dog aside, they gave what was left to Aquino. He lost forty pounds. He suffered two heart attacks. When he was not longing for revenge, he wanted to die.

His mother, deeply concerned, sent him a book, the memoirs of another prisoner. It was my story—*Born Again*.

At first Aquino looked at it with little appetite. Watergate was poorly understood outside America. Nonetheless, there were similarities in our careers. So Aquino read the book—and it touched him.

He read how I too had lost everything and entered the disorienting, mocking maze of prison. But God had shown me that such losses were not in vain as I found my true life in Christ.

Aquino began to search for the meaning I had found. A voracious reader, he poured over the Bible and other Christian books. He found great inspiration in a little classic, *The Imitation of Christ* by Thomas à Kempis. He was surprised to discover in reading the works of an early Filipino hero, José Rizal, that the same book had motivated his life and struggle for his country.

One night Aquino knelt in his jail cell and gave his life to Jesus Christ. Overcome with grief for his anger toward God, he begged forgiveness. His viewpoints, his life, most of all his bitterness—all changed. He had a sense that his life had suddenly moved into a different channel with another purpose.

As the late Jaime Cardinal Sin of the Philippines has said, it is hard for our doubting hearts to believe that spiritual power—which is peaceful, prayerful, humane, forgiving, willing to suffer on the side of the poor and oppressed—can change society. We know the gospel affects the lives of individuals, but can it make an impact on institutions and governments, where the heartless realities of power pierce like a knife? It is hard to fathom this.[1]

Nevertheless, it can happen. It does happen. One can never quite calculate how one conversion like Benigno Aquino's in a lowly prison cell may set in motion a train of events to shake a nation.

I met Benigno Aquino in 1980—a chance encounter, seemingly, on an airplane. He reached out to grasp my arm as we boarded the plane. "You're Mr. Colson," he exclaimed. "I must talk with you." Since we were blocking the aisle I offered him the empty seat next to mine. "I can't believe I am meeting you," he said. "I wanted to die in prison until I read your book." I knew when we had completed our flight, I had another Christian brother.

After eight years in prison Aquino had been released by Marcos under then President Carter's prodding. The grounds were humanitarian—he needed triple-bypass surgery. Aquino survived the heart operation and took a fellowship at Harvard. Marcos would not let him return to his own country.

Robert Shaplen, a foreign correspondent who had known Aquino for many years, wrote for the *New Yorker* magazine, "At fifty, he seemed to have acquired a new maturity, and, though he also retained his natural ebullience, a relative serenity that he had never had before. Some of his friends felt he had undergone something like religious conversion as a result of his years in prison...."[2]

Indeed he had. Yet that conversion took away none of his heartfelt concern for his nation. Ninoy, as his friends called him, vowed he would one day return to the Philippines. If he could run for office he believed he would be president. If Marcos threw him in prison, then he would be president of Prison Fellowship. "If I'm killed, I'll be with Jesus," he told me, smiling.

Marcos was using martial law as a cover while he raped the country. He and his business cronies were bleeding the nation dry, making huge profits through monopoly powers and putting the money into New York real estate and Swiss banks. Meanwhile, half the working population could not find jobs. The ugly scabs of slums, many without running water or flush toilets, spread across Manila and other cities.

Marxist guerrillas were quickly gaining ground, and the military, riven by corruption, seemed unable to stop them. They found it easier to savage poor peasants than to fight the Communists. Things had reached the point where anyone who helped the poor was under suspicion. Filipino army units arrested, killed, and tortured even Catholic priests and nuns who had chosen to work with the desperately poor. A few Catholics had, it is true, taken the side of the Marxists, but the vast majority simply ministered in the name of Jesus to those in need. Between the Marxist insurgency and the Marcos dictatorship, there was little room in the middle.

Aquino knew Marcos's ruthless side—he had, after all, suffered in solitary confinement. He also thought he knew of a better side; he believed he might reason with him to restore free elections. So in the summer of 1983 he decided, after much soul searching, to leave comfortable Cambridge and return home.

Shortly before leaving, Aquino testified at a congressional subcommittee: "It is true, one can fight hatred with a greater hatred, but ... it is more effective to fight hatred with greater Christian love.... I have decided to pursue my freedom struggle through the path of nonviolence, fully cognizant that this may be the longer and the more arduous road.... Only I will suffer solitary confinement once again, and possibly death.... But by taking the road of revolution, how many lives, other than mine, will have to be sacrificed?"[3]

It was August 21, 1983. Benigno Aquino rose in Taiwan at 5:00 A.M. after only four hours of sleep. His first act was prayer. He then called his wife Cory, still in Massachusetts. She read the Bible to him over the phone. He spoke briefly to each of his five children, and tears spilled down his cheeks. After hanging up he sat down and wrote each child a letter. "The one regret I have," he told his brother-in-law who was traveling with him, "is that Cory has had to suffer so much."

Though Aquino had tried to keep his flight to Manila a mystery to the government, the plane was jammed with journalists. Filipino passengers, startled to find themselves flying with a celebrity, mobbed him. One woman repeatedly kissed him while news cameras clicked and Aquino squirmed uncomfortably. He gave a series of interviews to the journalists on board. The mood was celebration. Aquino hoped to lead a march of 20,000 supporters to Marcos's lush Malacalang Palace.

Eventually, when the plane began its descent, the cabin sobered. Aquino went into the bathroom, removed the shirt to his cream-colored safari suit, and grimly put on a bulletproof vest.

Back in his seat he thoughtfully removed his watch and handed it to his brother-in-law. "I just want you to have it," he said. Then he sat quietly as the plane landed. His lips moved in silent prayer.

The airliner eased to a stop at the gate and the jetway crawled out to clamp its mouth to the door. Journalists and passengers pressed their foreheads to the windows, watching for signs of trouble. Suddenly they saw a blue van pull up. A contingent of uniformed soldiers carrying automatic weapons leaped out and circled the plane. Some of the passengers had stood up ready to deplane, but now a voice over the intercom asked them to be seated. "They're coming!" someone sang out from a window seat.

Three khaki-clad soldiers entered the cabin. Blinded by television lights and the commotion of photographers fighting for a good angle, they pushed down the aisle looking about them. The first soldier missed Aquino altogether, walking past his seat. But the second soldier, wearing sunglasses, recognized him and stopped. The third soldier leaned over, and Aquino smilingly took his hand. They exchanged a few words in Tagalog.

The soldiers slowly led Aquino through the crush to the front of the plane. Behind them came a sea of journalists, pushing, shouting. The jetway was jammed; no one could hear or see over the crush of bodies and the noisy confusion.

The soldiers escorted Aquino out of the plane door. But as soon as they turned the corner into the jetway, one of them opened the service door leading to a set of stairs descending to the tarmac below. The soldiers pushed Aquino through and slammed the door shut behind them. A soldier's body blocked the door window. Left inside, cameramen shouted, pushing and banging against the door. Nine seconds later, above the frantic noise, a shot rang out. People screamed, cursed. Then three more shots. Then a burst of automatic rifle fire.

At the foot of the stairs, sprawled on the pavement face down, his arms akimbo and blood oozing from his mouth, lay Aquino. He was dead, shot in the back of the head.

Two million people walked in the rain to his funeral. Soft warm drops from a gray sky glazed their faces, but they seemed not to notice. For hours they streamed through Manila streets, a seemingly endless mass of dazed people, moving as if by memory. Some wept. Some carried banners. But on the whole they were frighteningly silent.

Few Filipinos gave any credence to the military's story that a Communist-hired gunman had penetrated the tight airport security and shot Aquino, then died himself in a hail of soldier's bullets. They believed that their government had reached a new low; it had murdered, in cold blood and in front of the world, a man who had come in peace. It was an act so callous that it shocked many into action who had until then accepted corruption and violence with a cynical shrug.

Cardinal Sin gave an eloquent, moving sermon to those who found space in the crowded Santo Domingo Church. Among them was the frail-looking, grave woman who had read the Bible to Aquino on the day of his death: Cory Aquino. Privately Sin predicted, "This is the beginning, when people will be opening their eyes."

A few weeks later the government organized a rally in the affluent Makati district of Manila. No one quite knew why Marcos staged these affairs; the organizers sometimes slept through the speeches, and the crowds had to be bused in from distant suburbs where ward leaders could round up, at ten to twenty pesos a head, enough people with nothing to do. But this time the utterly unexpected happened. From the glass and chrome skyscrapers of the Philippines Wall Street poured tens of thousands of office workers. They had not been paid to attend, but then they were not cheering for Marcos. They carried hurriedly scrawled banners: "I love Ninoy," "Ninoy our Hero," "Justice for Aquino — Justice for All," "Who Killed our Hero?" The air rained colored paper and computer tapes. It was an unprecedented, spontaneous outburst of outrage and — yes, unmistakably — of joy. No one had ever seen anything like it in the Philippines — People Power. Aquino's death had awakened them.

Jaime Sin was a heavy-set, jovial man with a face as round as a wheel, a deep infectious laugh, and a rich sense of humor. He was appointed cardinal in 1983, the same year that Aquino died.

In 1984 the *New York Times* referred to Sin as the most popular man in the Philippines. He was certainly a lovable character and a remarkable preacher, but his popularity was due to more than that. The Philippines was disintegrating, its deep tradition of democracy degraded by a government that made less and less pretense of justice. Aquino's murder brought a wave of grief and revulsion.

Marcos himself was rumored to be desperately sick; it was not clear who ran the government on any given day. Communist guerrillas grew in strength. Yet the moderate opposition was a rats nest of infighting. Among this confusion only Sin and the Christian church he represented had credibility and moral authority.

Sin refused to serve on the official government commission investigating Aquino's murder, for he felt sure the commission would be a tool in the hands of the government. Instead he poured his energies into preaching the demands and privileges of the Kingdom of God. He sent pastoral letters criticizing the government for human-rights abuses; these were read in every Roman Catholic Church in the Philippines. Yet Sin made clear that he did not speak for opposition politicians. He spoke for God.

He saw his role as a spiritual, not a political leader. Sin had been studying the Book of Chronicles. He saw in the account of Israel's corrupt leaders a parallel with the grief his own nation was enduring. *When God wants to punish a people*, he reasoned, *He gives them unjust rulers. Like Marcos.* So the answer is for the people to repent, turn from their ways, be converted, and seek God.

Among the lush green islands Sin preached to legions of poor farmers as well as the stylishly dressed elite. His simple message took root. His battle cry was "Cor," which means "heart" — an acronym: C for conversion, the changed life created through repentance and forgiveness from God. O stood for the offering of obedient lives to God — for true conversion had to make a difference in behavior. R stood for reparation — for the "making right" required of true repentance. Sin called Filipinos to prayer and fasting. Bible studies and prayer groups spread, even in the military. As Sin told one visiting reporter, "You will see our churches filled up. There is no space even on weekdays.... They are complaining to God. They are bringing their sadness before the altar of God."

Throughout the Philippines people felt that change was coming. But along with hope there was much fear. People did not know how change would come or with how much blood.

Cardinal Sin walked through the familiar halls of Malacalang Palace wondering just what he would say to Marcos. A glance at the velvet upholstery, the mahogany paneling, and the rich heavy curtains reminded Sin that this world was well insulated from the climate of change he sensed throughout the Philippines. The ostentatious style smelled of money and privilege. What words would cut through the confidence of Marcos's political and business cronies?

Sin had talked to Marcos many times, to no avail. Marcos often promised to change or to investigate abuses. Then he would proceed to do the opposite of what he had promised. A crisis was coming for the Philippines. Sin felt it.

Marcos stood respectfully in welcome, though he seemed to totter slightly on his feet. His handshake was weak; his face looked gray and puffy. Nonetheless he was the familiar man: shrewd, genial, talkative, sidestepping questions when it suited him. Marcos was known even by those who hated him as the smartest, shrewdest politician in Philippine history. It was very difficult to be sure where truth ended and fiction began with Marcos. It was not certain Marcos knew or cared.

"The reason I have come," Cardinal Sin said when the pleasantries were done, "is this, Mr. President. Your term of office is due to end next year. Why are you calling for a snap election?"

Marcos had announced elections to be held early in February, 1986, just two months away. It was not clear why. The U.S. had been pressing him, but why do it on such short notice? Did he realize how unpopular he had become? Why run when he was so sick? Sin had come to try to understand what he was up to.

Marcos smiled at Sin. "I want to have a fresh mandate from the people," he said.

"It is very dangerous for you to call a snap election," Sin said. "You may lose. You will be forced to step down."

Marcos kept a smile stuck on his mouth, but his bland, puffy face looked as warm as a cobra's. "You think that you understand politics, which they never taught you in seminary. So you interfere. When you should support your government in its struggle against Communists, you instead disturb the peace by criticizing. But you do not understand the way things are done. I cannot lose an election to an opposition that is hopelessly divided. They will tear each other to pieces."

The two men stared frostily at each other. Sin was angry—at Marcos's insolent words and at his disregard for his own people's needs. He only cared about power, not the good he could have done with power. And he was so seemingly confident that he could control, through political maneuvers, the people's will.

Sin spoke slowly: "Sir, I will unite the opposition in order that there may be a fair election."

The two maintained a fierce stare. Did Marcos feel a slight pull of panic underneath his expressionless mask? Did he have a hint of what Sin could unleash? He gave no sign of it.

Sin stood. "Good-bye," he said. "And may the Lord come down to protect our people." Without a handshake he turned and left, his red robe swirling behind him, Marcos still in his chair.

Sin, in anger, had crossed a line. Until that time he had been very careful not to marry the church to the opposition. He had maintained the careful role of a church leader in the political realm: that of conscience, of reconciliation, of proclaiming God's good promises. But part of the risk of politics is that emotions become involved.

Sin was convinced only one person could unite the squabbling opposition: Cory Aquino, the quiet, self-effacing widow of the slain Ninoy. Sin knew her well. He knew of her deep Christian faith. She alone could raise the level of opposition above mere politics to a moral plane. She alone could ride on the wave of emotion that her husband's assassination had begun two and a half years before.

But she claimed no political aspirations. Sin met with her several times, urging her to stand for the presidency. She always said no. Then one day, after a huge worship service celebrated in Manila's Luneta Park, which six million people attended, Sin returned home to find Cory Aquino waiting for him.

She was the opposite of Marcos; disinterested in appearances, she wore no makeup, and her simple dress was yellow, her husband's favorite color. Yellow had become the symbol of those seeking to carry out the work he had begun.

"Why are you here?" Sin asked mildly.

"I have decided to run," she said quietly.

"Cory, under what political party? Who will be your running mate?"

"I will run alone," she said.

Sin knew that without a political organization her campaign would be hopeless. "Don't do that," he said. "You cannot organize a political party now. There is too little time. You run under UNIDO, with Laurel as your vice-president. Will you do that?"

"But Laurel is planning to run himself."

"I will get him to agree if you accept him first."

After a few moments of quiet reflection, Aquino said simply, "Yes, yes, I will run with him."

Sin's face broke into a wide and sunny smile. "God bless you. Out of your weakness this great man will come down. He has been insulting you, saying that women are only good for the bedroom. So you will win."

She fell to her knees in front of him, her hands clasped together, and Sin leaned down slightly to place his hand on her head and give his blessing. "I bless you and you will win." Cardinal Sin had now consciously crossed the line—to stay.

The Philippine election was remarkable for two reasons. The first was the outpouring of emotion that accompanied Cory Aquino wherever she went. Her motorcade was perpetually late because of the chanting crowds jamming the roads, the people swarming alongside her begging for a scrap of conversation or a handshake. She did not seem to care about the schedule: she always took time to talk to the lowliest person. Her campaign soon stood for more than a political faction; it became a festival of democracy. And it was accompanied by a great deal of prayer. Sin's preaching of repentance and conversion had made a deep impact on the nation, and now it bore fruit.

Democracy is not prescribed in the Bible, and Christians can and do live under other political systems. But Christians can hardly fail to love democracy, because of all systems it best assures human dignity, the essence of our creation in God's image.

Such a love for democracy was plain in the Philippines: in the cordons of nuns wrapping their arms around the aluminum ballot boxes as though they were protecting human life; in the crowds of fervent poll watchers, often from church groups; in the computer operators who walked off their vote-counting jobs because they saw the discrepancy between their count and the officially released results, and who were rushed to a nearby church for protection from the police. The enthusiasm, the tears, the confrontations all reflected a tremendous will for government of the people and for the people. Cory Aquino, in her calm, firm, common-sense manner—just the opposite of a glib, polished professional politician—seemed to embody democracy. She was a housewife pressed into politics by the need of her nation.

The other exceptional aspect of the election was the sheer cynicism and brutality of Marcos's party. They made very little attempt to hide what they were doing from foreign reporters, so American television audiences were shocked to witness ballot boxes stolen at gunpoint, votes purchased like potatoes, thousands of voters driven away from polling places by armed thugs. Filipinos were unable to see such reports; the state-controlled news calmly reported that everything was normal, that there were only scattered reports of fraud. But millions of Filipinos personally witnessed the election being stolen.

Sin had seen it coming and had issued a statement two weeks before: "If a candidate wins by cheating, he can only be forgiven by God if he renounces the office he has obtained by fraud. There will be no divine forgiveness for this act of injustice without a previous decision to repay the damage done."[4]

But apparently God's forgiveness was unimportant to those ruling the Philippines. They rigged the vote. All the passion for democracy and all the prayers of the people had not stopped them.

On February 14, one week after the election, the Marcos-dominated National Assembly laid all doubts about their objectivity to rest by proclaiming Ferdinand Marcos the electoral winner. Public anger was mounting and the danger of it erupting grew more likely each day. Aquino called a protesting political rally for the sixteenth, a Sunday. Small knots of marchers gathered at different points in the vast city of Manila, converging from all directions on Manila's downtown Luneta Park.

Many wore yellow T-shirts in memory of the slain Benigno Aquino. Yellow headbands proclaimed, "I love Ninoy." Marchers carried signs and banners and chanted, "Cory, Cory." The procession gradually grew as it entered the main city arteries. Supporters poured out of apartments, slums, churches. They did not stroll; they dog-trotted along, swinging their elbows. Mothers, children, old wizened men — it seemed as though half of Manila was marching, singing, chanting. The air of celebration that had marked Aquino's campaign had hardened into a tougher sense of determination.

Well over a million people reached the park together. Elbow to elbow they sang "Bayan Ko," the haunting, emotive melody of Philippine independence:

> *Even birds who freely fly*
> *When caged will struggle to escape.*

What more of a country endowed with nobility,
Would she not strive to break free?
The Philippines, my cherished land,
My home of sorrow and tears,
Always I dream to see you truly free.

Now, with such a mass of humanity together, the cry "Cory, Cory" seemed to saturate the air, the ground. Many wept.

This was the kind of crowd a politician might dream of. They would march anywhere, do anything, on command.

Yet Cory Aquino stood in front of the vast assemblage spread like a bright mosaic at her feet and spoke in her calm, rational, head-librarian manner. She did not send them to storm Malacalang Palace—though they would have gone. She asked them for a day of prayer.

She also called for a series of nonviolent protests—boycotting certain banks and businesses owned by Marcos cronies and setting up a "noise barrage" every evening after she spoke on the Catholic radio station. They were to do this patiently until the government conceded. "You have given a lot to the country," she said, "but in the coming days you will have to give more. We thought Election day was the day of our redemption, but it proved the start of our further struggle."

A young Catholic bishop read a statement issued by the bishops two days before: "The people have spoken. Or tried to. Despite the obstacles thrown in the way of their speaking freely, we the bishops believe what they attempted to say is clear enough. In our considered judgment the polls were unparalleled in the fraudulence of their conduct."

The church leaders supported nonviolent civil disobedience. "A government that assumes or maintains power through fraudulent means has no moral basis," they said. "If it does not of itself freely correct the evil it has inflicted on the people, then it is our serious moral obligation as a people to make it do so." Nonetheless they warned against "the enormous sin of fratricidal strife."

Some American reporters left the rally shaking their heads. How could this nonviolent, prayerful approach make a revolution?

During that tense, rumor-filled week, it seemed the reporters might be correct. Marcos might ride it out. He controlled the guns, after all.

Marcos did not, however, entirely control the men who carried the guns. Secret meetings were held, mainly by younger officers. They discussed the possibility of announcing their loyalty to Aquino whom they considered the duly elected president. A plan was hurriedly formed in consultation with the minister of defense, Juan Ponce Enrile.

The officers were a group who, years before, had begun questioning orders to make arrests without legal evidence or to use torture in interrogations. Their military training had given them no basis for judging how to respond to such orders. When was it right, if ever, for a military officer to refuse to obey?

The search for answers had led them to Christ. They began holding Bible classes and prayer meetings. As they studied the Bible their sense of moral outrage grew. They began demanding change and became known as the Reform Group.

Benigno Aquino's murder heightened their awareness that more than politics was at stake. Perhaps they intuitively grasped that the dignity of the individual, created in the image of God, was on trial. Now, with the election stolen, they felt it impossible to remain loyal to Marcos.

But Marcos discovered their plans to desert him and late Friday began to move loyal military units into position. By Saturday morning a watchful Enrile knew something was going on; he had reports of troops ferried into Manila. While eating a late breakfast with his daughter, Enrile received a warning telephone call from another cabinet minister. He suddenly realized that he would be arrested soon along with many others. He had to react within hours or face possible death.

They could flee the city. Or they could take a stand within Manila and appeal for popular support. There was no time to think through all the implications of the choices. Enrile elected to stay and at about 3:00 P.M. helicoptered into the ministry of defense headquarters at Camp Aguinaldo on the edge of town. Only a few hundred troops were on duty. It was virtually defenseless.

Enrile's first action was to call his wife. He asked her to reach Cardinal Sin and appeal to him for help.

At 6:30 that night, as darkness settled over Manila, Enrile and a much-respected general, Fidel Ramos, held a press conference in Camp Aguinaldo. Radio Veritas, the Catholic station, covered it live. Enrile explained their decision: "We can no longer support Marcos as our commander-in-chief—because of our honest belief that he did not receive the people's mandate in the election. I believe in my heart and mind that Mrs. Aquino was duly elected president of the Philippines.... We will never surrender, and if we are assaulted, we will all die together."

Death seemed a real possibility. Though they had stretched a thin defense force around the camp's perimeter, they were sitting ducks. As military men, they knew that they could be quickly overwhelmed by superior forces. They could only hope that somehow, something would turn in their favor.

At 9:00 that night it did. Sin's familiar warm voice suddenly came on Radio Veritas. He ordered all nuns into their chapels where they were to pray continuously until God delivered the Philippines. Then he spoke to *all* Christians. "Go to Camp Crame and Camp Aguinaldo. Lend your support to Enrile and Ramos. Protect them and bring them food; they have nothing to eat."

Within thirty minutes two million people were on the streets. Unarmed, often gathered as church groups, they simply waited, listening to their radios, praying, and singing through the long night. No one had told them how to carry out their unprecedented assignment to protect soldiers.

Catholic believers provided the impetus for this mass movement; but they were joined in the streets by Protestants. CONFES, an evangelical Protestant group formed to push for an honest election, was one of the earliest groups to make its way to the gates of the military camps. There, with barbed-wire fences for their backdrop, they organized into shifts for the vigil. They read Scripture, sang hymns, made signs. Everyone felt the tension. This was a protest that could end in blood.

The next day Marcos's troops began to come. One long column of tanks and trucks carried a regiment of marines, headed by a muscular, bronzed general, one of Marcos's strongest supporters. In the midday heat the tanks ground noisily over the Manila streets toward the camps. Thousands of civilians crowded around, shouting, beckoning. Some of the crowd began hurriedly pushing cars and buses into a major intersection ahead of the tanks. A barricade of dozens of vehicles forced the convoy to a temporary halt.

Groups of marines armed with automatic rifles leaped out of the trucks and jogged to the front. They took up menacing positions, guns ready. The general came forward with his bullhorn and ordered the people to disperse. The huge milling crowd, composed largely of women and children, instead moved closer. Some held out crosses; others offered flowers. Still others were praying. An old woman in a wheelchair cried out for the soldiers; kill her if they must, but not their own people.

The soldiers did not know what to do. None of these rebels threw anything at them or even insulted them. Apparently they had no fear. Could they shoot?

"We're all Filipinos!" shouted one woman. "What are you doing? Don't kill us!"

One slender, brave woman pushed her way between two bewildered soldiers right up to the general. She threw her arms around him, calling his name. "You have a wife and children too! Don't do it! Don't kill us in the name of a dictator."

The general gently pushed her away. For some time he nervously surveyed the masses of people in front of him. Finally, he ceremoniously took off his bulletproof vest. "We don't want to kill civilians," he told one of his aides. "Our quarrel is with Enrile and Ramos."

He climbed on top of a tank and with his bullhorn told the people that the tanks would have to pass. "We will not hurt you. We have orders to enter Camp Aguinaldo."

"No, no!" people cried. Many threw themselves to their knees and began praying out loud. The general ordered his men to start the tanks. The people prayed louder above the roaring engines. The tanks jerked forward, their treads creaking and clattering. There were high screams of horror; men held their heads, anticipating the moment when the first bodies would be crushed. But just as the lead tank reached the first kneeling bodies — many of them priests and nuns — it stopped. For just a moment there was virtual silence. Then the crowd let out a prolonged cheer.

The top of the tank opened and a helmeted, bemused soldier poked his head out, looked around at the masses of happy people, and shrugged his shoulders, as though to say, "What can we do about this?"

By Monday morning there were dozens of such tanks on the streets all around the military camps, stopped not by antitank missiles but by the bodies of praying Filipinos. Young soldiers sprawled on top of their beached vehicles eating food offered by the people who had stopped them.

On Tuesday Marcos fled the country, defeated.

※

Benigno Aquino was felled by an assassin's bullet. But what he represented could not be destroyed. In two and one half years Marcos was gone and Aquino's wife was president. Miraculously it was a bloodless transition.

Cory Aquino's first year in office was shaky at best; despite her personal popularity, this simple housewife, with faith of iron, narrowly survived several military coup attempts, communist uprisings, and attempts by Marcos supporters to destabilize her government—all while she was grappling to get control of a government that had been almost wholly corrupt. But democracy has survived.

I met with Cory Aquino in her office on a weekend in November 1986, She was to depart for her first trip to Japan. The press worldwide was speculating that her now defiant defense minister, Juan Enrile, would take over in her absence. Manila was abuzz with rumors. The young man who met me at the airport to drive me to Mrs. Aquino's office suggested I also visit Enrile: "He'll be president next week."

But Cory Aquino was at perfect peace. "I didn't seek this," she told me, "and I only want to serve my people. I simply have to put my trust in the Lord." Then she explained that she had given Cardinal Sin full instructions on what to say to the people if she were "unable to do so myself." I had the impression she could face death as resolutely as had her husband.

The next morning I went to Cardinal Sin's residence. We had met earlier when he addressed our International Conference in Nairobi—and we had become fast friends. I was delighted to discover at the chancery that the bishop had several months earlier instructed his entire staff to read *Born Again*. Several told me they had.

The cardinal, wearing a huge smile, swung open his door. "Welcome to the House of Sin, dear brother," he chuckled, enveloping me in a massive embrace.

During our conversation I expressed concern over the expected coup. Sin leaned back in his chair, rolled his eyes upward, and put both hands up, palms out. "There will be no coup, praise God," he said. Then with a mischievous expression he told me that he had met with Enrile the night before. "I've taken care of that, now you can do your part," he said, grinning. "You preach to those businessmen tonight from the Scripture." I was that evening to address a thousand conservative evangelicals at a major dinner. Many of them had been Enrile sympathizers. "You tell them to be born again—and pray for those in authority, for their Christian president."

There was no coup. Nearly a year after the revolution Jaime Cardinal Sin remained the most powerful individual in the Philippines.

The problems of the Philippines were not solved overnight, and its people continue to struggle. While the Communist insurgencies have subsided, violent Islamic separatists have taken their place, kidnapping and murdering innocents (including American missionary Ken Burnham in 2002).

Cardinal Sin died in 2005 at the age of seventy-six. The former Archbishop of Manila received state honors during his funeral mass. While his casket was draped in the Philippine flag, the flower arrangements contained no ribbons because the Church feared that political colors would mar Cardinal Sin's wake.

As for Corazon Aquino, she served for six years as president. Under her leadership, a new constitution was drafted and ratified in February of 1987. When she left office in 1992, Mrs. Aquino insisted on driving home in her own white Toyota Crown rather than the government-issued Mercedes as a public reminder that she was, once again, an ordinary citizen. Like Cardinal Sin, Mrs. Aquino took an active part in the revolt that led to the overthrow of President Estrada, and later condemned President Arroyo for engaging in election fraud.

Regardless of the future of Philippine politics, the revolution of February, 1986 will be remembered as one of the most remarkable church-state confrontation in the last century. The contrast with Nazi Germany in the thirties is striking. In Germany the church was institutionalized and lacked evangelical fervor and the emotional support of the populace; so Hitler could strike fast and dismember it before it could collect itself for opposition. In the Philippines, on the other hand, the church was strong, the masses were powerful, conversions were sweeping the islands, Benigno Aquino was a powerful martyr, and there was never any doubt that the remarkable Cardinal Sin was in charge. So in the Philippines the church prevailed, withdrawing its moral legitimization for a corrupt, repressive regime; it succeeded in holding the state "morally accountable before God to live up to its own claims," as one prominent pastor put it.[5]

But the church went further than simply withdrawing its support. It was the chief instrument in the overthrow of Marcos. In an earlier chapter we discussed an individual's right to disobey the state, but this story raises even more difficult questions as to the role of Christians as a body—the church. What are the grounds for disobedience? What form may it take? And what about the role of the clergy, which, as discussed in previous chapters, is called to preach the Good News and minister to the church, not form opposition political parties. And in the light of Scripture, can Christians actively advocate and participate in political revolutions? The apostle Paul does not equivocate in his instructions to the Romans. God has ordained government to preserve order; Paul offers no exception because even a bad government is a better alternative than no government—which results in chaos.

But Paul also says that government's authority is from God; it is a delegation. Therefore, governments—all governments—whether they acknowledge it or not, rule under God. But does God give an unrestricted delegation? Certainly not. As Jesus made clear with the coin, there are two realms—and Caesar is not to usurp what belongs to God. Any government that violates the law that is higher than its own is exceeding the legitimate authority God has granted.* As Dietrich Bonhoeffer put it, "If government persistently and arbitrarily violates its assigned task, then the divine mandate lapses."[6]

In that case the state becomes evil incarnate, as in Nazi Germany. Instead of acting as God's instrument for preserving life and order, it does the reverse, destroying life and order.

Then the church must resist. Though as argued earlier, the church's primary function is evangelization and ministering to spiritual needs; as the principal visible manifestation of the Kingdom of God, it must be the conscience of society, the instrument of moral accountability. Richard Neuhaus eloquently wrote that "the church can and should subject to moral questioning every political agenda or cause, thus keeping the entirety of human politics under the transcendent judgment of God."[7]

The real question then is not whether to resist, but how. The same principle applies with the individual Christian. Earlier I cited the example

---

*One eminent authority cautions that in interpreting Paul's word in Romans, a distinction must be made between government and nation. Government must always be respected, otherwise anarchy results; but the nation may attempt to venerate a culture or race. Donald Bloesch writes, "When the state is made to serve the aspirations of race or nation instead of the cause of justice for all, it becomes a demonic state warranting resistance and rejection by the Christian faith." Donald Bloesch, *Crumbling Foundations* (Grand Rapids, Mich.: Zondervan, 1984), 183.

of Daniel's refusing the king's choice food: Use the minimum resistance necessary to achieve the result.

The church's first duty then would be to publicly expose the state's immorality. Though I have argued that the clergy should avoid partisanship, it is not partisan to speak against unjust war—as the British bishops did against their own government bombing of civilian targets in World War II—corruption, oppression, the deprivation of civil liberties, or the taking of innocent lives.

In the West over the last thirty years, we have seen the rise of judicial power, which many of us have argued usurps the people's right of self-government. We are often ruled today, not by the laws the people pass, but by judicial fiats issued by judges who no longer respect *stare decisis* (judicial precedent), the body of law that has evolved over the years. In 1996, a group of thinkers—Robert Bork, Russell Hittinger, Hadley Arkes, Robert George, and myself—met to take part in a symposium called "The End of Democracy?" We confronted five decades of judicial decrees arrogating to the courts the final say on abortion, euthanasia, homosexuality, obscenity, and other fundamental questions of how we order our lives together. Some of us argued that if judicial imperialism continued, and eventually people lost their right of making their own legislative determination, that civil disobedience would be warranted.

The issuance of the document created a huge controversy. Interestingly enough, the loudest protest came from conservatives who declared that there would never be a situation in which Americans would rebel against their own government.

But one is reminded that this is precisely what Martin Luther King, Jr., did when he argued, in *Letter from a Birmingham Jail*, that an unjust law is no law at all. Abraham Lincoln made the same argument when, in 1857, the Supreme Court ruled on the case of a Missouri slave named Dred Scott. Scott's master, John Sandford, had taken him into the free state of Illinois. Because of the Missouri Compromise, which banished slavery in some states, slaves in free states could demand their freedom. Scott did.

Scott's owner challenged the constitutionality of the Missouri Compromise, arguing that slaves were private property protected by the Constitution and could not be taken away without due process. Congress, he argued, thus lacked the constitutional authority to ban slavery in Illinois or anywhere else.

The Supreme Court agreed. It not only sent Scott back into slavery, but also claimed he had never actually been free. The Court also ruled that Congress lacked the authority to forbid or abolish slavery in federal territories—meaning the Missouri Compromise was illegal.

As legal philosopher Robert George notes, "The Court had massively injected itself into the most divisive and morally charged issue of the day." Instead of ending the conflict over slavery, as the Court believed it was doing, it intensified it and heightened emotions (just as the Court did in 1973 when it ruled on *Roe v. Wade*).

Abraham Lincoln saw the *Dred Scott* decision as an outrage, not only because the Court came down on the wrong side, but because the Court claimed authority to decide for the other branches of government once and for all what the Constitution required. In so doing, it placed the other branches in a position of inferiority and subservience—something the Founders specifically rejected.

And once he was president, Lincoln ignored *Dred Scott*. His administration treated free blacks as citizens, issuing them passports and other documents. In open defiance of the ruling, he signed legislation that restricted slavery in the western territories.

To his critics, George writes, Lincoln was a lawless ruler who had no regard for the constitutional limits of his own power. But Lincoln saw himself following in the footsteps of another president. Thomas Jefferson also believed that the president and Congress were in no way inferior to the Supreme Court. Jefferson told a friend the Constitution "has wisely made all the departments co-equal and co-sovereign within themselves." In so doing, the Founders took into account fallen human nature. Both Jefferson and Lincoln believed the courts were quite capable of violating the Constitution—and undermining constitutional government.

Today, we have become so accustomed to the notion that the courts at every level have supreme authority that we're shocked at the very idea that a president or the Congress might stand up to the courts when they abuse their power. But we need to get over our shock, because never before in our history have judges been so out of control, beginning with *Roe v. Wade* right up to recent rulings by power-mad judges who are attempting to redefine marriage laws.

This is precisely the duty that Christians have always embraced: to be willing to stand for justice and in defense of a higher law, when the positive law is preventing the will of the people to be exercised, or when the law forbids the preaching of the Gospel. This is not a problem that will ever go away. In recent years in the West (especially in Canada, Australia, and Scandinavia), we have begun to see great hostility and even legal attacks directed against those who preach unpopular elements of Scripture — such as the biblical view of homosexuality.

As a second step the church should refuse to have any part in the state's immorality. For instance, when, in 1980, New York's Mayor Koch issued an executive order banning discrimination against hiring openly active homosexuals by private agencies that had city contracts, religious organizations faced a serious dilemma: Lose vital financial support or violate clear, biblical teaching. To their everlasting credit the Salvation Army forfeited $4.5 million in state contracts; Augdath Israel Temple, $513,000; and the Catholic Archdiocese of New York, $72 million. (In 1985, the New York State Court of Appeals invalidated Mayor Koch's order, declaring that the mayor lacked the authority to issue such a ban.)

But what if speeches and sermons and non-cooperation fail to deter the state? The church must take the next more severe measure of resistance lest its words be rendered hollow. In the midst of the American abolition campaign, the church used internal discipline and external pressure. The great evangelist Charles Finney refused communion to slaveholders. Others organized the Underground Railroad and rescued fugitive slaves from prison. Many ministers broke the law and were arrested; some were imprisoned.

But state endorsement of evil, even of an evil as egregious as slavery, does not give an unrestricted license to disobey any law; only the unjust law can properly be disobeyed. While active resistance may succeed, as it did with slavery and the civil rights movement, it may not, however, be enough in the face of the raw power modern totalitarian states have achieved. So what does the Christian do when all peaceable means fail? Is revolution ever justified?

Scottish reformation theologians like John Knox and Samuel Rutherford believed they could be, advocating the right of Christians to rise up against ungodly rulers. Many ministers in the colonies agreed as well; when they preached that the people had the authority to resist the king when the king violated God's commands, they were setting the stage for the American Revolution. After dumping tea in Boston Harbor the next step of resistance was the musket. A Boston preacher said that for a people to "arise unanimously and resist their prince, even to dethrone him, is not criminal but a reasonable way of vindicating their liberties and just rights."[8] John Adams observed, "The revolution was in the minds and hearts of the people, a change in their religious sentiments of their duties and obligations."[9]

Some Christian activists today loosely call for a new American Revolution just as the young radical youth movements did in the sixties. But as history reveals, revolution most often results, after the bodies are buried, in one form of tyranny replacing another. G. K. Chesterton summed it up well: "The real case against revolution is this: That there always seems to be much more to be said against the old regime than in favor of the new regime."[10]

So for the Christian, revolution is never to be lightly regarded. It is the most extreme form of disobedience. It could only be contemplated on the same justification as a just war; that is, that there must be a better alternative as a result of the revolution. Its advantages must outweigh the suffering, and the evil employed in the revolution must prevent a far greater evil than the status quo. This was the reasoning that caused Albert Einstein to abandon his pacifism in the face of Hitler's rise to power. "To prevent the greater evil, it is necessary that the lesser—the hated military—be accepted for the time being," Einstein contended.[11] It was this reasoning that caused Bonhoeffer to participate in the plot to assassinate Hitler.

For Christians to justify participation in revolution, therefore, they would have to be convinced that the state had become totally opposed to the purposes of God for the state and there was no other recourse to prevent massive evil.*

In light of this, then, what about the Philippines? What lessons can we draw from it?

Though Aquino's triumph is commonly called the February Revolution, that is, I believe, a misnomer. It was not the overthrow of an existing order, rather the replacement of a corrupt ruler, one who was clinging to power, in fact, by fraud and deceit, having reversed the outcome of a legitimate election. And the anti-Marcos forces were unarmed, engaging throughout in peaceful protest.

---

*During the 1980s, the Exodus from Egypt was often cited as a model for political action by liberation theologians, but they ignored the fact that in the Exodus, God did not overthrow the political system in Egypt. He extracted His own people from that system, taking them to Mount Sinai that they might worship Him.

Mrs. Aquino was following the will of a democratic electorate that had been thwarted by Marcos's tyranny. She was not overthrowing, but rather restoring and fulfilling a system that had been in place since 1946.

But regardless of whether it was properly labeled a revolution, did the church have grounds to take the leadership it did? When I was in Manila in late 1986 I talked with businessmen and politicians, both conservative and liberal. The conclusion was unanimous: If Marcos had remained in power the Philippines would have collapsed and fallen into the hands of Communist insurgents. Those I talked to believed that justified the revolution; but that alone would not be a basis for the church to act.

Nor would Mrs. Marcos's 3,500 pairs of shoes or the incredible greed of Marcos, who stashed away billions in U.S. and Swiss banks while half the populace was unemployed and starving.

While no one could ever develop a rigid formula, it seems to me that the combination of the Marcos regime's refusal to allow free elections, the suspension of civil liberties, the massive corruption of the governmental process, the trampling of human rights, and Marcos's own blasphemous, at times messianic pretensions, gave the church a mandate to act. Cardinal Sin acted heroically in mobilizing the church to say no to evil.

And in the first stage his approach was entirely biblical. By preaching repentance and conversion, he encouraged outbreaks of spiritual revival all across the Philippine islands. He called people to pray for their country.

But when Sin stared down Marcos, in the passion of the moment, he crossed an invisible divide. He did not just denounce raw injustice. He married the church to an opposition political movement. And when he created the UNIDO ticket, convincing Salvador Laurel to run with Cory Aquino, he momentarily left the sanctuary and entered the back rooms of power-brokering politics. For this he was immediately chastised by the Vatican and disciplined again in early 1987.

Sin later acknowledged his excess, issuing orders that all clergy would remain out of partisan, political camps. He also announced he himself would stay "in the background." And yet, some fifteen years later, in 2001, Sin once more involved himself in politics when Filipinos became fed up with the graft and corruption of then-President Joseph Estrada. Sin gave his blessing to massive street rallies, and Estrada was soon ousted from office. Gloria Macapagal Arroyo, whose father had once served as president of the Philippines, became the country's fourteenth president.

However one may evaluate Sin's political course, the overall picture is bright. A courageous cardinal, a widow, the Philippine church, and two million ordinary citizens opened a crack of light in the dark canopy that envelops so much of planet earth. Through their civil disobedience and resistance to evil, the Kingdom of God was made visible.

The late Francis Schaeffer once wrote, "If there is no place for civil disobedience, then the government has been made autonomous, and as such, it has been put in the place of the living God."[12]

The belief that government is autonomous, the ultimate repository of power, the solution to all of society's ills, is the greatest imposter of the twentieth century. As the next chapter demonstrates, Christians and the church have no higher calling than to expose it by every legitimate means.

24

THE POLITICAL ILLUSION

Governments are composed of persons who meet occasionally in a hall to make speeches and to write resolutions; of men studying papers at desks, receiving and answering letters and memoranda, listening to advice and giving it, hearing complaints and claims and replying to them; of clerks manipulating more papers; of inspectors, tax collectors, policemen, and soldiers. These officials have to be fed, and often they overeat. They would often rather go fishing, or make love, or do anything than shuffle their papers. They have to sleep. They suffer from indigestion and asthma, bile and palpitation, become bored, tired, careless, and have nervous headaches. They know what they happen to learn, they are aware of what they happen to observe, they can imagine what they happen to be interested in, they can accomplish only what they can command or persuade an unseen multitude to do.

WALTER LIPPMANN

What is so remarkable about the story of the Philippines is that millions of people believed more in the power of prayer than in the power of politics; they believed that the message "repent, be converted, and trust in Jesus" could topple even an authoritarian leader. They believed their deliverance was spiritual.

Such belief runs counter to the myth that all human problems are political and solvable by all-powerful human institutions. An extreme example was the prominent conservative Christian leader who declared in 1985, after Congress failed to pass his legislative agenda, "The only way to have a genuine spiritual revival is to have legislative reform ... I think we have been legislated out of the possibility of a spiritual revival."[1] Evidently, the work of the Kingdom of God had been defeated by a majority vote in the kingdoms of man.

I'm sure that individual didn't mean to deny the sovereignty of God, but his statement insinuates that nothing can be accomplished except through government. The late Jacques Ellul could well have been describing this leader when he wrote that politics has become "the supreme religion of the age."[2]

This political illusion springs from a diminishing belief in God and the growth of big government. What people once expected from the Almighty, they now expect from the almighty bureaucracy. That's a bad trade for anyone; but for the Christian, it's rank idolatry.

The media encourage the illusion. Stories of spiritual conversion, growth, and revival don't make good thirty-second news spots. While the everyday actions of ordinary citizens lack headline punch, politics offers confrontation, controversy, and scandal.* News coverage gravitates to political power centers, exalting the momentary, exulting in suspense. The public waits expectantly for the next installment in the unfolding political soap opera.

On one level media and government are natural antagonists; on another they are natural allies, depending on each other for their influence. News organizations concentrate their resources in political capitals; governments gear their policies and decisions for prime time audiences. The media spotlight politics and politics feeds the media. Because the illusion serves those with the power to perpetuate it, neither side cares to expose it.

The 1972 summit meetings between the Soviet Union and the United States provide a good illustration. All agreements had been reached before Mr. Nixon's arrival in Moscow; there was nothing further to be negotiated or discussed. The president, in fact, was so bored that he resorted to calling me in Washington every night to discuss domestic affairs—at length.

Though all the summit events were ceremonial, television cameras covered every one. Anchormen gave breathless blow-by-blow accounts of the five-day proceedings. To the viewer back home, world peace hung in the balance. (White House officials did everything possible to encourage that

---

*When religion does make the cover of *Time* or a spot on the network news, it is usually the result of scandal, as with the extraordinary, pre-election coverage in 2006 of Ted Haggard, former head of the National Association of Evangelicals, who was accused of sexual indiscretions. That's not a complaint; it's simply the way the news business works, which in turn is merely satisfying the public appetite. As John Sommerville, author of *How the News Makes Us Dumb*, puts it, "Religion celebrates what we believe to be settled and even eternal," but the news is about change and excitement. So reporters yawn when Christians go to church or volunteer at soup kitchens—but wake up at the first whiff of scandal.

impression.) So as the world watched anxiously, the two leaders met, discussed the weather in Moscow, and signed already confirmed documents.

The 1985 Reagan-Gorbachev summit in Geneva followed an identical format — except there were no prearranged agreements to be signed. More than three thousand journalists pounded the pavements of the beautiful Swiss city, desperate for something to film. Some, in a daring exposure of East-West competition, compared the fashions of Mrs. Gorbachev and Mrs. Reagan. Others analyzed Mrs. Reagan's anti-drug campaigns and Mrs. Gorbachev's interest in schoolchildren. Some cameramen shot footage of each other. A few gave up and went out for fondue.

In a rare moment, one network anchorman questioned whether the Geneva meetings actually warranted such coverage. Such a question treads perilously close to heresy. News is big business, after all, with hundreds of millions of dollars riding on Nielsen ratings. Network and cable personalities hold multimillion dollar contracts, and they, as well as many print journalists, enjoy the handsome rewards of celebrity. Even in nations with public-owned media, the illusion guarantees power, privilege, and access to the elite. These are not willingly surrendered.

This unwavering focus heightens both the promise and expectation of what government can do. Political rhetoric, therefore, must offer panaceas to all human ills. Can anyone recall a major candidate who did not claim he could solve any problem if elected?

President Gerald Ford and his opponent Jimmy Carter, for example, devoted an entire debate in the 1976 campaign to the question of who would balance the budget first. Ford insisted he would do so by 1979; the best Carter could promise was 1981.[3] In reality, of course, both men must have known that more than 80 percent of the federal budget — entitlement programs and other congressionally mandated outlays — was beyond their control. Neither candidate could have balanced the budget.

But politicians have little choice. Modern technology has reduced all issues to their lowest common denominator. Since there is no time to explain the complexities of the budget process, and since instant perceptions shape voter attitudes, politicians can do no more than create appealing visual impressions.

In his memoirs, former Budget Director David Stockman chided Reagan aides Baker and Meese for being more interested in the evening news broadcasts than in government policy. But perhaps they were more realistic. Policy has no meaning apart from how it is perceived, and that perception is heavily influenced by newscasters.

That is why Lyndon Johnson obsessively watched three evening news programs simultaneously on a three-console television set. He knew public reaction to the televised portrayal of Vietnam would influence opinion far more than battlefield strategies. He was right: the outcome of that war was decided in American living rooms.

To maintain the illusion, government attempts to shape, even manipulate public perceptions. One of my White House assignments was to do just that. I chaired a committee of White House staff who worked full time studying daily news briefings, monitoring public reactions to presidential speeches, taking daily polls, and feeding positive information to friendly reporters. Often we aggressively tried to manipulate public opinion.

For example, immediately after every presidential speech, I would unleash a small army of assistants who would call key leaders in every walk of life. We might make five hundred calls, each following the same script: "The president asked me to call to find out what you thought of his announced policy...." The reactions would be collated, typed, and within hours a report surveying the opinions of hundreds of leaders would be in the president's hands. We got helpful information, but we also influenced public reactions toward acceptance of our policy. To be told that the president wanted one's opinion flattered even the cynics. Those called rarely offered a critical reply; most could hardly wait to call their friends and casually mention that "by the way, the president just called" to ask their opinion.

Our efforts were at times singularly successful. During the weekend of August 15, 1971, President Nixon was closeted at Camp David with his key economic advisors. The economy was sluggish, the trade deficit rising, and both unemployment and inflation were approaching what were then unacceptable levels of 5 percent. Something had to be done. Nixon was trailing in the polls with only fifteen months until the election.

On Sunday morning the president decided on a bold stroke recommended by Treasury Secretary John Connally: wage and price controls, and closing the gold window, thus allowing the dollar to float in world markets.

I was stunned—but at the same time impressed with Mr. Nixon's boldness. For his entire political career the president had opposed economic controls; to make them work would require a massive bureaucracy. Other advisors were equally shocked, some predicting that the stock market would plummet. On one thing we all agreed: Mr. Nixon was taking the biggest gamble of his presidency. The policy's success would depend entirely on the public reaction—especially the stock market.

At 8:00 that evening the president announced his "new economic policy" on national television.* Even the news commentators were caught off guard. But before the president's speech was over, I was on the phone to the heads of the ten largest brokerage firms in the country. I knew most of them, and I knew how the pack mentality worked.

The first call was to an old friend. He thought the bottom might drop out of the market. I assured him he was wrong, that I had talked to five other brokerage firm heads and all were bullish.

Each call followed the same pattern, and by 9:30 I had spoken with the opinion leaders of Wall Street. Though most were unenthusiastic at the outset, they were quickly converted when told that everyone else expected the market to soar.

The next day it did—up 32.93 points, the largest single one-day rise in its history to that point. The media immediately declared the president's policy "the Nixon Rally," and as public support grew, the controls, mostly voluntary, succeeded—at least well enough to perk up the flagging economy just ahead of the 1972 election. It would have failed disastrously had the market turned down. (If I had not gone to prison for my part in Watergate, perhaps I should have for manipulating the stock market—not for personal but political profit. Such maneuvers, unfortunately, are not uncommon in the age of the political illusion.)

This manipulation of public attitudes by politicians is not a peculiarly American phenomenon. In the seventies President Nicolae Ceausescu of Romania, though a pragmatic and often ruthless ruler, was frequently photographed at the scene of fires or disasters. In deference to the media age, other Communist leaders, including Gorbachev and Castro, carefully cultivated favorable public images. Castro even agreed to extensive interviews with compliant American broadcasters to clean up his image in the U.S. Even in totalitarian societies the illusion has power.

With government policy so dependent on public reaction, it's little wonder that the celebrity syndrome has become such a major force in Western politics. During the debate on the farm bill of 1985, for example, a parade of

---

*We didn't discover until later—and to our considerable embarrassment—that the term *new economic policy* was not original. Lenin had first coined the phrase for his 1921 Plan.

farm groups, agricultural experts, and government officials appeared before the House committee. The press found little to cover. No one was excited and the bill was mired in committee.

So the committee chairman scheduled actresses Jane Fonda, Sissy Spacek, and Jessica Lange to testify. All three networks covered the hearings. The chairman later gushed, "I knew everyone would pay attention when they came."[4] The bill was whisked through committee and was passed by the House.

What were the qualifications of these stars? None had agricultural expertise. But in a fitting tribute to the media age, all three had *played* farm women in recent films. Celebrities, as *Time* film critic Richard Schickel has observed, have become "the chief agents of moral change in America."[5] Adds Robin Bronk of the Creative Coalition, a Hollywood outfit whose mission it is to help the glitterati speak out responsibly (and, incidentally, not make fools of themselves), "Basically, we live in a culture where celebrities are opinion leaders."

Unfortunately, they're right. The "farm wives" have been followed, in recent years, by Julia Roberts testifying about Rett Syndrome, Richard Gere about China's treatment of Tibet, and George Clooney about the tragedy of Darfur. Mary Tyler Moore, Michael J. Fox, and Christopher Reeve have testified about the need to fund diabetes research, Parkinson's, and cures for paralysis victims. These three have also spoken out — not always accurately — in favor of embryo-destructive research, as has Ron Reagan, Jr. But expertise is no longer the first priority of Congressmen intent on both votes and attention. As media expert Eric Denzenhall explains, "We're living in an age of optics. Expertise does not photograph well. Julia Roberts does." And what Julia Roberts says can change, overnight, the way people view an issue.

One politician who does care about expertise (as opposed to the illusion of it) is Ohio Senator George Voinovich. A few years ago, Voinovich boycotted a hearing of an Environmental and Public works subcommittee to protest the fact that Kevin Richardson of the Backstreet Boys band was testifying against a controversial coal mining technique known as mountaintop removal. "It's just a joke to think that this witness can provide members of the United States Senate with information on important geological and water quality issues," Voinovich fumed. "We're either serious about the issues or we're running a sideshow."

In a salute to the sideshow — I mean, celebrity power — most networks and cable channels now have daily segments titled "Celebrity Gossip,"

"Celebrity News," and "Access Hollywood" to keep up with both the personal and political antics of the glitterati. Webzines and Internet blogs are even faster, both in reporting the news and in gleefully poking holes in network and cable stories—such as Dan Rather's use of forged Texas Air National Guard documents to support his allegation that President George W. Bush had, thirty years before, shirked his duties.

One subtle danger of all this manipulation is that people no longer view their own circumstances as reality. Only what appears in print and on the screen is real. As Ellul put it, "The man of the present day does not believe in his own experiences, his own judgment and his own thought.... In his eyes, a fact becomes true when he has read an account of it in the paper and he measures the importance by the size of the headlines."[6]

And yet, "the news" is limited to whatever some editor decides to include in today's broadcast or newspaper. But what about the thousands of other events that took place on a particular day that were not included? Some of those events may ultimately be judged far more important than the ones that grabbed the day's headlines. As John Sommerville, author of *How the News Makes Us Dumb*, explains, "Historians may eventually tell us that the world turned a corner at just that time. Maybe in some embassy or boardroom or laboratory or monk's cell some lever was pulled that set history on a new course." But these historic moments will never be "news" because they went unnoticed when they actually occurred.

Living in such an environment, the individual gradually loses all sense of continuity. Whether a policy is good or bad, a success or failure, is of no account; all that matters is the emotion its instant image induces. No one remembers from one day to the next. On a Monday a president or a senator can announce that "air travel is safer from terror attacks." Everyone is happy. The next day it is disclosed that air travel is *not* safer—but nobody remembers (or if they do, it serves to make them even more cynical). And so on to the next night.

The process is mesmerizing. Images pile on images, day after day, anesthetizing the public so they feel individually impotent believing that all power resides in images they see on their television screens.* This eventually erodes their own sense of political responsibility and makes them easy prey to the appetite of an authoritarian state. Ellul believes that that consequence

---

*This point is developed at length by the late Neil Postman in his masterful book *Amusing Ourselves to Death: Public Discourse in the Age of Show Business* (New York: Viking, 1985).

is irresistible. Jewish philosopher Hannah Arendt would agree, writing that the chief characteristic of tyranny is isolation of the individual, denying him access to the public realm "where he would show himself, see and be seen, hear and be heard."[7]

"Even democracies need institutions and agencies through which the individual can resist the tendency of all central governments to grow larger, stronger, and more domineering."[8] For the only thing that stands between the multitudes and totalitarianism, says Ellul, are the mediating structures of society: families, small groups of citizens, churches, voluntary associations that are independent of and resistant to the collective state.

Long before the age of instant media, Tocqueville made the same point that if the American experiment were to succeed, it would require the continued help of voluntary associations.[9]

Of all these independent institutions, the church should be the one best able to expose the political illusion. For the message of a transcendent reality is a resounding warning against the futility of seeking immortality from the instruments and institutions of this life. Mastery of nature through technology has given modern man the illusion that he has mastered life itself. The message of the Kingdom is that only God is master of life. Attempts to create alternatives to His rule are futile.

Hannah Arendt, who spent much of her life studying man's attempts to construct his social and political environment, has pointed out how Western society first learned this painful lesson: "The fall of the Roman Empire plainly demonstrated that no work of mortal hands can be immortal, and it was accompanied by the rise of the Christian gospel of an everlasting individual life to its position as the exclusive religion of Western mankind. Both together made any striving for an earthly immortality futile and unnecessary."[10]

My own experiences have repeatedly confirmed this truth; one incident in particular left an indelible impression. It happened in Colombia, South America, in the spring of 1984 while I was visiting Prison Fellowship ministry leaders there.

Immediately after speaking to the inmates in the central prison in Bogotá, I was taken to meet the minister of justice. Several Prison Fellowship Colombia board members were with me. It was late in the day, and the minister had a packed schedule. His announced crackdown on drug traffickers was all over the front pages that day. His aide suggested that I be brief, and I assured him we would confine our visit to five minutes.

Minister Rodrigo Lara Bonilla was a handsome young man with intense, penetrating eyes. He bounded up from his chair to shake our hands and invited me to describe Prison Fellowship's ministry. His English was flawless, so I spoke rapidly. Five minutes into the meeting I thanked him for his courtesy, particularly for allowing me to visit his country's prisons, and I prepared to leave.

He leaned forward. "You've been in the prisons?" he asked. "What do you think of them?"

Did he not know what rat holes his prisons were? I wondered. Should I be politic or tell him the truth?

I blurted out, "They're dreadful, sir."

"Hah!" He slammed his palm on the polished table. "You are right; they are pigsties, unfit for humans. Corrupt too. The inmates pay more for food than people on the street."

I was startled. Bonilla had a reputation as a reformer; he was leading a massive assault on the biggest industry in Colombia, the drug traffic. But never had I heard an official be so critical of his own department.

"What do you think we should do?" he asked.

I outlined the reforms Prison Fellowship has advocated in many countries. Bonilla's mind was razor sharp, and he frequently interrupted with questions. Our discussion went on for about a half hour.

Then he leaned back in his chair. "Finally," he sighed, "I've met people who understand the problem. Will Prison Fellowship work with me, Mr. Colson? Send me someone who can help straighten out these holes."

I promised to send an expert to Colombia the next month.

Bonilla then summoned an aide, instructing him that the ministry was to extend full cooperation to Prison Fellowship. We would have open access to the prisons.

After we had photographs taken together, Bonilla embraced me. It was spontaneous, as if to seal our covenant to join together to clean up the horrors of Colombia's prisons. I gave him a Spanish edition of my book, *Life Sentence*, which he said he would read.

Outside the office, our Colombian directors were jubilant. "This man is the second most powerful man in the government, expected to be elected president in the next election," one said enthusiastically. Another exclaimed, "With his backing Prison Fellowship will be able to do anything!"

Two hours later I arrived at the penthouse apartment of one of Bogotá's leading businessmen, where I was to speak at a dinner gathering of business leaders and government officials. My host greeted me at the door, ashen faced. "Have you heard the news?" he asked. I shook my head.

He told me Rodrigo Lara Bonilla had been assassinated, shot to death by two gunmen—agents of the drug lords—as he was driven home from his office. I had been the minister's last appointment.

That night the president of Colombia declared the country in a state of siege. We were fortunate to get to the airport the next morning to catch our scheduled flight to the U.S. On the front page of the Bogotá newspaper was a grisly picture of the blood-spattered interior of Bonilla's Mercedes. On the seat, covered with shattered glass, was the copy of *Life Sentence*.

I was horrified at the death of this vigorous and brilliant young leader, saddened by the loss of a new friend. I was also sobered as I remembered our enthusiasm the day before. We had talked as if Bonilla's endorsement would assure Prison Fellowship's success.

A year later, in spite of the loss of this dynamic leader, we found that the ministry was actually flourishing, with more seminars going on in Colombian prisons than ever before. Though we had lost a friend and ally in a position of influence, the work of the Kingdom of God is not dependent on power in the kingdoms of man. "It is better to take refuge in the Lord than to trust in princes," wrote the psalmist.[11] Political kingdoms may rise and fall—but the Kingdom of God goes on forever.

Modern history is replete with similar lessons about the futility of putting ultimate trust in much-vaunted political systems. A greedy tyrant is overthrown in Nicaragua; the idealist replacing him promises liberation and hope for the oppressed. The people are jubilant. But in a short time the liberator becomes the oppressor himself, resplendent in his $3,500 designer glasses. When autocracy is replaced by bureaucracy, only the icons change.

When Mikhail Gorbachav brought in *perestroika*, the Russian people thought it was the beginning of freedom. Indeed, Yeltsin was elected president, and democratic reforms began. But unfortunately, the culture did not change. They had democracy, yes—but power was still concentrated in the hands of a few. Today, under Vladimir Putin, we are seeing a resumption of strong-arm tactics and the rise of the Russian mafia. Just so, the free market system has meant plenty of profits—for a few. While democracy has clearly made a huge difference in Russia—particularly the meltdown of the monolithic Soviet system—it is still a long way from really bringing the benefits to the people. The political change, dramatic though it has been in the former Soviet Union, has yet to really come to full flower. Changes like these do not come about easily.

Ideology, which in so many parts of the world has replaced true religion, is powerless as well. As Ellul points out, the promised utopias of the twentieth century, either Marxist or Fascist, are doomed because they accept the essential premises of current civilization and move with its lines of internal development: "Thus, utilizing what this world itself offers them, they become its slaves, although they think they are transforming it."[12] Even massive weapons of destruction fail to assure anything for today's mightiest governments. Wars reach no permanent solutions; there is no such thing as a lasting peace or, as Americans once so fondly believed, "a war to end all wars." Terrorists stalk the globe, and governments can do little to stop them.

Wars proliferate; political solutions fail; frustrations rise. Yet we continue to look to governments to resolve problems beyond their capability. The illusion persists.

Nowhere is that more evident than in one troubled corner of the world. But even there, in the midst of carnage, violence, and hatred, the example of a few people offers hope, pointing the way for civilization to emerge from its darkness.

25

THE INDESTRUCTIBLE KINGDOM

*That which man builds man destroys, but the city of God is built by
God and cannot be destroyed by man.*

AUGUSTINE

Before my first visit to Northern Ireland in 1977 I stopped in England. Perhaps I could gain insight into Ulster by discussing her problems with British politicians.[1]

In London my friend Michael Alison arranged a dinner for us with a number of the members of Parliament. As we convened in an elegant Westminster dining room, a page stepped through a side door, formally announcing, "Gentlemen, the Speaker."

With that, George Thomas strode into the room. He was a short, feisty Welshman, bubbling over with enthusiastic good humor. In his black knickers, white lace shirt, and powdered wig, he looked like he had emerged straight from the pages of *Punch*.

The beef Wellington matched the excellence of the conversation; seated next to George Thomas, I enjoyed myself immensely. After dessert I was asked to speak. I told the MPs about my conversion and responded to a number of questions. As the evening drew to a close, I said, "I've been answering questions all evening, gentlemen. Now I think it's only fair that we do a turnabout and I ask you one.

"I'm going to Belfast tomorrow for a series of meetings. Perhaps you could give me some insights into government policy and Ulster's political

---

This chapter is based on accounts of actual events in the day-to-day struggle of Northern Ireland; all the participants are real people, and the stories are told with their permission. In a few instances, however, events have been consolidated and chronology reconstructed somewhat for purposes of clarity.

solutions." I paused. "What are the answers to the struggles in Northern Ireland?"

Several MPs glanced at each other; others toyed with their silverware. George Thomas grinned and then spoke for the group.

"That's easy," he said. "There is no answer in Northern Ireland."

Northern Ireland. A small nation with just 1,685,000 people. Yet at the time of my visit, scarcely a week went by without a bombing, a shooting, or a riot. All told, between 1969 and 2001, 3,523 people were killed and tens of thousands more injured in what the people of Northern Ireland euphemistically called "the Troubles." The Troubles are centuries old and result from the clash between two deeply rooted traditions: the Roman Catholics who make up 43 percent of the population, and the Protestants who make up most of the other 57 percent. The Catholics tend to be Republicans who want Northern Ireland's six counties united with the Republic of Ireland and free of Great Britain's control. Protestants tend to be Loyalists, determined to keep their British allegiance.

The struggle is more political—a contest for power—than religious, however. As one wag put it, the combatants are Catholic atheists on one side and Protestant atheists on the other. And so deep is the conflict that it cannot be resolved by new political parties, British troops, or even the impassioned pleas of those who have suffered the most—the families of the slain.

Belfast, Northern Ireland's capital, lies between the chill waters of Belfast Lough and Lough Neagh. It is a gray industrial city of crowded nineteenth-century houses. Viewed from the air, the great shipbuilding cranes on the River Lagan stand like giant croquet wickets in the sea of gray and brick-red roofs. Smoke rises from tall chimneys nearby and blends with the low-hanging clouds that so often blanket the city.

When I visited downtown Belfast in 1977, nearly every block contained bomb-blackened, boarded-up buildings. Police stations of the Royal Ulster Constabulary were fortresses rolled in barbed wire, their thick, high walls tented with steel mesh to guard against the terrorists' habit of lobbing homemade bombs over the walls. Army vans filled with British soldiers were everywhere.

Yet the wartime setting was incongruous. Belfast was still a place of laughter, and the people were hospitable, friendly, and a bit apologetic about their country's reputation.

"Surely we're not as bad as you've heard we are?" a shopkeeper inquired anxiously. "We don't shoot strangers — just each other."

"Well, what do you think of the Troubles?" a cab driver asks. And when you apologize for not really understanding the complexity of the conflict, he responds cheerfully, "We don't understand it either."

Most would agree, however, that the current struggles began in August 1969 when British troops marched onto the streets of Belfast and Londonderry, or Derry, as Republicans call the ancient walled city in the north of Ulster.

The country is still divided, and the struggles are still taking place, albeit in a far more muted form compared to what went on before the Belfast Agreement of 1998. The fighting has stopped, the bombs are no longer exploding, and the IRA has largely shunned Sinn Fein, the public relations wing of the terrorist group. Protestant leader Ian Paisley has met with Catholic leaders and is struggling again for self-government.

Northern Ireland remains politically unsettled and it is difficult to form a responsible self-governing body, but nonetheless, it is light years ahead of where it was when I spent so much time there. The efforts of Catholics and Protestants working together emerged far more from Prison Fellowship and citizen groups than from political leaders, bringing a measure of stability and peace.

But back in 1969, unrest over civil rights and bottled-up bitterness had exploded into widespread rioting that the British government believed could be quelled only by a military presence. The soldiers' presence added to the tension. Sectarian shootings dominated the headlines, and the troops were targets of booby traps, ambushes, and bombings. The Protestant-controlled government, meeting at Stormont, the official government chambers, could do nothing.

Then came Bloody Sunday: January 30, 1972. British soldiers, attempting to break up a civil-rights rally in Londonderry, shot and killed thirteen demonstrators.

By mid-February retaliatory bombs were exploding in Northern Ireland at the rate of four a day. Those who survived each new blast lived in terror of the next. Citizens sometimes paid dearly just by going about their daily business, as did the six shoppers who died—and the 147 who were wounded—the day Irish Republican Army terrorists (IRA), left a gelignite bomb in a parked car in a busy Belfast shopping district.

Fifty-four days after Bloody Sunday, the Stormont government fell. British Prime Minister Heath declared Northern Ireland incapable of handling its own affairs and imposed direct rule from Westminster.

Thousands of bloody deaths followed in the decades ahead. One out of every twenty households felt the pain of either death or injury from the incessant shootings and bombings.

It isn't the grim statistics that tell the story of Northern Ireland, however. It is the lives of those who live, work, and survive there.

PEARL AND KAREN . . .

It was a Saturday evening in Belfast, September 25, 1982. As twenty-year-old Karen McKeown drove her mother, Pearl, home from a special service at their Protestant church, she was still humming the song the choir had sung: "I will enter into His courts with praise."

Mother and daughter talked about Karen's classes at Queen's University, Pearl's early shift the next morning at the hospital, the contact lens Karen had lost.

Pearl watched Karen, thinking her daughter had never looked prettier. Her dark hair was glossy and thick with a determined curl that Karen spent much of her energy trying to tame. Her new white sweater and skirt set off her dark eyes and pale complexion beautifully. *She has so much ahead of her,* Pearl thought proudly.

Karen dropped off her mother at home, waved good-bye, and headed back to the church to help clean up for Sunday services. She pulled into the church parking lot, got out, and was locking the car when a young man appeared by her side.

"I want you to know that I'm going to shoot you," he said, placing a heavy pistol against the base of Karen's neck.

He pulled the trigger.

The bullet ripped into Karen's neck and tore through her spinal column. She collapsed onto the concrete, bleeding and paralyzed, unable to breathe. Her assailant ran away into the night.

Friends in the church heard the crack of the gun and called the ambulance, which took Karen to the Royal Victoria Hospital. By the time Pearl and John McKeown arrived, their daughter was fighting for her life in intensive care.

Pearl refused to believe that Karen was the latest victim in Belfast's endless violence. Only as she sat day after day by her daughter's bedside did the full implication dawn.

Karen could still communicate, and Pearl would lean close to her face as she mouthed her words. It was through those words that Pearl learned the answers to the bloody bitterness of Northern Ireland.

One afternoon when she arrived to visit, she found Karen propped up on several crisp white hospital pillows with tubes coming out of her throat, nose, and arms. Machines, screens, and dials monitored her every breath.

Karen's eyes brightened when she saw her mother. "Mum," she mouthed, "could you squeeze my hands?"

Pearl gripped the slender fingers.

Karen's eyes fell. "I can't feel anything," she said. After a pause she continued, "But it doesn't matter. The only thing that matters is that we trust the Lord and never give the Devil a victory."

The inverted glass container of an intravenous tube was dripping a solution into Karen's veins, and the drug made her sleepy. Her eyelids batted a few times; then she drifted into sleep.

Pearl sat down in the armchair next to the bed, bowed her head, and wept. A few minutes later she looked up and discovered Karen awake again. "Mum," she whispered, "you think you have troubles. But just think about the troubles *his* mum has.

"When he said he was going to shoot me, I thought he was one of the boys from church, and I laughed," Karen continued. "It was as if the Lord put His arms around me. When I hit the ground I was still laughing."

Late that evening at home Pearl went into Karen's cluttered room and picked up her thick leather Bible. It had been a Christmas gift a year and a half earlier and was already worn, its pages marked with Karen's notes and underlinings. Pearl looked at the inside cover page where Karen had written, "To be a brave disciple is to be a bond slave to Jesus Christ, and to find that His service is perfect freedom."

In the Book of Job she found more notes. "This is not an explanation but an inspiration. Job's soul was a battleground without his knowledge. Could this be the reason for suffering today? In all cases, God is supreme and just. The Devil functions within God's purpose." Karen's underlining clotted the chapters of Job. "Though he slay me, yet will I hope in Him.... You will lie down, and no one will make you afraid."

Pearl's eyes filled with tears. Here in her daughter's strong, square script were notes that clearly prefigured what had happened. *If this is how Karen views suffering*, Pearl thought, *then this is how I must see what has happened to her.*

Meanwhile, the forensic results came back from the crime lab; the bullet taken from Karen's neck was from the same gun used to assassinate a prominent attorney. The gun could be traced to the INLA, the Irish National Liberation Army, a Catholic terrorist organization.

The next day Pearl went home, tired and frustrated, to pick up the mail before returning to Karen's bedside. A thin white envelope fell out of the stack of get-well cards and letters. The handwriting was unfamiliar. Her eyes went to the return address: Her Majesty's Prison, Magilligan.

She slit the envelope and unfolded the sheet inside. The writer explained that he had heard about Karen's attack through a Bible study in his prison. He was, he said, an ex-INLA prisoner who had become a Christian. He was no longer a member of the organization responsible for Karen's attack, but he wanted to ask Mrs. McKeown's forgiveness and permission to pray for Karen. Would she mind?

Pearl stared at the letter in her hand. The signature read "Liam McCloskey." She thought about her daughter's peaceful face, about the underlined verses in her Bible, and about her forgiving spirit and absolute trust in Christ. She realized Karen would welcome this man's request.

Pearl jotted a quick note to Liam McCloskey, enclosing an old photograph of Karen and telling him a little about her daughter and her faith.

LIAM...

Liam McCloskey had not always been part of a Bible-study group praying for Protestant victims of terrorism. For much of his violent young life he had been a member of the Irish National Liberation Army, an impatient, Marxist offshoot of the IRA — the same INLA that would later shoot Karen McKeown. But he had been changed unalterably during one of the most notorious chapters of Northern Ireland's troubled history.

In December 1977 Liam had been convicted of armed hijacking and robbery offenses. At the time he was in his early twenties—a freckled young man with reddish brown hair and a quick, whimsical laugh.

Liam began his ten-year sentence at Belfast's Maze Prison, the highest-security prison in the world, where the immense perimeter was rolled with huge coils of razor wire that could slit a man's skin in an instant. Its eight steel and concrete H-blocks were a forbidding reminder of both the desperation of those in the Maze and the determination of their captors. Though a good part of the prison population were deemed "ODCs"—Ordinary Decent Criminals—the Maze was packed with those convicted of terrorist offenses.

Liam shared a cell with Kevin Lynch, a childhood friend who now shared the same political goals. Inmates like Liam and Kevin had at one time been given a political-prisoner status, but in 1976 the British government had rescinded that designation, preferring not to allow paramilitaries—Protestant or Catholic—special privileges. Ever since, the paramilitaries had been trying to get the status reinstated.

They had started with blanket protests, during which the inmates refused to wear prison clothes. When this failed, they began what was called the dirty protest.

Prisoners on dirty protest refused to wash, refused to wear clothing, refused to leave their cells. They sat on the concrete floor, covered only by a blanket with a ragged hole cut out for the head. They smeared their excrement on the walls and rinsed their hands in their own urine. Their hair and beards grew long and knotted, streaked with filth. Uneaten food molded in the corners of their cells.

Though the men inside grew accustomed to the incredible stench, officers often vomited and fainted. Visitors were nonexistent. Periodically the inmates were forcibly washed down with fire hoses and moved to new cells while the old ones were cleansed and repainted. Then the cycle began again.

As the level of filth increased in the cellblock, so did the level of frustration. The inmates had broken the glass out of the narrow cell windows so they could smear excrement on the walls outside their cells. Orderlies used high-powered fire hoses to clean the walls.

Liam would wait until they had rolled up the hoses; then he would put his waste out. One morning as he was about to do so, an orderly came past his window. On an impulse Liam threw the filth at him. The man turned his face away just in time, but it struck his shoulder, hair, and the side of his head.

Liam got down from the window and waited for the warders. It wasn't long before he heard the sound of heavy boots. The door opened, and he was told to put on a pair of pants. Then he was marched down the hall.

He was told to face the wall, then instructed to turn around. As he did so, an orderly hit him in the face. When he fell to the ground in a ball, a sea of fists and boots punched and kicked him. He was then taken to the punishment block where orderlies washed him down with scrubbing brushes. A bristle from one of the brushes entered his ear, opening an old wound from childhood.

Liam continued on the dirty protest for years, with periodic washings. By Christmas Eve 1980 the protest had accomplished nothing. Liam began to pray for inner strength and to read the Bible. Yet outwardly he seemed as deeply committed to his political cause as ever. "I was trying to walk with God and Republicanism at the same time," he says. "But there appeared to be more and more contradictions between the two."

GLADYS...

While Liam McCloskey sat in his own filth on Christmas Eve 1980, Miss Gladys Blackburne was having her tea in a small Belfast flat and preparing to visit the Maze Prison. A retired schoolteacher in her midsixties, Miss Blackburne was an inch shy of five feet, with gently curled gray hair, sensible shoes, and a determined way about her.

In August 1969, when civil unrest erupted in Northern Ireland, Gladys Blackburne took her country's situation personally.

"I was desperately ashamed," she says. "The whole world was watching, and here in our land the name of Jesus was being dragged in the gutter. I wept and asked God to show me what I could do to honor His name."

Since then, Gladys had been doing what she believed God told her to do: to be the best citizen she could in her small troubled nation and to show the love of Christ to soldiers, as she was already doing with children, students, and other groups. That love was desperately needed. The soldiers were rotated out of Northern Ireland every few months; service there was too stressful for them to last much longer than that.

Whether they accepted her message or not, the soldiers loved Miss Blackburne. She had access to every army post in Northern Ireland, and when she wanted to visit soldiers in the field or injured men in the hospital, the army gladly gave her a lift. It was not unusual for Gladys to step out of a helicopter or an army lorry, handbag firmly in her grasp, and march off for a day of visiting soldiers.

She was also approved for a position on the Maze Prison Board of Visitors, a citizens' group set up to monitor the prison and report any irregularities or abuses. As such, she had access to any part of the prison, day or night.

On this Christmas Eve Miss Blackburne prayed about how God would have her celebrate the birth of His Son. *I must do something as near as possible to what Jesus did when He left His home in glory and was born in a Bethlehem stable*, she thought.

A stable, she repeated to herself. *Does God want me to go to the dirty protest where the cells smell like stables? I can't do that.* But Gladys Blackburne was not a person to take God's direction lightly. So she put on her coat and gloves, and prayed for the grace to be able to handle what she would find at the Maze.

She hitched a ride to the prison and cleared the laborious security checks at the main gate. Before she went to the cells of the dirty protesters, however, a prison officer took her aside.

"There's a Protestant lad in a different wing asking a lot of questions about Christianity," he said. "Why don't you visit him first?"

CHIPS ...

Chips McCurry was sitting on the edge of his bunk, head down, when his heavy cell door swung open. A Protestant paramilitary, Chips had been committed to terrorism since he was twelve years old—when the IRA murdered his father.

When he was sixteen he had joined the Ulster Volunteer Force, an illegal paramilitary organization passionately opposed to Republican attempts to bring about a unified Ireland. He was bent on inflicting as much pain as his family had suffered. But on February 19, 1976, when he carried out his first order, it was to assassinate a fellow Protestant suspected of spying within UVF ranks. Chips was convicted of murder and sent to the Maze.

He was by then a thin, solemn young man with wire-rimmed glasses and thick curly hair already flecked with gray. After several months in prison his exposure to Catholic inmates made him realize that families on both sides had been fractured by the violence. *There has to be an answer*, he thought. *It's a political situation. There must be a political solution.*

Chips began reading everything he could get his hands on—first a flirtation with fascism, then a stint as a Marxist. He studied smuggled guerrilla-warfare manuals, hoping to start a full-scale revolution when he got out.

His political search ended in disillusionment. Politics didn't offer any real answers. Perhaps religion did. *If there is a God*, he thought, *and if there is a hell, then I'm surely heading toward it. But there are so many different religions. These Christians can't have a monopoly on truth. If I ever come across the truth, then I'll follow it.*

So Chips began a new search, questioning both inmates and officers he knew were Christians. They, in turn, began to pray for him. Tracts arrived mysteriously in his cell. He threw them all away. His search for truth was philosophical and abstract. He wasn't looking for any kind of personal faith.

When Gladys Blackburne entered his cell on Christmas Eve, Chips recognized her. He had often seen her in the prison and knew, like most of the other inmates, that "if you don't want to hear the gospel, then you'd better run when you see Miss Blackburne coming."

But there was nowhere to run. Miss Blackburne took the chair at the small desk directly opposite Chip's cot and asked if she could read some Scriptures. Chips prepared himself for a recitation of the Christmas story. Instead, Miss Blackburne opened her Bible to Luke 23, the account of the Crucifixion. She stopped when she came to the words of the thief on the cross: "'Lord, remember me when you come into your kingdom.'"

"Now who was this thief calling 'Lord?'" Miss Blackburne asked Chips, her pale blue eyes looking intently into his. "Here was a man who had had a crown of thorns thrust onto His head. Here was a man who was spat upon, stripped, beaten, whipped, and so disfigured He was unrecognizable. Does that look like a Lord to you? But this thief called Him 'Lord'—because Jesus was still Lord on the cross."

Chip's eyes fell. He didn't know quite why, but Gladys Blackburne's words made him aware of all the hatred and bitterness that had consumed him for years. For the first time he caught a glimpse of a connection between Christ's death and himself. *Christ was perfect*, Chips thought. *And I am full of evil—the sin He had to die for.*

He looked at the small woman. "How do I become a Christian?" he asked.

"You need to accept Christ as Lord, just like the thief on the cross," she said. "You need to turn away from your sins and believe that He died for them. And you need to confess Him as Lord to others."

Confess Christ as Lord? Chips hesitated. He had taunted enough Christians himself to know how hard that was in prison.

Miss Blackburne didn't push it. "Let me show you one more verse," she said. "Then I need to go visit some other friends." She flipped the pages of her worn New Testament and read him John 6:37: " 'He who comes to me I will in no wise cast out.' "

"If you come to Christ," she said, "He will never let you go."

After Miss Blackburne left, Chips McCurry sat in his cell thinking. Finally, late that night, he knelt by his cot and committed his life to Jesus Christ. He had seen the self-perpetuating emptiness of violence and the impotence of political philosophy. He realized he had finally met the Truth.

The next morning, Christmas Day 1980, Chips woke early. A cold gray light pierced the thick concrete slates of his cell. His first thought was, *I'm not really a Christian.*

Then he remembered Miss Blackburne's words: "If you come to Christ, He will never let you go."

At the usual time Chips was released from his cell to go to the canteen for breakfast; there he smiled broadly as he stirred sugar into his tea. The man across the small table glared at him.

"What're you smilin' about?" he growled. "No one smiles in prison on Christmas morning."

Here I go, Chips thought. Aloud he said, "I've become a Christian."

The man exploded, his kindest incrimination being to call Chips a phony.

"Just wait and see," Chips told the man.

LIAM ...

That same Christmas morning, the Catholic prisoners in the Maze were preparing for their final protest. The dirty protests had achieved nothing;

paramilitaries were still denied political status. In pursuit of their objectives, the IRA leaders determined to turn the violence upon themselves.

Hunger strikes had been a revered form of protest for IRA faithful since the turn of the century. To threaten death by starvation was an act of defiance that could not be ignored—or so the IRA leaders thought.

A hunger strike held that fall had already ended in failure, however; no one died and no demands were met. So the IRA asked for volunteers to begin a new strike—to the death. One hundred of the Maze's seven hundred Catholic paramilitaries volunteered.

Liam McCloskey was one of those men.

At first Liam had wanted nothing to do with the hunger strikes, since he was questioning his political allegiance anyway. Then Liam's cellmate, Kevin, signed up for the strike. In spite of a knot of fear within him, Liam signed up as well.

Bobby Sands, leader of the Catholic inmates, was to begin the fast in early March. Shouting through his cell door to the others on the wing, he said there was a strong possibility he would die. But if he did, Sands said, it could be enough to "light the flame of freedom in the Irish people's hearts that would lead to British withdrawal and a Socialist Ireland."

Though attention to the hunger strike grew slowly, a county election in which Bobby Sands was elected to Parliament on April 9, 1981, gave it the boost it needed to capture the interest of the world press. Liam hoped the publicity would save Bobby's life, but it was not to be.

> Death [came] at last to convicted IRA Terrorist and Hunger Striker Robert (Bobby) Gerard Sands, 27, by virtue of his own will. His earthly remains were little more than a husk after a 66-day fast in the H-block section of Northern Ireland's Maze Prison....
>
> As the clanging of garbage can lids announced the news of Sands' death, gangs of Catholic youths once again rampaged through the streets, despite calls from the IRA itself for calm as the organization prepared its martyr's farewell.... One youngster blew himself up as he tried to plant a crudely made bomb ... a Belfast policeman was shot to death.... Heavy police protection was given to scores of British Members of Parliament.
>
> Sands' fatal hunger strike now appears to be only the prelude to a sustained movement by other Maze prisoners.... One senior Whitehall official repeated the government's refusal to compromise with the pris-

oners or to propose any solutions to the deeper problems in the near term. The situation was, he said, evoking centuries of bitterness, "a classic Irish tragedy from which at the moment there seems no escape."

The desperate death of Bobby Sands appears to be the start of a new chapter in just such a prolonged and dangerous tragedy.[2]

Then came Kevin's turn to strike. Liam was racked with doubts and questions. He refused to believe that his cellmate would die. Yet it had become apparent that the British government was digging in on the issue and that there was little hope of a solution. Liam also wrestled with the fact that he was next on the list. His fear of death made him hesitant, along with his own changing views and growing faith. *Since I have doubts about the rights and wrongs of killing,* he thought, *I won't be any good to Republicanism. And since I haven't fully accepted the Word of God, I'm no good to Him either. Better that I die than someone who would be of use to the movement.*

Kevin died. *My own hunger strike,* Liam thought, *will be my last act as a Republican, one way or another. Live or die.*

Liam began the strike on August 3, 1981, a Monday morning.

> Hundreds of families ... live in dread of the sudden news that their sons have volunteered to starve. When the name of the latest hunger volunteer, Liam McCloskey, 25, was announced last week, his [family] protested to the IRA that their son had a chronic ear infection that could cause early death. They dared to express their indignation.[3]

During the first two weeks of the strike, Liam's main problems were coldness and an almost overwhelming desire to eat one last pea, chip, or bean just to taste food again. Food was blown out of proportion in his mind.

> But after two weeks, the war of nerves becomes irrelevant. The trays keep arriving, but by now the prisoners have lost their craving for food. The stomach cramps and pains recede and eventually disappear. The prisoners concentrate instead on their daily five pints of water. Now their only concern is whether they can hold down the water without retching. A small bowl of salt is provided for each prisoner, and he can sprinkle in as much as he wants. When the hunger strikes are far along, the prisoners ask for carbonated water and the British grant the request.

This is the world of the zealots, where Irish youth are willing to starve themselves for their cause of driving the British out of Northern

Ireland. It is an astounding kind of sacrifice—a brutal, lingering death, full of hatred and martyrdom, so fanatical and Irish. The moment one striker dies, 50 volunteer to take his place.[4]

After four weeks, Liam was moved to the prison hospital. On his forty-second day of the strike, August 14, 1981, his eyes began to roll uncontrollably back and forth and he began to vomit green digestive fluid. Within a few days the vomiting eased, but by August 17 Liam was totally blind.

> At 42 days, almost exactly, a nightmarish experience occurs.... They are struck by something called nystagmus, a loss of muscular control due to severe vitamin deficiency. If they look sideways, their eyes begin to gyrate wildly and uncontrollably, first horizontally and then vertically. The prisoners struggle to stare straight forward, even cupping their hands against the sides of their heads, but they cannot help themselves....
>
> Now the end is not far off. Their speech is slurred, and they try not to talk because the sound of their own voices echoes in their heads. Their hearing is failing and visitors have to shout during normal conversations. They are slowly going blind. Even their sense of smell is failing.[5]

Liam began to pray. *There has to be a God*, he thought. *Life makes no sense without one.* He thought back on twenty-five years of life with nothing to show for it. *Can I go before God with nothing but a self-centered life of striving after sex, drink, and good times? And what about my involvement in Republicanism?*

If I had continued as I was outside of prison, he thought, *I would have taken life for that cause. Who was I that I should appoint myself judge, jury, and executioner of any man?*

Will my life even show up as a dot on eternity? he wondered. *Here I am, about to throw it all away for Ireland, like countless others who are prepared to do evil for Ireland or Ulster or Britain.*

By this time the hunger strike was falling apart. Ten men had died; one protester was taken off the strike by his mother, another by his wife. Liam's resolve weakened. Yet he felt he had to keep going for the sake of his fellow prisoners. He also decided it would be better to die than to live blind. Still, he prayed the prayer that had haunted him since he began the strike: "Not mine, but Thy will be done."

By August 26, his fifty-fourth day on the strike, Liam knew he would be in a final coma in a day or two. How great it would be to walk through a field of grass, to smell flowers, to see the waves lapping on the seashore. His thoughts were hazy and dreamlike.

DAVID ...

While Liam McCloskey lay dying in the Maze, a Protestant inmate in a prison on the other side of Belfast knelt in prayer for him. Yet anyone who knew David Hamilton would have said it most unlikely that he would pray for the recovery of a Catholic terrorist, for David had spent most of his life trying to eliminate enemies like Liam. His hatred of Catholics had started young.

David had grown up in Rathcoole, the largest government housing project in Europe, a product of a late-fifties Belfast slum-clearance program that moved the urban working class into the suburbs. Yet even with its bare concrete row houses and its maze of high-rise flats, Rathcoole was still a place where children played together happily.

David was one of those children, a sturdy Protestant boy with thick dark hair and startling blue eyes. He thrived on being "one of the boys," and in those days that meant playing football every afternoon with a gang his own age, including Catholic boys like Bobby Sands who lived just down the block—the same Bobby Sands who would later starve himself to death in the Maze.

But after the summer of 1969, when David was twelve years old, being one of the boys meant something else entirely. Suddenly the difference in religious beliefs mattered, and the Protestants, who made up roughly 60 percent of Rathcoole, let their unwanted neighbors know. Within months, thousands of Catholic families had fled to the Falls or Divas Flats or other places in the city where the Catholics were in control and the Protestants had moved out.

One afternoon David stole a ride into Belfast on the back of a lorry. On a downtown corner he spied Tom, an old friend he used to play with in Rathcoole every Sunday after Tom came home from Mass. Tom's family had moved away from Rathcoole some months ago and this was the first time David had seen his friend since then.

David raised his arm and yelled, "Hello, Tom."

Tom, who was standing with several other lads, looked at David like he had never seen him before. "Get away from me, you Orange bastard," he screamed, shaking his fist and letting loose a string of profanity. The other boys joined in.

David stared for a moment, then turned away, his heart pumping with anger and shame. From that moment on, his lighthearted spirit was replaced by a growing bitterness. Soon all Catholics were suspect; they were all probably members of the IRA, David thought.

We aren't doing enough to fight back, he thought. He had no faith in the British security forces, but he had observed the power of the street gangs in Rathcoole. Security came in aggression and numbers. So when the Ulster Volunteer Force came recruiting, David was one of the first of the boys in his gang to enlist. He was fifteen.

So David went from football to automatic weapons. He became an expert at robbing banks and post offices.

When he was seventeen, David was arrested for his paramilitary activities. While awaiting trial and sentencing, he was held at Long Kesh, an old air force base near Belfast where prisoners lived in wartime Nissen huts grouped into compounds. Long Kesh was a graduate school in terrorism for David.

One evening several of the prisoners, agitated by the home brew they were drinking (made by fermenting bits of fruit kept hidden from the officers), seized a man they suspected of being an informer. It was Charlie, a likable fellow David had just been talking to that afternoon. As Charlie pleaded his innocence, they held a mock court-martial, found him guilty, and pronounced sentence. Death.

Later that night, Charlie was murdered.

Despite his terrorist involvement, David had never seen murder before. He was scared. He had never been religious, but he began to pray desperately. He hated prison. He hated being separated from his family and his girlfriend. And now he was frightened of the violence. He promised God he would attend church every Sunday—the ultimate sacrifice—if God would just get him out of Long Kesh.

Shortly thereafter, his case came before the court and he was sentenced to five years in prison.

So much for praying, David thought.

But late that night as he lay in the solitary-confinement cell where just-sentenced prisoners were held, he spotted a bit of writing high in the corner of the white concrete wall next to his bunk. It was a name, written in precise block letters: Charlie—his friend who had been murdered.

There are worse fates than prison, David thought. *Charlie would gladly trade places with me now. Maybe God hasn't given me such a bad deal after all.*

But David wasn't ready to think much about God. If God did exist, He had nothing to do with the flesh-and-blood struggles of Northern Ireland. *All that church stuff's no use to me,* he thought. *I'm just a bad egg, and if I go to hell, I go to hell.*

So when he was unexpectedly released from prison, with a warning from the judge to stay out of paramilitary organizations, David ignored the warning. He married his girlfriend Roberta and promised her he wouldn't get involved with UVF again, though he had no intention of keeping his word.

One Friday evening David was showing a few of his mates how to assemble automatic weapons while Roberta was out shopping with her mother. They had gun parts spread all over the kitchen table, when suddenly the back door creaked open, and his wife and mother-in-law stood in the doorway.

His wife's eyes filled with tears of rage. "You promised!" she screamed. She turned and ran out the door, her mother close behind her. David didn't see her for a week. When she returned, nothing was said about the UVF. It had become an acknowledged reality but a closed subject.

Sometimes, however, his involvement could not be ignored. Like the night David and Roberta were sitting in a Chinese restaurant in Belfast eating chicken chow mien and three hooded IRA men stormed in the front door. In the sudden silence that followed their entrance, David threw down his tea cup and told Roberta to take cover under the table.

"It's me they want," he said.

He slid out of the booth, crashed past tables of terrified diners and through the double doors to the kitchen, shoving cooks and waiters aside in his effort to reach the back door. Behind him, he could hear people screaming as the gunmen followed.

David cursed when he reached the backdoor, a fortress of bolts and chains. He ripped them apart, tore the door open, and fled. As he scrambled up an outside wall and over the top, the gunmen began firing. The last thing he heard was his would-be assassins cursing their aim.

Then in 1978 the reality of David's paramilitary involvement burst into their lives again. David and dozens of other UVF men were arrested in their homes at 4:00 one morning in a police sweep. David ended up in the Crumlin Road Prison where he had spent the thoughtful night after Charlie's death several years earlier.

Months later an utterly alien thought entered David's mind: *Become a Christian.* David had been working in the prison laundry with a man named Trevor who was an outspoken Christian. David knew from listening to Trevor that becoming a Christian meant making a lot of changes. For starters, it would mean giving up the UVF, drinking, violence, and chasing women—the things that made his life meaningful.

He discarded the thought, but it kept returning. The next morning in the laundry he said, "Trevor, I'm thinking about becoming a Christian."

All that day while Trevor worked double time, David sat on a pile of towels reading gospel tracts. The other inmates taunted him.

"Thinkin' about becoming a member of the God squad?" they shouted.

By suppertime, David had made his decision. He returned to his cell and knelt to pray for the first time since childhood.

"If you want this life," he told God simply, "it's yours."

The next day he approached an IRA prisoner. The two men had never spoken but had come to blows one day in the laundry.

"I've become a Christian," David told the man.

"What are you tellin' me for?" the inmate sneered.

David looked him in the eye. "I figure that's as good a reason as any to start talkin' to you," he said.

In the days that followed David was shocked to find that God had taken away his hatred of IRA men. He joined a prayer group, and several of the members were former Catholic paramilitaries, now Christians. David still considered himself "a good Prod," but he found himself accepting Catholics as people, not faceless enemies.

Seeing years of hatred eradicated gave David new vigor and certainty about God's miraculous power in situations humanly impossible to resolve.

An IRA man serving time for three murders spoke to him one day. "I've been watchin' you," he said. "You must be the happiest man in this prison."

"That I am," David said. "I know God."

"How can you say that?" the other man sputtered.

David told how he had seen God work in his life and explained the gospel. The IRA man prayed to receive Christ, and he and David hugged there in the prison cell.

While such reconciliation was taking place between Protestants and Catholics within prison walls, the violence on the streets of Belfast was reaching spectacular proportions. It even extended across the Irish Sea to the British Parliament.

Airey M. S. Neave had been a Tory member of Parliament for twenty-five years. In 1976 Margaret Thatcher had appointed Neave to her shadow cabinet as spokesman for the affairs of Northern Ireland. Though he was consequently a natural target for terrorist violence, Neave had always firmly stated that British troops should remain in the strife-torn land.

Northern Ireland was not much on Neave's mind on the chill afternoon of March 30, 1979, as he prepared to leave the Parliament buildings in London. Margaret Thatcher was to formally open her campaign the next day, and Neave had been planning election strategy for months. He was tired.

As usual, he had left his blue Vauxhall in the five-story underground parking garage beneath the heavily guarded government buildings. He got into the car and slowly accelerated up the long ramp leading to the street with its famous silhouettes.

Less than fifty yards from Big Ben, Neave's car exploded. In the deadly stillness that followed, staff and members of Parliament came running from the House of Commons. A British reporter was one of the first to arrive. He wrote:

> The car was swollen like a balloon by the force of the blast. There was glass everywhere. The driver was still in his seat—almost standing—his face bloody and blackened. He was unrecognizable. His gray pinstripe trousers and black jacket were torn and ragged. I thought he looked dead, but a policeman who felt his pulse shouted, "He's still alive." Blood was running from the car and there was glass and mangled pieces of metal thrown up above the ramp into the yard."[6]

Airey Neave died forty minutes later.

That evening, telephones rang at Dublin newspaper offices. "We have a message for the British government," said a husky Irish voice. "Before you decide to have a general election, you had better state that you have decided not to stay in Ireland."

The next day Scotland Yard announced that both the Provisional IRA and the Irish National Liberation Army had claimed responsibility for the killing. Both claims were under investigation.

Protestant terrorists were not to be outdone by Catholic terrorists, as one of Belfast's most shocking murders proved.

Mervyn and Rosaleen McDonald, a young Catholic couple, lived on a Belfast street called Longlands Road. Though not politically active, the McDonalds had Republican ties. Rosaleen's father was a member of the political wing of the official faction of the IRA; Mervyn drank in a Republican bar. Those were reasons enough for them to be on a Protestant paramilitary death list.

One warm, hazy evening Mervyn was sitting at the kitchen table having dinner while Rosaleen watched the local television news in the main room. She held baby Margaret in her arms; two-and-a-half-year-old Seamus sat next to her on the sofa.

A white Austin pulled slowly up to the curb outside beyond the McDonalds' tall hedge. One man remained at the wheel; the other two got out. One had on a long overcoat.

The men knocked on the door and Rosaleen answered. "We're from the New Lodge. Is your husband in?" said one of the men. Thinking they were friends of her husband's family, who had connections on New Lodge Road, Rosaleen motioned them in.

Hearing strange voices, Mervyn got up from the dinner table and came to the doorway. As he did so, the man with the overcoat ripped a submachine gun from behind his back and fired at Mervyn, blowing off part of his face.

Clutching her baby, Rosaleen screamed, "Why us?"

The gunman turned toward her, tore the baby from her arms, pushed Rosaleen toward the sofa, and fired into her back. She fell in a pool of blood, while her children cried hysterically on the sofa.

The assassins left the house nonchalantly, climbed into the white Austin, and drove back to their base in Rathcoole. They agreed that their mission had been a success.

A neighbor found the McDonalds. Mervyn had been killed instantly; Rosaleen died four hours later—two more statistics in Northern Ireland's bitter toll.[7]

LIAM ...

When Liam McCloskey woke on Saturday morning, August 27, 1981, the fifty-fifth day of his hunger strike, he was considerably weaker. He was blind; his hearing was going.

His mother arrived. As soon as Liam went into a coma, she told him tearfully, she would have him fed intravenously. But by then it would be too late; his blindness would be permanent. She pleaded with him to end the strike before it was too late, since she was going to take him off it anyway.

Even in his weakened state, Liam was coherent enough to understand how supremely unfair he was being. His mother could not carry the responsibility for his death—or his blindness—on her conscience. He was trapped. He decided to end the strike.

"As I made that decision," he said later, "tears streamed out of my eyes. Tears of relief, tears of frustration, tears of sadness, tears of joy. I received a vitamin injection almost immediately and soon after some milk to drink.

"Waves of guilt washed over me as I sat eating, thinking about the men still on the hunger strike. So when the strike ended the Saturday of that week, I was a happy man. Even though it had ended in failure, no more would die that slow, lingering death."

Sectarian tensions were at their highest level since the early 1970s, when the region hovered on the verge of civil war. At the source of Ulster's new troubles is an apparent shift in IRA tactics. Having failed to win political concessions with hunger strikes, which disintegrated in the face of Prime Minister Margaret Thatcher's unyielding resistance and an erosion of support from families of participating prisoners (ten of whom died this year), the IRA has returned to the gun and stepped up its campaign of terror.

During the past three weeks, twelve people have been killed in Northern Ireland, including the 17-year-old son of an Ulster Defense Regiment soldier, and an 18-year-old Catholic youth who was shot as he walked home on the night of Bradford's murder. [The Rev. Robert Bradford, a Protestant member of Parliament and an evangelical Christian, was assassinated by IRA gunmen on November 17, 1981.] The IRA has also launched a series of bomb attacks in Britain. Four bombs have exploded in London during the past six weeks, killing three people.[8]

Liam's eyesight began to return, then his equilibrium. In the prison hospital he learned to walk again, rebuilding leg muscles deteriorated by the fast. He also began to think about resigning from the INLA.

"I was ripping myself apart inside," he says, "thinking about the men who had died, thinking about God, and the truths I had begun to discover on hunger strike.

"The first decision was to stop walking the way of Republicanism and the way of Jesus at the same time. It was impossible to walk both; one must override the other. I had to choose.

"I had reached the crossroads of life, and I took the way of Jesus. I found the rest I had long sought. Things became clearer in my mind. The Bible was no longer a book, but the way to God. I began to realize that God loved me and I loved God."

After Liam left the hospital, he was moved to a special H-block in the Maze for former protesters. He kept putting off his letter of resignation to the INLA, until one night he saw a television interview with the father of a young boy killed by an IRA bomb. The man said he forgave those who had planted the bomb and asked that no one retaliate.

There is a truly Christian man, thought Liam. *A beam of light in the darkness that engulfs this land. With people like that here, we are not beyond hope.*

He requested a transfer to Magilligan Prison, and it was granted. The night before he left he wrote his resignation to the INLA.

"As I left the Maze," says Liam, "it felt like a cloud lifting from me. I had left behind much of my old self in that place." He was finally ready to submit entirely to God, to pray with conviction, "Thy will be done."

As he was taken by van to Magilligan, he noticed the beauty of the countryside, and a wave of sadness swept over him. *People are dying together rather than living together to enjoy the land that God has given us all.*

Ready to be a force for reconciliation, Liam sought bold ways to show it. He decided to begin by breaking the stark lines of segregation between Protestants and Catholics in Magilligan Prison.

One place that segregation was already broken was in the Monday afternoon Bible study of Dr. Bill Holley, who later became one of Prison Fellowship's most faithful volunteers. His study was a proving ground for the unity to be found in Christ. Muscled inmates sporting "God & Ulster" tattoos up and down both arms shared Bibles with prisoners tattooed with "God & Ireland."

Several members of Dr. Holley's study had spent time in the Maze. Liam even became friends with UVF men and with Gerry, a former IRA man and now an outspoken Christian.

JIMMY ...

Another man who ended up in Dr. Holley's Bible study had traveled many of the same roads as the other prisoners. Short and muscular, with even white teeth and fine brown hair, Jimmy Gibson had gotten involved with the Protestant paramilitaries and was now in prison for attempted murder.

When he arrived at Magilligan, Jimmy wanted nothing to do with Christianity. He thought there probably was a God, but he certainly wanted nothing to do with Him. Certainly not with the things he was planning to do when he got out of prison. Retaliation against Catholic paramilitaries headed his list.

Jimmy respected the Christians at Magilligan, however. They weren't wishy-washy about their faith. He watched several of them closely—not only fellow Protestants, but Catholics like Gerry and Liam McCloskey, the slight, freckled prisoner who walked with a limp. Jimmy knew Liam had spent fifty-five days on a hunger strike; he also knew Liam had resigned from the INLA and become some sort of religious fanatic.

One day as Jimmy and two other Loyalist prisoners sat down for dinner, Liam limped toward their table, tray in hand. Jimmy's cellmate nodded at Liam.

"That's okay," he said. "You can sit here."

Jimmy kicked his mate under the table and felt his face grow hot. Liam sat down, said his grace, and took a forkful of beans. Excluding the prayer, the rest of the table followed suit.

The invisible line segregating Catholics from Protestants had been crossed.

Jimmy wasn't prepared to start a hunger strike of his own, so he continued to come to meals, despite the fact that Liam McCloskey did too—and his usual place was right next to Jimmy.

Slowly, as months went by, Jimmy began to see Liam as a person, not just a former hunger striker turned religious fanatic. Finally, one day Jimmy addressed him for the first time.

"What are you going to do to the other side when you get out?"

"Nothing," Liam responded.

I don't believe it, Jimmy thought to himself. He knew he couldn't give up the revenge he was plotting against his enemies.

Jimmy's inner turmoil continued to build until he knew he had to become a Christian. To tell God, "I reject You," would only mean God would reject him.

Finally Jimmy glumly told God he would give his life to Him. Later he went to Dr. Holley's Bible study. Liam, Gerry, and his other sworn enemies were jubilant, slapping him on the back and laughing. Jimmy was quiet—embarrassed—possibly the most miserable convert in Northern Ireland.

But the misery of his conversion didn't alter its veracity. Jimmy had thought it all through; he was ready to obey God's Word whatever it took. He hadn't come to Christianity to feel good; he came because it was true. He began speaking to Catholics and prison guards, whom he had hated equally. He began reading his Bible and telling others about his faith. He began learning how to forgive and seek reconciliation rather than plot revenge.

LIAM AND JIMMY . . .

One autumn evening as the men in the Magilligan Bible study met for prayer, a young girl named Karen McKeown headed their list. Dr. Holley had told them the week before about the young Protestant girl who had been shot by the INLA. Their prayer list always contained victims of the Troubles, but Liam had felt a special responsibility for Karen's suffering. He had written to her mother.

"I heard from Mrs. McKeown," Liam said, passing Karen's picture around the circle. "I haven't been able to stop thinking about her."

The group bowed their heads and joined hands. Then, one by one, the former terrorists—Catholic and Protestant—prayed for Karen McKeown and her family, asking that God heal this latest young victim of Belfast's violence.

Liam closed the prayer with the words he had first prayed during his months on the hunger strike. "Not ours, Lord, but Thy will be done."

PEARL AND KAREN ...

By the end of her second week in the hospital, Karen slept a little more each day. Pearl treasured the moments she was awake. By the third week, meningitis set in, and Karen slipped into a coma.

Then, early one morning while the rain fell outside the hospital windows, Pearl watched her daughter die.

Shortly after that, another letter arrived from Liam McCloskey.

"Pearl, we make strange friends in this troubled land. It is to the glory of God and He who makes it possible. Remember John 8:51, 'And I tell you most solemnly. Whoever keeps My Word will never see death.' Karen has left us, and even though it was no choice of mine, yet you can make a conscious decision in your own mind to see it as a gift of God. Your beautiful daughter to our beautiful Father who knows best. Surely the peace of Christ will be yours."

In the summer of 1983 Prison Fellowship conducted its first international conference in Belfast, Northern Ireland. At a time when travelers were passing up the troubled country, we decided it was a fitting backdrop for the theme of our conference: "In Christ, Reconciliation."

The work of Christians like Dr. Bill Holley and Gladys Blackburne and the reality of Christ in the lives of former terrorists clearly portrayed the power of God to bring unity. The struggles of Belfast represented the unresolved conflicts throughout our world. Northern Ireland illustrated both the hope and the desperate needs.

The highlight of the conference came one evening during a meeting open to the public. Hundreds of townspeople — both Protestant and Catholic — streamed into Queen's University's elegant Whitlow Hall, donated for the occasion. Clearly our ministry in Northern Ireland's prisons had captured the interest of many of Ulster's citizens.

Liam McCloskey and Jimmy Gibson had been furloughed from prison to be with us for the week. Their presence, more than anything else, evidenced the reconciling nature of the gospel. That evening, each told how he had come to know Christ. Liam concluded by putting his thin arm around Jimmy's muscular shoulders.

"My hope is to believe that God is changing the hearts of men like myself and Jimmy," Liam said. "That's the only hope I have for peace in Northern

Ireland. Before, if I had seen Jimmy on the street, I would have shot him. Now he's my brother in Christ. I would die for him."

As members of the audience murmured in disbelief, James McIlroy, director of Prison Fellowship for Northern Ireland, took the microphone.

"There's a woman I'd like you to meet," he said, motioning to someone in the back row. A lithe, energetic woman began to thread her way toward the front.

As she did, James briefly told the story of Pearl and Karen McKeown; of Karen's death at the hands of an INLA gunman; of Pearl's friendship through the mail with Liam, the former INLA terrorist; how Pearl and Liam had grown to love one another as mother and son, though they had never met.

Pearl climbed the stage steps and walked slowly toward Liam, arms outstretched. They hugged. Then Pearl held Liam's hand as she tearfully explained how Karen's death had been to God's glory.

"Liam told me his prayer is now that of St. Francis," she said. " 'Lord, make me an instrument of your peace. Where there is hatred, let me sow love. Where there is injury, pardon. Where there is death, life. Where despair, hope. Where there is darkness, light. Where there is sadness, joy.'

"And Liam *has* been God's instrument of peace to me," she concluded in a choked voice. "For he is the one who has showed me how to love God again."

By now tears glistened in many eyes as the audience strained to capture the incredible tableau: the two former terrorists, Catholic and Protestant, once sworn enemies, now standing together as brothers in Christ; the bereaved Protestant mother and the Catholic terrorist, holding hands.

Such is the reconciling power of God in Northern Ireland.

What is the answer to the troubles of Northern Ireland? Nothing in its chaotic history suggests there are political answers. George Thomas was right that night at our dinner in London: politically speaking, "There is no answer in Northern Ireland." But when every political effort of men and their institutions has been frustrated, when the kingdoms of man are utterly impotent, it is then that the power of the Kingdom of God, in all its glory, breaks into the dark stream of history. And it is the citizens of the Kingdom of God who carry that light into the darkness—which cannot overcome it. Thus these

Christians of Northern Ireland—and many others—continue the witness of the indestructible Kingdom in the midst of their nation's struggles.

After Chips McCurry was released from prison in 1985, he studied at Baptist College in conjunction with Queen's University. When a BBC radio program interviewed Chips and an ex-IRA man together, Chips told the story of his conversion. Gladys Blackburne happened to hear the broadcast and was thrilled; until then, she had not known the results of her Christmas Eve visit with him in 1980.

Perhaps it is Chips who best articulates the problems—and the solution—for Northern Ireland.

"I spent almost ten years in prison. I saw guys fighting, dying for God and Ulster. Or for God and Ireland. What would happen if either side got what they wanted? You see that politics can't bring any lasting solutions.

"The only thing that will make any lasting peace, the only things that will bridge the gulf between the Catholics and the Protestants here is for people to give up violence and learn forgiveness. The only way that can possibly happen is through Jesus Christ."

EPILOGUE

*The light shines in the darkness, and the darkness
has not overcome it.*

JOHN 1:5 [RSV]

The story of Northern Ireland is told here in part because it is a metaphor for what is happening all over the world. While on the surface it was (and is) a religious war, the conflict is, in reality, a long-standing struggle for political and economic power.

We have seen the same destructive confrontations in the Middle East between Jews and Muslims and between Muslims and Christians (including, tragically, up to a million Chaldean Christians in Iraq, who are regularly brutalized by their Sunni, Kurd, and Shia neighbors). We've witnessed endless conflicts in the Balkans. We stood helplessly by and watched the bloody genocide in Rwanda, where thousands were slaughtered as the United Nations did nothing.

We spent the summer of 2006 watching a bloody battle between Israel and Syrian-backed Hezbollah terrorists that killed some 1,400 combatants and civilians alike. As I write, the war in Iraq is still raging, with no end in sight. The West watches uneasily as unpredictable rulers in Iran and Venezuela flex their muscles and make threats. In Sudan, the slaughter of innocents goes on — victims of brutal Muslim leaders.

In North Korea, millions have starved under a gangster leader. Tens of thousands of others have been thrown into gulags over trivial or trumped-up reasons. There they are tortured, see their children murdered, and have medical experiments performed on them. In Communist China, Christians are imprisoned, tortured, and killed for their faith; in Russia, Communist leaders are gone, replaced by criminal gangs and mobsters. All over the world, international sex traffickers have destroyed the lives of millions of women and children.

Much of the world lives under the thumb of tyranny; here in the West, people are enslaved by more subtle—and often unacknowledged—tyrants. In America's inner cities, a generation is in bondage to drugs and poverty; many see crime as their only way out and end up in the wasteland of America's prisons. Meanwhile, more affluent Americans embrace the false gods of materialism and hedonism. Man's basest passions have unleashed a plague called AIDS, which has killed tens of millions the world over; the number of sexually transmitted diseases multiply with frightening regularity, leaving pain, sterility, and despair in their wake.

Millions more are addicted to Internet pornography, which has led to a horrific increase in the sexual exploitation of children and attacks on young girls naive enough to arrange meetings with men they meet on MySpace. Americans dread the consequences of millions of illegal aliens flooding over our borders, many of them criminals; others fearfully wonder where embryo-destructive research, cloning, and other medical research will take humanity.

With the fall of the Soviet empire, the menace of all-out nuclear war has dissolved. But the Soviets have been replaced by another, perhaps deadlier menace. Nothing threatens the world today more than Islamic radicalism. In Indonesia, England, Spain, Italy, and the United States, Islamo-fascists, fueled by hatred of the West, have murdered thousands of innocents.

During my days working in the White House some thirty years ago, I often came home feeling nauseated after meetings about national security, in which we spent the afternoon hearing about possible nuclear attacks, first-strike survivability, and the policy of Mutually Assured Destruction (MAD), which shaped every decision we made. I used to come home and tell my wife, Patty, "I don't know if I can take this, because we are making decisions that could, by one miscalculation, obliterate this country!"

Now consider: The entire MAD policy assumed that leaders on both sides of the Cold War—the Americans and the Soviets—were reasonable, rational people. Today it's a totally different ballgame. When it comes to Islamic fanatics, one cannot assume rationality. One must assume, based on their past behavior, that they are *irrational*—that if they ever got their hands on nuclear weapons, they'd be willing to use them.

I have come to the sobering conclusion that we are in greater danger of a nuclear strike today than we were during the Cold War. I am not alone in believing that terrorists will attempt to buy or build what they need—and then, a mushroom cloud will rise once again, this time over the United States or Israel.

At the dawn of the twenty-first century, a great irony persists. Technology has given man power he has never known before; giant institutions, such as the United Nations, offer panaceas for all human ills. But never has man seemed less able to devise political strategies to produce order and harmony among people. The proudest pretensions of the strongest nations are mocked by a handful of bomb-laden terrorists willing to die in order to kill strangers on a train, subway, or jet. Korea, Lebanon, Darfur, Iran, China, and dozens of places like them are but open sores on the body politic, reminding us that even in this age of technological wonders, modern governments have devised nothing to cure the unbridled passions of man.

Is there no hope?

Like any author, I would like to end this book on a triumphant note, announcing that ultimate peace and harmony can be achieved through human efforts. But that utopian illusion is shattered by the splintered history of the human race. Governments rise; even the most powerful fall. The battle for people's hearts and minds will continue.

Where then is hope? It is in the fact that the Kingdom of God has come to earth—the Kingdom announced by Jesus Christ in that obscure Nazareth synagogue two thousand years ago. It is a Kingdom that comes not in a temporary takeover of political structures, but in the lasting takeover of the human heart by the rule of a holy God.

Certainly, as I hope this book has shown, the fact that God reigns can be manifest through political means, whenever the citizens of the Kingdom of God bring His light to bear on the institutions of the kingdoms of man. But His rule is even more powerfully evident in ordinary, individual lives, in the breaking of cycles of violence and evil, in the paradoxical power of forgiveness, in the actions of those little platoons who live by the transcendent values of the Kingdom of God in the midst of the kingdoms of this world, loving their God and loving their neighbor.

Thus in the midst of the dark and habitual chaos of earth, a light penetrates the darkness. It cannot be extinguished; it is the light of the Kingdom of God. His Kingdom *has* come, in His people today, and it is yet to come as well, in the great consummation of human history. Today, as we endure a tremendous clash of civilizations, we must remember the truths of the Kingdom. While the battles rage over the earth, we can take heart—not in the fleeting fortunes of men or nations, but rather in the promise so beautifully captured in Handel's *Messiah*.

Stop. Listen. Over the din of the conflict, if you listen carefully, you will hear the chorus echoing in the distance: "The kingdom of this world has become the kingdom of our Lord and of His Christ."

Listen. For in that glorious refrain is man's one hope.

> Let us then ... rejoice that we see around us at every hand the decay of the institutions and instruments of power, see intimations of empires falling to pieces, money in total disarray, dictators and parliamentarians alike nonplussed by the confusion and conflicts which encompass them. For it is precisely when every earthly hope has been explored and found wanting, when every possibility of help from earthly sources has been sought and is not forthcoming, when every recourse this world offers, moral as well as material, has been explored to no effect, when in the shivering cold the last faggot has been thrown on the fire and in the gathering darkness every glimmer of light has finally flickered out, it's then that Christ's hand reaches out, sure and firm. Then Christ's words bring their inexpressible comfort, then His light shines brightest, abolishing the darkness forever. So finding in everything only deception and nothingness, the soul is constrained to have recourse to God Himself and to rest content with Him.[1]

WITH GRATITUDE
(1987 EDITION)

If this book accomplishes nothing more than to cause readers to turn to Richard John Neuhaus's *Naked Public Square*, I shall consider my labors well rewarded. Of the thirty or more books I studied in preparation for writing *Kingdoms in Conflict*, Neuhaus's work was second only to Augustine's classic *The City of God*. I am thus deeply indebted to Richard. My prayer is that what I have written will in some way contribute to his heroic struggle to defend religious values in Western culture.

I'm also indebted to esteemed theologian Dr. Carl F. H. Henry, my beloved friend, for both his various writings on church and state issues and for his critique of this manuscript. When I asked Carl for his counsel, the publisher's deadline was imminent and he was leaving in twelve hours for an extended teaching trip. I was astonished to discover the entire manuscript in my office the next day, thoroughly reviewed. With characteristic generosity and devotion, he had simply stayed up all night to read it.

I'm also profoundly grateful to Jacques Ellul, the French sociologist and critic, for his many prophetic works, most significantly *The Political Illusion* and *The Presence of the Kingdom*. These are classic commentaries on our times and, in what is in itself a sad commentary on our times, are out of print. Also of tremendous importance was Donald Bloesch's *Crumbling Foundations*.

Paul Johnson's *Modern Times* was a great inspiration as well. If my writing has aroused in the reader's mind a desire to know more of the philosophical undercurrents of this century, I could recommend nothing more highly than this insightful, provocative critique.

In the "For Further Reading" section, I've listed other contemporary writers and their works that greatly assisted me in the reference section to follow, in the hope that readers will go deeper into the complex and crucial issues of church, state, and the Kingdom of God.

As with *Loving God*, this book was the result of a team effort: My wonderfully gifted editorial associate, Ellen Santilli Vaughn, who assisted with certain chapters of *Loving God*, was this time my colleague in the fullest sense, as the title page properly acknowledges. It is a joy to work closely with one who combines keen editorial skills with such an uplifting Christian spirit.

Kenneth Myers, editor of *This World: A Journal of Religion and Public Life*, provided research help with early drafts and wise theological counsel throughout. So did David Coffin, a doctoral candidate at Westminster Theological Seminary and head of Berea Ministries.

Tim Stafford, another *Loving God* collaborator, provided tremendous assistance with the Prologue, the material on the Philippines, and particularly with his fascinating research and reporting of the events leading up to World War II.

My very talented friend Jim Manney, editor of *New Covenant Magazine*, provided outstanding research for the Christianity and Marxism material. My research assistant, Michael Gerson, did a brilliant job, providing provocative research and well-reasoned drafts. Elizabeth Leahy, director of the Prison Fellowship Information Center, gave invaluable and exhaustive help, excavating mounds of obscure sources and cites—without ever losing her smile.

But the most important member of the team was my editor, Judith Markham. Judith edited *Loving God*; and, in spite of the pain an editor's surgery causes any writer, we ended up good friends. I also gained enormous admiration for Judith's ability—her availability was the deciding factor in my selection of a publisher. She did not disappoint me. Judith Markham is, in my opinion, the master craftsman of her trade.

I was enormously helped as well by my extremely competent executive secretary, Grace McCrane, who tamed this manuscript through, in some cases, ten or more drafts, offering important suggestions and helpful additions throughout. She was assisted with typing of early drafts by Patti Perkins. I am grateful as well to Margaret Shannon, who provided the idea and initial research for the Clivedon material, as well as to Jim Park, Prison Fellowship Oklahoma area director, for his research into Collinsville.

In addition to Carl Henry, Richard Neuhaus, and theologian Arthur Lindsley, several of my Prison Fellowship colleagues read and critiqued the manuscript. I'm particularly grateful to Dan Van Ness, president of Justice Fellowship, and his colleague David Coolidge, who as a church-state student himself, offered excellent and insightful suggestions throughout. I'm indebted as well to Prison Fellowship president Gordon Loux, who from the beginning of our ministry has been my closest confidant and friend. A word of thanks is also due to Ron Nikkel, executive director of Prison Fellowship International, for his consistent encouragement, and to Fellowship

Communications president Nelson Keener and my executive assistant, Jim Jewell, for their help with contract matters and book promotion.

The support of my family, especially Patty, the helpmate God has given me, proved indispensable to this book. Five months before the deadline I was hospitalized for major surgery. Patty and my daughter, Emily Colson Boehme, were faithfully at my side during the month I spent in the hospital; my sons Wendell and Chris also came from great distance to offer encouragement, as did my mother and stepfather. I wonder if I would have made it without them.

Patty then nursed me through the two months of recovery only to lose me to long days—and nights—as I labored over this manuscript. There are far easier callings than to be married to those who periodically feel compelled to take pen in hand; but without Patty's consistent encouragement, *Kingdoms in Conflict* could not have been written.

Finally, my gratitude to all those in Prison Fellowship who encourage and support me; to the teachers who have given so unstintingly of their time; and to the readers of my books who frequently encourage me with their letters. And of course most important, my eternal gratitude goes to the One who guides my hand across the page. May this book glorify Him in every way.

CHARLES W. COLSON
June 20, 1987

POSTSCRIPT: For the second edition, *God & Government*, a special debt of gratitude is due to Anne Morse, my very faithful colleague who undertook the Herculean task of going through *Kingdoms in Conflict* line by line, updating, refreshing, and helping me compose copy that speaks to 2007 as opposed to 1987. The interesting thing is that while many of the illustrations had to be changed and updated, many others did not. They are of timeless value. Most significantly, we found that none of the teaching about the relationship of church and state, God and government, public life and religion, had to be altered. Those judgments are made on the basis of the eternal verities of the biblical worldview and stood the test of time, and will continue to.

I owe a debt also to Tim Stafford, who helped rewrite the prologue.

CHARLES W. COLSON
April, 2007

NOTES

CHAPTER 1: KINGDOMS IN CONFLICT

1. Paul Vitz, *Psychology as Religion: The Cult of Self-Worship* (Grand Rapids, Mich.: Eerdmans, 1977), 114. Quoted in Donald G. Bloesch, *Crumbling Foundations* (Grand Rapids, Mich.: Zondervan, 1984), 67.

2. Justice William O. Douglas's opinion in *Zorach v. Clauson*, 343 U.S. 306 (April 28, 1952) is cited in Robert T. Miller and Ronald B. Flowers, *Toward Benevolent Neutrality: Church, State, and the Supreme Court*, rev. ed. (Waco, Texas: Markham Press Fund, 1977), 327.

3. Jack Kroll, "The Most Famous Artist," *Newsweek* (March 9, 1987), 64.

4. Justice Goldberg's dissenting opinion in *Abington Township School District v. Schempp*, 374 U.S 203 (June 17, 1963) is cited in Miller and Flowers, *Toward Benevolent Neutrality*, 372.

5. Walter Shapiro, "Politics and the Pulpit," *Newsweek* (September 17, 1984), 24.

6. Ronald Reagan's speech at an ecumenical prayer breakfast in Dallas Texas is quoted in Jeremiah O'Leary, "Reagan Declares that Faith Has Key Role in Political Life," *Washington Times* (August 24, 1984).

7. Shapiro, "Politics and the Pulpit," 24.

8. Mario M. Cuomo, "Religious Belief and Public Morality: A Catholic Governor's Perspective," a paper presented to the Department of Theology at the University of Notre Dame (September 13, 1984), 12.

9. *New York Times* (April 10, 1983). Quoted in a speech given by Stephen V. Monsma, "The Promises and Pitfalls of Evangelical Political Involvement," (October 17, 1986).

10. Will Durant, *Caesar and Christ: A History of Roman Civilization from Its Beginnings to A.D. 337* (New York: Simon and Schuster, 1944), 164.

11. St. Augustine, *City of God* (Garden City, N.Y.: Image/Doubleday, 1958), 88.

12. *London Times* editorial: "Evil in the Air," (May 12, 1983), 15A

13. Quoted in Richard John Neuhaus, *The Naked Public Square* (Grand Rapids, Mich.: Eerdmans, 1984), 95.

14. Quoted in Neuhaus, *Naked Public Square*, 115.

15. Adam Michnik, *Letters from Prison and Other Essays* (Berkeley, Calif.: University of California Press, 1986). Quoted in Norman Davies, "True to Himself and His Homeland," *New York Times Book Review* (October 5, 1986).

16. Vernon J. Bourke, "Introduction," in St. Augustine, *City of God*, 9 – 10.

17. "Indian Leader Urges Gandhi to 'Stamp Out' Missionaries," *Presbyterian Journal* (November 20, 1985), 6.

CHAPTER 2: AFTER THE FEAST

1. This chapter is based on several studies of Hemingway's life, the most helpful of which were John Killinger, *Hemingway and the Dead Gods* (Lexington, Ky.: The University of Kentucky Press, 1960), and A. E. Hotchner, *Papa Hemingway: The Ecstasy and Sorrow* (New York: Quill, 1983).

2. "Hero of the Code," *Time* (July 14, 1961), 87.

3. Killinger, *Hemingway and the Dead Gods*, 69.

4. Maurice Natanson, "Jean-Paul Sartre's Philosophy of Freedom," *Social Research*, XIX (September 1952), 378.

5. E. L. Allen, *The Self and Its Hazards: A Guide to the Thought of Karl Jaspers* (London: Hodder and Stoughton, 1953), 7.

CHAPTER 3: CROSSING THE RUBICON

1. The information in this chapter is based on news reports and an interview with Jerry and Sis Levin conducted by Ellen Santilli Vaughn (April 9, 1987).

CHAPTER 4: FAITH AND THE EVIDENCE

1. Quoted in R. C. Sproul, *If There Is a God, Why Are There Atheists?* (Minneapolis: Dimension Books, 1978), 48.

2. Harry Blamires, *The Christian Mind* (Ann Arbor, Mich.: Servant Books, 1963), 44.

3. Lincoln Kinnear Barnett, *The Universe and Dr. Einstein* (New York: William Morrow, 1968), 114 (emphasis in the original).

4. Paul C. Davies, *The Edge of Infinity: Where the Universe Came From and How It Will End* (New York: Simon & Schuster, 1982), 169.

5. Arthur Eddington, as quoted in Hugh Ross, "Astronomical Evidences for a Personal, Transcendent God," in *The Creation Hypothesis*, ed. J. P. Moreland (Downers Grove, Ill.: InterVarsity, 1994), 145-46.

6. George Smoot, quoted in *Current Biography*,' Vol. 55, No. 4 (April 1994), reprinted at http://aether.lbl.gov/www/personnel/Smoot-bio.html.

7. Jerry Bergman, Ph.D., "Arno A. Penzias: Astrophysicist, Nobel Laureate," *Perspectives in Science and Christian Faith* (September 1994).

8. Bergman, "Arno A. Penzias."

9. Bergman, "Arno A. Penzias."

10. Carl Sagan, *Cosmos* (New York: Random House, 1980), 4.

11. Eugene Mallove, "Gravity: Is the Force that Makes the Apple Fall the Clue to Creation?" *Washington Post* (March 3, 1985), C-1-a.

12. Bertrand Russell, *The Autobiography of Bertrand Russell*, a letter to Lady Ottoline Morrell dated August 11, 1918 (Boston: Little, Brown, 1968), 121.

13. Quoted in Joseph Frank, *Dostoyevsky: Years of Ordeal* (Princeton, N.J.: Princeton University Press, 1983), 159.

14. Jeremiah 22:16.

15. Paul Johnson, "A Historian Looks at Jesus," unpublished speech (1986).

16. "Conversation with an Author: Mortimer J. Adler, Author of *How to Think About God*," *Book Digest Magazine* (September 1980).

17. Mortimer Adler, *A Second Look in the Rearview Mirror: Further Autobiographical Reflections of a Philosopher at Large* (New York: Macmillan, 1992).

CHAPTER 5: NEITHER APE NOR ANGEL

1. Aleksandr I. Solzhenitsyn, *The Cancer Ward* (New York: Dell, 1968).

2. Paul Johnson, "The Necessity for Christianity," *Truth*, 1:1 (1985), 2.

3. Peter Singer, "Sanctity of Life or Quality of Life?" *Pediatrics* (July 1983), 129.

4. Quoted in Thomas Molnar, *Utopia: The Perennial Heresy* (London: Tom Stacey, 1972), 4.

5. William Golding, *Lord of the Flies* (New York: Wide View/Paragrees Books, 1954).

6. E. L. Epstein, "Notes on *Lord of the Flies*," in Golding, *Lord of the Flies*, 186.

7. Armando Valladares, *Against All Hope* (New York: Knopf, 1986), 4.

8. Valladares, *Against All Hope*, 135.

9. Paul Johnson, *Modern Times: The World from the Twenties to the Eighties* (New York: Harper & Row, 1983), 11.

10. Charles Murray, "No, Welfare Really Isn't the Problem," *Public Interest* (Summer 1986), 10.

11. Leszek Kolakowski, "The Idolatry of Politics," *New Republic* (June 16, 1986), 29–36.

12. Quoted in James V. Schall, *Christianity and Politics* (Boston: St. Paul Editions, 1981), 295.

13. Molnar, *Utopia*, 7.

CHAPTER 6: KING WITHOUT A COUNTRY

1. Luke 4:18, in which Jesus quotes Isaiah 61:1–2. The story that follows is related in Luke 4:20–30.

2. Matthew 6:33.

3. St. Augustine, *The Confessions of St. Augustine*, translated and edited by J. G. Pilkington (New York: Liveright, 1943), 1.

4. Acts 16:30.

5. Edmund Clowney, "The Politics of the Kingdom," *Westminster Theological Journal* 41 (Spring 1979), 302.

CHAPTER 7: POLITICS OF THE KINGDOM

1. Paul Johnson, "The Family as an Emblem of Freedom," *Emblem of Freedom: The American Family in the 1980s*, edited by Carl A. Anderson and William J. Gribbon (Durham, N.C.: Carolina Academic Press, 1981), 23.

2: Robert Rector, panel discussion, "The Collapse of Marriage and the Rise of Welfare Dependence," Lecture # 959, The Heritage Foundation, (May 22, 2006). *www.heritage.org/Research/Welfare/hl959.cfm*

3: Barbara Dafoe Whitehead, panel discussion, "The Collapse of Marriage and the Rise of Welfare Dependence," Lecture # 959, The Heritage Foundation, (May 22, 2006). *www.heritage.org/Research/Welfare/hl959.cfm*

4: U.S. Census Bureau, "Current Population Survey, March Annual Social and Economic Supplements, 2004 and earlier."

5: Rector, Heritage.

6: Dafoe, Heritage.

7: Dafoe, Ibid.

8. Stanton E. Samenow, *Inside the Criminal Mind* (New York: New York Times Book Co., 1984).

9. James Q. Wilson and Richard J. Herrnstein, *Crime and Human Nature* (New York: Simon and Schuster, 1985).

10. Carl F. H. Henry: "The Modern Flight from the Family," *The Emblem of Freedom, the American Family in the 1980s*, edited by Carl A. Anderson and William J. Gribbon (Durham, N.C.: North Carolina Academic Press, 1981), 46.

11. Romans 13:4.

12. 1 Peter 2:14.

13. Quoted in Michael Harrington, *The Politics at God's Funeral* (New York: Penguin, 1983), 107.

14. Jay Marcellus Kik, *Church and State in the New Testament* (Grand Rapids, Mich.: Baker, 1962), 20.

15. Exodus 18:13.

16. Exodus 18:15–16.

17. 1 Timothy 2:2.

18. Robert Nisbet, *The Quest for Community* (New York: Oxford University Press, 1953).

19. Robert L. Saucy, *The Church in God's Program* (Chicago: Moody Press, 1972), 91.

20. Floyd Filson, *Jesus Christ the Risen Lord* (Nashville: Abingdon Press, 1956), 253.

21. Jacques Ellul, *The Presence of the Kingdom* (New York: Seabury Press, 1948/1967), 47.

22. Pope John Paul II, "Opening Address at Puebla" (1979). In *The Pope and Revolution: John Paul II Confronts Liberation Theology*, edited by Quintin L. Quade (Washington, D.C.: Ethics and Public Policy Center, 1982).

23. Edmund Clowney, "The Politics of the Kingdom," *Westminster Theological Journal* 41:2 (Spring 1979), 306.

24. Clowney, "Politics of the Kingdom," 307.

CHAPTER 8: FOR THE GOOD OF THE NATION

1. This chapter was based on a number of studies of Wilberforce's life and the fight for the abolition of the slave trade in England. Several of the most helpful sources were: Robin Furneaux, *William Wilberforce* (London: Hamilton, 1974); John Pollock, *Wilberforce* (New York: St. Martin's Press, 1978); William Wilberforce, *Real Christianity*, a modern edition edited by James Houston (Portland: Multnomah, 1982); Ernest Marshall Howse, *Saints in Politics: The Clapham Sect* (Unwin, 1974); Garth Lean, *God's Politician: William Wilberforce's Struggle* (London: Darton, Longman and Todd, 1980).

CHAPTER 9: THE CROSS AND THE CROWN

1. Acts 17:6–7.

2. F. F. Bruce, *The Spreading Flame: The Rise and Progress of Christianity from Its First Beginnings to the Conversion of the English* (Grand Rapids, Mich.: Eerdmans, 1958), 293.

3. Etienne Gilson's "Foreword," quoting Fustel de Coulanges, in St. Augustine, *The City of God* (New York: Image/Doubleday, 1958), 15.

4. Alexis de Tocqueville, *The Old Regime and the French Revolution*, translated by Stuart Gilbert (Garden City: Doubleday/Anchor Books, 1955), 149.

5. Tocqueville, *The Old Regime and the French Revolution*, 149.

6. Romans 13:5, 7.

7. Edmund Clowney, "The Politics of the Kingdom," *Westminster Theological Journal* (Spring 1979), 306.

8. Harold J. Berman, "Atheism and Christianity in the Soviet Union," in *Freedom and Faith: The Impact of Law on Religious Liberty*, edited by Lynn R. Buzzard (Westchester, Ill.: Crossway Books, 1982), 127–43.

9. Quoted from the "Offices of the Congregation for the Doctrine of the Faith," Rome, the Vatican (June 3, 2003), www.vatican.va/roman_curia/congregations-unions_en.html.

10. Justice Janice Rogers Brown, quoted in "California Supreme Court Orders Catholic Charities to Pay for Birth Control," *Christianity Today Library*, compiled by Ted Olsen (March 1, 2004), www.ctlibrary.com/ct/2004/marchweb-only/3-1-22.0.html.

11. Joseph Starrs, quoted in *WorldNetDaily*, www.wnd.com/news/article.asp?ARTICLE_ID =37375.

12. Information from www.breakpoint.org/ listingarticle.asp?ID=1540.

13. William Blake, "And Did Those Feet," *The Norton Anthology of Poetry*, 3d ed. (New York: W. W. Norton, 1983), 266.

14. Oscar Cullman, *The State in the New Testament* (New York: Scribner's, 1956), 91.

15. Hugh T. Kerr, ed., *Compendium of Luther's Theology* (Philadelphia: Westminster Press, 1966), 218.

16. Carl F. H. Henry, "The Gospel for the Rest of Our Century," *Christianity Today* (January 17, 1986), 25–31.

17. Charles Colson, *How Now Shall We Live?* (Wheaton, Ill.: Tyndale, 1999).

18. Quoted in Neuhaus, *Naked Public Square*, 61.

19. "James Madison's Memorial and Remonstrance, 1785," in Edwin S. Gaustad, ed., *A Documentary History of Religion in America: Vol. I* (Grand Rapids, Mich.: Eerdmans, 1982), 262–63.

20. Quoted in A. James Reichley, *Religion in American Public Life* (Washington, D.C.: The Brookings Institute, 1985), 105.

21. Reichley, *Religion in American Public Life*, 360.

CHAPTER 10: ROOTS OF WAR (PART I)

1. The following sources were particularly useful in the research of this chapter: Eberhard Bethge, *Dietrich Bonhoeffer* (New York: Harper & Row, 1977); John Conway, *The Nazi Persecution of the Churches* (New York: Basic Books, 1968); Arthur C. Cochrane, *The Church's Confession Under Hitler* (Allison Park, Penn.: Pickwick, 1977); Richard Gutteridge, *Open Thy Mouth for the Dumb! The German Evangelical Church and the Jews* (New York: Barnes and Noble, 1976); Dietmar Schmidt, *Pastor Niemoller* (New York: Doubleday, 1959); William Shirer, *A Berlin Diary* (New York: Knopf, 1941).

CHAPTER 11: ROOTS OF WAR (PART II)

1. This chapter is based on a number of studies on England and the thirties, including: Neville Chamberlain, *In Search of Peace* (Salem, N.H.: Ayer, facsimile of 1939 edition); Keith Middlemas, *The Strategy of Appeasement: The British Government and Germany, 1937–1939* (New York: Times Books, 1972); John W. Wheeler-Bennett, *Munich: Prologue to Tragedy* (Duell, 1962); David Dilks, *Neville Chamberlain* (New York: Cambridge University Press, 1984); Martin Gilbert and Richard Gott, *The Appeasers* (Boston: Houghton Mifflin, 1963).

CHAPTER 12: YEAR ZERO

1. Many of the historical details in this chapter are taken from William Manchester, *American Caesar: Douglas MacArthur 1880–1964* (Boston: Little, Brown, 1978). See especially chapter 7, "At High Port," for additional information.

2. Quoted in John Lukacs, *1945: Year Zero* (Garden City: Doubleday, 1978), 239.

3. Paul Johnson, *Modern Times: The World from the Twenties to the Eighties* (New York: Harper & Row, 1983), 430.

4. Friedrich Nietzsche, *The Gay Science*, as quoted in Michael Harrington, *The Politics at God's Funeral* (New York: Penguin Books, 1983), 85.

5. Quoted in Robert Byrne, *The Other 637 Best Things Anybody Ever Said* (New York: Fawcett Crest, 1984), 6.

6. James V. Schall, *Christianity and Politics* (Boston: St. Paul Editions, 1981), 102.

7. Harrington, *The Politics at God's Funeral*, 85.

8. This study, "Issues in Criminal Justice Reform: Faith-Based Initiatives," is available at the *Center for Research on Religion and Civil Society*'s website: referenced at www.justice fellowship.org/generic.asp?ID=478.

9. "Americans United for Separation of Church and State vs. Prison Fellowship Ministries," referenced at www.prisonfellowship .org/media/ifi/Docs/IFI_Decision_%20Judge_ Pratt.pdf (filed June 2, 2006)

10. "Americans United for Separation of Church and State vs. Prison Fellowship Ministries," referenced at www.prisonfellowship. org/media/ifi/Docs/IFI_Decision_%20Judge_ Pratt.pdf (filed June 2, 2006)

11. "Opening Remarks, Commission on Safety and Abuse in America's Prisons" (July 19, 2005), www.prisoncommission.org/statements/ brown_devon.pdf.

CHAPTER 13: MARXISM
AND THE KINGDOM OF GOD

1. Walter Kaufmann, ed. and trans., *The Portable Nietzsche* (New York: Penguin Books, 1954), 95.

2. Paul Johnson, *Modern Times: The World from the Twenties to the Eighties* (New York: Harper & Row, 1983), 50.

3. Prabhu Isaac, *For Christ in the Wilderness* (Solid Rock Publications), www.breakpoint.org/generic.asp?ID=2513.

4. Mark Early, "A Modern Auschwitz: North Korea's Camp 22," www.breakpoint.org/listing article.asp?ID=3227.

5. Mindy Belz, "The Party Rules," *World Magazine* online archives (March 15, 1997), www.worldmag.com/articles/162.

6. Julia Duin, "Christian Persecution Growning," *Washington Times*, at the website of Assyrian International News Agency (December 15, 2005), www.aina.org/news/20051215124541.htm.

7. Erin McCormick, "The Cost for Christ, and Christmas, around the World," *Prison Fellowship* (December 21, 2005), www.wilberforce.org/article.asp?ID=1040.

8. McCormick, "The Cost for Christ."

9. Charles Colson, "Murder in the Outposts," *Prison Fellowship* (April 1, 1996), www.breakpoint.org/listingarticle.asp?ID=4250.

10. Joseph Mindszenty, *Mindszenty* (New York: Macmillan, 1974).

11. Quoted in George Seldes, *Great Thoughts* (New York: Ballantine, 1985), 241.

12. Seldes, *Great Thoughts*, 397.

13. "Christ Would Never Approve that Man Be Considered Merely as a Means of Production," *New York Times* (June 10, 1979), 1:6.

14. "Urged the Government to Honor the Cause of Fundamental Human Rights, Including the Right to Religious Liberty," *New York Times* (June 6, 1979), 1:3.

15. "Told Poles to Set a Christian Example Even If It Means Risking Danger," *New York Times* (June 7, 1979), 8:1.

16. Evangelical Press News Service (November 21, 1981).

17. Much of this section of chapter 13 was borrowed and adapted from Chuck Colson, *Being the Body* (Nashville, W Publishing Group, 2001). The story is told in greater detail there.

18. Stefan Wyszynski, *The Freedom Within: The Prison Notes of Stefan Cardinal Wyszynski* (New York: Harcourt Brace Jovanovich, 1982), 12.

19. Jacques Ellul, "Lech Walesa and the Social Force of Christianity," *Kattalagete* (June 1982), 6.

20. Wyszynski, *The Freedom Within*, 26.

21. Beth Spring, "Campus Crusade Director Describes Government Harassment of Evangelicals," *Christianity Today* (February 7, 1986), 52–53. Most of the details concerning Jimmy Hassan were drawn from this article.

22. The information on Nicaragua was drawn from Humberto Belli, *Breaking Faith: The Sandinista Revolution and Its Impact on Freedom and Christian Faith in Nicaragua* (Westchester, Ill.: Crossway Books, 1985).

23. Benjamin Cortes quoted in Belli, *Breaking Faith*, 158.

24. Belli, *Breaking Faith*, 212.

25. Belli, *Breaking Faith*, 152.

26. Belli, *Breaking Faith*, 161.

27. Belli, *Breaking Faith*, 162.

28. The story of Poland's school children and the crucifixes was gathered from articles in the following issues of the *New York Times*: (March 8, 1984), I, 15:1; (March 9, 1984), I, 1:3; (March 10, 1984), I, 24:1; (March 11, 1984), I, 3:4; (March 14, 1984), I, 1:1; (March 15, 1984), I, 4:3.

CHAPTER 14: CONFLICT AND
COMPROMISE IN THE WEST

1. *Stone v. Graham*, 449 U.S. 39 (1980), cited in Robert T. Miller and Ronald B. Flowers, *Toward Benevolent Neutrality: Church, State, and the Supreme Court*, rev. ed. (Waco, Tex.: Markham Press Fund, 1977), 327.

2. Material regarding the Marian Guinn case was taken from a wide variety of news stories and wire reports, a transcript of a CBS *60 Minutes* interview (April 22, 1984), and a number of articles, including Lynn Buzzard, "Is Church Discipline and Invasion of Privacy?" *Christianity Today* (November 9, 1984), 37–39; and "Marian and the Elders," *Time* (March 26, 1984).

3. 1 Corinthians 5:9.

4. 1 Timothy 5:20.

5. Richard John Neuhaus, *The Naked Public Square*, (Grand Rapids, Mich.: Eerdmans, 1984), 142.

6. Nat Hentoff, "Religion on School Property," *Washington Post* (November 1, 1984), A–25.

7. The information from the Dayton Christian School case was taken from William Bentley, "Secularism: Tidal Wave of Repression," in *Freedom and Faith*, edited by Lynn L. Buzzard (Westchester, Ill.: Crossway Books, 1982).

8. Dorthey Korber, "No Adverse Reaction to Prayer Ban," from an undated California newspaper clipping.

9. Jonathan Kalstrom, "Fire and Brimstone: An Atheist Takes on Small Town America," *Liberty* (January/February 1987), 22–25; and *NFD Journal* (August 1986), 14.

10. *New York Times* (March 6, 1984), II, 6:1.

11. *Zorach v. Clauson*, 343 U.S. 306 (April 28, 1952). Cited in Miller and Flowers, *Toward Benevolent Neutrality*, 327.

12. *Abington Township School District v. Schempp*, 374 U.S. 203 (June 17, 1963). Cited in Miller and Flowers, *Toward Benevolent Neutrality*, 372.

13. *United States v. Seeger* (no. 50); *United States v. Jakobson* (no. 51); *Peter v. United States* (no. 29) 380 U.S. 163 (March 8, 1965). Cited in Miller and Flowers, *Toward Benevolent Neutrality*, 177.

14. Richard John Neuhaus, "Moral Leadership in Post-Secular America," *Imprimis*, 2:7 (July 1982), 3.

15. Will Herberg, *Protestant, Catholic, Jew: An Essay in American Religious Sociology* (Chicago: University of Chicago Press, 1983), 269.

16. John F. Kennedy, "For the Freedom of Man," inaugural address, Washington, D.C., January 20, 1961. Quoted in *Vital Speeches of the Day*, February 1, 1961.

17. Daniel Bell, *The Cultural Contradictions of Capitalism* (New York: Basic Books, 1978), 77.

18. Quoted in James Hitchcock, *What Is Secular Humanism?* (Ann Arbor, Mich.: Servant Books, 1982), 66.

19. Hitchcock, *What Is Secular Humanism?* 66.

20. Jack Kroll, "The Most Famous Artist," *Newsweek* (March 9, 1987), 64.

21. Kroll, "The Most Famous Artist," 64.

22. Quoted in David Brock, "A Philosopher Hurls Down a Stinging Moral Gauntlet," *Insight* (May 11, 1987), 12.

23. Robert N. Bellah, et al., *Habits of the Heart: Individualism and Commitment in American Life* (New York: Harper & Row, 1985), 281.

24. Meg Greenfield, "The Grinches vs. the Creche," *Newsweek* (December 24, 1984), 72.

25. "Creation Trial: Less Circus, More Law," *Washington Post* (December 21, 1981), A–3-b.

26. Carl Sagan, *Cosmos* (New York: Random House, 1980), 4.

27. "The Week," *National Review* (May 8, 1987), 16.

28. G. K. Chesterton, *The End of the Armistice* (New York: Sheed and Ward, 1936), 121–22.

29. Quoted in Martin E. Marty, "A Profile of Norman Lear: Another Pilgrim's Progress," *Christian Century* (January 21, 1987), 57.

30. Paul C. Vitz, *Censorship: Evidence of Bias in Our Children's Textbooks* (Ann Arbor, Mich.: Servant Books, 1986).

31. Vitz, *Censorship*, 15.

32. Vitz, *Censorship*, 16.

33. Vitz, *Censorship*, 3.

34. Vitz, *Censorship*, 16.

35. Joseph Sobran, "Pensees: Notes for the Reactionary of Tomorrow," *National Review* (December 31, 1985), 48.

36. Richard John Neuhaus, "The Naked Public Square," *Christianity Today* (October 5, 1984), 32.

37. Henry Hyde, *For Every Idle Silence* (Ann Arbor, Mich.: Servant Books, 1985), 12–13.

38. Donald G. Bloesch, *Crumbling Foundations* (Grand Rapids, Mich.: Zondervan, 1984), 83–84.

39. Quoted in Neuhaus, *Naked Public Square*, 260.

40. Bloesch, *Crumbling Foundations*, 19.

41. "Persecution Next Step—Roberts," *Washington Times* (April 6, 1987).

42. Quoted in Sydney E. Ahlstrom, *A Religious History of the American People* (New Haven, Conn.: Yale University Press, 1972), 954.

43. Walter Shapiro, "Politics and the Pulpit," *Newsweek* (September 17, 1984), 24.

44. *New York Times* (August 14, 1984), A–21.

45. *New York Times* (August 14, 1984), A–21.

46. Mario M. Cuomo, "Religious Belief and Public Morality: A Catholic Governor's Per-

spective," a paper presented to the Dept. of Theology at the University of Notre Dame (September 13, 1984).

47. The information and citations concerning St. John the Divine Cathedral are drawn from Kenneth L. Woodward and Deborah Witherspoon, "The Awakening of a Cathedral," *Newsweek* (June 16, 1986), 59–60.

CHAPTER 15: THE NAKED PUBLIC SQUARE

1. Walter Shapiro, "Ethics: What's Wrong?" *Time* (May 25, 1987), 14.

2. Ezra Bowen, "Ethics: Looking to Its Roots," *Time* (May 25, 1987), 26.

3. Elwood McQuaid, "Lying as a Lifestyle," *Moody Monthly* (July/August 1987), 8.

4. C. S. Lewis, *The Abolition of Man* (New York: Macmillan, 1974), 35.

5. Richard John Neuhaus, *The Naked Public Square* (Grand Rapids, Mich.: Eerdmans, 1984), 86.

6. Neuhaus, *Naked Public Square*, 89.

7. Neuhaus, *Naked Public Square*, 153.

8. Arthur Schlesinger, *The Vital Center* (New York: Houghton Mifflin, 1962), 188. Quoted in Neuhaus, *Naked Public Square*, 91.

9. Peter L. Berger, "Religion in Post-Protestant America," *Commentary* 81:5 (May 1986), 44.

10. Russell Kirk, *The Roots of American Order* (LaSalle, Ill.: Open Court, 1974), 81.

11. Will Durant, *Caesar and Christ: A History of Roman Civilization from Its Beginnings to* A.D. *337* (New York: Simon and Schuster, 1944), 164.

12. Etienne Gilson, "Foreword," in St. Augustine, *The City of God* (New York: Image/Doubleday, 1958), 19.

13. Edmund Burke, *Reflections on the Revolution in France*. Quoted in *The Portable Conservative Reader* (New York: Penguin, 1982), 27.

14. A. James Reichley, *Religion in American Public Life* (Washington, D.C.: Brookings Institute, 1986), 9.

15. Kirk, *Roots of American Order*, 17.

16. Quoted in Sydney E. Ahlstrom, *A Religious History of the American People* (New Haven, Conn.: Yale University Press, 1972), 386.

17. Will and Ariel Durant, *The Lessons of History* (New York: Simon and Schuster, 1968), 50.

18. Boris Rumer, "Soviet Writers Decry Loss of Spiritual Values in Society," *Christian Science Monitor* (October 7, 1986), 1.

19. Rumer, "Soviet Writers Decry Loss of Spiritual Values in Society," 1.

20. Walter Lippmann, *A Preface to Morals* (New York: Time, 1929), 134.

21. Aleksandr I. Solzhenitsyn, *A World Split Apart: Commencement Address Delivered at Harvard University, June 8, 1978* (New York: Harper & Row, 1978), 49.

CHAPTER 16: BENEFITS OF THE KINGDOM

1. Arthur Brooks, "Who Really Cares: The Surprising Truth About Compassionate Conservativism," Basic Books, scheduled for release Nov. 24, 2006

2. *Westminster Confession of Faith*, XX, 2.

3. John 13:34.

4. Quoted in Richard John Neuhaus, *The Naked Public Square* (Grand Rapids, Mich.: Eerdmans, 1984), 178.

5. *The Religion and Society Report*, 3:9 (September 1986), 5.

6. Matthew 5:13–14.

7. Quoted in George F. Will, *Statecraft as Soulcraft: What Government Does* (New York: Simon and Schuster, 1983), 129.

8. See Matthew 25:14–30 and Luke 16:10–31 for discussion of this issue.

9. James Q. Wilson, "Crime and American Culture," *The Public Interest* 70 (Winter 1983), 22.

10. Paul Johnson, *Modern Times: The World from the Twenties to the Eighties* (New York: Harper & Row, 1983), 246–47.

11. Edwin J. Orr, *The Flaming Tongue: The Impact of 20th Century Revivals* (Chicago, Ill.: Moody Press, 1973), 17–18.

12. Etienne Gilson, "Foreword," in St. Augustine, *The City of God* (New York: Image/Doubleday, 1958), 32.

13. Neuhaus, *Naked Public Square*.

CHAPTER 17: CHRISTIAN PATRIOTISM

1. Joseph Sobran, "Pensees: Notes for the Reactionary of Tomorrow," *National Review* (December 31, 1985), 50.

2. Donald Bloesch, *Crumbling Foundations* (Grand Rapids, Mich.: Zondervan, 1984), 38.

3. Bloesch, *Crumbling Foundations*, 73.

4. G. K. Chesterton, *The Victorian Age in English Literature* (New York: Holt, 1913), 43.

5. James V. Schall, "The Altar as the Throne," in Stanley Atkins and Theodore McConnell, eds., *Churches on the Wrong Road* (Chicago: Regnery, 1986), 231–32.

6. Harry Blamires, *The Christian Mind* (Ann Arbor, Mich.: Servant Books, 1963/1978), 3.

7. Jacques Ellul, *Presence in the Kingdom* (New York: Seabury Press, 1948/1967), 119.

8. Romans 13:1; 1 Timothy 2:2.

9. Acts 5:29.

10. St. Augustine, *City of God* (Garden City, N.Y.: Image/Doubleday, 1958).

11. Quoted in Richard John Neuhaus, *The Naked Public Square* (Grand Rapids, Mich.: Eerdmans, 1984), 209.

12. St. Augustine, *City of God*.

13. C. S. Lewis, *The Four Loves* (New York: Harcourt, Brace, World, 1960), 41.

14. Quoted in Neuhaus, *Naked Public Square*, 237.

15. Neuhaus, *Naked Public Square*, 75.

16. Quoted in Lynn Buzzard and Paula Campbell, *Holy Disobedience: When Christians Must Resist the State* (Ann Arbor, Mich.: Servant Books, 1984), 123.

17. Daniel 1–3.

18. Paraphrase of Daniel 3:16–18.

19. Acts 4:19–20.

20. Charles Mendies, in an interview with Ellen Santilli Vaughn (September 1986).

21. Daniel 1:8.

22. Quoted in A. James Reichley, *Religion in American Public Life* (Washington, D.C.: Brookings Institute, 1986), 104.

CHAPTER 18: LITTLE PLATOONS

1. "Brother Can You Spare a Song?" *Newsweek* (October 28, 1985), 95.

2. "Brother Can You Spare a Song?" 95.

3. Quoted in George F. Will, *Statecraft as Soulcraft: What Government Does* (New York: Simon and Schuster, 1983), 129.

4. Cited in March Bell, "A Justice Department Commission is Escalating the War Over Pornography," *Eternity* (May 1986), 15–21.

5. "ACLU Reports, Deplores Antipornography Drive," *Washington Post* (February 24, 1986), A–12.

6. This story is told in more detail in Jack Eckerd, *Finding the Right Prescription* (Old Tappan, N.J.: Revell, 1987).

7. Quoted in "Personalities" section of *Philadelphia Inquirer*.

CHAPTER 19: THE PROBLEM OF POWER

1. John Naisbitt, *Megatrends: Ten New Directions Transforming Our Lives* (New York: Warner Books, 1983).

2. Paul Tournier, *The Violence Within*. Quoted in Cheryl Forbes, *The Religion of Power* (Grand Rapids, Mich.: Zondervan, 1983), 17.

3. *Newsweek* (September 6, 1971), 16.

4. George Orwell, *1984* (New York: New American Library, 1961), 217.

5. C. P. Snow, *The Masters* (New York: Scribner's, 1982).

6. Richard J. Foster, *Money, Sex and Power* (New York: Harper & Row, 1985), 175.

7. John Milton, *Paradise Lost and Paradise Regained* (New York: New American Library, 1968), 54.

8. Luke 22:26.

9. Mark 10:44.

10. Quoted in Sydney E. Ahlstrom, *A Religious History of the American People* (New Haven, Conn.: Yale University Press, 1972), 386.

11. 2 Corinthians 12:9–10.

12. Anthony Campolo, *The Power Delusion* (Wheaton, Ill.: Victor Books, 1984).

13. Numbers 12:3.

CHAPTER 20: CHRISTIANS IN POLITICS

1. "America's Question and Answer Man," *Newsweek* (June 15, 1987), 56.

2. Robert L. Dabney, *Discussions*, vol. 2, edited by C. R. Vaughan (Harrisburg, Virginia: Sprinkle Publications, 1982), 408.

3. Stephen Monsma, "The Promises and Pitfalls of Evangelical Political Involvement," a speech (October 17, 1986), 9.

4. Andrew Sinclair, *Prohibition: The Era of Excess* (Boston: Little, Brown, 1962).

5. Monsma, "The Promises and Pitfalls of Evangelical Political Involvement," 15–16.

6. St. Augustine, *City of God*, (Garden City, N.Y.: Image/Doubleday, 1958), 88.

7. Harry Blamires, *The Christian Mind* (London: S.P.C.K., 1963), 25.

8. Vernon Grounds, "Crosscurrents," *Moody Monthly* (July/August 1986), 80.

9. Personal letter from Richard John Neuhaus (June 8, 1987).

10. "Vatican Statement on Respect for Human Life in Its Origins and on the Dignity of Procreation: A Reply to Certain Questions of the Day" (1987), 37.

11. Quoted in Joseph Laitin, "Web of Lies," *Washington Post* (October 5, 1986), C–6.

12. *McDaniel vs. Paty*, 435 U.S. 618.

13. "Christopher Dawson: His Interpretation of History," *Modern Age* (Summer 1979), 263.

14. U.S. Bishops' paper on nuclear war, *The Challenge of Peace: God's Promise and Our Response* (May 3, 1983), from the National Conference of Catholic Bishops is discussed in William McNeal, *New York Times* (December 26, 1982), E–3.

15. McNeal, *New York Times* (December 26, 1982), E–3.

16. Russell Kirk, "Promises and Perils of 'Christian Politics,'" *Intercollegiate Review* (Fall/Winter 1982), 15.

17. Kirk, "Promises and Perils of 'Christian Politics,'" 23.

18. Roman Catholic Polish bishops' statement (June 23, 1985).

19. Exodus 21–22.

CHAPTER 21: SIGNS OF THE KINGDOM

1. Richard W. Larsen, "A One-Eyed Angel," *Seattle Times* (April 14, 1985).

CHAPTER 22: PERILS OF POLITICS

1. Quoted in *Christianity Today* (September 5, 1986), 54.

2. Vernon Grounds, "Authentic Piety," *The Other Side* 21:7 (October 1985), 56–57.

3. George Marsden, *Reformed Journal* (November 1986), 3.

4. Quoted in *Christianity Today* (September 5, 1986), 54.

5. Exodus 18:21.

6. James Skillen, "The Bible, Politics and Democracy," a speech delivered at Wheaton College (November 7–8, 1985), 5.

7. McKendree Langley, *The Practice of Political Spirituality* (Jordan Station, Ontario, Canada: Paideia Press, 1984).

8. C. S. Lewis, *God in the Dock* (Grand Rapids, Mich.: Eerdmans, 1970), 198.

9. Quoted by Colman McCarthy, "For Bennett, A Failing Grade in History," *Washington Post* (September 22, 1985), G–8.

10. Interviews with Ronald Reagan after his meeting with the Religious Roundtable in Dallas (August 22, 1980).

11. A. James Reichley, *Wall Street Journal* (November 25, 1985), 28.

12. Quoted in *Journal of Law and Religion*, 2:1 (1984), 71.

13. "Keeping the Church Doors Open," *Christianity Today* (March 21, 1986), 14.

14. *Time* (September 2, 1985), 58.

15. Kent R. Hill, "Religion and the Common Good: In Defense of Pluralism," *This World* (Spring 1987), 83.

16. James V. Schall, "The Altar as the Throne," in Stanley Atkins and Theodore McConnell, eds., *Churches on the Wrong Road* (Chicago: Regnery, 1986), 233.

17. Donald Bloesch, *Crumbling Foundations* (Grand Rapids, Mich.: Zondervan, 1984), 39.

18. Bloesch, *Crumbling Foundations*, 40.

19. Richard Wurmbrand, *Marx and Satan* (Chicago: Crossway, 1986), appendix.

20. Bloesch, *Crumbling Foundations*, 39.

21. Myron Augsburger, *Christianity Today* (January 17, 1986), 21-I.

CHAPTER 23: PEOPLE POWER

1. Jaime Cardinal Sin, from a press conference of the Prison Fellowship International Triennial Symposium in Nairobi, Kenya (August 3, 1986).

2. Robert Shaplan, "Letter from the Philippines," *New Yorker* (February 2, 1985), 61.

3. Benigno Aquino, testimony before the House Foreign Affairs Committee (June 20, 1983).

4. Jaime Cardinal Sin, "A Call to Conscience," a pastoral letter (January 1986).

5. Myron Augsburger, *Christianity Today* (January 17, 1986), 21-I.

6. Quoted in Lynn Buzzard and Paula Campbell, *Holy Disobedience: When Christians Must Resist the State* (Ann Arbor, Mich.: Servant Books, 1984), 142.

7. Richard John Neuhaus, *Religion and Society Report* 3:6 (June 1986), 2.

8. Jonathan Mayhew, *A Discourse Concerning Limited Resistance and Non-Resistance* (Boston, 1750).

9. Buzzard and Campbell, *Holy Disobedience*, 58–59.

10. G. K. Chesterton, *Sidelights on New London and Newer New York*, (New York: Dodd and Mead, 1932), 191.

11. Quoted in David R. Weber, *Civil Disobedience in American History* (Ithaca, N.Y.: Cornell University Press, 1978), 244.

12. Francis Schaeffer, *The Complete Works of Francis A. Schaeffer: A Christian Worldview*, vol. 5 (Westchester, Ill.: Crossway, 1981), 491.

CHAPTER 24: THE POLITICAL ILLUSION

1. "Leaders of the Christian Right Announce Their Next Step," *Christianity Today* (December 13, 1985), 65.

2. Jacques Ellul, *The New Demons* (New York: Seabury Press, 1975), 167.

3. *Time* (November 1, 1976), 20.

4. "The Farm Act," *Washington Post* (May 7, 1985), B–1; and "Actresses Appeal for Aid to Farmers," *New York Times* (May 7, 1985), 8.

5. Richard Schickel, *Intimate Strangers: The Culture of Celebrity* (New York: Doubleday, 1985).

6. Jacques Ellul, *The Presence of the Kingdom* (New York: Seabury Press, 1948/1967), 100.

7. Quoted in Parker J. Palmer, *Company of Strangers: Christians and the Renewal of America's Public Life* (New York: Crossroads Publishing, 1981), 80.

8. Alexis de Tocqueville, quoted in Palmer, *Company of Strangers*.

9. Tocqueville, *Democracy in America*. Cited in Arendt, *Company of Strangers*, 80.

10. Quoted in Palmer, *Company of Strangers*.

11. Psalm 118:9.

12. Ellul, *Presence of the Kingdom*, 35.

CHAPTER 25: THE INDESTRUCTIBLE KINGDOM

1. The information in this chapter is based on interviews conducted by Ellen Santilli Vaughn (April 1986).

2. George Russell, "Shadow of a Gunman," *Time* (May 18, 1981), 52–54.

3. Robert Ajemian, "Ready to Die in the Maze," *Time* (August 17, 1981), 47.

4. Ajemian, "Ready to Die in the Maze," 46.

5. Ajemian, "Ready to Die in the Maze," 47.

6. *New York Times* (March 31, 1979), 1.

7. Based on an account in Jack Holland, *Too Long a Sacrifice* (New York: Dodd and Mead, 1981), 84–89.

8. Guy Garcia, "Edging Toward the Abyss," *Time* (November 30, 1981), 58.

EPILOGUE

1. Malcolm Muggeridge, *The End of Christendom* (Grand Rapids, Mich.: Eerdmans, 1980), 56.

FOR FURTHER READING

I would like to acknowledge the following works, which were especially useful in the research and preparation of this book. This is by no means intended to be an exhaustive bibliography on the issues of church and state, religion and politics—but readers will find these sources useful in their own further study.

St. Augustine. *The Confessions, The City of God, and On Christian Doctrine*. Chicago: University of Chicago, Great Books Series, Encyclopedia Brittanica, 1952.

Belli, Humberto. Breaking Faith: The Sandinista Revolution and Its Impact on Freedom and Christian Faith in Nicaragua. Westchester, Ill.: Crossway, 1985.

Berger, Peter. "Religion in Post-Protestant America." *Commentary* 81:5 (May 1986).

———. *The Sacred Canopy*. Garden City, N.Y.: Anchor, 1968.

Blamires, Harry. *The Christian Mind*. Ann Arbor, Mich.: Servant, 1963.

Bloesch, Donald. *Crumbling Foundations*. Grand Rapids, Mich.: Zondervan, 1984.

Bright, John. *The Kingdom of God*. Nashville: Abingdon, 1953.

Buzzard, Lynn, and Paula Campbell. *Holy Disobedience: When Christians Must Resist the State*. Ann Arbor: Servant, 1984.

Campolo, Anthony. *The Power Delusion*. Wheaton, Ill.: Victor, 1983.

Christianity Today Institute. For its extraordinarily useful summary of *The Christian as Citizen*. Christianity Today, 1985.

Clowney, Edmund. "The Politics of the Kingdom." *Westminster Theological Journal* 41 (Spring 1979).

Cullman, Oscar. *The State in the New Testament*. New York: Scribner's, 1956.

Durant, Will, and Ariel Durant. *The Lessons of History*. New York: Simon and Schuster, 1968.

Ellul, Jacques. *The Presence of the Kingdom*. New York: Seabury, 1948/1967.

———. *The New Demons*. New York: Seabury, 1975.

———. *The Political Illusion*. Translated by Konrad Keller. New York: Vintage, 1972.

Forbes, Cheryl. *The Religion of Power*. Grand Rapids, Mich.: Zondervan, 1983.

Herberg, Will. Protestant, Catholic, Jew: An Essay in American Religious Sociology. Chicago: University of Chicago, 1983.

Johnson, Paul. Modern Times: The World from the Twenties to the Eighties. New York: Harper & Row, 1983.

Jones, E. Stanley. The Unshakable Kingdom and the Unchanging Person. Nashville: Abingdon, 1972.

Kik, J. Marcellus. *The Story of Two Kingdoms*. New York: Nelson, 1963.

Kirk, Russell. "Promises and Perils of 'Christian Politics'." *Intercollegiate Review* (Fall/Winter 1982).

———. "Religion in the Civil Social Order." *Modern Age* (Fall 1984).

———. *The Roots of American Order*. LaSalle, Ill.: Open Court, 1974.

Mott, Stephen. *Biblical Ethics and Social Change*. New York: Oxford University, 1982.

Neuhaus, Richard John. *The Naked Public Square*. Grand Rapids, Mich.: Eerdmans, 1984.

———. *Unsecular America*. Grand Rapids, Mich.: Eerdmans, 1986.

Reichley, A. James. *Religion in American Public Life*. Washington, D.C.: Brookings Institute, 1985.

Runner, Evan. Especially his "Preface" to McKendree R. Langley, *The Practice of Political Spirituality*. Jordan Station, Ontario: Paideia, 1984.

Schaeffer, Francis. *How Should We Then Live?* Old Tappan, N.J.: Revell, 1976.

Schall, James V. "The Altar as the Throne." *Churches on the Wrong Road*. Chicago: Regnery, 1986.

———. *Christianity and Politics*. Boston: St. Paul Editions, 1981.

Skillen, James. "The Bible, Politics and Democracy: What Does Biblical Obedience Entail for American Political Thought?" In The Bible, Politics and Democracy. Edited by *Richard John Neuhaus*. Grand Rapids: Eerdmans, 1987.

Sproul, R. C. *If There Is a God, Why Are There Atheists?* Minneapolis: Dimension, 1978.

———. *Classical Apologetics*. Grand Rapids, Mich.: Zondervan, 1984.

Valladares, Armando. *Against All Hope*. New York: Knopf, 1986.

Vos, Gerhardus. *Biblical Theology: Old and New Testaments*. Grand Rapids, Mich.: Eerdmans, 1984.

Wood, James E., Jr. *Nationhood and the Kingdom*. Nashville: Broadman, 1977.

INDEX